D0131630

About this Book

This book starts where it's likely to start—at the beg........g ensures that you learn the fundamental concepts of the TCP/IP network protocol so that you can set up and administer your own TCP/IP network.

By following the book's examples, you will learn how to use various utilities, set up network database files, and navigate the network. You will learn about the Open Systems Interconnection (OSI) Layers and command network architectures.

Who Should Read this Book?

Anyone interested in learning to use the TCP/IP will find something of value in this book. This book is aimed at helping the novice; in addition, it can be used by experienced TCP/IP users as a tune-up and reference.

This book covers the TCP/IP from the basics—such as OSI, architectures, and the Internet—to more advanced subjects, such as administrative utilities.

This book is for you, if one or more of the following is true:

☐ You are interested in learning more about TCP/IP and the Internet.

☐ You've just heard that your company is about to make TCP/IP the standard network protocol.

☐ You need to learn how to navigate and administer your TCP/IP network.

Conventions

To help guide you through the daily topics and draw your attention to important information, several special easy-to-see icons are used in this book.

Note: Here you will find interesting information that can make your use of the shell more effective.

Tip: Read tips for useful shortcuts and techniques for being more efficient with the shell.

Caution: Cautions focus your attention on problems or side effects that can occur in specific situations.

Each day ends with a Q&A section containing answers to common questions relating to that day's material. There is also a Workshop at the end of each day. The Workshop contains quiz questions (and some Workshops contain exercises). To check quiz answers, refer to Appendix F.

Teach Yourself TCP/IP in 14 Days

Teach Yourself
TCP/IP
in 14 Days

Tim Parker

SAMS
PUBLISHING

201 West 103rd Street, Indianapolis, Indiana 46290

This one is for my grandparents.
Eheu fugaces labuntur anni

International Standard Book Number: 0-672-30549-6

Library of Congress Catalog Card Number: 94-66278

97   96   4

Interpretation of the printing code: the rightmost double-digit number is the year of the book's printing; the rightmost single-digit, the number of the book's printing. For example, a printing code of 94-1 shows that the first printing of the book occurred in 1994.

Composed in MCPdigital by Macmillan Computer Publishing

Printed in the United States of America

Publisher
Richard K. Swadley

Associate Publisher
Jordan Gold

Acquisitions Manager
Stacy Hiquet

Managing Editor
Cindy Morrow

Acquisitions Editor
Grace Buechlein

Development Editor
Scott Parker

Production Editor
Mary Inderstrodt

Copy Editor
Howard Peirce

Editorial Coordinator
Bill Whitmer

Editorial Assistants
Carol Ackerman
Sharon Cox
Lynette Quinn

Technical Reviewer
Mark Edmead

Marketing Manager
Gregg Bushyeager

Book Designer
Alyssa Yesh

Director of Production and Manufacturing
Jeff Valler

Imprint Manager
Juli Cook

Manufacturing Coordinator
Paul Gilchrist

Production Analysts
Angela Bannan
Dennis Clay Hager
Mary Beth Wakefield

Graphics Image Specialists
Teresa Forrester
Clint Lahnen
Tim Montgomery
Dennis Sheehan
Greg Simsic
Susan VandeWalle
Jeff Yesh

Page Layout
Elaine Brush
Ayanna Lacey
Michelle M. Mitchell
Casey Price
Kim Scott
Scott Tullis

Proofreading
Carol L. Bowers
Georgiana Briggs
Michael Brumitt
Brian-Kent Proffitt
Beth Rago

Indexer
Rebecca Mayfield

About the Author

Tim Parker

Tim Parker started programming computers 20 years ago and began writing about programs five years later. Since then, he has published more than 500 articles and nine books on the subject. He has held roles as columnist and editor with some of the most popular computer magazines and newsletters.

Educated at the University of Toronto and the University of Ottawa, he pursued a doctoral degree in chemistry at the Ottawa-Carleton Institute for Graduate Work and Research. Along the way, computers became an integral part of his research. A desire to explain the cryptic world of computer science led him to his writing career. Although a freelance writing and programming career is not the most stable, Tim has never been short of work.

Tim was a founding columnist and reviewer for Computer Language Magazine, a columnist with UNIX Review, and has contributed to dozens of other magazines such as *UNIX World, Data Based Advisor, Compute!,* and *Microsystems Journal.* He is currently the Technical Editor of *SCO World* magazine, editor of the newsletter *UNIQUE: The UNIX Systems Information Source,* a frequent contributor to *UNIX Review* magazine, and a columnist with *MacLean-Hunter Publications.* He covers UNIX, DOS, and Macintosh platforms. His books on UNIX have been very well-received and are used in courses taught world-wide.

He is the president of his own consulting company, which specializes in technical writing and training, software development, and software quality testing. He is a pilot, scuba diver, and white-water kayaker. Tim currently lives in Kanata, Ontario with a temperamental network of too many PCs and workstations.

Overview

Contents

Acknowledgments

Writing books is supposed to get easier with practice. This is my ninth book, and although I no longer worry about grammar or writing style, this one had its own unique problems. Most of the problems hinge on the simple fact that explaining TCP/IP is impossible without getting into a fair level of detail, most of which is—simply put—quite dull. There is no easy way to spice up details of a complex communications protocol, but I have tried to make the subject as readable as possible.

TCP/IP is not a single protocol but a family of related protocols that perform dedicated tasks. Explaining these protocols means delving into detail without going to the point that the reader's eyes glaze over. It's a tricky line to tread, and I hope I've managed it to your satisfaction. This book covers everything you need to know as a newcomer to TCP/IP, while also providing enough information as you progress into the advanced levels. From there, the level of detail multiplies and the original design documents are the best sources of information.

This book took a lot of effort to complete, in part because of its lack of practical material. There was also a considerable amount of work from several people at Sams Publishing. The editors at Sams have worked hard to produce a readable, well-presented book. They are to be thanked and congratulated for their efforts.

Several vendors kindly provided software for my use during the writing of this book. Thanks to the Santa Cruz Operation, ftp Software, NetManage, and Microsoft.

On a personal level, thanks go to my parents for understanding why I couldn't visit as often as I would have liked. Thanks also to Yvonne for tolerating all the late nights and weekends that were spent in front of a screen instead of with her. The result of all the effort is a book I am proud of and hope you find useful.

Preface

I first encountered TCP/IP a decade ago when a client lead me into a room with a bunch of UNIX-based computers, a stack of network boards, a roll of coaxial cable, and a pile of diskettes. My instructions were simple: Install a TCP/IP network that works. Unfortunately, there was no documentation along with the boards or software. A quick visit to the university library proved that few books were available on the subject; those that were left a lot to be desired. Eventually, through trial and error, I got the system working. In the process, I learned a great deal about the quirkiness of TCP/IP and UNIX.

TCP/IP is a family of protocols that covers a wide variety of tasks, all intertwined and interrelated in some way. There has been a steady increase in the number of TCP/IP networks as both the Internet and the UNIX operating systems have grown in popularity. UNIX and TCP/IP have been interwoven from the start of the protocol's history, which shows itself in the number of configuration files and architecture of TCP/IP. The last few years have seen TCP/IP implementations for almost every hardware platform and operating system available. Luckily, they are (almost) all compatible.

Several books have been written about TCP/IP, although none really suits the requirements for beginning users. There are a few excellent TCP/IP reference books that give precise details of the protocols, but they fail to give a solid overview—in easily understood terms—for newcomers. Finally the opportunity to write the TCP/IP book I'd like to have had 10 years ago came along. The result is now in your hands.

Introduction

So you've just been told you are on a TCP/IP network, you are the new TCP/IP system administrator, or you have to install a TCP/IP system. But you don't know very much about TCP/IP. That's where this book comes in. You don't need any programming skills, and no familiarity with operating systems is assumed. Even if you've never touched a computer before, you should be able to follow the material.

This book is intended for beginning through intermediate users and covers all the protocols involved in TCP/IP. Each protocol is examined in a fair level of detail to show how it works and how it interacts with the other protocols in the TCP/IP family. Along the way, this book shows you the basic tools required to install, configure, and maintain a TCP/IP network. It also shows you most of the user utilities that are available.

Because of the complex nature of TCP/IP and the lack of a friendly user interface, there is a lot of information to look at. Throughout the book, the role of each protocol is shown separately, as is the way it works on networks of all sizes. The relationship with large internetworks (like the Internet) is also covered.

Each day's text in the book adds to the complexity of the system, building on the material in the earlier chapters. Although some chapters seem to be unrelated to TCP/IP at first glance, all the material is involved in an integral manner with the TCP/IP protocol family. The last few days cover the installation and troubleshooting of a network.

By the time you finish this book, you will understand the different components of a TCP/IP system, as well as the complex acronym-heavy jargon used. Following the examples presented, you should be able to install and configure a complete TCP/IP network for any operating system and hardware platform.

Open Systems, Standards, and Protocols

Today's text covers some important information, including the following:

- [ ] What an open system is and how it handles networking
- [ ] Why standards are required and how they are developed
- [ ] Protocols in general and the OSI protocol in detail

Open Systems

This is a book about a protocol called TCP/IP, so why bother looking at open systems and standards? Because the background of TCP/IP grew out of the need to develop a standardized communications procedure that would inevitably be used on a variety of platforms. Therefore, a little background helps put the design of TCP/IP into perspective.

More importantly, open systems have become *de rigueur* in the current competitive market. The term *open system* is bandied around as a solution for all problems. Understanding what an open system really implies leads to a better awareness of TCP/IP's role.

In a similar vein, the use of standards ensures that a protocol such as TCP/IP is the same on each system. Developing a standard is not a trivial process, but one that involves the interrelationship of many different protocols. Knowing the interactions between TCP/IP and the other components layers of a communications system is important for proper configuration and optimization.

If you're in a rush to get started, you can skip these sections. In doing so, however, you might miss the fundamental concepts upon which TCP/IP relies, as well as some important terminology that you'll have to check for when you encounter it later.

What is an Open System?

There are many definitions of open systems, but a single concise definition is far from being accepted. For most people, an open system is best defined as one for which the architecture is not a secret. The description of the architecture may have been published or is readily available to others who want to build products for the platform. The definition applies equally well to hardware and software.

When more than a single vendor begins producing products for a platform, customers have a choice. You don't particularly like Nocrash Software's network monitoring software? No problem, because FaultFree Software's product runs on the Nocrash hardware and you like its fancy interface much better. The primary idea, of course, is a move away from proprietary platforms to one that is multivendor.

A decade ago, open systems were virtually nonexistent. Every hardware manufacturer had their product lines, and you were practically bound to that manufacturer for all your software and hardware needs. Some companies took advantage of the captive market, charging outrageous prices or forcing unwanted configurations on their customers. The ground swell of resentment grew to the point that customers began forcing the issue.

UNIX is a classic example of an open software platform. UNIX has been around for 30 years. Its source code is understood and is available to anyone who wants it. UNIX can be ported to run on many hardware platforms, eliminating proprietary dependencies. The attraction of UNIX is not the operating system's features themselves but simply the fact that a UNIX user can run software from other UNIX platforms, that files are compatible (except for disk formats of course), and that there is a wide variety of vendors selling products for UNIX.

The growth of UNIX pushed the large hardware manufacturers to the open systems principle, resulting in most manufacturers licensing the right to produce a UNIX version for their own hardware. This step let customers combine different hardware systems into larger networks, all running UNIX and working together. Users could move between machines almost transparently, ignorant of the actual hardware platform they were on. This open systems networking, originally of prime importance only to the largest corporations and governments, is now a key element in even the smallest company's computer strategy.

> **Note:** Although UNIX is a copyrighted work now owned by X/Open, the details of the operating system have been published and are readily available to any developer who wants to produce applications or hardware that work with the operating system. UNIX is quite unique in this respect.

The term *open system networking* means many things, depending on whom you ask. It is easy to see why people want open systems networking, though. There are three services that are widely used and account for the highest percentage of network traffic: file transfer, electronic mail, and remote login.

File transfer enables users to quickly and efficiently share files, without excessive duplication or concerns about the transport method. Network file transfers are much faster than an overnight courier crossing the country, and usually faster than copying a file on a diskette and carrying it across the room. File transfer is also extremely convenient, which not only pleases users but also eliminates time delays while waiting for material.

Electronic mail has mushroomed to a phenomenally large service, not just within a single business but worldwide. Internet carries millions of messages from people in government, private industry, educational institutions, and private interests. Electronic mail is cheap (no paper, envelopes, or stamps) and fast (around the world in 60 seconds or so). It is also an obvious extension of the computer-based world we work in.

Remote login enables a user who is based on one system to connect through a network to any other system that will accept him as a user. This may be in the next workgroup, the next state, or in another country. Remote logins enable users to take advantage of particular hardware and software in another location, as well as to run applications on another machine.

Architectures

To understand networking protocols, it is useful to know a little about networks. A quick look at the most common network architectures will help later in this book when you read about routing. The term *network* usually means a set of computers and peripherals (printers, modems, plotters, scanners, and so on) that are connected together by some medium. The connection may be direct (through a cable) or indirect (through a modem). The different devices on the network communicate with each other through a predefined set of rules (the protocol).

The devices may be in the same room or scattered through a building. They can be separated by many miles through the use of dedicated telephone lines, microwaves, or similar systems. They can even be scattered around the world, again connected by long-distance communications media. The layout of the network (the actual devices and the manners in which they are connected to each other) is called the *network topology*. For the purposes of this book, there are three topologies that are important: bus, ring, and hub.

The bus network is the simplest, comprising a single main communications pathway with each device attached to the main path at some point. An example of a bus network is shown in Figure 1.1. Each device on the pathway has a special identifying number, or address, that lets the device know that incoming information is for that device. Typically the pathway is a cable, with each computer and peripheral attached to the cable by a connector so that signals on the cable pass through the connector and then on down the cable to the next device if the connector's software decides the message is not for it (based on the device's address).

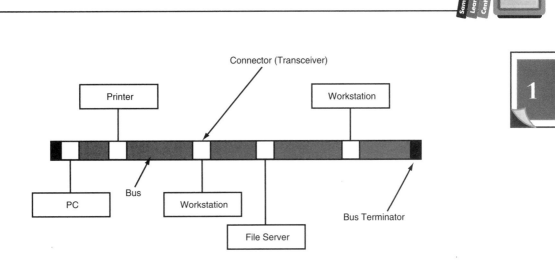

Figure 1.1. *A schematic of a bus network.*

A bus network is seldom a straight cable but is usually twisted around walls and buildings as needed. It does have a single pathway from one end to the other, with each end being terminated in some way. Figure 1.1 shows a logical representation of the network, meaning it has simplified the actual physical appearance of the network into a schematic with straight lines and no real scale to the connections. A physical representation of the network would show how it goes through the walls, around desks, and so on. Most devices on the bus network can send or receive data along the bus by packaging a message with the intended recipient's address.

A ring network topology is often drawn as its name suggests, shaped like a ring. A typical ring network schematic is shown in Figure 1.2. The term *ring* is a misnomer, though, because ring networks don't have an unending cable like a bus network with the two terminators joined together. Instead, ring refers to the design of the central unit that handles the network's message passing.

You may have heard the term *token ring network* before, but you might be disappointed to find no physical ring cable architecture. In a Token Ring network, the central control unit is called a Media Access Unit or MAU. The MAU has a ring circuit inside it (for which the network topology is named). The ring inside the MAU serves as the bus for devices to obtain messages.

Note: Despite the almost automatic assumption that a ring network has a backbone with the ends of the cable joined to form a loop, there is no real cabling ring at all. The ring name derives from the construction of the central control unit.

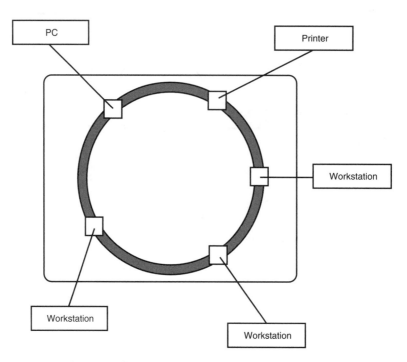

Figure 1.2. *A schematic of a ring network.*

A hub network uses a main cable much like the bus network, which is called the *backplane*. The hub topology is shown in Figure 1.3. From the backplane, a set of connections lead to a set of ports, into which devices are plugged. The cables to a connection point are often called *drops*, because they drop from the backplane to the ports.

Hub networks have become popular, in part because they are easy to set up and maintain. They also can be the least expensive system in many installations, which adds to their attraction. The backplane can extend across a considerable distance just like a bus network, whereas the ports, or connection points, are usually grouped in a set placed in a box or panel. There many be many panels or connection boxes attached to the backplane.

Layers

Writing a single software package that accomplishes every task required for communications between different computers would be a nightmarish task. Apart from having to cope with the different hardware architectures, simply writing the code for all the applications one would desire would result in a program that was far too large to execute or maintain.

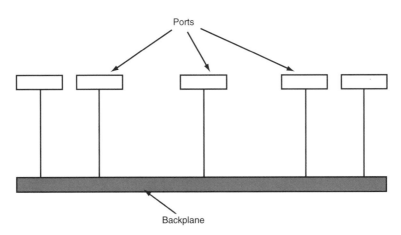

Figure 1.3. *A schematic of a hub network.*

Dividing all the requirements into groups is a sensible approach, much as a programmer breaks code into logical chunks. With open systems communications, groups were quite obvious. One group would deal with the transport of data, another with the packaging of messages, another with end-user applications, and so on. Each group of related tasks was called a *layer*.

> **Note:** The layers of an architecture are meant to be stand-alone, independent entities. They usually cannot perform any observable task without interacting with other layers, but from a programming point of view they are self-contained.

Of course, some crossover of functionality could be expected, and several different approaches to the same division of layers were proposed. One that became adopted as a standard was the Open Systems Interconnection Reference Model (which is discussed in more detail in the next section). The OSI Reference Model (OSI-RM) uses seven layers, as shown in Figure 1.4. The TCP/IP architecture is similar, but only involves five layers because it combines some of the OSI functionality in two layers into one. For now, though, consider the seven-layer OSI model.

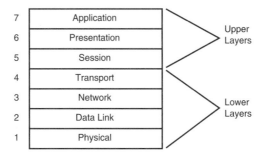

Figure 1.4. *The OSI Reference Model showing all seven layers.*

The application, presentation, and session layers are all application-oriented in that they are responsible for presenting the interface to the user. All three are independent of the layers below them and are totally oblivious to the means by which data gets to the application.

The lower four layers deal with the transmission of the data, covering the packaging, routing, verification, and transmission of each data group. The lower layers don't worry about the type of data they receive or send to the application but deal simply with the task of sending it. They don't differentiate between the different applications in any way.

The following sections explain each layer so that the architecture of the OSI-RM can be understood (and later contrasted to the architecture of TCP/IP).

Application Layer

The *application layer* is the end-user interface to the OSI system. It is where the applications, such as electronic mail, USENET readers, or database display modules, reside. The application layer's task is to display received information and send the user's new data to the lower layers.

In distributed applications, such as client-server systems, the application layer is where the client application resides. It communicates through the lower layers to the server.

Presentation Layer

The *presentation layer's* task is to isolate the lower layers from the application's data format. It converts the data from the application into a common format, often called the *canonical representation.* The presentation layer processes machine-dependent data from the application layer into a machine-independent format for the lower layers.

It is in the presentation layer that file formats and even character formats (ASCII and EBCDIC, for example) are lost. The conversion from the application data format takes place through a "common network programming language" (as it is called in the OSI Reference Model documents) that has a structured format.

The presentation layer does the reverse for incoming data. It is converted from the common format into application-specific formats, based on the type of application the machine has instructions for. If the data comes in without reformatting instructions, the information may not be assembled in the correct manner for the user's application.

Session Layer

The *session layer* organizes and synchronizes the exchange of data between application processes. It works with the application layer to provide simple data sets called *synchronization points* that let an application know how the transmission and reception of data is progressing. In simplified terms, the session layer can be thought of as a timing and flow control layer.

The session layer is involved in coordinating communications between different applications, letting each know the status of the other. An error in one application (whether on the same machine or across the country) is handled by the session layer to let the receiving application know that the error has occurred. The session layer can resynchronize applications that are currently connected to each other. This can be necessary when communications are temporarily interrupted, or when an error has occurred that results in loss of data.

Transport Layer

The *transport layer,* as its name suggests, is designed to provide the "transparent transfer of data from a source end open system to a destination end open system," according to the OSI Reference Model. The transportation layer establishes, maintains, and terminates communications between two machines.

The transport layer is responsible for ensuring that data sent matches the data received. This verification role is important in ensuring that data is correctly sent, with a resend if an error was detected. The transport layer manages the sending of data, determining its order and its priority.

Network Layer

The *network layer* provides the physical routing of the data, determining the path between the machines. The network layer handles all these routing issues, relieving the higher layers from this issue.

The network layer examines the network topology to determine the best route to send a message, as well as figuring out relay systems. It is the network layer only that sends a message from source to target machine, managing other chunks of data that pass through the system on its way to another machine.

Data Link Layer

The *data link layer,* according to the OSI reference paper, "provides for the control of the physical layer, and detects and possibly corrects errors which may occur." In practicality, the data link layer is responsible for correcting transmission errors induced during transmission (as opposed to errors in the application data itself, which are handled in the transport layer).

The data link layer is usually concerned with signal interference on the physical transmission media, whether through copper wire, fiber-optic cable, or microwave. Interference is common, resulting from many sources, including cosmic rays and stray magnetic interference from other sources.

Physical Layer

The *physical layer* is the lowest layer of the OSI model and deals with the "mechanical, electrical, functional, and procedural means" required for transmission of data, according to the OSI definition. This is really the wiring or other transmission form.

When the OSI model was being developed, a lot of concern dealt with the lower two layers, because they are, in most cases, inseparable. The real world treats the data link layer and the physical layer as one combined layer, but the formal OSI definition stipulates different purposes for each. (TCP/IP includes both the data link and physical as one layer, recognizing that the division is more academic than practical.)

Terminology and Notations

Both OSI and TCP/IP are rooted in formal descriptions, presented as a series of complex documents that define all aspects of the protocols. In order to define OSI and TCP/IP, several new terms were developed and introduced into use; some (mostly OSI terms) are rather unusual. You might find the term *OSI-speak* used to refer to some of these rather grotesque definitions, much as *legalese* refers to legal terms.

To better understand the details of TCP/IP, it is necessary to deal with these terms now. You won't see all these terms in this book, but you may encounter them when reading manuals or online documentation. Therefore, all the major terms are covered here.

Note: Many of the terms used by both OSI and TCP/IP may seem to have multiple meanings, but there is a definite attempt to provide a single, consistent definition for each word. Unfortunately, the user community is slow to adopt new terminology, so there is a considerable amount of confusion.

Packets

To transfer data effectively, many experiments have shown that creating a uniform chunk of data is better than sending characters singly or in widely varying sized groups. Usually these chunks of data will have some information ahead of them (the *header*) and sometimes an indicator at the end (the *trailer*). These chunks of data are called *packets* in most synchronous communications systems.

The amount of data in a packet and the composition of the header will change depending on the communications protocol, as well as some system limitations, but the concept of a packet always refers to the entire set (including header and trailer). The term *packet* is often used in the computer industry, sometimes when it shouldn't be.

Warning: You will see the word "packet" used as a generic reference to any group of data packaged for transmission. As an application's data passes through the layers of the architecture, each adds more information. The term "packet" is often used at each stage. Treat the term as a generalization for any data with additional information, instead of the specific result of only one layer's addition of header and trailer. This goes against the efforts of both OSI and the TCP governing bodies but helps keep your sanity intact!

Subsystems

A *subsystem* is the collective of a particular layer across a network. For example, if there are 10 machines connected together, each running the seven-layer OSI model, all 10 application layers are the application subsystem, all 10 data link layers are the data link subsystem, and so on. As you might have already deduced, with the OSI Reference Model there will be seven subsystems.

It is entirely possible (and even likely) that all the individual components in a subsystem will not be active at one time. Using the 10-machine example again, only three may have the data link layer actually active at any moment in time, but it is the cumulative of all the machines that make up the subsystem.

Entities

A layer may have more than one part to it. For example, the transport layer may have routines that verify checksums as well as routines that handle resending packets that didn't transfer correctly. Not all these routines will be active at once, because they may not be required at any moment. The active routines, though, are called entities. The word *entity* was adopted in order to find a single term that could not be confused with another computer term such as module, process, or task.

N Notation

The notations (N), (N+1), (N+2), and so on are used to identify a layer and the layers that are related to it. (Refer to Figure 1.4.) If the transport layer is layer N, the physical layer is N-3 and the presentation layer is N+2. With OSI, N always has a value of 1 through 7, inclusive. One reason this notation was adopted was to allow writers to refer to other layers without having to write out their names every time. It also makes flow charts and diagrams of interactions a little easier to draw. The terms N+1 and N-1 are commonly used in both OSI and TCP (for the layer above and below the current layer, respectively), as you will see.

To make things even more confusing, many OSI standards refer to a layer by the first letter of its name. This can lead to a real mess for the casual reader, because S-entity, 5-entity, and layer 5 all refer to the session layer.

N-Functions

Each layer performs N-functions. The functions are the different things that the layer does. Therefore, the functions of the transport layer are the different tasks that the layer provides. For most purposes in this book, functions and entities mean the same thing.

N-Facilities

This uses the hierarchical layer structure to express the idea that one layer provides a set of facilities to the next higher layer. This is sensible, because the application layer expects the presentation layer to provide a robust, well-defined set of facilities to it. In OSI-speak, the (N+1)-entities assume a defined set of N-facilities from the N-entity.

Services

The entire set of N-facilities provided to the (N+1)-entities is called the N-service. In other words, the service is the entire set of N-functions provided to the next higher layer. Services may seem similar to functions, but there is a formal difference between the two. The OSI documents go to great lengths to provide detailed descriptions of services, with a "service definition standard" (as it is called by OSI) for each layer. This was necessary during the development of the OSI standard so that the different tasks involved in the communications protocol could be assigned to different layers, and so that the functions of each layer are both well-defined and isolated from other layers.

The service definitions are formally developed from the bottom layer (physical), upward to the top layer. The advantage to this approach is that the design of the N+1 layer can be based on the functions performed in the N layer, avoiding two functions that accomplish the same task in two adjacent layers.

An entire set of variations on the service name have been developed to apply these definitions, some of which are in regular use:

> An N-service user is a user of a service provided by the N layer to the next higher (N+1) layer.
>
> An N-service provider is the set of N-entities that are involved in providing the N layer service.
>
> An N-service access point (often abbreviated to N-SAP) is where an N-service is provided to an (N+1)-entity by the N-service-provider.
>
> N-service data is the packet of data exchanged at an N-SAP.
>
> N-service data units (N-SDUs) are the individual units of data exchanged at an N-SAP (so that N-service-data is made up of N-SDUs). ·

These terms are visually represented in Figure 1.5. Another common term is *encapsulation,* which is the addition of control information to a packet of data. The control data contains addressing details, checksums for error detection, and protocol control functions.

Making Sense of the Jargon

It is important to remember that all these terms are used in a formal description, because a formal language is usually the only method to adequately describe something as complex as a communications protocol. It is possible, though, to fit these terms together so that they make a little more sense when you encounter them. An example should help.

Figure 1.5. *Service providers and service users communicate through service access points.*

The session layer has a set of session functions. It provides a set of session facilities to the layer above it, the presentation layer. The *session layer* is made up of *session entities*. The *presentation layer* is a user of the services provided by the session layer (layer 5). A *presentation entity* is a user of the services provided by the session layer and is called a *presentation service user.*

The *session service provider* is the collection of session entities that are actively involved in providing the presentation layer with the session's services. The point at which the session service is provided to the presentation layer is the *session service access point,* where the session service data is sent. The individual bits of data in the session service data are called *session service data units.*

Confusing? Believe it or not, after a while you will begin to feel more comfortable with these terms. The important ones to know now are that a layer provides a set of entities through a service access point to the next higher layer, which is called the *service user.* The data is sent in chunks called service data, made up of service data units.

Queues and Connections

Communications between two parties (whether over a telephone, between layers of an architecture, or between applications themselves) takes place in three distinct stages: establishment of the connection, data transfer, and connection termination.

Communications between two OSI applications in the same layer is through queues to the layer beneath them. Each application (more properly called a service user) has two queues, one for each direction to the service provider of the layer beneath (which controls the whole layer). In OSI-speak, the two queues provide for simultaneous (or *atomic*) interactions between two N-service action points.

Data, called *service primitives,* is put in to and retrieved from the queue by the applications (service user). A service primitive can be a block of data, an indicator that something is required or received, or a status indicator. As with most aspects of OSI, a lexicon has been developed to describe the actions in these queues:

A *request primitive* is when one service submits a service primitive to the queue (through the N-SAP) requesting permission to communicate with another service in the same layer.

An *indication primitive* is what the service provider in the layer beneath the sending application sends to the intended receiving application to let it know that communications is desired.

A *response primitive* is sent by the receiving application to the layer beneath's service provider to acknowledge the granting of communications between the two service users.

A *confirmation primitive* is sent from the service provider to the final application to indicate that both applications on the layer above can now communicate.

An example may help clarify the process. Assume two applications in the presentation layer want to communicate with each other. They can't do so directly (according to the OSI model) so must go through the layer below them. These steps are shown in Figure 1.6.

The first application sends a request primitive to the service provider of the session layer and waits. The session layer's service provider removes the request primitive from the inbound queue from the first application and sends an indication primitive to the second application's inbound queue.

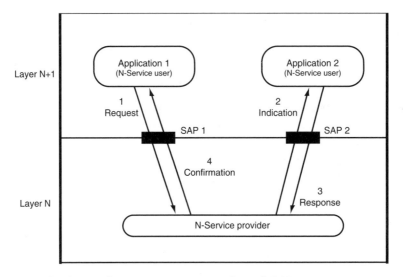

Figure 1.6. *Two applications communicate through SAPs using primitives.*

The second application takes the indication primitive from its queue to the session service provider and decides to accept the request for connection by sending a positive response primitive back through its queue to the session layer. This is received by the session layer service provider, and a confirmation primitive is sent to the first application in the presentation layer. This is a process called *confirmed service* because the applications wait for confirmation that communications are established and ready.

OSI also provides for *unconfirmed service,* which has a request primitive being sent to the service provider, sending the indication primitive to the second application. The response and confirmation primitives are not sent. This is a sort of a "get ready, 'cause here it comes whether you want it or not" communications, often referred to as *send and pray.*

When two service users are using confirmed service to communicate, they are considered connected. There are two applications talking to each other, aware of what the other is doing with the service data. OSI refers to the establishment and maintenance of *state information* between the two, or the fact that each knows then the other is sending or receiving. OSI calls this *connection-oriented* or *connection-mode* communications.

Connectionless communications is when service data is sent independently, as with unconfirmed service. The service data is self-contained, possessing everything a receiving service user needs to know. These service data packets are often called *datagrams.* The application that sends the datagram has no idea who receives the datagram and how it is handled, whereas the receiving service users have no idea who sent it (other than information that might be contained within the datagram itself). OSI calls this *connectionless-mode.*

OSI (and TCP/IP) use both connected and connectionless systems between layers of their architecture. Each has its benefits and ideal implementations. All these communications are between applications (service users) in each layer, using the layer beneath to communicate. There are lots of service users, and this process is going on all the time. It's quite amazing when you think about it.

Standards

We don't question the need for rules in a board game. If we didn't have rules, each player could be happily playing as it suits him, regardless of whether his play was consistent with that of others. The existence of rules ensures that each player plays the game in the same way, which may not be as much fun as a free-for-all. However, when a fight over a player's actions arises, the written rules clearly indicate who is right. The rules are a set of standards by which a game is played.

Standards prevent a situation arising in which two seemingly compatible systems really are not. For example, 10 years ago when CP/M was the dominant operating system, the 5.25-inch floppy was used by most systems. The floppy from a Kaypro II, however, couldn't be read by an Osbourne I because the tracks were laid out in a different manner. A utility program could convert between the two, but that extra step was a major annoyance for machine users.

When the IBM PC became the platform of choice, the 5.25-inch format used by the IBM PC was adopted by other companies to ensure disk compatibility. The IBM format became a de-facto standard, one adopted because of market pressures and customer demand.

Setting Standards

Creating a standard in today's world is not a simple matter. Several organizations are dedicated to developing the standards in a complete, unambiguous manner. The most important of these is the International Organization for Standardization, or ISO (often called the International Standardization Organization to fit their acronym, although this is incorrect). The ISO consists of standards organizations from many countries who try to agree on international criterion. The American National Standards Institute (ANSI),

British Standards Institute (BSI), Deutsches Institut fur Normung (DIN), and Association Francaise du Normalization (AFNOR) are all member groups. The ISO developed the Open Systems Interconnection (OSI) standard that is discussed throughout this book.

Each nation's standards organization can create a standard for that country, of course. The goal of ISO, however, is to agree on worldwide standards. Otherwise, incompatibilities could exist that wouldn't allow one country's system to be used in another. (An example of this is with television signals: the U.S. relies on NTSC, whereas Europe uses PAL—systems that are incompatible with each other).

Curiously, the language used for most international standards is English, even though the majority of participants in a standard's committee are not from English-speaking countries. This can cause quite a bit of confusion, especially since most standards are worded in an awkward manner to begin with.

The reason most standards involve awkward language is that to unambiguously describe something can be very difficult, sometimes necessitating the creation of new terms that the standard defines. Not only must the concepts be clearly defined, but the absolute behavior is necessary, too. With most things that standards apply to, this means using numbers and physical terms to provide a concrete definition. Defining a two-by-four piece of lumber simply necessitates the use of a measurement of some sort, and similarly defining computer terms requires mathematics.

Simply defining a method of communications, such as TCP/IP, would be fairly straightforward if it weren't for the complication of defining it for open systems. The use of an open system adds another difficulty because all aspects of the standard must be machine-independent. Imagine trying to define a two-by-four without using a measurement we are familiar with, such as inches; or if inches were adopted, it would be difficult to define inches in an unambiguous way (which indeed is what happens, because most units of length are defined with respect to the wavelength of a particular kind of coherent light).

Computers communicate through bits of data, but those bits may represent characters, numbers, or something else. Numbers could be integers, fractions, or octal representations. Again, we must define the units. You can see that the complications mount, one on top of the other.

To help define a standard, an abstract approach is usually used. In the case of OSI, the meaning (called the semantics) of the data transferred (the abstract syntax) is first dealt with, whereas the exact representation of the data in the machine (the concrete syntax) and the means by which it is transferred (transfer syntax) is handled separately. The separation of the abstract lets the data be represented as an entity, without concern for what it really means. It's a little like treating your car as a unit instead of an engine, transmission, steering wheel, and so on. The abstraction of the details to a simpler whole makes it easier to convey information. ("My car is broken" is abstract, whereas "the power steering fluid has all leaked out" is concrete.)

To describe systems in an abstract manner, it is necessary to have a language that meets the purpose. Most standards bodies have developed such a system—the most commonly used, ISO's Abstract Syntax Notation One, frequently shortened to ASN.1. It is suited especially for describing open systems networking. Thus, it's not surprising to find it used extensively in the OSI and TCP descriptions. Indeed, ASN.1 was developed concurrently with the OSI standards when it became necessary to describe upper-layer functions.

The primary concept of ASN.1 is that all types of data, regardless of type, size, origin, or purpose, can be represented by an object that is independent of the hardware, operating system software, or application. The ASN.1 system defines the contents of a datagram protocol header—the chunk of information at the beginning of an object that describes the contents to the system. (Headers are discussed in more detail in the section titled "Protocol Headers," later today.)

Part of ASN.1 describes the language used to describe objects and data types (such as a data description language in database terminology). Another part defines the basic encoding rules that deal with moving the data objects between systems. ASN.1 defines data types that are used in the construction of data packets (datagrams). It provides for both structured and unstructured data types, with a list of 28 supported types.

> **Note:** Don't be too worried about learning ASN.1 in this book. This book refers to it in passing in only a couple of places. It is useful, though, to know that the language is provided for the formal definition of all the aspects of TCP/IP.

Internet Standards

When the Defense Advanced Research Projects Agency (DARPA) was established in 1980, a group was formed to develop a set of standards for the Internet. The group, called the Internet Configuration Control Board (ICCB) was reorganized into the Internet Activities Board (IAB) in 1983, whose task was to design, engineer, and manage the Internet.

In 1986, the IAB turned over the task of developing the Internet Standards to the Internet Engineering Task Force (IETF), while the long-term research was assigned to the Internet Research Task Force (IRTF). The IAB retained final authorization over anything proposed by the two task forces.

The last step in this saga was the formation of the Internet Society in 1992, wherein the IAB was renamed the Internet Architecture Board. This group is still responsible for existing and future standards, reporting to the board of the Internet Society.

After all that, what happened during the shuffle? Almost from the beginning, the Internet was defined as "a loosely-organized international collaboration of autonomous, interconnected networks," which supported host-to-host communications "through voluntary adherence to open protocols and procedures" defined in a technical paper called the Internet Standards, RFC 1310.2. That definition is still used today.

The IETF continues to work on refining the standards used for communications over the Internet through a number of *working groups,* each one dedicated to a specific aspect of the overall Internet protocol suite. There are working groups dedicated to network management, security, user services, routing, and many more things. It is interesting that the IETF's groups are considerably more flexible and efficient than those of, say, the ISO, whose working groups can take years to agree on a standard. In many cases, the IETF's groups can form, create a recommendation, and disband within a year or so. This helps continuously refine the Internet standards to reflect changing hardware and software capabilities.

Creating a new Internet standard (which happened with TCP/IP) follows a well-defined process, shown schematically in Figure 1.7. It begins with a request for comment (RFC). This is usually a document containing a specific proposal, sometimes new and sometimes a modification of an existing standard. RFCs are widely distributed, both on the network itself and to interested parties as printed documents.

The RFC is usually discussed for a while on the network itself, where anyone can express an opinion, as well as in formal IETF working group meetings. After a suitable amount of revision and continued discussion, an *internet draft* is created and again distributed. This draft is close to final form, providing a consolidation of all the comments the RFC generated.

The next step is usually a *proposed standard,* which remains as such for at least six months. During this time, the Internet Society requires at least two independent and interoperable implementations to be written and tested. Any problems arising from the actual tests can then be addressed. (In practice, it is usual for many implementations to be written and given a thorough testing.)

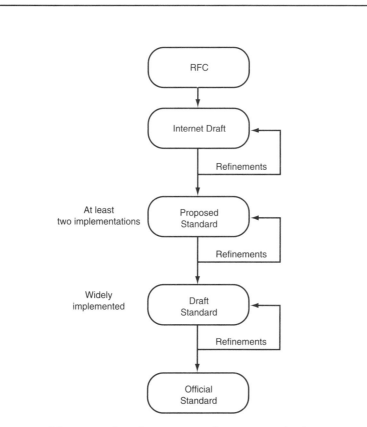

Figure 1.7. *The process for adopting a new Internet standard.*

After the testing and refinement process is completed, a *draft standard* is written, which remains for at least four months, during which time many more implementations are developed and tested. The last step—after many months—is the adoption of the standard, at which point it is implemented by all sites that require it.

Protocols

Diplomats follow rules when they conduct business between nations, which we see referred to in the media as protocol. Diplomatic protocol requires that you don't insult your hosts and that you do respect local customs (even if that does mean you have to eat some unappetizing dinners!). Most embassies and commissions have specialists in protocol, whose function is to ensure that everything proceeds smoothly when communications are taking place. The protocol is a set of rules that must be followed in order to "play the game," as career diplomats are fond of saying. Without the protocols, one side of the conversation may not really understand what the other is saying.

Similarly, computer protocols define the manner in which communications take place. If one computer is sending information to another and they both follow the protocol properly, the message will get through, regardless of what type of machines they are and what operating system they run (the basis for open systems). As long as the machine has software that can manage the protocol, communications are possible. Essentially, a computer protocol is a set of rules that coordinates the exchange of information.

Protocols have developed from very simple processes ("I'll send you one character, you send it back, and I'll make sure the two match") to elaborate, complex mechanisms that cover all possible problems and transfer conditions. A task such as sending a message from one coast to another can be very complex when you consider the manner in which it moves. A single protocol to cover all aspects of the transfer would be too large, unwieldy, and overly specialized. Therefore, a number of protocols have been developed, each handling a specific task.

Combining several protocols, each with their own dedicated purposes, would be a nightmare if the interactions between the protocols was not clearly defined. The concept of a layered structure was developed to help keep each protocol in its place and to define the manner of interaction between each protocol (essentially, a protocol for communications between protocols!).

As you saw earlier, the International Organization for Standardization (ISO) has developed a layered protocol system called Open Systems Interconnection (OSI). The OSI defines a protocol as "a set of rules and formats (semantic and syntactic), which determines the communication behavior of (N)-entities in the performance of (N)-functions." You may remember that N represents a layer and that an entity is a service component of a layer.

When machines communicate, the rules are formally defined and account for possible interruptions or faults in the flow of information, especially when the flow is connectionless (no formal connection between the two machines exists). In such a system, the capability to properly route and verify each packet of data (datagram) is vitally important. As discussed earlier, the data sent between layers is called a service data unit (SDU), so OSI defines the analogous data between two machines as a protocol data unit (or PDU).

The flow of information is controlled by a set of actions that define the state machine for the protocol. OSI defines these actions as protocol control information (or PCI).

Breaking Data Apart

It is necessary to introduce a few more terms commonly used in OSI and TCP, but luckily they are readily understood because of their real-world connotations. These terms are necessary because data doesn't usually exist in manageable chunks. The data might have to be broken down into smaller sections, or several small sections can be combined into a large section for more efficient transfer. The basic terms are

Segmentation is the process of breaking an N-service data unit (N-SDU) into several N-protocol data units (N-PDUs).

Reassembly is the process of combining several N-PDUs into an N-SDU (the reverse of segmentation).

Blocking is the combination of several SDUs (which may be from different services) into a larger PDU within the layer in which the SDUs originated.

Unblocking is the breaking up of a PDU into several SDUs in the same layer.

Concatenation is the process of one layer combining several N-PDUs from the next higher layer into one SDU (similar to blocking except occurring across a layer boundary).

Separation is the reverse of concatenation, so that a layer breaks apart a single SDU into several PDUs for the next layer higher (similar to unblocking except across a layer boundary).

These six processes are shown in Figure 1.8.

Finally, here is one last set of definitions that deal with connections:

Multiplexing is when several connections are supported by a single connection in the next lower layer (so three presentation service connections could be multiplexed into a single session connection).

Demultiplexing is the reverse of multiplexing, in which one connection is split into several connections for the layer above it.

Splitting is when a single connection is supported by several connections in the layer below (so the data link layer may have three connections to support one network layer connection).

Recombining is the reverse of splitting, so that several connections are combined into a single one for the layer above.

Multiplexing and splitting (and their reverses, demultiplexing and recombining) are different in the manners in which the lines are split. With multiplexing, several connections combine into one in the layer below. With splitting, however, one connection may be split into several in the layer below. As you might expect, each has its importance within TCP and OSI.

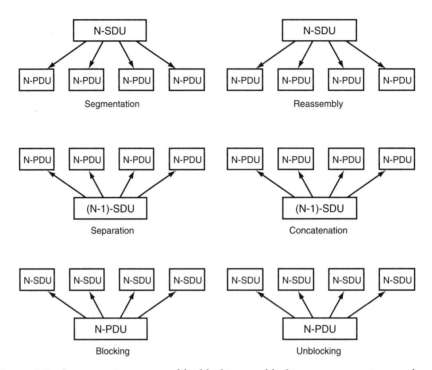

Figure 1.8. *Segmentation, reassembly, blocking, unblocking, concatenation, and separation.*

Protocol Headers

Protocol control information is information about the datagram to which it is attached. This information is usually assembled into a block that is attached to the front of the data it accompanies, and is called a *header* or *protocol header*. Protocol headers are used for transferring information between layers, as well as between machines. As mentioned earlier, the protocol headers are developed according to rules laid down in the ISO's Abstract Syntax Notation One document set.

When a protocol header is passed to the layer beneath, the datagram including the layer's header is treated as the entire datagram for that receiving layer, which adds its own protocol header to the front. Thus, if a datagram started at the application layer, by the time it reaches the physical layer, it would have seven sets of protocol headers on it. These layer protocol headers are used when moving back up the layer structure, stripped off as the datagram moves up. An illustration of this is shown in Figure 1.9.

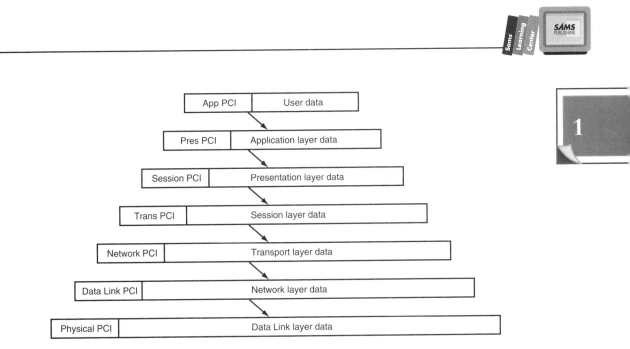

Figure 1.9. *Adding each layer's PCI to user data.*

It is easier to think of this process as layers on an onion. The inside is the data that is to be sent. As it passes through each layer of the OSI model, another layer of onion skin is added. When finished moving through the layers, there are several protocol headers enclosing the data. When the datagram is passed back up the layers (probably on another machine), each layer peels off the protocol header that corresponds to the layer. When it reaches the destination layer, there is only the data left.

This process makes sense because each layer of the OSI model requires different information from the datagram. By using a dedicated protocol header for each layer of the datagram, it is a relatively simple task to remove the protocol header, decode its instructions, and pass the rest of the message on. The alternative would be to have a single large header that contained all the information, but this would take longer to process. The exact contents of the protocol header are not important right now, but this book examines them later when looking at the TCP protocol.

As usual, OSI has a formal description for all this, which states that the N-user data to be transferred is prepended with N-protocol control information (N-PCI) to form an N-protocol data unit (N-PDU). The N-PDUs are passed across an N-service access point (N-SAP) as one of a set of service parameters comprising an N-service data unit (N-SDU). The service parameters comprising the N-SDU are called N-service user data (N-SUD), which is prepended to the (N-1)PCI to form another (N-1)PDU.

For every service in a layer, there is a protocol for it to communicate to the layer below it (remember that applications—services—communicate through the layer below, but not directly). The protocol exchanges for each service are defined by the system, and to a lesser extent by the application developer who is hopefully following the rules of the system.

Protocols and headers may sound a little complex or overly complicated for the task that must be accomplished, but considering the original goals of the OSI model, it is generally acknowledged that this is the best way to go. (Many a sarcastic comment has been made about OSI and TCP that claim the header information is much more important than the data contents. In some ways this is true, because without the header the data would never get to its destination.)

Summary

Today's text has thrown a lot of terminology at you, most of which you will see frequently in the days to come. In most cases, a gentle reminder of the definition will accompany the first occurrence of the terms in each day's text. To understand the relationships between the different terms, though, you may have to refer back to today's lesson.

You now have the basic knowledge to relate TCP/IP to the OSI's layered model, which will help you understand what TCP/IP does (and how it goes about doing it). Tomorrow, you'll look at the history of TCP/IP and the growth of the Internet.

Q&A

Q What are the three main types of network architecture? What are their primary characteristics?

A The three network architectures are bus, ring, and hub. There are others, but these three describe the vast majority of all local area networks.

A *bus network* is a length of cable that has a connector for each device directly attached to it. Both ends of the network cable are terminated. A *ring network* has a central control unit called a Media Access Unit to which all devices are attached by cables. A *hub network* has a backplane with connectors leading through another cable to the devices.

## 1

Q What are the seven OSI layers and (in one phrase) their responsibility?

A The OSI layers (from the bottom up) are as follows:

Physical: transmits data

Data Link: corrects transmission errors

Network: provides the physical routing information

Transport: verifies data is correctly transmitted

Session: synchronizes data exchange between upper and lower layers

Presentation: converts network data to application-specific format

Application: end-user interface

Q What are the differences between segmentation and reassembly, and concatenation and separation?

A Segmentation is the breaking apart of a large N-service data unit (N-SDU) into several smaller N-protocol data units (N-PDUs), and reassembly is the reverse.

Concatenation is the combination of several N-PDUs from the next higher layer into one SDU. Separation is the reverse.

Q Define multiplexing and demultiplexing. How are they useful?

A Multiplexing is when several connections are supported by a single connection. According to the formal definition, this applies to layers (so that three presentation service connections could be multiplexed into a single session connection). However, it is a term generally used for all kinds of connections, such as putting four modem calls down a single modem line. Demultiplexing is the reverse of multiplexing, in which one connection is split into several connections.

Multiplexing is a key to supporting many connections at once with limited resources. A typical example is a remote office with 20 terminals, each of which is connected to the main office by a telephone line. Instead of requiring 20 lines, they can all be multiplexed into three or four. The amount of multiplexing that is possible depends on the maximum capacity of each physical line.

Q How many protocol headers are added by the time an OSI-based e-mail application (in the application layer) has sent a message to the physical layer for transmission?

A Seven, one for each OSI layer. More protocol headers may be added by the actual physical network system. As a general rule, each layer adds its own protocol information.

Workshop

The Workshop provides quiz questions to help you solidify your understanding of the material covered. Some Workshop sections of this book also contain exercises to provide you with experience in using what you've learned. Try to understand the quiz and exercise answers before continuing on to the next chapter. Answers are provided in Appendix F, "Answers."

Quiz

1. What does each of the following primitives do?

   service primitive
   request primitive
   indication primitive
   response primitive
   confirmation primitive

2. What is a Service Access Point? How many are there per layer?

3. Explain the process followed in adopting a new Internet Standard for TCP/IP.

Exercises

1. Provide definitions for each of the following terms:

   packet
   subsystem
   entity
   service
   layer
   ISO
   ASN.1

2. Use diagrams to show the differences between segmentation, separation, and blocking.

2

TCP/IP and the Internet

Before proceeding into a considerable amount of detail about TCP/IP, the Internet, and the Internet Protocol, it is worthwhile to try and complete a quick outline of TCP/IP. Then, as the details are discussed, they can be placed in the broader outline more easily, thereby leading to a complete understanding in the next two chapters.

Just what is TCP/IP? It is a software-based communications protocol used in networking. Although the name TCP/IP implies that the entire scope of the product is a combination of two protocols—Transmission Control Protocol and Internet Protocol—the term TCP/IP is usually not a single entity combining two protocols, but a larger set of software programs that provide network services such as remote logins, remote file transfers, and electronic mail. TCP/IP provides a method for transferring information from one machine to another. A communications protocol should handle errors in transmission, manage the routing and delivery of data, and control the actual transmission by the use of predetermined status signals. TCP/IP accomplishes all of this.

Note: TCP/IP is not a single product. It is a catch-all name for a family of protocols that use similar behaviors. The term TCP/IP usually refers to a protocol within the family, not TCP and IP only.

In Day 1, you saw that the OSI model is composed of seven layers. You can overlay the TCP/IP programs on this model to give a rough idea of where they all reside. Figure 2.1 shows the basic elements of the TCP/IP system. You will see that TCP/IP is not involved in the bottom two layers of the OSI model (Data Link and Physical), but begins in the Network layer where the Internet Protocol (IP) resides. In the Transport layer, the Transmission Control Protocol (TCP) is involved. Above this, the utilities and protocols that make up the rest of the TCP/IP suite are built using the TCP and IP layers for their communications system. There are two transport systems involved, namely TCP and User Datagram Protocol (UDP). Each has its strengths, which you will see later. The routing of messages is performed by the Internet Protocol in the Network layer.

Warning: A note of caution about TCP/IP: Despite the fact that TCP/IP is an open protocol, there are many companies who have modified it for their own networking system. There can be incompatibilities because of these modifications, which, even though they may adhere to the official standards, might have other aspects that cause problems. Luckily, these problems are not rampant, but you should be careful when choosing a TCP/IP product to ensure its compatibility with existing software and hardware.

Telnet - Remote Login
FTP - File Transfer Protocol
SMTP - Simple Mail Transfer Protocol
X - X Windows System
Kerberos - Security
DNS - Domain Name System
ASN - Abstract Syntax Notation
SNMP - Simple Network Management Protocol

NFS - Network File Server
RPC - Remote Procedure Calls
TFTP - Trivial File Transfer Protocol
TCP - Transmission Control Protocol
User Datagram Protocol
IP - Internet Protocol
ICMP - Internet Control Message Protocol

Figure 2.1. *TCP/IP suite and OSI layers.*

TCP/IP is dependent on the concept of clients and servers. This has nothing to do with a file server being accessed by a diskless workstation or PC. The term *client/server* has a simple meaning in TCP/IP: It refers to any device that initiates communications as the client, and the device that answers as the server. The server is responding (serving) the client's requests.

A Quick Overview of TCP/IP Components

To understand the role that the many components of the TCP/IP protocol family plays, it is useful to know what you can do over a TCP/IP network. Then, once the applications are understood, the protocols are a little easier to comprehend. The following list is not exhaustive but mentions the primary user applications that TCP/IP provides.

Telnet

The Telnet program provides a remote login capability. This lets a user on one machine log onto another machine and act as though he or she were directly in front of the second machine. The connection can be anywhere on the local network or on another network anywhere in the world, as long as the user has permission to log onto the remote system.

File Transfer Protocol

The File Transfer Protocol (FTP) enables a file on one system to be copied to another system. The user doesn't actually log in as a full user to the machine he or she wants to access, as with telnet, but instead uses the FTP program to enable access. Again, the correct permissions are necessary to provide access to the files. Once the connection to a remote machine has been established, FTP enables you to copy one or more files to your machine. (The term *transfer* implies that the file is moved from one system to another, but the original is not affected. Files are copied.)

Simple Mail Transfer Protocol

The Simple Mail Transfer Protocol (SMTP) is used for the transferring of electronic mail. Transparent to the user, SMTP connects to different machines and transfers the mail messages, much like FTP transfers files.

Kerberos

Kerberos is a widely supported security protocol that uses a special device called an *authentication server*, which validates passwords and encryption schemes. Kerberos is one of the more secure encryption systems used in communications and is quite common in UNIX.

Domain Name Server

The Domain Name Server (DNS) enables a device with a common name to be converted to a special network address. For example, a system called joes_workstation cannot be accessed by a network across the country unless some method of checking the local machine's names is available. The DNS provides a conversion from the common local name to the unique physical address of the device's network connection.

Abstract Syntax Notation

You saw Abstract Syntax Notation (ASN.1) in the first chapter. It is a language used in both OSI and TCP/IP to define standards. ASN.1 provides unambiguous definitions for terms used in those standards.

Simple Network Management Protocol

The Simple Network Management Protocol (SNMP) uses the User Datagram Protocol (UDP) as a transport mechanism. It uses different terms from TCP/IP, working with managers and agents instead of clients and servers. An agent provides information about a device, whereas a manager communicates across a network.

Network File Server

The Network File Server (NFS) is a set of protocols developed by Sun Microsystems to transparently enable multiple machines to access each other's directories. They accomplish this by using a distributed filesystem scheme. NFS systems are common in large corporate environments, which use UNIX workstations.

Remote Procedure Calls

Remote Procedure Calls (RPCs) are functions that enable an application to communicate with another machine (the server). They provide for programming functions, return codes, and predefined variables to support distributed computing.

Trivial File Transfer Protocol

The Trivial File Transfer Protocol (TFTP) is a very simple, unsophisticated file transfer protocol that lacks any security. It uses UDP as a transport.

Transmission Control Protocol

Transmission Control Protocol (the TCP part of TCP/IP) is a communications protocol that provides reliable transfer of data. It is responsible for assembling data passed from higher-layer applications into standard packets and ensuring the data is transferred correctly.

User Datagram Protocol

User Datagram Protocol (UDP) is a connectionless-oriented protocol, meaning it does not provide for the retransmission of datagrams (unlike TCP, which is connection-oriented). UDP is not very reliable, but it does have particular purposes. If the applications that use UDP have reliability checking, the shortcomings of UDP can be overcome.

Internet Protocol

The Internet Protocol (IP) is responsible for moving the packets of data assembled by either TCP or UDP across networks. It uses a set of unique addresses for every device on the network to determine routing and destinations.

Internet Control Message Protocol

The Internet Control Message Protocol (ICMP) is responsible for checking and generating messages on the status of devices on a network. It can be used to inform other devices of a failure in one particular machine. ICMP and IP usually work together.

TCP/IP History

The architecture of TCP/IP is often called the Internet architecture because TCP/IP and the Internet are so closely interwoven. Yesterday, you saw how the Internet standards were developed by the Defense Advanced Research Projects Agency (DARPA) and eventually passed on to the Internet Society.

The Internet was originally proposed by the precursor of DARPA, called the Advanced Research Projects Agency (ARPA), as a method of testing the viability of packet-switching networks. (When ARPA's focus became military in nature, the name change was effected.) During its tenure of the project, ARPA foresaw a network of leased lines connected by switching nodes. The network was called ARPAnet and the switching nodes were called Internet Message Processors or IMPs.

The ARPAnet was initially to be comprised of four IMPs located at the University of California at Los Angeles, the University of California at Santa Barbara, the Stanford Research Institute, and the University of Utah. The original IMPs were to be Honeywell 316 minicomputers.

The contract for the installation of the network was won by Bolt, Beranek, and Newman (BBN), a company which was to have a strong influence on the development of the network in the following years. The contract was awarded in late 1968, followed by testing and refinement over the next five years.

> **Note:** Bolt, Beranek, and Newman (BBN) made many suggestions for the improvement of the Internet and the development of TCP/IP, for which their names are often associated with the protocol.

In 1971, ARPAnet entered into regular service. Machines used the ARPAnet by connecting to an IMP using the "1822" protocol—so called because that was the number of the technical paper describing the system. During the early years, the purpose and utility of the network was widely (and sometimes heatedly) discussed, leading to refinements and modifications as users requested more functionality from the system.

A commonly recognized need was the capability to transfer files from one machine to another, as well as the capability to support remote logins. Remote logins would enable a user in Santa Barbara to connect to a machine in Los Angeles over the network, and function as though he or she were in front of the UCLA machine. The protocol then in use on the network wasn't capable of handling these new functionality requests, so new protocols were continually developed, refined, and tested.

Remote login and remote file transfer were finally implemented in a protocol called the Network Control Program (NCP). Later, electronic mail was added through the File Transfer Protocol (FTP), and together with NCP's remote logins and file transfer, formed the basic services for ARPAnet.

By 1973, it was clear that NCP was unable to handle the volume of traffic and proposed new functionality. A project was begun in order to develop a new protocol. The birth of the TCP/IP and gateway architectures were first proposed in 1974. The published article by Cerf and Kahn described a system that provided a standardized application protocol that also used end-to-end acknowledgments.

Neither of these concepts were really novel at the time, but more importantly (and with considerable vision), Cerf and Kahn suggested that the new protocol be independent of the underlying network and computer hardware. Also, they proposed universal connectivity throughout the network. These two ideas were radical in a world of proprietary hardware and software because they would enable any kind of platform to participate in the network. The protocol was developed and became known as TCP/IP.

A series of RFCs (Request for Comments, part of the process for adopting new Internet Standards) was issued in 1981, standardizing on TCP/IP Version 4 for the ARPAnet. In 1982, TCP/IP supplanted NCP as the dominant protocol of the growing network, which was now connecting machines across the continent. It is estimated that a new computer was connected to ARPAnet every 20 days during its first decade. (That may not seem like much compared to the current estimate of Internet's size doubling every year, but in the early eighties it was a phenomenal growth rate.)

During the development of ARPAnet, it became obvious that non-military researchers could use the network to their advantage, enabling faster communications of ideas, as well as faster physical data transfer. A proposal to the National Science Foundation lead to funding for the Computer Science Network in 1981, joining the military with educational and research institutes to refine the network. This led to the splitting of the network into two different networks in 1984. The MILNET was dedicated to unclassified military traffic, whereas the ARPAnet was left for research and other non-military purposes.

ARPAnet's growth and subsequent demise came with the approval for the Office of Advanced Scientific Computing to develop wide access to supercomputers. They created NSFNET to connect six supercomputers spread across the country through T-1 lines (which operated at 1.544 Mbps). The Department of Defense finally declared ARPAnet obsolete in 1990, when it was officially dismantled.

Berkeley UNIX Implementations and TCP/IP

TCP/IP became important when the Department of Defense started including the protocols as military standards, which were required for many contracts. TCP/IP became popular primarily because of the work done at UCB (Berkeley). UCB had been a center of UNIX development for years, but in 1983 they undertook to release a new version that incorporated TCP/IP as an integral element. That version—4.2BSD (Berkeley System Distribution)—was made available to the world as public domain software.

The popularity of 4.2BSD spurred the popularity of TCP/IP, especially as more sites connected to the growing ARPAnet. Berkeley released an enhanced version (which included the so-called Berkeley Utilities) in 1986 as 4.3BSD. An optimized TCP implementation followed in 1988 (called 4.3BSD/Tahoe). Practically every version of TCP/IP available today has its roots (and much of its code) in the Berkeley versions.

> **Note:** Despite the demise of Berkeley Software Distribution's UNIX version in 1993, the BSD and UCB developments are an integral part of TCP/IP and will continue to be used as part of the protocol family's naming system.

OSI and TCP/IP

The adoption of TCP/IP didn't conflict with the OSI standards because the two developed concurrently. In some ways, TCP/IP contributed to OSI, and vice versa.

Several important differences do exist, though, which arise from the basic requirements of TCP/IP:

- [ ] A common set of applications
- [ ] Dynamic routing
- [ ] Connectionless protocols at the networking level
- [ ] Universal connectivity
- [ ] Packet-switching

The differences between the OSI architecture and that of TCP/IP relates to the layers above the transport level, and those at the network level. OSI has both the session layer and the presentation layer, whereas TCP/IP combines both into an application layer. The requirement for a connectionless protocol also required TCP/IP to combine the OSI's physical and link layer into a network level. A schematic view of TCP/IP's layered structure (compared with OSI's seven layer model) is shown in Figure 2.2. TCP/IP calls the different network level elements *subnetworks*.

Figure 2.2. *The OSI and TCP/IP layered structures.*

> **Note:** OSI and TCP/IP are not incompatible, but they aren't perfectly compatible, either. They both have a layered architecture, but the OSI architecture is much more rigorously defined and the layers are more independent that TCP/IP's.

Some fuss was made about the network level combination, although it soon became obvious that the argument was academic as most implementations of the OSI model combined the physical and link levels on an intelligent controller (such as a network card). The combination of the two layers into a single layer had one major benefit: It enabled a subnetwork to be designed that was independent of any network protocols, because TCP/IP was oblivious to the details. This enabled proprietary, self-contained networks to implement the TCP/IP protocols for connectivity outside their closed systems.

The layered approach gave rise to the name TCP/IP. The transport layer uses the Transmission Control Protocol (TCP) or one of several variants such as the User Datagram Protocol (UDP). (There are other protocols in use, but TCP and UDP are the most common.) There is, however, only one protocol for the network level—the Internet Protocol (IP). This is what assures the system of universal connectivity, one of the primary design goals.

There is a considerable amount of pressure from the user community to abandon the OSI model (and any future communications protocol that is developed that conforms to it) in favor of TCP/IP. The argument hinges on some obvious reasons:

☐ TCP/IP is up and running, and has a proven record.

☐ TCP/IP has an established, functioning management body.

☐ There are thousands of applications that currently use TCP/IP and its well-documented application programming interfaces.

☐ TCP/IP is the basis for most UNIX systems, which are gaining the largest share of the operating system market (other than desktop single-user machines, such as the PC and Macintosh).

☐ TCP/IP is vendor-independent.

Arguing rather strenuously against TCP/IP, surprisingly enough, is the U.S. government—the very body that sponsored it in the first place. Its primary argument is that TCP/IP is not an internationally adopted standard, whereas OSI has that recognition. The Department of Defense has even begun to move its systems away from the TCP/IP protocol set. A compromise will probably result, with some aspects of OSI adopted into the still-evolving TCP/IP protocol suite.

TCP/IP and Ethernet

For many people, the terms TCP/IP and Ethernet go together almost automatically, primarily for historical reasons, as well as the simple fact that there are more Ethernet-based TCP/IP networks than any other type. Ethernet was originally developed at XEROX's Palo Alto Research Center (PARC) as a step towards an electronic office communications system and has since grown in capability and popularity.

Ethernet is a hardware system, providing for the Data Link and Physical layers of the OSI model. As part of the Ethernet standards, issues such as cable type and broadcast speeds are established. There are several different versions of Ethernet, each with a different data transfer rate. The most common is Ethernet Version 2, also called 10Base5, Thick Ethernet, and IEEE 802.3 (after the number of the standard that defines the system adopted by the Institute of Electrical and Electronic Engineers). This system has a 10 megabit-per-second rate.

There are several commonly used variants of Ethernet, such as Thin Ethernet (called 10Base2), which can operate over thinner cable (such as the coaxial cable used in cable television systems) and Twisted-Pair Ethernet (10BaseT), which uses simple twisted-pair wires similar to telephone cable. The latter variant is popular for small companies because it is inexpensive, easy to wire, and has no strict requirements for distance between machines.

> **Note:** It is usually easy to tell which type of Ethernet network is being used by checking the connector to a network card. If it has a telephone-style plug, it is 10BaseT. The cable for 10BaseT looks the same as telephone cable. If the network has a D-shaped connector with many pins in it, it is 10Base5. A 10Base2 network has a connector similar to a cable TV coaxial connector, except it locks into place. The 10Base5 connector is always circular.
>
> The size of a network is also a good indicator. 10Base5 is used in large networks with many devices and long transmission runs. 10Base2 is used in smaller networks, usually with all the network devices in fairly close proximity. Twisted-pair (10BaseT) networks are often used for very small networks with a few dozen devices maximum in a close proximity.

Ethernet and TCP/IP work well together, with Ethernet providing the physical cabling (layers one and two) and TCP/IP the communications protocol (layers three and four) that is broadcast over the cable. The two have their own processes for packaging information: TCP/IP uses 32-bit addresses, whereas Ethernet uses a 48-bit scheme. The two work together, however, because of one component of TCP/IP called the Address Resolution Protocol, which converts between the two schemes. (ARP is discussed in more detail in the section called "Address Resolution Protocol.")

Ethernet relies on a protocol called Carrier Sense Multiple Access with Collision Detect (CSMA/CD). To simplify the process, a device checks the network cable to see if anything is currently being sent. If it is clear, the device sends its data. If the cable is busy (carrier detect), the device waits for it to clear. If two devices transmit at the same time (a collision), the devices know—because of their constant comparison—of the cable traffic to the data in the sending buffer. If a collision happens, the devices wait a random amount of time before trying again.

Internet

As ARPAnet grew out of a military-only network to add subnetworks in universities, corporations, and user communities, it became know as the Internet. There is no single network called the Internet, however. The term refers to the collective network of subnetworks. The one things they all have in common is TCP/IP as a communications protocol.

As described in Day 1, the organization of the Internet and adoption of new standards is controlled by the Internet Advisory Board (IAB), which among other things, coordinates several task forces including the Internet Engineering Task Force (IETF) and Internet Research Task Force (IRTF). In a nutshell, the IRTF is concerned with ongoing research, whereas the IETF handles the implementation and engineering aspects associated with the Internet.

A body that has some bearing on the IAB is the Federal Networking Council (FNC), which serves as an intermediary between the IAB and the government. The FNC has an advisory capacity to the IAB and its task forces, as well as the responsibility for managing the government's use of the Internet and other networks. Because the government was responsible for funding the development of Internet, they retain a considerable amount of control, as well as sponsor some research and expansion of the Internet.

The Structure of the Internet

As mentioned earlier, the Internet is not a single network but a collection of networks that communicate with each other through gateways. For the purposes of today's text, a *gateway* (sometimes called a *router*) is defined as a system that performs relay functions between networks, as shown in Figure 2.3. The different networks connected to each other through gateways are often called subnetworks, because they are a smaller part of the larger overall network. Take care not to assume this means that a subnetwork is small or dependent on the larger network. Subnetworks are complete networks, but they are connected through a gateway as a part of the larger internetwork, or in this case the Internet.

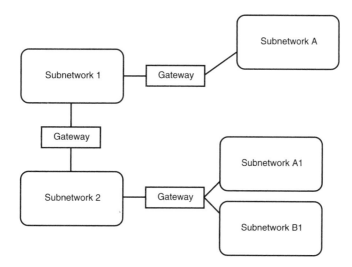

Figure 2.3. *Gateways act as relays between subnetworks.*

With TCP/IP, all interconnections between physical networks are through gateways. An important point to remember for use later is that gateways route information packets based on their destination network name, not the destination machine. Gateways are supposed to be completely transparent to the user, which also alleviates the gateway from handling user applications (unless the machine that is acting as a gateway is also someone's work machine or a local network server, as is often the case with small networks). Put simply, the gateway's sole task is to receive a Protocol Data Unit (PDU) from either the internetwork or the local network and either route it on to the next gateway or pass it into the local network for routing to the proper user.

Gateways work with any kind of hardware and operating system, as long as they are designed to communicate with the other gateways they are attached to (which in this case means that a gateway uses TCP/IP). Whether the gateway is leading to just a Macintosh network, a set of IBM PCs, or mainframes from a dozen different companies doesn't matter to the gateway or the PDUs it handles.

Note: There are actually several types of gateways, each performing a difference type of task. Day 7 looks at the different gateways in more detail.

In the United States, the Internet has the NFSNET as its backbone, as shown in Figure 2.4. Among the primary networks connected to the NFSNET are NASA's Space Physics Analysis Network (SPAN), the San Diego Supercomputer Network (SDSCNET), the Computer Science Network (CSNET), and a host of smaller user-oriented networks such as Because It's Time Network (BITNET) and UUNET, who provide connectivity through gateways for smaller sites that can't or don't want to establish a direct gateway to the Internet.

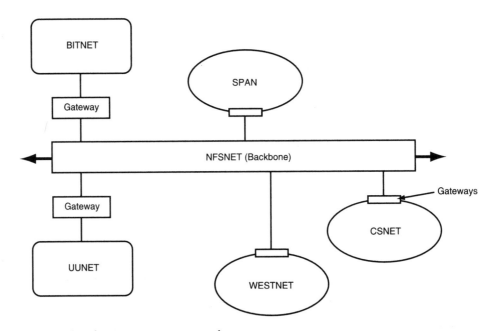

Figure 2.4. *The U.S. Internet network.*

The NFSNET backbone is comprised of approximately 3,000 research sites, connected by T-3 leased lines running at 44.736 megabits per second. Tests are currently underway to increase the operational speed of the backbone to enable more throughput and accommodate the rapidly increasing number of users. Several technologies are being field-tested, including Synchronous Optical Network (SONET), Asynchronous Transfer Mode (ATM), and ANSI's proposed High-Performance Parallel Interface (HPPI). These new systems can produce speeds approaching 1 gigabit per second.

The Internet Layers

Most internetworks, including the Internet, can be thought of as a layered architecture (yes, even more layers!) to simplify understanding. The layer concept helps in the task of developing applications for internetworks, too. The layering also shows how the different parts of TCP/IP work together. The more logical structure brought about by using a layering process has already been seen in the first chapter for the OSI model, so applying it to the Internet makes sense. Be careful to think of these layers as conceptual only; they are not really physical or software layers as such (unlike the OSI or TCP/IP layers).

It is convenient to think of the Internet as having four layers. This layered Internet Architecture is shown in Figure 2.5. These layers should not be confused with the architecture of each machine, as described in the OSI seven-layer model, but as a method of seeing how the internetwork, network, TCP/IP, and the individual machines work together. Independent machines reside in the subnetwork layer at the bottom of the architecture, connected together in a local area network (LAN) and referred to as the subnetwork, a term you saw in the last section.

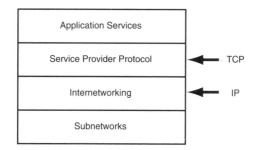

Figure 2.5. *The Internet architecture.*

On top of the subnetwork layer is the internetwork, which provides the functionality for communications between networks through gateways. Each subnetwork uses gateways to connect to the other subnetworks in the internetwork. It is in the internetwork layer that data gets transferred from gateway to gateway until it reaches its destination and then passes into the subnetwork layer. The internetwork layer runs the Internet Protocol.

The Service Provider Protocol layer is responsible for the overall end-to-end communications of the network. This is the layer that runs the Transmission Control Protocol (TCP) and other protocols. It handles the data traffic flow itself and ensures reliability for the message transfer.

The top-most layer is the Application Services layer, which supports the interfaces to the user applications. This layer interfaces to electronic mail, remote file transfers, and remote access. There are several protocols used in this layer, many of which you'll read about later.

To see how the Internet Architecture layer model works, a simple example is useful. Assume an application on one machine wants to transfer a datagram to an application on another machine in a different subnetwork. Without all the signals between layers and simplifying the architecture a little, the process is shown in Figure 2.6. The layers in the sending and receiving machines are the OSI layers, with the equivalent Internet Architecture layers indicated.

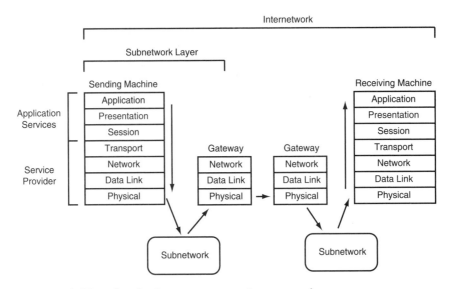

Figure 2.6. *Transfer of a datagram over an internetwork.*

The data is sent down the layers of the sending machine, assembling the datagram with the Protocol Control Information (PCI) as it goes. From the physical layer, the datagram (which is sometimes called a *frame* after the data link layer has added its header and trailing information) is sent out to the local area network. The LAN routes the information to the gateway out to the internetwork. During this process, the LAN has no concern about the message contained in the datagram. Some networks, however, do alter the header information to show, among other things, the machines it has passed through.

From the gateway, the frame passes from gateway to gateway along the internetwork until it arrives at the destination subnetwork. At each step, the gateway analyzes the datagram's header to determine if it is for the subnetwork the gateway leads to, and if not, routes the datagram back out over the internetwork. This analysis is performed in the Physical layer, eliminating the need to pass the frame up and down through different layers on each gateway. The header may be altered at each gateway to reflect its routing path.

When the datagram is finally received at the destination subnetwork's gateway, the gateway recognizes that the datagram is at its correct subnetwork and routes it into the local area network and eventually to the target machine. The routing is accomplished by reading the header information. When the datagram finally reaches the destination machine, it passes up through the layers with each layer stripping off its PCI header, and then passing the result on up. At long last, the application layer on the destination machine processes the final header and passes the message to the correct application.

If the datagram was not data to be processed but a request for a service such as a remote file transfer, the correct layer on the destination machine would decode the request and route the file back over the internetwork to the original machine.

Internetwork Problems

Not everything goes smoothly when transferring data from one subnetwork to another. All manner of problems can occur, despite the fact that the entire network is using one protocol. A typical problem is a limitation on the size of the datagram. The sending network may support datagrams of 1,024 bytes, but the receiving network might only use 512-byte datagrams (because of a different hardware protocol, for example). This is where the processes of segmentation, separation, reassembly, and concatenation—that were mentioned in the last chapter—become important.

The actual addressing methods used by the different subnetworks can cause conflicts when routing datagrams. Because communicating subnetworks might not have the same network control software, the network-based header information might differ, despite the fact that the communications methods are based on TCP/IP. An associated problem occurs when dealing with the differences between physical and logical machine names. In the same manner, a network that requires encryption instead of clear-text datagrams may affect the decoding of header information. Therefore, differences in the security implemented on the subnetworks can affect datagram traffic. These differences can all be resolved with software, but the problems associated with addressing methods can become considerable.

Another common problem is the different networks' tolerance for timing problems. Time-out and retry values may differ, so when two subnetworks are trying to establish communications, one may have given up and moved on to another task while the second is still waiting patiently for an acknowledgment signal. Also, if two subnetworks are communicating properly and one gets busy and has to pause the communications process for a short while, the amount of time before the other network assumes a disconnection and gives up may be important. Coordinating the timing over the internetwork can become very complicated.

Routing methods and the speed of the machines on the network may affect the internetwork's performance, too. If a gateway is managed by a particularly slow machine, the traffic coming through the gateway may back up, causing delays and incomplete transmissions for the entire internetwork. Developing an internetwork system that can dynamically adapt to loads and reroute datagrams when a bottleneck occurs is very important.

There are other factors to consider, such as network management and troubleshooting information, but you should begin to see that simply connecting networks together without due thought will not work. The many different network operating systems and hardware platforms require a logical, well-developed approach to the internetwork. This is outside the scope of TCP/IP, which is simply concerned with the transmission of the datagrams. The TCP/IP implementations on each platform, however, must be able to handle the problems mentioned.

Internet Addresses

Network addresses are analogous to mailing addresses, in that they tell a system where to deliver a datagram. Three terms commonly used in the Internet relate to addressing: name, address, and route.

Note: The term *address* is often generically used with communications protocols to refer to many different things. It can mean a destination, a port of a machine, a memory location, an application, and more. Take care when you encounter the term to make sure you know what it is really referring to.

A *name* is a specific identification of a machine, a user, or an application. It is usually unique and provides an absolute target for the datagram. An *address* typically identifies where the target is located, usually as its physical or logical location in a network. A *route* tells the system how to get a datagram to the address.

You'll use the recipient's name often, either specifying a user name or a machine name, and an application will do the same thing transparently to you. From the name, a network software package called the *name server* will try to resolve the address and the route, making that aspect unimportant to you. When you send electronic mail, you simply indicate the recipient's name, relying on the name server to figure out how to get the mail message to them.

Using a name server has one other primary advantage besides making the addressing and routing unimportant to the end user: It gives the system or network administrator a lot of freedom to change the network as required, without having to tell each user's machine about any changes. As long as an application can access the name server, any routing changes can be ignored by the application and users.

Naming conventions differ depending on the platform, the network, and the software release, but here is a typical Ethernet-based Internet subnetwork as an example. There are several types of addressing you need to look at, including the local area network system, as well as the wider internetwork addressing conventions.

Subnetwork addressing

On a single network, there are several pieces of information necessary to ensure the correct delivery of data. The primary components are the physical address and the data link address.

Physical Addresses

Each device on a network that will communicate with others has a unique *physical address,* sometimes called the *hardware address.* On any given network, there will be only one occurrence of each address; otherwise the name server will have no way of identifying the target device unambiguously. For hardware, the addresses are usually encoded into a network interface card, set either by switches or by software. With respect to the OSI model, the address is located in the physical layer.

In the physical layer, the analysis of each incoming datagram (more accurately a protocol data unit or PDU) is performed. If the recipient's address matches the physical address of the device, the datagram can be passed up the layers. If the addresses don't match, the datagram is ignored. Keeping this analysis in the bottom-most layer of the OSI model prevents unnecessary delays, because otherwise the datagram would have to be passed up to other layers for analysis.

The length of the physical address varies depending on the networking system, but Ethernet and several others use 48 bits in each address. For communications to occur, two address are required: one each for the sending and receiving devices.

The IEEE is now handling the task of assigning universal physical addresses for subnetworks (a task previously performed by Xerox, as it developed Ethernet). For each subnetwork, the IEEE assigns an organization unique identifier (OUI) that is 24-bits long, enabling the organization to assign the other 24 bits however it wants. (Actually, two of the 24 bits assigned as an OUI are control bits, so only 22 bits identify the subnetwork. Because this provides 2 to the exponent 22 combinations, it is possible to run out of OUIs in the future if the current rate of growth is sustained.)

The format of the organization unique identifier is shown in Figure 2.7. The least significant bit of the address (lowest bit number) is the individual or group address bit. If the bit is set to 0, the address refers to an individual address; a setting of 1 means that the rest of the address field identifies a group address that needs further resolution. If the entire OUI is set to 1s, the address has a special meaning. All stations on the network are assumed to be the destination.

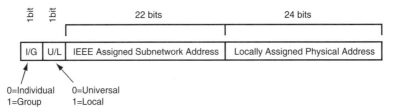

Figure 2.7. *Layout of the organization unique identifier.*

The second bit is the *local* or *universal* bit. If set to 0, it has been set by the universal administration body. This is the setting for IEEE assigned OUIs. If the second bit has a value of 1, the OUI has been locally assigned and would cause addressing problems if decoded as an IEEE-assigned address.

The remaining 22 bits make up the physical address of the subnetwork, as assigned by the IEEE. The second set of 24 bits identify local network addresses and are administered locally. If an organization were to run out of physical addresses (there are about 16 million addresses possible from 24 bits), the IEEE has the capacity to assign a second subnetwork address.

The combination of 24 bits from the OUI and 24 locally assigned bits is called a media access control (MAC) address. When a packet of data is assembled for transfer across an internetwork, there will be two sets of MACs, one from the sending machine and one for the receiving machine.

Data Link Address

The IEEE Ethernet standards (and several other allied standards) use another address called the link layer address (abbreviated as LSAP for link service access point). The LSAP identifies the type of link protocol used in the data link layer. As with the physical addresses, a datagram will carry both sending and receiving LSAPs. The IEEE also enables a code that identifies the EtherType assignments, which identifies the upper layer protocol (ULP) running on the network (almost always a LAN).

Ethernet Frames

The layout of information in each transmitted packet of data differs depending on the protocol, but it is instructive to examine one to see how the addresses and related information are prepended to the data. This section uses the Ethernet system as an example because of its wide use with TCP/IP. It is quite similar to other systems, as well.

A typical Ethernet frame (remember that a frame is the term for a network-ready datagram) is shown in Figure 2.8. The preamble is a set of bits that are used primarily to synchronize the communication process and account for any random noise in the first few bits that are sent. At the end of the preamble is a sequence of bits that are the start frame delimiter (SFD), which indicate that the frame follows immediately.

Preamble	Recipient Address	Sender Address	Type	Data	CRC
64 Bits	48 Bits	48 Bits	16 Bits	Variable Length	32 Bits

Figure 2.8. *The Ethernet frame.*

The recipient and sender addresses follow in IEEE 48-bit format, followed by a 16-bit type indicator that is used to identify the protocol. The data follows the type indicator. The Data field is between 46 and 1,500 bytes in length. If the data is actually less than 46 bytes, it is padded with 0s until it is 46 bytes long. Any padding is not counted in the calculations of the data field's total length, which is used in one part of the IP header. The next chapter covers IP headers.

At the end of the frame is the cyclic redundancy check (CRC) count, which is used to ensure that the frame's contents have not been modified during the transmission process.

Each gateway along the transmission route calculates a CRC value for the frame and compares it to the value at the end of the frame. If the two match, the frame can be sent farther along the network or into the subnetwork; but if they differ, a modification to the frame must have happened and the frame is discarded (to be later retransmitted by the sending machine when a timer expires).

In some protocols, such as the IEEE 802.3, the overall layout of the frame is the same, but slight variations in the contents are used. With 802,3, the 16 bits used by Ethernet to identify the protocol type are replaced with a 16-bit value for the length of the data block. Also, the data area itself is prepended by a new field. This book looks at several different protocols in detail.

IP Addresses

TCP/IP uses a 32-bit address to identify a machine on a network and the network to which it is attached. IP addresses identify a machine's connection to the network, not the machine itself—an important distinction. Whenever a machine's location on the network is moved, the IP address must be changed, too. The IP address is the set of numbers many people see on their workstations or terminals, such as 127.40.8.72, which uniquely identifies the device.

IP (or Internet) addresses are assigned only by the Network Information Center (NIC), although if a network is not connected to the Internet, that network can determine its own numbering. For all Internet accesses, though, the IP address must be registered with the NIC.

There are four formats for the IP address, each used depending on the size of the network. The four formats, Class A through Class D, are shown in Figure 2.9. The class is identified by the first few bit sequences, shown in the figure as 1 bit for Class A and up to 4 bits for Class D. The class can be determined from the first 3 (high-order) bits. In fact, in most cases, the first 2 bits are enough, because there are few Class D networks.

Class A addresses are for large networks that have many machines. The 24 bits for the local address (also frequently called the host address) are needed in these cases. The network address is kept to 7 bits, which limits the number of networks that can be identified.

Class B addresses are for intermediate sized networks, with 16-bit local or host addresses and 14-bit network addresses. Class C network have only 8 bits for the local or host address, limiting the number of devices to 256. There are 21 bits for the network address.

Finally, Class D networks are used for multicasting purposes, when a general broadcast to more than one device is required. The lengths of each section of the IP address have been carefully chosen to provide maximum flexibility in assigning both network and local addresses.

Figure 2.9. *The four IP address class structures.*

IP addresses are four sets of 8 bits, for a total 32 bits. You often represent these bits as separated by a period for convenience, so the IP address format can be thought of as `network.local.local.local` for Class A through to `network.network.network.local` for Class C. The IP addresses are usually written out in their decimal equivalents, instead of the long binary strings. This is the familiar host address number network users are used to seeing, such as `147.10.13.28`, which would indicate that the network address is `147.10` and the local or host address is `13.28`. Of course, the actual address is a set of 1s and 0s. The decimal notation used for IP addresses is properly called *dotted quad notation*—a bit of trivia for your next dinner party.

The IP addresses can be translated to common names and letters. This can pose a problem, though, because there must be some method of unambiguously relating the physical address, the network address, and a language-based name (such a `tpci_ws_4` or `bobs_machine`). The section later today titled, "Domain Name System," looks at this aspect of address naming.

From the IP address, a network can determine if the data is to be sent out through a gateway. Obviously, if the network address is the same as the current address (routing to a local network device, called a *direct host*), the gateway is avoided; but all other network addresses are routed to a gateway to leave the local network (*indirect host*). The gateway receiving data to be transmitted to another network must then determine the routing from the data's IP address and an internal table that provides routing information.

As mentioned, if an address were set to all 1s, the address applies to all addresses on the network. (See the previous section titled, "Physical Addresses.") The same rule applies to IP addresses, so that an IP address of 32 1s is considered a broadcast message to all networks and all devices. It is possible to broadcast to all machines in a network by altering the local or host address to all 1s, so that the address 147.10.255.255 for a Class B network (identified as network 147.10) would be received by all devices on that network (255.255 being the local addresses composed of all 1s); but the data would not leave the network.

Warning: There are two contradictory ways to indicate broadcasts. The later versions of TCP/IP use 1s, but earlier BSD systems use 0s. This causes a lot of confusion. All the devices on a network must know which broadcast convention is used, otherwise datagrams can be stuck on the network forever!

A slight twist is coding the network address as all 0s, which means the originating network, or the local address is being set to 0s—which refers to the originating device only (usually used only when a device is trying to determine its IP address). The all-zero network address format is used when the network IP address is not known, but other devices on the network still can interpret the local address. If this were to be transmitted to another network, it can obviously cause confusion! By convention, no local device is given a physical address of 0.

It is possible for a device to have more than one IP address if it is connected to more than one network, as is the case with gateways. These devices are called *multihomed*, because they have a unique address for each network they are connected to. In practice, it is best to have a dedicate machine for a multihomed gateway; otherwise the applications on that machine can get confused about which address they should use when building datagrams!

Two networks can have the same network address if they are connected by a gateway. This can cause problems for addressing, because the gateway must be able to differentiate which network the physical address is on. This problem will be looked at again in the next section.

Address Resolution Protocol

Determining addresses can be difficult because every machine on the network may not have a list of all the addresses of the other machines or devices. Sending data from one machine to another if the recipient's machine physical address is not known can cause a problem if there is no resolution system for determining the addresses. Having to constantly update a table of addresses on each machine would be a network administration nightmare. The problem is not restricted to machine addresses within a small network, because if the remote destination network addresses are unknown, routing and delivery problems will also occur.

The Address Resolution Protocol (ARP) helps solve these problems. ARP's job is to convert IP addresses to physical addresses (network and local) and in doing so, eliminates the need for applications to know about the physical addresses. Essentially, ARP is a table with a list of the IP addresses and their corresponding physical addresses. The table is called an *ARP cache*. The layout of an ARP cache is shown in Figure 2.10. Each row corresponds to one device, with information for each device:

IF Index:	The physical port (interface)
Physical Address:	The physical address of the device
IP Address:	The IP address corresponding to the physical address

	IF INDEX	PHYSICAL ADDRESS	IP ADDRESS	TYPE
Entry 1				
Entry 2				
Entry 3				
Entry n				

Figure 2.10. *The ARP cache address translation table layout.*

Mapping Type

The mapping type is one of four possible values indicating the status of the entry in the ARP cache. A value of 2 means the entry is invalid, a value of 3 means the mapping is dynamic (the entry may change), a value of 4 means static (the entry doesn't change), and finally, a value of 1 means none of the above.

When the ARP receives a recipient device's IP address, it searches the ARP cache for a match. If it finds one, it returns the physical address. If the ARP cache doesn't find a match for an IP address, it sends a message out on the network. The message, called an *ARP request,* is a broadcast that is received by all devices on the local network. (You may remember a broadcast has all 1s in the address.) The ARP request contains the IP address of the intended recipient device. If a device recognizes the IP address as belonging to it, the device sends a reply message containing its physical address back to the machine that generated the ARP request, which places the information into its ARP cache for future use. In this manner, the ARP cache can determine the physical address for any machine based on its IP address.

Whenever an ARP request is received by an ARP cache, it uses the information in the request to update its own table. Thus, the system can accommodate changing physical addresses and new additions to the network dynamically without having to generate an ARP request of its own. Without the use of an ARP cache, all the ARP requests and replies would generate a lot of network traffic, which can have a serious impact on network performance. There are some simpler network schemes that abandon the cache and simply use broadcast messages each time. This is feasible only when the number of devices is low enough to avoid network traffic problems.

The layout of the ARP request is shown in Figure 2.11. When an ARP request is sent, all fields in the layout are used except the Recipient Hardware Address (which the request is trying to identify). In an ARP reply, all the fields are used.

Figure 2.11. *The ARP request and ARP reply layout.*

This layout, which will be combined with the network system's protocols into a protocol data unit (PDU), has several fields. The following sections describes these fields.

Hardware Type

The hardware type identifies the type of hardware interface. Legal values are as follows.

Type	Description
1	Ethernet
2	Experimental Ethernet
3	X.25
4	Proteon ProNET (Token Ring)
5	Chaos
6	IEEE 802.X
7	ARCnet

Protocol Type

The protocol type identifies the type of protocol the sending device is using. With TCP/IP, these protocols are usually an EtherType, for which the legal values are as follows.

Decimal	Description
512	XEROX PUP
513	PUP Address Translation
1536	XEROX NS IDP
2048	Internet Protocol (IP)
2049	X.75
2050	NBS
2051	ECMA
2052	Chaosnet
2053	X.25 Level 3

continues

Decimal	Description
2054	Address Resolution Protocol (ARP)
2055	XNS
4096	Berkeley Trailer
21000	BBN Simnet
24577	DEC MOP Dump/Load
24578	DEC MOP Remote Console
24579	DEC DECnet Phase IV
24580	DEC LAT
24582	DEC
24583	DEC
32773	HP Probe
32784	Excelan
32821	Reverse ARP
32824	DEC LANBridge
32823	AppleTalk

If the protocol is not EtherType, other values are allowed.

Hardware Address Length

The length of each hardware address in the datagram, given in bytes.

Protocol Address Length

The length of the protocol address in the datagram, given in bytes.

Operation Code (Opcode)

The Opcode indicates whether the datagram is an ARP request or an ARP reply. If it is a request, the value is set to 1. If the datagram is a reply, the value is set to 2.

Sender Hardware Address

This is the hardware address of the sending device.

Sender IP Address

This is the IP address of the sending device.

Recipient Hardware Address

This is the hardware address of the recipient device.

Recipient IP Address

This is the IP address of the recipient device.

Two (or more) networks connected by a gateway can have the same network address. The gateway has to determine to which network the physical address or IP address corresponds. The gateway can do this with a modified ARP called the Proxy ARP (sometimes called Promiscuous ARP). A proxy ARP creates an ARP cache consisting of entries from both networks, with the gateway able to transfer datagrams from one network to the other. The gateway has to manage the ARP requests and replies that cross the two networks.

An obvious flaw with the ARP system is that if a device didn't know its own IP address, there would be no way to generate requests and replies. This can happen when a new device (typically a diskless workstation) is added to the network. The only address the device is aware of is the physical address set either by switches on the network interface or by software. A simple solution is the Reverse Address Resolution Protocol (RARP), which works the reverse of ARP, sending out the physical address and expecting back an IP address. The reply containing the IP address is sent by an RARP server, a machine that can supply the information. Although the originating device sends the message as a broadcast, RARP rules stipulate that only the RARP server can generate a reply. (Many networks assign more than one RARP server, both to spread the processing load and to act as a backup in case of problems.)

The Domain Name System

Instead of using the full 32-bit IP address, many systems adopt more meaningful names for their devices and networks. Network names usually reflect the organization's name (such as `tpci.com` and `bobs_cement`). Individual device names within a network can range from descriptive names on small networks (such as `tims_machine` and `laser_1`) to more complex naming conventions on larger networks (such as `hpws_23` and `tpci704`). Translating between these names and the IP addresses would be practically impossible on an Internet-wide scale.

To solve the problem of network names, the Network Information Center maintains a list of network names and the corresponding network gateway addresses. This system grew from a simple flatfile list (which was searched for matches) to a more complicated system called the Domain Name System (DNS) when the networks became too numerous for the flatfile system to function efficiently.

The Domain Name System uses a hierarchical architecture, much like the UNIX filesystem. The first level of naming divides networks into the category of subnetworks, such as `com` for commercial, `mil` for military, `edu` for educational, and so on. Below each of these is another division that identifies the individual subnetwork, usually one for each organization. This is called the *domain name* and is unique. The organization's system manager can further divide the company's subnetworks as desired, with each network called a *subdomain*. For example, the system `merlin.abc_corp.com` has the domain name `abc_corp.com`, whereas the network `merlin.abc_corp` is a subdomain of `merlin.abc_corp.com`. A network can be identified with an *absolute name* (such as `merlin.abc_corp.com`) or a *relative name* (such as `merlin`) that uses part of the complete domain name.

There are seven first-level domain names established by the NIC so far. These are

`.arpa`	An ARPAnet-Internet identification
`.com`	Commercial company
`.edu`	Educational institution
`.gov`	Any governmental body
`.mil`	Military
`.org`	Anything that doesn't fall into one of the other categories

The NIC also allows for a country designator to be appended. There are designators for all countries in the world, such as `.ca` for Canada and `.uk` for the United Kingdom.

The Domain Name System uses two systems to establish and track domain names. A *name resolver* on each network examines information in a domain name. If it can't find the full IP address, it queries a *name server,* which has the full NIC information available. The name resolver tries to complete the addressing information using its own database, which it updates in much the same manner as the ARP system (discussed earlier) when it must query a name server. If a queried name server cannot resolve the address, it can query another name server, and so on, across the entire internetwork.

There is a considerable amount of information stored in the name resolver and name server, as well as a whole set of protocols for querying between the two. The details, luckily, are not important to an understanding of TCP/IP, although the overall concept of the address resolution is important when understanding how the Internet translates between domain names and IP addresses.

Summary

Today, you saw the relationship of OSI and TCP/IP layered architectures, a history of TCP/IP and the Internet, the structure of the Internet, Internet and IP addresses, and the Address Resolution Protocol. Using these concepts you can move on to look at the TCP/IP family of protocols in more detail.

Day 3 begins with the Internet Protocol, showing how it is used and the format of its header information. The rest of the chapter covers gateway information necessary to piece together the rest of the protocols. Gateways are also revisited in Day 7.

Q&A

Q Explain the role of gateways in internetworks.

A Gateways act as relays between networks, passing datagrams from network to network, checking for a destination address. Networks talk to each other through gateways.

Q Expand the following TCP/IP protocol acronyms: DNS, SNMP, NFS, RPC, TFTP.

A DNS is the Domain Name Server, which allows a common name to be used instead of an IP address. SNMP is the Simple Network Management Protocol, used to provide information about devices. NFS is the Network File Server, a protocol that allows machines to access other filesystems as if they were part of their own. RPC is the Remote Procedure Call protocol, which enables applications to communicate. TFTP is the Trivial File Transfer Protocol, a simple file transfer system with no security.

Q Name the Internet's advisory bodies.

A The Internet Advisory Board (IAB) controls the Internet. The Internet Engineering Task Force (IETF) handles implementations of protocols on the Internet, and the Internet Research Task Force (IRTF) handles research.

Q What does ARP do?

A The Address Resolution Protocol converts IP addresses to physical device addresses.

Q What are the four IP address classes and their structures?

A The four IP address classes and their structures are as follows:

Class A for large networks: Network address = 7 bits, local address = 24 bits.
Class B for mid-size networks: Network address = 14 bits, local address = 16 bits.
Class C for small networks: Network address = 21 bits, local address = 8 bits.
Class D for multicast addresses, using 28 bits. Class D networks are seldom encountered.

Workshop

The Workshop provides quiz questions to help you solidify your understanding of the material covered. Some Workshop sections of this book also contain exercises to provide you with experience in using what you've learned. Try to understand the quiz and exercise answers before continuing on to the next chapter. Answers are provided in Appendix F, "Answers."

Quiz

1. Draw the layered architectures of both the OSI Reference Model and TCP/IP. Show how the layers correspond in each diagram.

2. Show the layered Internet architecture, explaining each layer's purpose.

3. Show how a datagram is transferred from one network, through one of more gateways, to the destination network. In each device, show the layered architecture and how high up the layered structure the datagrams goes.

4. Draw the IP header and an Ethernet frame, showing the number of bits used for each component. Explain each component's role.

5. Explain what an ARP Cache is. What is its structure and why is it used?

TCP/IP Protocols

Yesterday, you looked at the history of TCP/IP and the Internet in some detail; now you can move on to the Internet Protocol, the "IP" part of TCP/IP. A good understanding of IP is necessary to continue on to TCP, because the IP is the component that handles the movement of datagrams. Knowing how a datagram must be assembled and how it is moved through the networks will help you understand how the higher-level layers work with IP.

Today's text contains, unfortunately, even more detail on headers, protocols, and messaging. This information is necessary to understand when dealing with the applications and their interactions with IP, as well as troubleshooting the system. While we don't go into exhaustive detail, there is enough here that you can refer back to today's text whenever needed.

Internet Protocol

The Internet Protocol (IP) is a primary protocol of the OSI model, as well as an integral part of TCP/IP (as the name suggests). Although the word "Internet" appears in the protocol's name, it is not restricted to use with the Internet. It is true that all machines on the Internet will use or understand IP, but IP can be used on dedicated networks that have no relation to Internet at all. IP defines a protocol, not a connection.

The Internet Protocol's main tasks are the addressing of datagrams of information between computers and managing the fragmentation process of these datagrams. The protocol has a formal definition of the layout of a datagram of information and the formation of a header composed of information about the datagram. IP is responsible for the routing of a datagram, determining where it will be sent, as well as alternate routes in case of problems.

Another important aspect of IP's purpose has to do with "unreliable" delivery of a datagram. Unreliable in the IP sense means that the delivery of the datagram is not guaranteed, because it may get delayed, misrouted, or mangled in the breakdown and reassembly of message fragments. Internet Protocol has nothing to do with flow control or reliability: There is no inherent capability to verify that a sent message is correctly received. IP does not have a checksum for the data contents of a datagram, only for the header information. The verification and flow control tasks are left to other components in the layer model. (For that matter, IP doesn't even properly handle the forwarding of datagrams. IP has the capability to make a guess as to the best routing to move a datagram to the next node along a path, but does not inherently verify that the chosen path is the fastest or most efficient route.) Part of the IP system defines how gateways manage datagrams, how and when they should produce error messages, and how to recover from problems that may arise.

In Day 1 of this book, you saw how data can be broken into smaller sections for transmission and then reassembled at another location. IP provides for a maximum packet size of 65,535 bytes. The protocol has the capability to automatically divide a datagram of information into smaller datagrams if necessary, using the principles you saw in Day 1.

When the first datagram of a larger message that has been divided arrives at the destination, a *reassembly timer* is started. If all the pieces of the entire datagram are not received by the time the timer has reached a predetermined value, all the datagrams that have been received are discarded. The receiving machine knows the order in which the pieces are to be reassembled because of a field in the IP header. One consequence of this process is that a fragmented message has a lower chance of arrival than an unfragmented message, which is why most applications try to avoid fragmentation whenever possible.

The Internet Protocol is connectionless, meaning it doesn't worry about which nodes a datagram passes through along the path, or even at which machines the datagram starts and ends. This information is in the header, but the process of analyzing and passing on a datagram has nothing to do with IP analyzing the sending and receiving IP addresses. IP handles the addressing of a datagram with the full 32-bit Internet address, even though the transport protocol addresses use 8 bits.

The Internet Protocol Datagram Header

It is tempting to compare the Internet Protocol to a hardware network such as Ethernet because of the basic similarities in packaging information. In Day 2, you saw how Ethernet assembles a frame by combining the application data with a header block containing address information. The Internet Protocol does the same, except the contents of the header are specific to that protocol. When Ethernet receives an IP-assembled datagram, it adds its header to the front to create a frame—a process called *encapsulation*. The primary difference is that Ethernet's header contains the physical addresses of the destination machine, whereas the IP header contains the IP addresses. You may recall that the translation between the two addresses is performed by the Address Resolution Protocol.

> **Note:** *Encapsulation* is the process of adding something to the start (and sometimes the end) of data. It provides details about the data that is enclosed.

The datagram is the transfer unit used by IP, sometimes more specifically called an Internet datagram, or IP datagram. The Internet Protocol header uses six 32-bit words (24 bytes) when all the optional fields are included. The shortest header uses five words (20 bytes). To understand all the fields in the header, it is useful to remember that IP has no hardware dependence but must account for all versions of IP software it can encounter. The IP header layout is shown schematically in Figure 3.1. The different fields in the IP header can now be examined in more detail.

Figure 3.1. *The IP header layout.*

Version Number

This is a 4-bit field that contains the IP version number the protocol software supports. The version number is required so that receiving software will know how to decode the rest of the header, which changes with each new release of the IP standards. The current version is 4.

Part of the protocol stipulates that the receiving software must first check the version number before proceeding. If the software cannot handle the version, it rejects the datagram.

Header Length

This 4-bit field reflects the total length of the IP header, given in 32-bit words. The shortest header is five words, but the use of optional fields may increase the header size. To properly decode the header, IP must know when the header ends and the data begins, which is why this field is included. (There is no start-of-data marker.)

Type of Service

The 8-bit service type field instructs IP how to process the datagram properly. The field's 8 bits are read and assigned, as shown in Figure 3.2. The first 3 bits indicate the datagram's precedence, with a value from 0 (normal) through 7 (network control). The higher the number, the more important the datagram. Most implementations of TCP/IP and practically all hardware that uses TCP/IP ignores this field, treating all datagrams with the same priority.

Precedence (3 bits)	Delay	Thru	Rel	Not Used

Figure 3.2. *The 8-bit service type field layout.*

The next 3-bit flags control the delay, throughput, and reliability of the datagram. If the bit is set to 0, the setting is normal. A bit set to 1 implies low delay, high throughput, and high reliability in order of the flags. The last 2 bits of the field are not used.

For most purposes, the values of all the bits in the service type field are set to 0 because differences in delay, throughput, and reliability between machines are virtually non-existent unless a special network has been established. Although these flags would be useful in establishing the best routing method for a datagram, no currently available UNIX-based IP system bothers to evaluate the bits in these fields. (Although it is conceivable that the code could be modified for high-security or high-reliability networks.)

Datagram Length

This field gives the total length of the datagram, including the header, in bytes. The length of the data area itself can be computed by subtracting the header length from this value. The size of the total datagram length field is 16 bits, hence the 65,535 bytes maximum length of a datagram (including the header). This field is used to determine the length to be passed to the transport protocol to set the total frame length.

Identification

This field holds a number that is a unique identifier created by the sending node. This number is required when reassembling fragmented messages, ensuring that the fragments of one message are not intermixed with others.

Flags

The flags field is a 3-bit field, the first bit of which is left unused. The remaining 2 bits are dedicated to flags called DF (Don't Fragment) and MF (More Fragments), which control the handling of the datagrams when fragmentation is desirable.

If the DF flag is set to 1, the datagram cannot be fragmented under any circumstances. If the current node cannot send the datagram on without fragmenting it, and this bit is set to 1, the datagram will be discarded and an error message will be sent back to the sending device.

If the MF flag is set to 1, the current datagram is followed by more packets (often called *subpackets*), which must be reassembled to re-create the full message. The last fragment, that is sent as part of the larger message, has its MF flag set to 0 (off) so that the receiving device will know when to stop waiting for datagrams. Because the order of the fragments arrival may not correspond to the order in which they send, the MF flag is used in conjunction with the Fragment Offset (see the next section) to indicate to the receiving device the full extent of the message.

Fragment Offset

If the MF (More Fragments) flag bit is set, the fragment offset contains the position in the complete message of the submessage contained within the current datagram. This enables IP to reassemble fragmented packets in the proper order.

Offsets are always given relative to the beginning of the message. This is a 13-bit field, so offsets are calculated in units of 8 bytes, corresponding to the maximum packet length of 65,535 bytes.

Time to Live (TTL)

This field gives the amount of time in seconds that a datagram may remain on the network before it is discarded. This is set (usually to 15 or 30 seconds) by the sending node.

The TCP/IP standards stipulate that the field must be decreased by at least one second for each node that processes the packet, even if the processing time was less than one second. Also, when a datagram is received by a gateway, the arrival time is tagged so that if the datagram must wait to be processed, that time counts against its TTL. Hence, if a gateway is particularly overloaded and can't get to the datagram in short order, the timer may expire while awaiting processing and the datagram abandoned.

If the field becomes 0, the datagram must be discarded by the current node; but a message is sent to the sending machine if the packet is dropped. This rule prevents packets from endlessly circulating through networks.

Transport Protocol

This field holds the identification number of the transport protocol to which the packet has been handed. The numbers are defined by the Network Information Center. There are currently about 50 protocols. ICMP is number 1, and TCP is number 6. The full list of numbers is not necessary here.

Header Checksum

The number in this field is a checksum for the protocol header field (but not the data fields) to enable faster processing. Because the Time to Live (TTL) field is decremented at each node, the checksum also will change. The algorithm takes the ones-complement of the 16-bit sum of all 16-bit words.

This is a fast, efficient algorithm, but it will miss some unusual circumstances such as the loss of an entire 16-bit word that contains only 0s. However, because the data checksums used by both TCP and UDP cover the entire packet, these types of errors usually can be caught because the frame is assembled for the network transport.

Sending Address and Destination Address

These fields contain the 32-bit IP addresses of the sending and destination devices. These fields are established when the datagram is created and are not altered during the routing.

Options

The Options field is optional, composed of several different codes of variable length. If more than one option is used in the datagram, the options appear consecutively in the IP header. All the options are controlled by a byte that is usually divided into three fields: a 1-bit copy flag, a 2-bit option class, and a 5-bit option number. The copy flag is used to stipulate how the option is handled when fragmentation is necessary in a gateway. When the bit is set to 0, the option should be copied only to the first datagram but not to subsequent ones. If the bit is set to 1, the option is copied to all the datagrams.

The option class and option number indicate the type of option and its particular value. At present, there are only two option classes set. (With only 2 bits to work with in the field, a maximum of four options could be set.) When the value is 0, the option applies to datagram or network control. A value of 2 means it is for debugging or administration purposes. Values of 1 and 3 are unused. Currently supported values for the option class and number are given in Table 3.1.

Table 3.1. Valid option class and numbers for IP headers.

Option Class	Option Number	Description
0	0	Marks the end of the options list
0	1	No option (used for padding)
0	2	Security options (military purposes only)
0	3	Loose source routing
0	7	Activates routing record (adds fields)
0	9	Strict source routing
2	4	Timestamping active (adds fields)

Of most interest to us are options that enable the routing and timestamps to be recorded. These are used to provide a record of a datagram's passage across the internetwork, which can be useful for diagnostic purposes. Both these options add information to a list contained within the datagram. (The timestamp has an interesting format: It is expressed in milliseconds since midnight, Universal Time. Unfortunately, because most systems have widely differing time settings—even when corrected to Universal Time—the timestamps should be treated with a little suspicion.)

There are two kinds of routing indicated within the options field: loose and strict. *Loose routing* provides a series of IP addresses that the machine must pass through, but it enables any route to get to each of these addresses (usually gateways). *Strict routing* enables no deviations from the specified route. If the route can't be followed, the datagram is abandoned. Strict routing is frequently used to test routes but rarely for transmission of user datagrams.

Padding

The content of the padding area depends on the options selected. The padding is usually used to ensure that the datagram header is a round number of bytes.

A Datagram's Life

When an application must send a datagram out on the network, it performs a few simple steps. First, it constructs the IP datagram within the legal lengths stipulated by the local IP implementation. The checksum is calculated for the data and then the IP header is constructed. Next, the first "hop" of the route to the destination must be determined to route the datagram to the destination machine directly over the local network, or to a gateway if the internetwork is used. If routing is important, this information is added to the header using an option. Finally, the datagram is passed to the network for its manipulation of the datagram.

As a datagram passes along the internetwork, each gateway performs a series of tests. After the network layer has stripped off its header, the gateway calculates the checksum and verifies the integrity of the datagram. If the checksums don't match, the datagram is discarded and an error message is returned to the sending device. Next, the time-to-live field is decremented and checked. If the datagram has expired, again it is discarded and an error message is sent. After determining the next hop of the route, either by analysis of the target address or from a specified routing instruction within the options field of the IP header, the datagram is rebuilt with the new time-to-live value and new checksum.

If fragmentation is necessary because of an increase in the datagram's length or a limitation in the software, the datagram is divided and new datagrams with the correct header information are assembled. If a routing or timestamp is required, it is added as well. Finally, the datagram is passed back to the network layer.

When the datagram is finally received at the destination device, the system performs a checksum calculation and, assuming the two sums match, checks to see if there are other fragments. If more datagrams are required to reassemble the entire message, the system waits, meanwhile running a timer to ensure that the datagrams arrive within a reasonable time. Even if all the parts of the larger message have arrived but the device can't reassemble them before the time-to-live timer reaches 0, the datagram is discarded and an error message is returned to the sender. Finally, the IP header is stripped off and the message passed up the layers. If a reply was required, it is then generated and sent back to the sending device.

When extra information is added to the datagram for routing or timestamp recording, the length can increase. Handling all these conditions is part of the Internet Protocol's forte, for which practically every problem has a resolution system.

Internet Control Message Protocol (ICMP)

Days 1 and 2 showed how problems can occur in routing. Time-to-live may expire, fragmented datagrams may not arrive with all segments intact, a gateway may misroute a datagram, and so on. Letting the sending device know of a problem with the datagram is important, as is correctly handling error conditions within the network routing itself. It is for this task that the Internet Control Message Protocol (ICMP) was developed.

ICMP is an error-reporting system. It is an integral part of the Internet Protocol and must be included in every implementation. This provides for consistent, understandable error messages and signals across the different versions. It is useful to think of ICMP as one IP package talking to another IP package across the network: In other words, ICMP is the IP communications system. Messages generated by ICMP are treated by the rest of the network as any other datagram. ICMP messages have a header built in the same manner as a user applications' and are not differentiated until a receiving machine processes the datagram properly.

In almost all cases, error messages sent by ICMP are routed back to the original datagram's sending machine. This is because only the sender's and destination devices' IP addresses are included in the header; and because the error won't mean anything to the destination device, the sender is the logical recipient of the error message. The sender can then determine from the ICMP message the type of error that occurred and establish how to best resend the failed datagram.

ICMP messages go through two encapsulations: when they are incorporated into a regular IP datagram and then into the network frame. This is shown in Figure 3.3. ICMP headers have a different format than IP headers, and the format differs slightly depending on the type of message. However, all ICMP headers start with the same three fields: a message type, a code field, and a checksum for the ICMP message. Figure 3.4 shows the layout of the ICMP message.

Usually, any ICMP message that is reporting a problem with delivery also will include the header and first 64 bits of the data field from the datagram for which the problem occurred. Including the 64 bits of the original datagram accomplishes two things. It enables the sending device to match the datagram fragment to the original datagram by comparison. Also, because most of the protocols involved are defined at the start of the datagram, the inclusion of the original datagram fragment allows for some diagnostics.

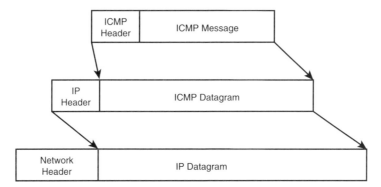

Figure 3.3. *Two-step encapsulating an ICMP message.*

Type (8 bits)	Code (8 bits)	Checksum (16 bits)
Parameters		
Data...		

Figure 3.4. *The layout of an ICMP message.*

The 8-bit message type field can have one of the following values.

Value	Description
0	Echo Reply
3	Destination Not Reachable
4	Source Quench
5	Redirection Required
8	Echo Request
11	Time-To-Live Exceeded
12	Parameter Problem
13	Timestamp Request
14	Timestamp Reply

Value	Description
15	Information Request (now obsolete)
16	Information Reply (now obsolete)
17	Address Mask Request
18	Address Mask Reply

The code field expands on the message type. The checksum is calculated in the same manner as the IP header checksum.

The layout of the ICMP message is slightly different for each type. Figure 3.5 shows the layouts of each type of ICMP message header. The Destination Unreachable and Time Exceeded messages are self-explanatory, although they are used in other circumstances, too, such as when a datagram must be fragmented but the Don't Fragment bit flag is set. This would result in a Destination Unreachable message.

Figure 3.5. *ICMP message header layouts.*

The Source Quench message is used to control the rate at which datagrams are transmitted, although this is a very rudimentary form of flow control. When a device receives a Source Quench message, it should reduce the transmittal rate over the network until the Source Quench messages cease. The messages are typically generated by a gateway or host that has either a full receiving buffer or has slowed the processing of incoming datagrams because of other factors. If the buffer is full, the device is supposed to issue a Source Quench message for each datagram that is discarded. Some implementations will issue Source Quench messages when the buffer exceeds a certain percentage to slow down reception of new datagrams and enable the device to clear the buffer.

Redirection messages are sent to a gateway in the path when a better route is available. For example, if a gateway has just received a datagram from another gateway but on checking its datafiles finds a better route, it will send the redirection message back to that gateway with the IP address of the better route. When a redirection message is sent, an integer is placed in the code field of the header to indicate the conditions for which the rerouting apply. A value of 0 means that datagrams for any device on the destination network should be redirected. A value of 1 indicates that only datagrams for the specific device should be rerouted. A value of 2 implies that only datagrams for the network with the same type of service (read from one of the IP header fields) should be rerouted. Finally, a value of 3 reroutes only for the same host with the same type of service.

The Parameter Problem message is used whenever a semantic or syntactic error has been encountered in the IP header. This can happen when options are used with incorrect arguments. When a Parameter Problem message is sent back to the sending device, the Parameter field in the ICMP error message contains a pointer to the byte in the IP header that caused the problem. (See Figure 3.5.)

Request or reply types are commonly used for debugging purposes. When a request is sent, a device or gateway down the path will send a reply back to the specified device. These request-reply pairs are useful for identifying routing problems, failed gateways, or network cabling problems. The simple act of processing an ICMP message also acts as a check of the network, because each gateway or device along the path must correctly decode the headers and then pass the datagram along. Any failure along the way could be with the implementation of the IP software. A commonly used request-reply system is the ping command. (See Day 6.) The ping command sends a series of requests and waits for replies.

Timestamp requests and replies enable the timing of message passing along the network to be monitored. When combined with strict routing, this can be useful in identifying bottlenecks. Address mask requests and replies are used for testing within a specific network or subnetwork.

Gateway-to-Gateway Protocols

Gateways need to know what is happening to the rest of the network in order to route datagrams properly and efficiently. This includes not only routing information but also the characteristics of subnetworks. For example, if one gateway is particularly slow but is the only access method to a subnetwork, other gateways on the network can tailor the traffic to suite.

A gateway-to-gateway protocol is used to exchange routing information between devices. It is important to not confuse routing information, which contains addresses, topology, and details on routing delays, with the algorithms used to make routing information. Usually the routing algorithms are fixed within a gateway and not modified. Of course, as the routing information changes, the algorithm will adapt the chosen routes to reflect the new information.

Gateway-to-gateway protocols are primarily for autonomous (self-complete) networks. An autonomous system uses gateways that are connected in one large network, such as one might find in a large corporation. There are two kinds of gateways that must be considered in an autonomous network. The gateways between smaller subnetworks help tie the small systems into the larger corporate network, but the gateways for each subnetwork are usually under the control of one system (usually in the IS department). These gateways are considered autonomous because the connections between gateways is constant and seldom changes. These gateways communicate through an *interior gateway protocol,* or IGP.

Large internetworks such as the Internet are not as static as corporate systems. Gateways may change constantly as the subsidiary networks make changes and the communications routes between gateways are more subject to change, too. For widely spread companies, there may be gateways spread throughout the country (or the world) that are all part of the same corporate network but use the Internet to communicate. The communications between these gateways is slightly different than when they are all physically connected together. These gateways communicate through an *exterior gateway protocol,* or EGP.

There are fewer rules governing IGPs than EGPs simply because the IGP can handle custom-developed applications and protocols within its local network. When Internet is used for gateway-to-gateway communications, the messages must conform to the internetwork standards. Also, when connecting two subnetworks, it is possible to send only one message to the subnetwork gateway through EGP, which can then be duplicated, modified, and propagated to all gateways on the internal system using IGP. EGP has formalized rules governing its use.

Since EGP was developed to enable remote systems to exchange routing information and status messages, the protocol is heavily based in requests or commands followed by replies. The four EGP commands and their possible responses are shown in Table 3.2.

Table 3.2. EGP commands.

Command Name	Command Description	Response Name	Response Description
Request	Request that a neighbor become a gateway	Confirm/Refuse	Agree or refuse the request
Cease	Request the termination as a neighbor	Cease-Ack	Agree to termination
Hello	Request confirmation of routing to neighbor (neighbor reachability)	IHU	Confirms the routing
Poll	Request the neighbor provide network information (network information reachability)	Update	Provides network

To understand Table 3.2 properly, you must understand the concept of *neighbor* to an internetwork. Gateways are neighbors if they share the same subnetwork. They may be gateways to the same network (such as Internet) or work with different networks. When the two want to exchange information, they must first establish communications between each other; the two gateways are essentially agreeing to exchange routing information. This process is called *neighbor acquisition.*

Warning: Don't think that neighbor means that networks have to be next to each other. They are connected by a gateway, but the networks can be on different continents. The term neighbor has to do with connections, not geography.

3

The process of becoming neighbors is formal, because one gateway may not wish to become a neighbor at that particular time (for any number of reasons but usually because the gateway is busy). It begins with a Request, which is followed by either an acceptance (Confirm) or refusal (Refuse) from the second machine. If the two gateways are neighbors, either can break the relationship with a Cease message.

After two gateways become neighbors, they assure each other that they are still in contact by occasionally sending a Hello message, to which the second gateway responds with an IHU (I Heard You) message as soon as possible. These Hello-IHU messages can be sent at any time, and with several gateways involved on a network the number of Hello messages can become appreciable as the gateways continue to remain in touch. This process is called *neighbor reachability*.

The other message pair sent by EGP is network reachability, in which case one gateway sends a Poll message and expects an Update message in response. The response contains a list of networks that can be reached through that gateway with a number representing the number of hops that must be made to reach the networks. By assembling the Update messages from different neighbors, a gateway can decide the best route to send a datagram.

Finally, there is an error message that is returned whenever the gateway cannot understand an incoming EGP message.

The layout of the different messages used by EGP are shown in Figure 3.6. The fields have the following meanings described after Figure 3.6.

Vers	Type	Code	Status
Checksum		System No.	
Sequence No.		Hello Interval	
Poll Interval			

Neighbor Acquisition

Vers	Type	Code	Status
Checksum		System No.	
Sequence No.		Not Used	
Source Network IP Address			

Poll

Vers	Type	Code	Status
Checksum		System No.	
Sequence No.			

Neighbor Reachability

Vers	Type	Code	Status
Checksum		System No.	
Sequence No.		Reason	
Error Message			

Error Message

Figure 3.6. *EGP Message Format.*

Version Number—the EGP release number

Type—the type of message

Code—the subtype of message (Table 3.3)

Status—combined with "code," provides more information (Table 3.3)

Checksum—checksum of the entire message

System Number—an assigned number identifying the system

Sequence Number—an incremental number that is used for all command-response pairs to ensure the pairs match

The reason field of the error message may contain one of the following integers:

0—Unspecified error

1—Bad EGP header

2—Bad EGP data field

3—Reachability information not available

4—Excessive polling

5—No response received to a poll

Through a combination if the message type, code, and status fields, the purpose and meaning of the EGP message can be more accurately determined. Table 3.3 shows all codes and status values.

Table 3.3. EGP messages.

Type	Description	Code	Description	Status	Description
1	Update	0		0	Indeterminate
				1	Up
				2	Down
				128	Unsolicited
2	Poll	0		0	Indeterminate
				1	Up
				2	Down

continues

Table 3.3. continued

Type	Description	Code	Description	Status	Description
3	Neighbor Acquisition	0	Request	0	Not specified
		1	Confirm	1	Active mode
		2	Refuse	2	Passive mode
		3	Cease	3	Insufficient Resources
		4	Cease-Ack	4	Prohibited
				5	Shutting Down
				6	Parameter Problem
				7	Protocol Violation
5	Neighbor Reachability	0	Hello	0	Indeterminate
		1	I Heard You	1	Up
				2	Down
8	Error	0		0	Indeterminate
				1	Up
				2	Down
				128	Unsolicited

The Status field can indicate whether a gateway is up or down. In the down state, the gateway will not perform any routing. The Neighbor Acquisition status indicator can show whether the machine is active or passive. When passive, the gateway will not generate any Hello commands, but it will respond to them. At least one neighbor has to be in the active state to issue the Hellos.

When a list of networks and their distances must be added to an EGP header, it is done in the format shown in Figure 3.7. The number of distances in the list is specified, followed by entries with the same format giving the distance (number of hops) to the gateway, the number of networks that can be reached through that gateway, and the network addresses. The number of internal and external gateways in the EGP header tell the gateway how many entries are in the list.

Figure 3.7. *Routing Information in an EGP header.*

Using EGP, gateways can update each other and keep their routing tables current. A similar scheme is used for IGP, although the messages can be custom designed by the network manager and application development team because they are not transmitted over the Internet.

Internet Protocol Support in Different Environments

The University of California at Berkeley was given a grant in the early 1980s to modify its UNIX operating system to included support for the Internet Protocol. The BSD4.2 UNIX release already offered support for TCP and IP, as well as the Simple Mail Transfer Protocol (SNMP) and Address Resolution Protocol (ARP); but funded by DARPA's funds, BSD4.3 was developed to provide more complete support.

The BSD4.2 support for IP was quite good but proved to be limited to use in small local area networks. To increase the capabilities, BSD added retransmission capabilities, time-to-live information, and redirection messages. Other features were added, too, but these changes enable BSD4.3 to work with larger networks, internetworks (connections between different networks) and wide area networks connected by leased lines.

With the strong support for IP amongst the UNIX community, it was inevitable that manufacturers of other software operating systems would produce software that allowed their machines to interconnect to the UNIX IP system.

This section examines several different hardware and software systems, focusing on the most widely used. Much of this will be of interest only if you have the particular platform discussed (DEC VAX users tend not to care about interconnectivity to IBM SNA platforms), so you can be selective about the sections you read. In some cases, you will use one package (from each platform, later in this book) as an application example and for screen captures. These products are mentioned in this section now and will be covered in more detail when they are actually used.

MS-DOS

PCs came onto the scene when TCP/IP was already in common use, so it was not surprising to find interconnection software rapidly introduced. In many ways, the PC was a perfect platform as a stand-alone machine with access through a communications package to other, larger, systems. The PC was perfect for a client/server environment.

There are many PC-based versions of TCP/IP. The most widely used packages come from FTP Software, The Wollongong Group, and Beame and Whiteside Software, Inc. All the packages feature interconnection to other machines using TCP/IP, whereas most add other useful features list FTP and mail routing.

FTP Software's PC/TCP is one of the most widely used. PC/TCP supports the major network interfaces: Packet Driver, IBM's Adapter Support Interface (ASI), Novell's Open Data Link Interface (ODI), and Microsoft/3Com's Network Driver Interface Specification (NDIS). All four LAN interfaces are discussed in more detail in the section titled "Local Area Networks," later today.

The design of PC/TCP covers all seven layers of the OSI model, developed in such a manner that components can be configured as required to support different transport mechanisms and applications. Typically, the Packet Driver, ASI, ODI, or NDIS module has a generic PC/TCP kernel on top of it, with the PC/TCP application on top of that.

PC/TCP enables the software to run both TCP/IP and another protocol, such as DECnet, Novell NetWare, and LAN Manager, simultaneously. This can be useful for enabling a PC to work within a small LAN workgroup, as well as within a larger network, without switching software.

Microsoft Windows

There are several TCP/IP products appearing for Microsoft's Windows, most of which are ports of DOS products. Although these tend to work well, a totally Windows-designed product tends to have a slight edge in terms of integration with the Windows environment. Some later versions of Windows (such as Windows for Workgroups and the upcoming Windows 4.0) have some TCP/IP capabilities built in to the distribution software.

One Windows-designed product is NetManage's Chameleon TCP/IP for Windows. It offers a complete port of TCP/IP and additional software utilities to enable a PC that is running Windows to integrate into a TCP/IP network. Chameleon offers terminal emulation, Telnet, FTP, electronic mail, DNS directory services, and NFS capabilities. There are several versions of Chameleon, depending on whether NFS is required or not.

Windows NT

Windows NT is ideally suited for TCP/IP because it is designed to act as a server and gateway. Although Windows NT is not inherently multiuser, it does work well as a TCP/IP access device. Windows NT includes support for the TCP/IP protocols as a network transport, although the implementation does not include all the utilities usually associated with TCP/IP.

Among the add-on products available for Windows NT, NetManage's Chameleon32 is a popular package. Similar to the Microsoft Windows version, Chameleon32 offers versions for NFS. The behavior of Chameleon32 is very similar to the Windows version, and will be covered later in this book.

OS/2

IBM's OS/2 platform has a strong presence in corporations because of the IBM reputation and OS/2's solid performance. Not surprisingly, TCP/IP products are popular in these installations. Although OS/2 differs from DOS in many ways, it is possible to run DOS-based ports of TCP/IP software under OS/2. A better solution is to run a native OS/2 application. Several TCP/IP OS/2-native implementations are available, including a solid product from IBM itself.

Macintosh

Except for versions of UNIX that run on the Macintosh, the Macintosh and UNIX worlds have depended on versions of TCP/IP to keep them connected. With many corporations now wanting their investment in Macintosh computer to serve double duty as X terminals onto UNIX workstations, TCP/IP for the Mac has become even more important.

Macintosh TCP products are available in several forms, usually as an add-on application or device driver for the Macintosh operating system. An alternative is Tenon Intersystem's MachTen product line, which enables a UNIX kernel and the Macintosh operating system to co-exist on the same machine, providing compatibility between UNIX and the Macintosh file system and Apple events.

3

The AppleTalk networking system enables Macs and UNIX machines to interconnect to a limited extent, although this requires installation of AppleTalk software on the UNIX host—something many system administrators are reluctant to do. Also, because AppleTalk is not as fast and versatile as Ethernet and other network transports, this solution is seldom favored.

A better solution is simply to install TCP/IP on the Macintosh using one of several commercial packages available. Apple's own MacTCP software product can perform the basic services but must be coupled with software from other vendors for the higher-layer applications. MacTCP also requires a Datagram Delivery Protocol to Internet Protocol (DDP-to-IP) router to handle the sending and receiving of DPP and IP datagrams.

Apple's MacTCP functions by providing the Physical through Transport layers of the architecture. MacTCP allows for both LocalTalk and Ethernet hardware and supports both IP and TCP, as well as a number of other protocols. Running on top of MacTCP is the third-party application, which uses MacTCP's function calls to provide the final application for the user. Functions such as Telnet and FTP protocols are supported with add-on software, too.

DEC

Digital Equipment Corporation's minicomputers were for many years a mainstay in scientific and educational research, so an obvious development for DEC and third-party software companies was to introduce IP software. Most DEC machines run either VMS or Ultrix (DEC's licensed version of UNIX). Providing IP capabilities to Ultrix was a matter of duplicating the code developed at Berkeley, but VMS was not designed for IP-type communications, relying instead on DEC's proprietary network software.

DEC's networking software is the Digital Network Architecture (DECnet). The first widely used version was DECnet Phase IV (introduced in 1982), which used industry-standard protocols for the lower layers but was proprietary in the upper layers. The 1987 release of DECnet Phase V provided a combined DECnet IV and OSI system that allowed new OSI protocols to be used within the DECnet environment.

DEC announced the ADVANTAGE-NETWORKS in 1991 as an enhancement of DECnet Phase V, adding support for the Internet Protocols. With the ADVANTAGE-NETWORKS, users could choose between the older, DEC-specific DECnet, OSI, or IP schemes. ADVANTAGE-NETWORKS is DECs attempt to provide interoperability, providing the DEC-exclusive DECnet system for LAN use, and the TCP/IP and OSI systems for WANs and system interconnection between different hardware types.

Users of VMS systems can connect to the UNIX environment in several ways. The easiest is to use a software gateway between the VMS machine and a UNIX machine. DEC's TCP/IP Services for VMS performs this function, as do several third-party software solutions, such as the Kermit protocol from Columbia University, Wollongong Group's WIN/TCP, and TGV's MultiNet. The advantage of the third-party communications protocol products like Kermit is that they don't have to be connected to a UNIX machine, because any operating system that supports the communications protocol will work.

ADVANTAGE-NETWORKS users have more options available, many from DEC. Because the protocol is already embedded in the network software, it makes the most sense to simply use it because it comes if it fits into the system architecture. Because of internal conversion software, ADVANTAGE-NETWORKS can connect from a DECnet machine using either the DECnet or the OSI protocols.

IBM's SNA

IBM's Systems Network Architecture (SNA) is in widespread use for both mainframes and minicomputers. Essentially all IBM equipment provides full support for IP and TCP, as well as many other popular protocols. There is native IBM software available for each machine, and several third-party products have appeared (usually at a lower cost than IBM's).

IBM's UNIX version, AIX (which few people know stands for Advanced Interactive Executive), has the TCP/IP software built in, enabling any machine that can run AIX (from workstation to large minicomputer) to interconnect through IP with no additional software. The different versions of AIX have slightly different support, so users should check before blindly trying to connect AIX machines.

For large systems like mainframes, IBM has the 3172 Interconnect Controller, which sits between the mainframe and a network. The 3172 is a hefty box that handles high-speed traffic between a mainframe channel and the network, offloading the processing for the communications aspect from the mainframe processor. It can connect to Ethernet or Token Ring networks and through additional software to DEC's DECnet.

IBM mainframes running either MVS or VM can run software appropriately called TCP/IP for MVS and TCP/IP for VM. These products provide access from other machines running TCP/IP to remotely access the mainframe operating system, usually over a LAN. The software enables the calling machine (actually the client in a client/server scheme) to act as a 3270-series terminal to MVS or VM. FTP is provided for file transfers with automatic conversion from EBCDIC to ASCII. An interface to PROFS is available. Both TCP/IP software products support SMTP for electronic mail.

Local Area Networks

LANs are an obvious target for TCP/IP, because TCP/IP helps solve many interconnection problems between different hardware and software platforms. To run TCP/IP over a network, the existing network and transport layer software must be replaced with TCP/IP, or the two merged together in some manner so that the LAN protocol can carry TCP/IP information within its existing protocol (encapsulation).

Whichever solution is taken for the lower layer, a higher-layer interface also must be developed, which will reside in the equivalent of the data link layer, communicating between the higher-layer applications and the hardware. This interface enables the higher layers to be independent of the hardware when using TCP/IP, something that many popular LAN operating systems are not currently able to claim.

There are three interfaces (which have been mentioned by name earlier today) currently in common use. The Packet Driver interface was the first interface developed to meet these needs. 3Com Corporation and Microsoft developed the Network Driver Interface Specification (NDIS) for OS/2 and 3Com's networking software. NDIS provides a driver to communicate with the networking hardware and a protocol driver that acts as the interface to the higher layers. Novell's Open Data Link Interface (ODI) is similar to NDIS.

For single-vendor, PC-based networks, there are several dedicated TCP/IP packages available, such as Novell's LAN WorkPlace, designed to enable any NetWare system to connect to a LAN using an interface hardware card and a software driver.

Summary

Today's text started with an in-depth look at the TCP/IP protocol family with the Internet Protocol. You read about what IP is and how it does its task of passing datagrams between machines. The construction of the IP datagram and the format of the IP header have been shown in detail. The construction of the IP header is important to many TCP/IP-family protocol members, so you can use this knowledge throughout the rest of the book. You also looked at the Internet Control Message Protocol (ICMP), an important aspect of the TCP/IP system. Finally, you looked at the Exterior Gateway Protocol, used to provide destination information for gateways.

Tomorrow, you'll move to the next-higher layer in the TCP/IP layered architecture and look at the Transmission Control Protocol (TCP) itself. You'll also look at the related User Datagram Protocol (UDP). TCP and UDP form the basis for all TCP/IP protocols.

Q&A

Q Why does the IP header have a Time-to-Live field?

A The easiest way to answer this is to consider what would happen without the field. A datagram with faulty information in the IP header could circulate around a network forever, forwarding from one gateway to another in the search of a destination. With a Time-to-Live field, the number of bounces the datagram makes is limited. This has been proven to have an important effect on network traffic.

Q Give a one sentence description of ICMP.

A ICMP is an error reporting system that communicates between different IP-based devices, providing information about status changes and failed devices.

Q What is a neighbor in the IP sense?

A Neighbors are connected through a gateway. There is no physical restriction on the distance between neighbors. However, all neighbors share gateways.

Q How is an ICMP message datagram constructed?

A The ICMP message, which may include part of the datagram that causes an ICMP message to be generated, has an ICMP header attached to the front of it. This is then passed to IP, which encapsulates it within an IP header. Finally, a network header is added when the datagram is sent over the network.

Q What are the four EGP message formats and what are they used for?

A The four message EGP message formats are neighbor acquisition, neighbor reachability, poll message, and error message. The neighbor acquisition and neighbor reachability messages are used to provide information about devices attached to a gateway, which can help a system determine routing for a datagram. The poll message is a request for information from another gateway. The error message is used to send status information about failed gateways.

Workshop

The Workshop provides quiz questions to help you solidify your understanding of the material covered. Some Workshop sections of this book also contain exercises to provide you with experience in using what you've learned. Try to understand the quiz and exercise answers before continuing on to the next chapter. Answers are provided in Appendix F, "Answers."

Quiz

1. Explain why IP is important to the proper transmission of data.

2. Show the construction of the IP header and the meaning of each element within the header structure.

3. ICMP headers are quite small. Show the structure of a typical message header and the meaning of the bits within it.

4. Explain the different EGP message formats and when they are used.

5. Show the EGP message format, explaining the contents of the header and the network reachability information.

TCP/IP In More Detail

Yesterday's text examined the Internet Protocol (IP) in considerable detail. The Internet Protocol handles the lower-layer functionality. Now you can look at the transport layer, where Transmission Control Protocol (TCP) comes into play.

TCP is one of the most widely used transport layer protocols, expanding from its original implementation on the ARPAnet to connect commercial sites all over the world. On Day 1, you looked at the OSI seven-layer model, which bears a striking resemblance to TCP/IP's layered model; so it is not surprising that many of the features of the OSI transport layer were based on TCP.

In theory, a transport layer protocol could be a very simple software routine, but TCP cannot be called simple. Why use a transport layer that is as complex as TCP? The most important reason depends on IP's unreliability. As seen yesterday, IP does not guarantee delivery of a datagram; it is a connectionless system. IP simply handles the routing of datagrams; and if problems occur, IP discards the packet without a second thought (generating an error message back to the sender in the process). The task of ascertaining the status of the datagrams sent over a network and handling the resending of information if parts have been discarded falls to TCP, which can be thought of as "riding shotgun" over IP.

Most users think of TCP and IP as a tightly knit pair, but TCP can (and frequently is) used with other transport protocols. For example, TCP or parts of it are used in the File Transfer Protocol (FTP) and the Simple Mail Transfer Protocol (SMTP), both of which do not use IP.

What is TCP?

The Transmission Control Protocol provides a considerable number of services to the IP layer and the upper layers. Most importantly, it provides a connection-oriented protocol to the upper layers that enable an application to be sure that a datagram sent out over the network was received in its entirety. In this role, TCP acts as a message-validation protocol providing reliable communications. If a datagram is corrupted or lost, it is usually TCP (not the applications in the higher layers) that handles the retransmission.

> **Note:** TCP is not a piece of software. It is a communications protocol.

TCP manages the flow of datagrams from the higher layers, as well as incoming datagrams from the IP layer. It has to ensure that priorities and security are respected. TCP must be capable of handling the termination of an application above it that was expecting incoming datagrams, as well as failures in the lower layers. TCP also must maintain a state table of all data streams in and out of the TCP layer. The isolation of these services in a separate layer enables applications to be designed without regard to flow control or message reliability. Without the TCP layer, each application would have to implement the services themselves, which is a waste of resources.

TCP resides in the transport layer, positioned above IP but below the upper layers and their applications, as shown in Figure 4.1. TCP resides only on devices that actually process datagrams, ensuring that the datagram has gone from the source to target machines. It does not reside on a device that simply routes datagrams, so there is no TCP layer in a gateway. This makes sense, because on a gateway the datagram has no need to go higher in the layered model than the IP layer.

Figure 4.1. *TCP provides end-to-end communications.*

Because TCP is a connection-oriented protocol responsible for ensuring the transfer of a datagram from the source to destination machine (end-to-end communications), TCP must receive communications messages from the destination machine to acknowledge receipt of the datagram. The term *virtual circuit* is usually used to refer to the handshaking that goes on between the two end machines, most of which are simple acknowledgment messages (either confirmation of receipt or a failure code) and datagram sequence numbers.

Following a Message

To illustrate the role of TCP, it is instructive to follow a sample message between two machines. The processes are simplified at this stage, to be expanded upon later today. The message originates from an application and is passed to TCP from the next higher layer in the architecture through some protocol (often referred to as an *upper-layer protocol,* or *ULP,* to indicate that it resides above TCP). The message is passed as a *stream*—a sequence of individual characters sent asynchronously. This is in contrast to most protocols, which use fixed blocks of data. This can pose some conversion problems with applications that handle only formally constructed blocks of data or insist on fixed-size messages.

TCP receives the stream of bytes and assembles them into *TCP segments,* or packets. In the process of assembling the segment, header information is attached. Each segment has a checksum calculated and embedded within the header, as well as a sequence number if there is more than one segment in the entire message. The length of the segment is usually determined by TCP or by a system value set by the system administrator.

If two-way communication is required (such as with Telnet or FTP), and prior to passing the segment to IP for routing, a connection (virtual circuit) between the sending and receiving machines is established. This process starts with the sending TCP software issuing a request for a TCP connection with the receiving machine. In the message is a unique number (called a *socket number*) that identifies the sending machine's connection. The receiving TCP software assigns its own unique socket number and sends it back to the original machine. The two unique numbers then define the connection between the two machines until the virtual circuit is terminated.

After the virtual circuit is established, TCP sends the segment to the IP software, which then issues the message over the network as a datagram. After winding its way over the network, the receiving machine's IP passes the received segment up to the recipient machine's TCP layer, where it is processed and passed up to the applications above it using an upper-layer protocol.

If the message was more than one segment long, the receiving TCP software reassembles the message using the sequence numbers contained in each segment's header. If a segment is missing or corrupt (which can be determined from the checksum), TCP returns a message with the faulty sequence number in the body. The originating TCP software can then resend the bad segment.

If only one segment is used for the entire message, after comparing the segment's checksum with a newly calculated value, the receiving TCP software can generate either a positive acknowledgment (ACK) or a request to resend the segment and route it back to the sending layer.

The receiving machine's TCP implementation can perform a simple flow control to prevent buffer overload. It does this by sending a *window value* to the sending machine, following which the sender can send only enough bytes to fill the window. After that, the sender must wait for another window value to be received. This provides a handshaking protocol between the two machines, although it does slow down the transmission time and slightly increase network traffic.

> **Note:** The use of a sliding window is more efficient than a single block send and acknowledgment scheme because of delays waiting for the acknowledgment. By implementing a sliding window, several blocks can be sent at once. A properly configured sliding window protocol will provide a much higher throughput.

As with most connection-based protocols, timers are an important aspect of TCP. The use of a timer ensures that an undue wait is not involved while waiting for an ACK or an error message. If the timers expire, an incomplete transmission is assumed. Usually an expiring timer before the sending of an acknowledgment message will cause a retransmission of the datagram from the originating machine.

Timers can cause some problems with TCP. The specifications for TCP provide for the acknowledgment of only the highest datagram number that has been received without error, but this cannot properly handle fragmentary reception. If a message is composed of several datagrams that arrive out of order, the specification states that TCP cannot acknowledge the reception of the message until all the datagrams have been received. So even if all but one datagram in the middle of the sequence has been successfully received, a timer may expire and cause all the datagrams to be resent. With large messages, this can cause an increase in network traffic.

If the receiving TCP software receives duplicate datagrams (as may occur with a retransmission after a timeout or due to a duplicate transmission from IP), the receiving version of TCP will discard any duplicate datagrams, without bothering with an error message. After all, the sending system cares only that the message was received—not how many copies were received.

TCP does not have a *negative acknowledgment* (NAK) function, relying on a timer to indicate lack of acknowledgment. If the timer has expired after sending the datagram without receiving an acknowledgment of receipt, the datagram is assumed to have been lost and is retransmitted. The sending TCP software keeps copies of all unacknowledged datagrams in a buffer until they have been properly acknowledged. When this happens, the retransmission timer is stopped and the datagram is removed from the buffer.

TCP supports a *push* function from the upper-layer protocols. A push is used when an application wants to immediately send data and confirm that a message passed to TCP has been successfully transmitted. To do this, a *push flag* is set in the ULP connection, instructing TCP to forward any buffered information from the application to the destination as soon as possible (as opposed to holding it in the buffer until it is ready to transmit it).

Ports and Sockets

All upper-layer applications that use TCP (or UDP) have a port number that identifies the application. In theory, port numbers can be assigned on individual machines, or however the administrator desires, but some conventions have been adopted to allow better communication between TCP implementations. This enables the port number to identify the type of service that one TCP system is requesting from another. Port numbers can be changed, although this can cause difficulties. Most systems maintain a file of port numbers and their corresponding service.

Typically, port numbers above 255 are reserved for private use of the local machine, but numbers below 255 are used for frequently used processes. A list of frequently used port numbers is published by the Internet Assigned Numbers Authority. The commonly used port numbers on this list are shown in Table 4.1. The numbers 0 and 255 are reserved.

Table 4.1. Frequently used TCP port numbers.

Port Number	Process Name	Description
1	TCPMUX	TCP Port Service Multiplexer
5	RJE	Remote Job Entry
7	ECHO	Echo
9	DISCARD	Discard
11	USERS	Active Users
13	DAYTIME	Daytime
17	Quote	Quotation of the Day
19	CHARGEN	Character generator
20	FTP-DATA	File Transfer Protocol—Data

Port Number	Process Name	Description
21	FTP	File Transfer Protocol—Control
23	TELNET	Telnet
25	SMTP	Simple Mail Transfer Protocol
27	NSW-FE	NSW User System Front End
29	MSG-ICP	MSG-ICP
31	MSG-AUTH	MSG Authentication
33	DSP	Display Support Protocol
35		Private Print Servers
37	TIME	Time
39	RLP	Resource Location Protocol
41	GRAPHICS	Graphics
42	NAMESERV	Host Name Server
43	NICNAME	Who Is
49	LOGIN	Login Host Protocol
53	DOMAIN	Domain Name Server
67	BOOTPS	Bootstrap Protocol Server
68	BOOTPC	Bootstrap Protocol Client
69	TFTP	Trivial File Transfer Protocol
79	FINGER	Finger
101	HOSTNAME	NIC Host Name Server
102	ISO-TSAP	ISO TSAP
103	X400	X.400
104	X400SND	X.400 SND
105	CSNET-NS	CSNET Mailbox Name Server
109	POP2	Post Office Protocol v2

continues

Table 4.1. continued

Port Number	Process Name	Description
110	POP3	Post Office Protocol v3
111	RPC	Sun RPC Portmap
137	NETBIOS-NS	NETBIOS Name Service
138	NETBIOS-DG	NETBIOS Datagram Service
139	NETBIOS-SS	NETBIOS Session Service
146	ISO-TP0	ISO TP0
147	ISO-IP	ISO IP
150	SQL-NET	SQL NET
153	SGMP	SGMP
156	SQLSRV	SQL Service
160	SGMP-TRAPS	SGMP TRAPS
161	SNMP	SNMP
162	SNMPTRAP	SNMPTRAP
163	CMIP-MANAGE	CMIP/TCP Manager
164	CMIP-AGENT	CMIP/TCP Agent
165	XNS-Courier	Xerox
179	BGP	Border Gateway Protocol

Each communication circuit in to and out of the TCP layer is uniquely identified by a combination of two numbers, which together are called a *socket*. The socket is composed of the IP address of the machine and the port number used by the TCP software. There is a socket on both the sending and receiving machines. Because the IP address is unique across the internetwork and the port numbers will be unique to the individual machine, the socket numbers will also be unique across the entire internetwork. This enables a process to talk to another process across the network, based entirely on the socket number.

> **Note:** TCP uses the connection (not the protocol port) as fundamental elements. A completed connection has two end points. This enables a protocol port to be used for several connections at the same time (multiplexing).

The last section examined the process of establishing a message. During the process, the sending TCP requests a connection with the receiving TCP, using the unique socket numbers. This process is shown in Figure 4.2. If the sending TCP wants to establish a Telnet session from its port number 350, the socket number would be composed of the source machine's IP address and the port number (350), and the message would have a destination port number of 23 (Telnet's port number). The receiving TCP will have a source port of 23 (Telnet) and a destination port of 350 (the sending machine's port).

Figure 4.2. *Setting up a virtual circuit with socket numbers.*

The sending and receiving machines maintain a port table, which lists all active port numbers. The two machines involved will have reversed entries for each session between the two. This is called *binding* and is shown in Figure 4.3. The source and destination numbers are simply reversed for each connection in the port table. Of course, the IP addresses, and hence the socket number, will be different.

If the sending machine is requesting more than one connection, the source port numbers would be different, even though the destination port numbers might be the same. For example, if the sending machine were trying to establish three Telnet sessions simultaneously, the source machine port numbers might be 350, 351, and 352, while the destination port numbers would all be 23.

Figure 4.3. *Binding entries in port tables.*

It is possible for more than one machine to share the same destination socket—a process called *multiplexing*. In Figure 4.4, three machines are establishing Telnet sessions with a destination. They all use destination port 23, which is port multiplexing. Because the datagrams emerging from the port have the full socket information (with unique IP addresses), there is no confusion as to which machine a datagram is destined.

Figure 4.4. *Multiplexing one destination port.*

When multiple sockets are established, it is conceivable that more than one machine will send a connection request with the same source and destination ports. However, the IP addresses for the two machines will be different, so the sockets are still uniquely identified despite identical source and destination port numbers.

TCP Communications with the Upper Layers

TCP must communicate with applications in the upper layer and a network system in the layer below. There are several messages defined for the upper-layer protocol to TCP communications, but there is no defined method for TCP to talk to lower layers (usually, but not necessarily, IP). TCP expects the layer beneath it to define the communication method. It is usually assumed that TCP and the transport layer communicate asynchronously.

The TCP to upper-layer protocol (ULP) communication method is well-defined, consisting of a set of *service request primitives.* The primitives involved in ULP to TCP communications are shown in Table 4.2.

Table 4.2. ULP-TCP service primitives.

Command	Parameters Expected
ULP to TCP Service Request Primitives	
ABORT	Local connection name
ACTIVE-OPEN	Local port, remote socket
	Optional: ULP timeout, timeout action, precedence, security, options
ACTIVE-OPEN-WITH- DATA	Source port, destination socket, data, data length, push flag, urgent flag
	Optional: ULP timeout, timeout action, precedence, security
ALLOCATE	Local connection name, data length
CLOSE	Local connection name
FULL-PASSIVE-OPEN	Local port, destination socket
	Optional: ULP timeout, timeout action, precedence, security, options
RECEIVE	Local connection name, buffer address, byte count, push flag, urgent flag
SEND	Local connection name, buffer address, data length, push flag, urgent flag
	Optional: ULP timeout, timeout action

continues

Table 4.2. continued

Command	Parameters Expected
STATUS	Local connection name
UNSPECIFIED-PASSIVE-OPEN	Local port
	Optional: ULP timeout, timeout action, precedence, security, options

TCP to ULP Service Request Primitives

Command	Parameters Expected
CLOSING	Local connection name
DELIVER	Local connection name, buffer address, data length, urgent flag
ERROR	Local connection name, error description
OPEN-FAILURE	Local connection name
OPEN-ID	Local connection name, remote socket, destination address
OPEN-SUCCESS	Local connection name
STATUS RESPONSE	Local connection name, source port, source address, remote socket, connection state, receive window, send window, amount waiting ACK, amount waiting receipt, urgent mode, precedence, security, timeout, timeout action
TERMINATE	Local connection name, description

Passive and Active Ports

TCP enables two methods to establish a connection: active and passive. An *active* connection establishment happens when TCP issues a request for the connection, based on an instruction from an upper-level protocol that provides the socket number. A *passive* approach happens when the upper-level protocol instructs TCP to wait for the arrival of connection requests from a remote system (usually from an active open instruction). When TCP receives the request, it assigns a port number. This enables a connection to proceed rapidly, without waiting for the active process.

There are two passive open primitives. A *specified passive open* creates a connection when the precedence level and security level are acceptable. An *unspecified passive open* opens the port to any request. The latter is used by servers that are waiting for clients of an unknown type to connect to it.

TCP has strict rules about the use of passive and active connection processes. Usually a passive open is performed on one machine, whereas an active open is performed on the other with specific information about the socket number, precedence (priority), and security levels.

Although most TCP connections are established by an active request to a passive port, it is possible to open a connection without a passive port waiting. In this case, the TCP that sends a request for a connection will include both a local socket number and the remote socket number. If the receiving TCP is configured to allow the request (based on the precedence and security settings, as well as application-based criteria), the connection can be opened. This process is looked at again in the section titled "TCP and Connections."

TCP Timers

TCP uses several timers to ensure that excessive delays are not encountered during communications. Several of these timers are elegant, handling problems that are not immediately obvious at first analysis. Each of the timers used by TCP is examined in the following sections, which reveal its role in ensuring data is properly sent from one connection to another.

Retransmission Timer

The retransmission timer manages retransmission timeouts (RTOs), which occur when a preset interval between the sending of a datagram and the returning acknowledgment is exceeded. The value of the timeout tends to vary, depending on the network type, to compensate for speed differences. If the timer expires, the datagram is retransmitted with an adjusted RTO, which is usually increased exponentially to a maximum preset limit. If the maximum limit is exceeded, connection failure is assumed and error messages are passed back to the upper-layer application.

Values for the timeout are determined by measuring the average time data takes to be transmitted to another machine and the acknowledgment received back, which is called the *round trip time*, or RTT. From experiments, these RTTs are averaged by a formula that develops an expected value, called the *smoothed round trip time*, or SRTT. This value is then increased to account for unforeseen delays.

Quiet Timer

After a TCP connection is closed, it is possible for datagrams that are still making their way through the network to attempt to access the closed port. The quiet timer is intended to prevent the just-closed port from reopening again quickly and receiving these last datagrams.

The quiet timer is usually set to twice the maximum segment lifetime (the same value as the Time-To-Live field in an IP header), ensuring that all segments still heading for the port have been discarded. Typically, this can result in a port being unavailable for up to 30 seconds, prompting error messages when other applications attempt to access the port during this interval.

Persistence Timer

The persistence timer handles a fairly rare occurrence. It is conceivable that a receive window will have a value of 0, causing the sending machine to pause transmission. The message to restart sending may be lost, causing an infinite delay. The persistence timer waits a preset time and then sends a 1-byte segment at predetermined intervals to ensure that the receiving machine is still clogged.

The receiving machine will resend the zero window size message after receiving one of these status segments, if it is still backlogged. If the window is open, a message giving the new value is returned and communications resumed.

Keep-Alive Timer and Idle Timer

Both the keep-alive timer and the idle timer were added to the TCP specifications after their original definition. The keep-alive timer sends an empty packet at regular intervals to ensure that the connection to the other machine is still active. If no response has been received after sending the message, by the time the idle timer has expired, the connection is assumed to be broken.

The keep-alive timer value is usually set by an application, with values ranging from 5 to 45 seconds. The idle timer is usually set to 360 seconds.

Note: TCP uses adaptive timer algorithms to accommodate delays. The timers adjust themselves to the delays experienced over a connection, altering the timer values to reflect inherent problems.

Transmission Control Blocks and Flow Control

TCP has to keep track of a lot of information about each connection. It does this through a Transmission Control Block (TCB), which contains information about the local and remote socket numbers, the send and receive buffers, security and priority values, and the current segment in the queue. The TCB also manages send and receive sequence numbers.

The TCB uses a number of variables to keep track of the send and receive status and to control the flow of information. These variables are shown in Table 4.3.

Table 4.3. TCP send and receive variables.

Variable Name	Description
Send Variables	
SND.UNA	Send Unacknowledged
SND.NXT	Send Next
SND.WND	Send Window
SND.UP	Sequence number of last urgent set
SND.WL1	Sequence number for last window update
SND.WL2	Acknowledgment number for last window update
SND.PUSH	Sequence number of last pushed set
ISS	Initial send sequence number

continues

Table 4.3. continued

Variable Name	Description
	Receive Variable
RCV.NXT	Sequence number of next received set
RCV.WND	Number of sets that can be received
RCV.UP	Sequence number of last urgent data
RCV.IRS	Initial receive sequence number

Using these variables, TCP controls the flow of information between two sockets. A sample connection session helps illustrate the use of the variables. It begins with Machine A wanting to send five blocks of data to Machine B. If the window limit is seven blocks, a maximum of seven blocks can be sent without acknowledgment. The SND.UNA variable on Machine A will indicate how many blocks have been sent but are unacknowledged (5), and the SND.NXT variable will have the value of the next block in sequence (6). The value of the SND.WND variable will be 2 (seven blocks possible, minus five sent), so only two more blocks could be sent without overloading the window. Machine B will return a message with the number of blocks received, and the window limit will be adjusted accordingly.

The passage of messages back and forth can become quite complex as the sending machine forwards blocks unacknowledged up to the window limit, waiting for acknowledgment of earlier blocks that have been removed from the incoming cue, and then sending more blocks to fill the window again. The tracking of the blocks becomes a matter of bookkeeping, but with large window limits and traffic across internetworks that sometimes cause blocks to go astray, the process is, in many ways, remarkable.

TCP Protocol Data Units

As mentioned earlier, TCP must communicate with IP in the layer below (using an IP-defined method) and applications in the upper layer (using the TCP-ULP primitives). TCP also must communicate with other TCP implementations across networks. To do this, it uses Protocol Data Units (PDUs), which are called *segments* in TCP parlance.

The layout of the TCP PDU (commonly called the header) is shown in Figure 4.5.

Figure 4.5. *The TCP Protocol Data Unit.*

## 4

The different fields are as follows:

Source port: A 16-bit field that identifies the local TCP user (usually an upper-layer application program).

Destination port: A 16-bit field that identifies the remote machine's TCP user.

Sequence number: A number indicating the position of the current block's position in the overall message. This number is also used between two TCP implementations to provide the initial send sequence (ISS) number.

Acknowledgment number: A number that indicates the next sequence number expected. In a backhanded manner, this also shows the sequence number of the last data received; it shows the last sequence number received plus 1.

Data offset: The number of 32-bit words that are in the TCP header. This field is used to identify the start of the data field.

Reserved: A 6-bit field reserved for future use. The 6 bits must be set to 0.

Urg flag: If on (a value of 1), indicates that the urgent pointer field is significant.

Ack flag: If on, indicates that the acknowledgment field is significant.

Psh flag: If on, indicates that the push function is to be performed.

rst flag: If on, indicates that the connection is to be reset.

Syn flag: If on, indicates that the sequence numbers are to be synchronized. This flag is used when a connection is being established.

Fin flag: If on, indicates that the sender has no more data to send. This is the equivalent of an end-of-transmission marker.

Window: A number indicating how many blocks of data the receiving machine can accept.

Checksum: Calculated by taking the 16-bit one's complement of the one's complement sum of the 16-bit words in the header (including pseudo-header) and text together.

Urgent pointer: Used if the urg flag was set; it indicates the portion of the data message that is urgent by specifying the offset from the sequence number in the header. No specific action is taken by TCP with respect to urgent data: the action is determined by the application.

Options: Similar to the IP header option field, it is used for specifying TCP options. Each option consists of an option number (1 byte), the number of bytes in the option, and the option values. Only three options are currently defined for TCP:

0	End of option list
1	No operation
2	Maximum segment size

Padding: Filled to ensure that the header is filled to a 32-bit multiple.

Following the PDU or header is the data. The options field has one useful function: to specify the maximum buffer size a receiving TCP implementation can accommodate. Because TCP uses variable-length data areas, it is possible for a sending machine to create a segment that is longer than the receiving software can handle.

The checksum field calculates the checksum based on the entire segment size, including a 96-bit pseudoheader that is prefixed to the TCP header during the calculation. The pseudoheader contains the source address, destination address, protocol identifier, and segment length. These are the parameters that are passed to IP when a send instruction is passed, and also the ones read by IP when delivery is attempted.

TCP and Connections

TCP has many rules imposed on how it communicates. These rules and the processes that TCP follows to establish a connection, transfer data, and terminate a connection are usually presented in state diagrams. (Because TCP is a state-driven protocol, its actions depend on the state of a flag or similar construct.) Avoiding overly complex state diagrams is difficult, so flow diagrams can be used as a useful method for understanding TCP.

Establishing a Connection

A connection can be established between two machines only if a connection between the two sockets does not exist, both machines agree to the connection, and both machines have adequate TCP resources to service the connection. If any of these conditions are not met, the connection cannot be made. The acceptance of connections can be triggered by an application or a system administration routine.

When a connection is established, it is given certain properties that are valid until the connection is closed. Typically, these will be a precedence value and a security value. These settings are agreed upon by the two applications when the connection is in the process of being established.

In most cases, a connection is expected by two applications, so they issue either active or passive open requests. Figure 4.6 shows a flow diagram for a TCP open. The process begins with Machine A's TCP receiving a request for a connection from its ULP, to which it sends an active open primitive to Machine B. (Refer back to Table 4.2 for the TCP primitives.) The segment that is constructed will have the SYN flag set on (set to 1) and will have a sequence number assigned. The diagram shows this with the notation *SYN SEQ 50* indicating that the SYN flag is on and the sequence number (Initial Send Sequence number or ISS) is 50. (Any number could have been chosen.)

Figure 4.6. *Establishing a connection.*

The application on Machine B will have issued a passive open instruction to its TCP. When the SYN SEQ 50 segment is received, Machine B's TCP will send an acknowledgment back to Machine A with the sequence number of 51. Machine B will also set an Initial Send Sequence number of its own. The diagram shows this message as *ACK*

51; SYN 200 indicating that the message is an acknowledgment with sequence number 51, it has the SYN flag set, and has an ISS of 200.

Upon receipt, Machine A sends back its own acknowledgment message with the sequence number set to 201. This is *ACK 201* in the diagram. Then, having opened and acknowledged the connection, Machine A and Machine B both send connection open messages through the ULP to the requesting applications.

It is not necessary for the remote machine to have a passive open instruction, as mentioned earlier. In this case, the sending machine provides both the sending and receiving socket numbers, as well as precedence, security, and timeout values. It is common for two applications to request an active open at the same time. This is resolved quite easily, although it does involve a little more network traffic.

Data Transfer

Transferring information is straightforward, as shown in Figure 4.7. For each block of data received by Machine A's TCP from the ULP, TCP encapsulates it and sends it to Machine B with an increasing sequence number. After Machine B receives the message, it acknowledges it with a segment acknowledgment that increments the next sequence number (and hence indicates that it received everything up to that sequence number). Figure 4.7 shows the transfer of only one segment of information—one each way.

Figure 4.7. *Data transfers.*

The TCP data transport service actually embodies six different subservices:

Full duplex: Enables both ends of a connection to transmit at any time, even simultaneously.

Timeliness: The use of timers ensures that data is transmitted within a reasonable amount of time.

Ordered: Data sent from one application will be received in the same order at the other end. This occurs despite the fact that the datagrams may be received out of order through IP, as TCP reassembles the message in the correct order before passing it up to the higher layers.

Labeled: All connections have an agreed-upon precedence and security value.

Controlled flow: TCP can regulate the flow of information through the use of buffers and window limits.

Error correction: Checksums ensure that data is free of errors (within the checksum algorithm's limits).

Closing Connections

To close a connection, one of the TCPs receives a close primitive from the ULP and issues a message with the FIN flag set on. This is shown in Figure 4.8. In the figure, Machine A's TCP sends the request to close the connection to Machine B with the next sequence number. Machine B will then send back an acknowledgment of the request and its next sequence number. Following this, Machine B sends the close message through its ULP to the application and waits for the application to acknowledge the closure. This step is not strictly necessary; TCP can close the connection without the application's approval, but a well-behaved system would inform the application of the change in state.

After receiving approval to close the connection from the application (or after the request has timed out), Machine B's TCP sends a segment back to Machine A with the FIN flag set. Finally, Machine A acknowledges the closure and the connection is terminated.

An abrupt termination of a connection can happen when one side shuts down the socket. This can be done without any notice to the other machine and without regard to any information in transit between the two. Aside from sudden shutdowns caused by malfunctions or power outages, abrupt termination can be initiated by a user, an application, or a system monitoring routine that judges the connection worthy of termination. The other end of the connection may not realize an abrupt termination has occurred until it attempts to send a message and the timer expires.

Figure 4.8. *Closing a connection.*

To keep track of all the connections, TCP uses a connection table. Each existing connection has an entry in the table that shows information about the end-to-end connection. The layout of the TCP connection table is shown in Figure 4.9.

	STATE	LOCAL ADDRESS	LOCAL PORT	REMOTE ADDRESS	REMOTE PORT
Connection 1					
Connection 2					
Connection 3					
Connection n					

Figure 4.9. *The TCP connection table.*

The meaning of each column is as follows:

State: The state of the connection (closed, closing, listening, waiting, and so on).

Local address: The IP address for the connection. When in a listening state, this will be set to 0.0.0.0.

Local port: The local port number.

Remote address: The remote's IP address.

Remote port: The port number of the remote connection.

User Datagram Protocol (UDP)

TCP is a connection-based protocol. There are times when a connectionless protocol is required, so UDP is used. UDP is used with both the Trivial File Transfer Protocol (TFTP) and the Remote Call Procedure (RCP). Connectionless communications don't provide reliability, meaning there is no indication to the sending device that a message has been received correctly. Connectionless protocols also do not offer error-recovery capabilities—which must be either ignored or provided in the higher or lower layers. UDP is much simpler than TCP. It interfaces to IP (or other protocols) without the bother of flow control or error-recovery mechanisms, acting simply as a sender and receiver of datagrams.

Note: UDP is connectionless; TCP is based on connections.

The UDP message header is much simpler than TCP's. It is shown in Figure 4.10. Padding may be added to the datagram to ensure that the message is a multiple of 16 bits.

Source Port (16 bits)	Destination Port (16 bits)
Length (16 bits)	Checksum (16 bits)
Data...	

Figure 4.10. *The UDP header.*

The fields are as follows:

Source port: An optional field with the port number. If a port number is not specified, the field is set to 0.

Destination port: The port on the destination machine.

Length: The length of the datagram, including header and data.

Checksum: A 16-bit one's complement of the one's complement sum of the datagram, including a pseudoheader similar to that of TCP.

The UDP checksum field is optional; but if it isn't used, there is no checksum applied to the data segment because IP's checksum applies only to the IP header. If the checksum is not used, the field should be set to 0.

Summary

Today, you've looked at TCP in reasonable detail. Combined with the information in the last three days, you now have the theory and background necessary to better understand TCP/IP utilities, such as Telnet and FTP, as well as other protocols that use or closely resemble TCP/IP, such as SMTP and TFTP.

The details of TCP/IP will be revisited later in this book, but you can proceed to actually using TCP/IP and its toolset.

Q&A

Q Define multiplexing and how it would be used to combine three source machines to one destination machine. Relate to port numbers.

A Multiplexing was explained in some detail on Day 1. It refers to combining several connections into one. Three machines could each establish source ports to one machine using only one receiving port. The port numbers for the sending machines would all be different, but all three would use the same destination port number. This was shown in Figure 4.4.

Q What one word best describes the difference between TCP from UDP?

A Connections. TCP is connection-based, whereas UDP is connectionless.

Q What are port numbers and sockets?

A A port number is used to identify the type of service provided. A socket is the address of the port a on which connection is established. There is no inherent physical relationship between the two, although many machines assign certain sockets for particular services (port numbers).

Q Describe the timers used with TCP.

A The retransmission timer is used to control the resend of a datagram. The quiet timer is used to delay the reassignment of a port. The persistence timer is used to test a receive window. Keep-alive timers send empty data to keep a connection alive. The idle timer is the amount of time to wait for a disconnection to be terminated after no datagrams are received.

Q What are the six data transport subservices offered by TCP?

A The subservices are full duplex, timeliness, ordered, labeled, controlled flow, and error correction.

Workshop

The Workshop provides quiz questions to help you solidify your understanding of the material covered. Some Workshop sections of this book also contain exercises to provide you with experience in using what you've learned. Try to understand the quiz and exercise answers before continuing on to the next chapter. Answers are provided in Appendix F, "Answers."

Quiz

1. Draw a diagram showing the binding of port tables when three machines are sending information to each other.

2. Draw the TCP protocol data unit (PDU) and explain the meaning of each field.

3. Use a diagram to show the signals involved with two machines establishing a TCP connection. Then, show how data is transferred. Finally, show the termination process.

4. What is a TCP connection table? How is it used?

5. Draw the UDP header and explain the fields it contains.

6. What are the advantages of using UDP over TCP? When would you not want to use UDP?

5

Telnet and FTP

In the last four days you have seen the architecture of TCP/IP, as well as both the Internet Protocol and the Transmission Control Protocol in considerable detail. Building on these two protocols is a layer of application-layer protocols that are commonly associated with TCP/IP. Day 4 looks at the most common application layer protocol: Telnet, File Transfer Protocol (FTP), Trivial File Transfer Protocol (TFTP), and Simple Mail Transfer Protocol (SMTP), as well as a suite of tools called the Berkeley r-utilities.

To cover all four protocols in complete detail would require several hundred pages, so today's text examines the protocols' most important aspects, including their purposes, their relations to TCP and IP, their control codes and behavior, and typical usage examples. Each of the four protocols has advantages that make it ideally suited for a particular purpose. Hopefully, by the end of the day, you will understand why they are used and how they fit into the TCP/IP world.

Telnet

The Telnet (telecommunications network) program is intended to provide a remote login or virtual terminal capability across a network. In other words, a user on machine *A* should be able to log into machine *B* anywhere on the network, and as far as the user is concerned, it appears that the user is seated in front of machine *B*. The Telnet service is provided through TCP's port number 23. (See Table 4.1 for the TCP port numbers.)

Telnet was developed because at one time the only method of allowing one machine to access another was to establish a link using communications devices such as modems or networks into dedicated ports. This is a little more complicated than might appear at first glance because of the wide diversity of terminals and computers, each with its own control codes and terminal characteristics. When directly connected to a server, the server's CPU must manage the translation of terminal codes between the two, which puts a hefty load on the server CPU. With several remote logins active, a server CPU can spend an inordinate amount of time managing the translations.

Telnet alleviates this problem by embedding the terminal characteristic sequences within the Telnet protocol. When two machines communicate using Telnet, Telnet itself can determine and set the communications and terminal parameters for the session during the connection phase, and includes the capability not to support a service that one end of the connection cannot handle. When a connection has been established by Telnet, both ends have agreed upon a method for the two machines to exchange information, taking the load off the server CPU for a sizable amount of this work.

Usually, Telnet involves a process on the server that accepts incoming requests for a Telnet session. On UNIX systems, this process is called `telnetd`. The client (the end that is doing the calling) runs a program, usually called `telnet`, that attempts the connection to the server. A relative of `telnet` is the program `rlogin`, which is common on UNIX machines and that you will look at later today; see "The Berkeley Utilities."

> **Note:** The `rlogin` program provides almost identical functionality to Telnet and adds support for the UNIX environment. Many machines, especially UNIX workstations, act as both client and server simultaneously, allowing a user to log into other machines on the network and other users to log into the user's machine.

Telnet Connections

The Telnet protocol uses the concept of a *network virtual terminal,* or *NVT,* to define both ends of a Telnet connection. Each end of the connection has a logical keyboard and printer. The logical printer can display characters, while the logical keyboard can generate characters. The network printer is usually a terminal screen, while the logical keyboard is usually the user's keyboard, although it could be a file or other input stream. These terms are also used in the File Transfer Protocol (FTP) and Simple Mail Transfer Protocol (SMTP). Figure 5.1 illustrates the NVT and logical keyboard and printer.

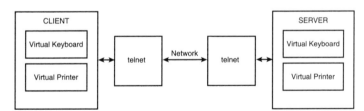

Figure 5.1. *A network virtual terminal for Telnet.*

The Telnet protocol treats the two ends of the connection as network virtual terminals. The two programs at either end (telnet and telnetd) manage the translation from virtual terminal to actual physical devices. The concept of virtual terminals enables Telnet to interconnect to any type of device, as long as a mapping is available from the virtual codes to the physical device. One advantage of this approach is that some physical devices cannot support all operations, so the virtual terminal will not have those codes. When the two ends are establishing the connection, the lack of these codes is noted and sequences that would use them are ignored. This process is straightforward: one end asks whether the function is supported and the other replies either positively or negatively. If it is supported, the necessary codes are sent. The list of supported functions is quickly covered in this manner.

When a connection is established through Telnet, telnetd starts a process on the server for running applications. Every keystroke in a Telnet session must go through several different processes, as shown in Figure 5.2. Each keystroke goes through telnet, telnetd, and the application. Some applications want to communicate through a terminal device, so the remote system runs a pseudo-TTY driver that acts like a terminal to the application. If a windowed interface such as X or Motif is used on the host and remote machine, the systems must be instructed to allow windowing information to be passed back and forth, otherwise the remote machine will try to open the windows on the server.

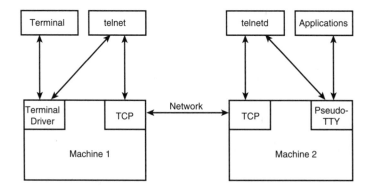

Figure 5.2. *A Telnet connection.*

To start Telnet, you must provide either the name or the IP address of the machine to be connected with. The name can be used only if the system has a means of resolving the name into its IP address, such as with the Domain Name System. A port name can usually be used, too, to connect to a specific service, but this is encountered infrequently by most users. If no name, address, or port is specified, Telnet will enter its command mode and wait for specific instructions. When the connection is established, a user ID and password will be requested. You can log in with any user ID that would be valid on the remote system (it does not have to be the same user ID you have on the local system).

> **Warning:** You can use a machine name as part of the Telnet command only if the system has a means of resolving the name to its IP address. If not, no connection will be established, although Telnet may remain in command mode. To exit, use Ctrl+D or the break sequence displayed as part of the start-up message.

You can enter Telnet's command mode at any time, usually by using the Ctrl+] key combination (hold down Ctrl and press the right bracket key). If you are currently connected to an active session when you enter command mode, Telnet will wait for you to issue a command, execute it, and then return to the session automatically. Command mode lets you enter commands relative to the client (the machine you are physically in front of) instead of the server.

Once the connection is successfully established, your session behaves as though you were on the remote machine, with all valid commands of that operating system. All instructions are relative to the server, so a directory command shows the current directory on the server, not the client. To see the client's directory, you would have to enter command mode. A sample Telnet login and logout session calling from one UNIX workstation (called `tpci_server`) to another (called `tpci_hpws4`, a name that can be resolved by the name server) follows:

```
tpci_hpws2> telnet tpci_hpws4
Trying...
Connected to tpci_hpws4.
Escape character is '^]'.
HP-UX tpci_hpws4 A.09.01 A 9000/720 (ttys2)
login: tparker
password: xxxxxxxx
tpci_hpws4-1> pwd
/u1/tparker
tpci_hpws4-2> cd docs
tpci_hpws4-3> pwd
/u1/tparker/docs
```

```
tpci_hpws4-2> <Ctrl+d>
Connection closed by foreign host.
tpci_hpws2>
```

Once you are connected to the remote machine, the session behaves exactly as though you were on that machine. To log out of the remote session, simply issue the logout command (in the previous example, the UNIX Ctrl+D combination), and you are returned to your local machine. The `telnet` program is useful when you are on an underpowered machine or terminal and you want to use another machine's processing capabilities, or if another machine has a particular tool that you don't want to load on your local machine.

If the calling and receiving workstations use a graphical user interface (GUI) such as Motif, you must instruct both ends to use the local terminal for windowing (because you wouldn't be able to see a window on the remote terminal). Locally, a program is run that instructs the operating system to enable other machines to display directly onto the screen, while the remote must have an instruction to redirect windowing commands to the local screen. Many UNIX systems would perform this function like this:

```
tpci_server-1> xhost +
tpci_server-2> telnet tpci_hpws4
Trying...
Connected to tpci_hpws4.
Escape character is '^]'.
HP-UX tpci_hpws4 A.09.01 A 9000/720 (ttys2)
login: tparker
password: xxxxxxxx
tpci_hpws4-1> setenv DISPLAY tpci_server:0.0
tpci_hpws4-2> <Ctrl+d>
Connection closed by foreign host.
tpci_server-3>
```

The UNIX `xhost +` instruction tells the local machine to enable the remote system to control windows on the local screen. The instruction `setenv DISPLAY machine_name` executed on the remote sets the shell environment variable to the local screen. Whenever a window must be opened (as when a Motif application is run) the windowing will appear on the local screen while the processing is conducted on the remote. These examples are for UNIX, but a similar sequence will work on other machines and GUIs.

Telnet Commands

A number of service options are available when a Telnet session is established. Their values can be changed during the course of a Telnet session if both ends agree (one end may be prevented from enabling or disabling a service because of administrator or resource settings). There are four verbs used by the Telnet protocol to offer, refuse, request, and prevent services: `will`, `won't`, `do`, and `don't`, respectively. The verbs are designed to be paired. To illustrate how these are used, consider the following Telnet session, which has the display of these verbs turned on using the telnet command `toggle options`:

```
tpci_server-1> telnet
telnet> toggle options
Will show option processing.
telnet> open tpci_hpws4
Trying...
Connected to tpci_hpws4.
Escape character is '^]'.
SENT do SUPPRESS GO AHEAD
SENT will TERMINAL TYPE (don't reply)
SEND will NAWS (don't reply)
RCVD do 36 (reply)
sent wont 36 (don't reply)
RECD do TERMINAL TYPE (don't reply)
RCVD will SUPPRESS GO AHEAD (don't reply)
RCVD do NAWS (don't reply)
Sent suboption NAWS 0 80 (80) 0 37 (37)
Received suboption Terminal type - request to send.
RCVD will ECHO (reply)
SEND do ECHO (reply)
RCVD do ECHO (reply)
SENT wont ECHO (don't reply)
HP-UX tpci_hpws4 A.09.01 A 9000/720 (ttys2)
login:
```

A partial set of Telnet command codes is shown in Table 5.1. Additional codes are used to represent printer functions, such as horizontal and vertical tabs and form feeds, but these have been left off the table for brevity's sake. Part of the Telnet command code set includes six terminal functions (IP, AO, AYT, EC, EL, and GA), which are common across most terminal definitions, so they are formally defined in the Telnet standard.

Table 5.1. Telnet command codes.

Code	Value	Description
Abort Output (AO)	245	Runs process to completion but does not send the output
Are you there (AYT)	246	Queries the other end to ensure an application is functioning
Break (BRK)	243	Sends a break instruction
Data Mark	242	Data portion of a Sync

continues

Table 5.1. continued

Code	Value	Description
Do	253	Asks for the other end to perform or an acknowledgment that the other end is to perform
Don't	254	Demands the other end stop performing or confirms that the other end is no longer performing
Erase Character (EC)	247	Erases a character in the output stream
Erase Line (EL)	248	Erases a line in the output stream
Go Ahead (GA)	249	Indicates permission to proceed when using half-duplex (no echo) communications
Interpret as Command (IAC)	255	Interprets the following as a command
Interrupt Process (IP)	244	Interrupts, suspends, aborts, or terminates the process
NOP	241	No operation
SB	250	Subnegotiation of an option
SE	240	End of the subnegotiation
Will	251	Instructs the other end to begin performing or confirms that this end is now performing
Won't	252	Refuses to perform or rejects the other end performing

Telnet commands are sent in a formal package called a *command,* as shown in Figure 5.3. Typically, the command will contain 2 or 3 bytes: the Interpret as Command (IAC) instruction, the command code being sent, and any optional parameter to the command. The options supported by Telnet are shown in Table 5.2.

Interpret As Command (IAC)	Command Code	Options
		(Optional)

Figure 5.3. *The Telnet command structure.*

Table 5.2. Supported Telnet option codes.

Code	Description
0	Binary transmission
1	Echo
2	Reconnection
3	Suppress Go Ahead (GA)
4	Approximate message size negotiation
5	Status
6	Timing mark
7	Remote controlled transmission and echo
8	Output line width
9	Output page length
10	Output carriage-return action
11	Output horizontal tab stop setting

continues

Table 5.2. continued

Code	Description
12	Output horizontal tab stop action
13	Output form feed action
14	Output vertical tab stop setting
15	Output vertical tab stop action
16	Output line feed action
17	Extended ASCII characters
18	Logout
19	Bytes macro
20	Data entry terminal
21	SUPDUP
22	SUPDUP output
23	Send location
24	Terminal type
25	End of Record
26	TACACS user identification
27	Output marking
28	Terminal location number
29	3270 regime
30	X.3 PAD (Packet assembly and disassembly)
31	Window size

If you refer to the code previous listing with the options toggled on, some of the commands can be understood more clearly now. For example, will ECHO (which would be transmitted as values 255 251 1) instructs the other end to begin echoing back characters it receives. The command won't ECHO (the command would be 255 252 1) indicates that the sender will not echo back characters or wants to stop echoing.

> **Note:** The use of ASCII characters and small tables of commands and options makes it relatively easy to follow Telnet communications.

TN3270

Many mainframes use EBCDIC, whereas most smaller machines rely on ASCII. This can cause a problem when trying to Telnet from EBCDIC-based machines to ASCII-based machines, because the codes being transferred will not be accurate. To correct this, a Telnet application called TN3270 was developed, which provides translation between the two formats.

When TN3270 is used to connect between two machines, Telnet itself establishes the initial connection, and then one end sets up for translation. If an ASCII machine is calling an EBCDIC machine, the translation between the two formats is conducted at the EBCDIC (server) end unless there is a gateway between them, in which case the gateway can perform the translation.

File Transfer Protocol (FTP)

The *File Transfer Protocol,* usually called *FTP,* is a utility for managing files across machines without having to establish a remote session with Telnet. FTP enables you to transfer files back and forth, manage directories, and access electronic mail. FTP is not designed to enable access to another machine to execute programs, but it is the best utility for file manipulation.

The File Transfer Protocol uses two TCP channels. TCP port 20 is the data channel, whereas port 21 is the command channel. FTP is different from most other file transfer programs in that it uses two channels, enabling simultaneous transfer of FTP commands and data. It also differs in one other important aspect: FTP conducts all file transfers in the foreground, instead of the background. FTP does not use spoolers or queues. By using TCP, FTP eliminates the need to worry about reliability or connection management, because FTP can rely on TCP to perform these functions properly.

In FTP parlance, the two channels that exist between the two machines are called the *protocol interpreter,* or *PI,* and the *data transfer process,* or *DTP.* The PI transfers instructions between the two implementations using TCP data channel 21, and the DTP transfers files on TCP data channel 20. This is shown in Figure 5.4.

5

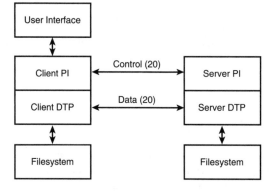

Figure 5.4. *FTP two-channel connections.*

FTP is similar to Telnet in that it uses a server program that runs continuously and a separate program that is executed on the client. On UNIX systems, these programs are named *FTPD* and *FTP*, respectively (similar to `telnetd` and `telnet`).

FTP Commands

FTP's internal protocol commands are four-character ASCII sequences terminated by a newline character. Some of the codes require parameters after them. One primary advantage to using ASCII characters for commands is that a user can observe the command flow and understand it easily. This helps considerably in the debugging process. Also, it makes it possible for a knowledgeable user to communicate directly with the FTP server component without invoking the client portion (in other words, communicating with FTPD without using FTP on a local machine).

FTP commands used by the protocol are summarized in Table 5.3. These commands provide for the connection process, password checking, and the actual file transfers. These are not to be confused with the commands available to a user.

Table 5.3. FTP internal commands.

Command	Description
ABOR	Abort previous command
ACCT	User account ID
ALLO	Allocate storage for forthcoming operation
APPE	Append incoming data to an existing file
CDUP	Change to parent directory
CWD	Change working directory
DELE	Delete file
HELP	Retrieve information
LIST	Transfer list of directories
MKD	Make a directory
MODE	Set transfer mode
NLST	Transfer a directory listing
NOOP	No operation
PASS	User password
PASV	Request a passive open
PORT	Port address
PWD	Display current directory
QUIT	Terminate the connection
REIN	Terminate and restart a connection
REST	Restart marker (restart transfer)
RETR	Transfer copy of file
RMD	Remove a directory
RNFR	Old pathname for rename command
RNTO	New pathname for rename command

continues

5

Table 5.3. continued

Command	Description
SITE	Provides service specifics
SMNT	Mount a file system
STAT	Returns status
STOR	Accept and store data
STOU	Accept data and store under different name
STRU	File structure
SYST	Query to determine operating system
TYPE	Type of data
USER	User ID

FTP also uses simple return codes to indicate transfer conditions. Each return code is a three-digit number, the first of which signifies a successful execution (the first digit is 1, 2, or 3) or a failure (the first digit is 4 or 5). The second and third digits specify the return code or error condition in more detail. The FTP return codes are shown in Table 5.4 and Table 5.5. The third-digit codes are not included because there are many of them and they can vary between implementations.

Table 5.4. FTP reply code first digits.

First Digit	Description
1	Action initiated. Expect another reply before sending a new command.
2	Action completed. May send a new command.
3	Command accepted but on hold due to lack of information.
4	Command not accepted or completed. Temporary error condition exists. Command may be reissued.
5	Command not accepted or completed. Reissuing command will result in same error (don't reissue).

Table 5.5. FTP reply code second digits.

Second Digit	Description
0	Syntax error or illegal command
1	Reply to request for information
2	Reply that refers to connection management
3	Reply for authentication command
4	Not used
5	Reply for status of server

FTP enables file transfers in several formats, which are usually system-dependent. The majority of systems (including UNIX systems) have only two modes: text and binary. Some mainframe installations add support for EBCDIC, while many sites have a local type that is designed for fast transfers between local network machines (the local type may use 32- or 64-bit words). Text transfers use ASCII characters separated by carriage-return and newline characters, whereas binary enables transfer of characters with no conversion or formatting. Binary mode is faster than text and enables for the transfer of all ASCII values (necessary for nontext files). On most systems, FTP will start in text mode, although many system administrators now set FTP to binary mode for their user's convenience. FTP cannot transfer file permissions, because these are not specified as part of the protocol.

> **Warning:** Before transferring files with FTP, make sure you are using the correct transfer mode. Transferring a binary file as ASCII will result in garbage! Check with your system administrator if you are unsure of the mode, or watch the messages FTP returns to see the mode used.

FTP Connections

FTP is usually started with the name or address of the target machine. As with Telnet, the name must be resolvable into an IP address for the command to succeed. The target machine also can be specified from the FTP command line.

When FTP connects to the destination, you must be able to log in as though connecting through Telnet. Some systems allow an *anonymous* or *guest* login for FTP file transfers (usually using your login name as a password is a record of your access; see the section titled, "Anonymous FTP Access"), while most require you to have regular access to the machine. On large networks where a system such as Yellow Pages (YP) or Network Information Services (NIS) is used, logins are usually permitted on most machines. If YP or NIS is not employed, you must be in the valid user file to obtain FTP access. As with Telnet, you can log into the remote with a different user ID from your local machine login. To transfer files, you must have the proper permissions on the remote.

After logging in using FTP, you are not actually on the remote machine. You are still logically on the client, so all instructions for file transfers and directory movement must be with respect to your local machine and not the remote one. Note that this is the opposite of Telnet (a distinction that causes considerable confusion among newcomers to FTP and Telnet).

Warning: Remember that all references to files and directories are relative to the machine that initiated the FTP session. If you are not careful, you can accidentally overwrite existing files.

The process followed by FTP when a connection is established is as follows:

1. *Login:* Verifies the user ID and password
2. *Define directory:* Identifies the starting directory
3. *Define file transfer mode:* Defines the type of transfer
4. *Start data transfer:* Enables user commands
5. *Stop data transfer:* Closes the connection

These steps are performed in sequence for each connection. A user has a number of commands available to control FTP; the most frequently used commands are summarized in Table 5.6.

Table 5.6. FTP user commands.

FTP Command	Description
ascii	Switches to ASCII transfer mode
binary	Switches to binary transfer mode
cd	Changes directory on the server
close	Terminates the connection
del	Deletes a file on the server
dir	Displays the server directory
get	Fetches a file from the server
hash	Displays a pound character for each block transmitted
help	Displays help
lcd	Changes directory on the client
mget	Fetches several files from the server
mput	Sends several files to the server
open	Connects to a server
put	Sends a file to the server
pwd	Displays the current server directory
quote	Supplies an FTP command directly
quit	Terminates the FTP session

Using FTP is similar to using Telnet, except that all movements of files are relative to the client. Therefore, *putting* a file is moving it from the client to the server, whereas *getting* a file is the reverse. A sample FTP session follows:

```
tpci_hpws1-1> ftp tpci_hpws4
Connected to tpci_hpws4.
220 tpci_hpws4 FTP server
➥(Version 1.7.109.2 Tue Jul 28 23:32:34 GMT 1992) ready.
Name (tpci_hpws4:tparker):
331 Password required for tparker.
Password:
230 User tparker logged in.
Remote system type is UNIX.
Using binary mode to transfer files.
```

```
ftp> pwd
257 "/u1/tparker" is current directory.
ftp> <Ctrl+d>
tpci_hpws1-2>
```

A debugging option is available from the command line by adding -d to the command. This displays the command channel instructions. Instructions from the client are shown with an arrow as the first character, whereas instructions from the server have three digits in front of them. A PORT in the command line indicates the address of the data channel on which the client is waiting for the server's reply. If no PORT is specified, channel 20 (the default value) is used. Unfortunately, the progress of data transfers cannot be followed in the debugging mode. A sample session with the debugging option enabled is shown here:

```
tpci_hpws1-1> ftp -d
ftp> open tpci_hpws4
Connected to tpci_hpws4.
220 tpci_hpws4 FTP server
➡(Version 1.7.109.2 Tue Jul 28 23:32:34 GMT 1992) ready.
Name (tpci_hpws4:tparker):
---> USER tparker
331 Password required for tparker.
Password:
---> PASS qwerty5
230 User tparker logged in.
---> SYST
215 UNIX Type: L8
Remote system type is UNIX.
---> Type I
200 Type set to I.
Using binary mode to transfer files.
ftp> ls
---> PORT 47,80,10,28,4,175
200 PORT command successful.
---> TYPE A
200 Type set to A.
---> LIST
150 Opening ASCII mode data connection for /bin/ls.
total 4
-rw-r-----  1 tparker  tpci    2803  Apr 29 10:46 file1
-rw-rw-r--  1 tparker  tpci    1286  Apr 14 10:46 file5_draft
-rwxr-----  2 tparker  tpci   15635  Mar 14 23:23 test_comp_1
-rw-r-----  1 tparker  tpci      52  Apr 22 12:19 xyzzy
Transfer complete.
---> TYPE I
200 Type set to I.
ftp> <Ctrl+d>
tpci_hpws1-2>
```

You will notice in the previous code how the mode changes from binary to ASCII to send the directory listing, and then back to binary (the system default value). You can see how the two systems communicate to display the status messages that appear, without the debugging option active.

FTP Third-Party Transfers

FTP enables a transfer to occur through a third machine positioned between the client and the server. This procedure is known as a *third-party transfer* and is sometimes necessary to obtain proper permissions to access the remote machine. Figure 5.5 shows the schematic of a third-party transfer, with the control connection made through a third machine.

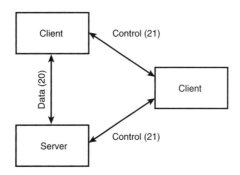

Figure 5.5. *Third-party FTP transfers.*

When setting up a third-party connection, the client opens the control connections between the remote machine and the second client that handles the control channel. Only the control channel goes through the second client, whereas the data channel goes directly between the two ends.

When a transfer request is submitted, it is transferred through the second client, which checks permissions and then forwards the request to the server. The data transfer can take place directly because the permissions were checked on the control channel.

Anonymous FTP Access

FTP requires a user ID and password to enable file-transfer capabilities, but there is a more liberal method of allowing general access to a file or directory, called *anonymous FTP*. Anonymous FTP removes the requirement for a login account on the remote machine, usually allowing the login anonymous with a password of either guest or the user's actual login name. The following session shows the use of an anonymous FTP system:

```
tpci_hpws4-1> ftp uofo.edu
Connected to uofo.edu.
220 uofo.edu FTP server (Version 1.7.109.2 Tue Jul 28 23:32:34 GMT 1992) ready.
Name (uofo:username): anonymous
331 Guest login ok, send userID as password.
Password: tparker
230 Guest login ok, access restrictions apply.
ftp> <Ctrl+d>
tpci_hpws4-2>
```

If the remote system is set to allow anonymous logins, you will be prompted for a password and then given a warning about access limitations. If there is a file on the remote system you require, a get command will transfer it. Anonymous FTP sites are becoming common, especially with the expanding interest in the Internet.

Trivial File Transfer Protocol (TFTP)

The Trivial File Transfer Protocol (TFTP) is one of the simplest file transfer protocols in use. It differs from FTP in two primary ways: it does not log on to the remote machine and it uses the User Datagram Protocol (UDP) connectionless transport protocol instead of TCP. By using UDP, TFTP does not monitor the progress of the file transfer, although it does have to employ more complex algorithms to ensure proper data integrity. By avoiding logging on to the remote, user access and file permission problems are avoided. TFTP uses the TCP port identifier number 69, even though TCP is not involved in the protocol.

TFTP has few advantages over FTP. Usually, it is not used for file transfers between machines where FTP could be used instead, although TFTP is useful when a diskless terminal or workstation is involved. Typically, TFTP is used to load applications and fonts into these machines, as well as for bootstrapping. TFTP is necessary in these cases because the diskless machines cannot execute FTP until they are fully loaded with an operating system. TFTP's small, executable size and memory requirements make it ideal for inclusion in a bootstrap, the system requiring only TFTP, UDP, and a network driver, all of which can be provided in a small EPROM.

TFTP handles access and file permissions by imposing restraints of its own. On most UNIX systems, for example, a file can be transferred only if it is accessible to all users on the remote (both read and write permissions are set). Because of the lax access regulations, most system administrators will impose more control over TFTP (or ban its use altogether), otherwise it would be quite easy for a knowledgeable user to access or transfer files that could constitute a security violation.

TFTP transfers can fail for many reasons, because practically any kind of error encountered during a transfer operation will cause a complete failure. TFTP does support some basic error messages, but it cannot handle simple errors like insufficient resources for a file transfer or even a failure to locate a requested file.

TFTP Commands

The important instructions in TFTP's command set are shown in Table 5.7. It is similar to FTP's, but differs in several important aspects because of the connectionless aspect of the protocol. Most noticeable is the `connect` command, which simply determines the remote's address instead of initiating a connection.

Table 5.7. TFTP's command set.

TFTP Command	Description
binary	Uses binary mode for transfers
connect	Determines the remote's address
get	Retrieves a file from the remote
put	Transfers a file to the remote
trace	Displays protocol codes
verbose	Displays all information

TFTP allows both text and binary transfers, as does FTP. As with both Telnet and FTP, TFTP uses a server process (TFTPD on a UNIX system) and an executable usually called TFTP. A sample TFTP session is shown here, with full trace options and binary transfers turned on:

```
tpci_hpws1-1> tftp
tftp> connect tpci_hpws4
tftp> trace
Packet tracing on.
tftp> binary
Binary mode on.
tftp> verbose
```

```
Verbose mode on.
tftp> status
Connected to tpci_hpws4.
Mode: octet Verbose: on Tracing: on
Rexmt-interval: 5 seconds, Max-timeout: 25 seconds
tftp> get /usr/rmaclean/docs/draft1
getting from tpci_hpws4:/usr/rmaclean/docs/draft1 to /tmp/draft1 [octet]
sent RRQ <file=/usr/rmaclean/docs/draft1, mode=octet>
received DATA <block1, 512 bytes>
send ACK <block=1>
received DATA <block2, 512 bytes>
send ACK <block=3>
received DATA <block4, 128 bytes>
send ACK <block=3>
Received 1152 bytes in 0.2 second 46080 bits/s]
tftp> quit
tpci_hpws1-2>
```

TFTP Packets

TFTP uses UDP as a transport protocol, so TFTP can use the UDP header to encapsulate TFTP protocol information. TFTP uses the UDP source and destination port fields to set the two ends of the connection. It accomplishes this by the use of *TFTP Transfer Identifiers,* or *TIDs,* which are created by TFTP and passed to UDP, which then places them in the headers.

As with Telnet and FTP, TFTP uses *port binding,* wherein the sending machine selects a TID and the remote is set to port number 69 (TFTP's port number). The remote machine will respond with an acknowledgment of a connection request, a source port of 69, and the destination TID sent in the request.

TFTP uses five types of Protocol Data Units, which are referred to as *packets* in the TFTP lexicon. These packets are given in Table 5.8. Their layout is shown in Figure 5.6. Error messages supported by TFTP are shown in Table 5.9.

Table 5.8. TFTP Protocol Data Unit codes.

Code	OpCode	Description
ACK	4	Acknowledgment
DATA	3	Send Data
Error	5	Error
RRQ	1	Read request
WRQ	2	Write request

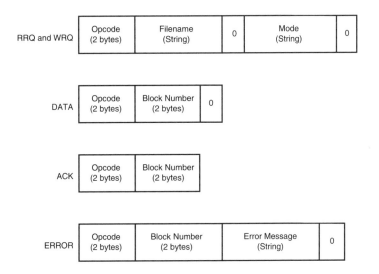

Figure 5.6. *TFTP packet layouts.*

Table 5.9. TFTP error messages and codes.

Code	Description
0	Not defined
1	File not found
2	Permissions prevent access
3	Disk full or allocation limit exceeded
4	Illegal TFTP operation requested
5	Unknown transfer number

The packet layouts for both RRQ and WRQ have a mode field, which indicates the type of transfer. There are three modes currently available to TFTP:

☐ *NetASCII:* Standard ASCII codes

☐ *Byte:* 8-bit bytes and binary information

☐ *Mail:* Indicates the destination is a user not a file (information is transferred as NetASCII)

The last block in all packets contains between 0 and 511 bytes of data, labeled 0 in Figure 5.6. This pads out the block of data to 512 bytes.

The communications process used by TFTP begins with the client sending an RRQ or WRQ request to the server through UDP. As part of the request, a transaction number, the filename, and a code to identify the transmission mode to be used is specified. The transaction number is used to identify future transactions in the sequence.

Because there is no connection between the two, the client sets a timer and waits for a reply from the server. If one doesn't arrive before the timer expires, another request is sent. After an ACK is received, a DATA packet is transmitted, to which another ACK or an ERROR is received. If there are several packets to be transferred, they are constructed so they have a length of 512 bytes and an incrementing sequence number. The process terminates when a DATA packet with a length of less than 512 bytes is received by the server. For each packet sent, TFTP waits for an acknowledgment before sending the next, a system known as *flip-flop protocol.*

Simple Mail Transfer Protocol (SMTP)

The Simple Mail Transfer Protocol (SMTP) is the defined Internet method for transferring electronic mail. SMTP is similar to FTP in many ways, including the same simplicity of operation. SMTP uses TCP port number 25.

Most UNIX systems use a program called sendmail to implement SMTP (as well as several other mail protocols). The sendmail program acts as both a client and a server system, usually running in background as a daemon. Users do not interact with sendmail directly, but use a front-end mail program such as mail, mailx, or Mail. These mail system interfaces pass the message to sendmail for forwarding.

SMTP uses spools or queues. When a message is sent to SMTP, it places it in a queue. SMTP attempts to forward the message from the queue whenever it connects to remote machines. If it cannot forward the message within a specified time limit, the message is returned to the sender or removed.

SMTP Commands

SMTP data transmissions use a simple format. All the message text is transferred as 7-bit ASCII characters. The end of the message is indicated by a single period on a line by itself. (If for some reason a line in the message begins with a period, a second one is added by the protocol to avoid confusion with the end-of-message indicator.)

SMTP has a simple protocol command set, listed in Table 5.10. Using these protocol elements, mail is transferred with a minimum of effort.

Table 5.10. The SMTP protocol command set.

Command	Description
DATA	Message text
EXPN	Expansion of a distribution list
HELO	Used in connection establishment to exchange identifiers
HELP	Request for help
MAIL	The sender's address
NOOP	No operation
RCPT	The message destination address (more than one may be provided)
RSET	Terminates the current transaction
SAML	Sends a message to the user's terminal and send mail
SEND	Sends a message to the user's terminal
SOML	Either sends a message to the user's terminal or send mail
TURN	Changes the sending direction (reverse sending and receiving roles)
VRFY	Verifies the user name

When a connection is established, the two SMTP systems exchange authentication codes. Following this, one system will send a MAIL command to the other to identify the sender and provide information about the message. The receiving SMTP will return an acknowledgment, after which a RCPT is sent to identify the recipient. If more than one recipient at the receiver location is identified, several RCPT messages will be sent, but the message itself is only transmitted once. After each RCPT, there is an acknowledgment. A DATA command is followed by the message lines until a single period on a line by itself indicates the end of the message. The connection is closed with a QUIT command.

The sender and recipient address fields use standard Internet formats, involving the user name and domain name (such as tparker@tpci.com). The domain may be replaced by other information as a direct connection is established, or if there is a forwarding machine in the path. SMTP uses the Domain Name System (DNS) for all addresses.

The Berkeley Utilities

The University of California at Berkeley was instrumental in the development of TCP/IP and contributed many utility programs to the application tool set. These are usually known by the term *Berkeley r-Utilities.* They are called r-utilities because they all start with the letter r (for remote). Most of the utilities are UNIX-specific, although they have since all been ported to other operating systems.

The *hosts.equiv* and *.rhosts* Files

To correctly enable machines to communicate over networks, access rights for machines and users must be set. Usually, when logging in to another machine, a user must supply a user ID and a password. When you log into many machines, retyping this information can be tedious and time-consuming. It also can be a security problem, because it is easy to write a program that monitors network connections for this information. A way to enable fast access without actually logging in and preventing interception of passwords is clearly useful in some cases.

The system administrator can decide that all login names used on other machines whose name is in the file hosts.equiv are allowed access on the local machine. This enables a protocol that is querying a machine for access to check the hosts.equiv file for the requesting machine's name and if it is found, grant access to the user on the remote machine. The user would have the same access rights as on his or her home machine.

If the protocol doesn't find an entry in the hosts.equiv file, it can check another file maintained in a user's home directory called .rhosts. A user can control who has access to his or her login name with the file .rhosts in his or her home directory, enabling other users to log in as if they were that user. The .rhosts file must be owned by the user (or root) and not allow write access to all users (on a UNIX system, the "other" permission cannot be *write*). A .rhosts file consists of a line for each user to be allowed into the home directory. The line consists of a machine name and a login name. A sample .rhosts file is shown here:

```
tpci_hpws1 rmaclean
tpci_hpws1 bsmallwood
tpci_hpws3 ychow
```

```
tpci_hpws3 bsmallwood
tpci_hpws4 glessard
tpci_hpws4 bsmallwood
tpci_sunws1 chatton
merlin tparker
merlin ahoyt
merlin lrainsford
```

This file would allow user `bsmallwood` to log in from three different machines.

rlogin

The `rlogin` command (for *remote login*) enables a user to log into another machine. It is very similar in functionality to Telnet, although the protocol is much simpler. There is a background program running on the server called rlogind, while the program `rlogin` resides on the client.

The `rlogin` protocol begins a session by sending three character strings, separated by zeros. The first string is the user's login ID (on the client), the second string is the login name for the server (usually, but not always the same as the login name on the client), and the third string is the login name and transmission rate of the user's terminal (such as `wyse60/19200`). When received on the server, the strings can be converted to environment variables (such as UNIX's TERM terminal variable). You cannot log into the remote machine with a different user ID, as the system does not prompt for the login name. It will prompt for a password, however.

After the login process is completed, `rlogin` doesn't use any protocol. Every character you type on the client machine is sent to the server, and every server-generated character is displayed on your console. The only ways to exit to your local machine are either by closing the connection by using Ctrl+D, or by entering the escape character on a line by itself. By default, the escape character is a tilde (~).

Some versions of `rlogin` enable a shell escape, a temporary suspension of the `rlogin` session and a return to the operating system, by using ~!.

rsh

The `rsh` utility (remote shell) lets you execute commands on a remote machine. As with most Berkeley utilities, the background process called `rshd` is involved. Executing a command on a remote machine is a matter of adding `rsh` and the machine name to the front of the command line, such as rsh `tpci_hpws3` who or rsh `tpci_sunws1` tar xvf / dev/rct0 (using UNIX examples). The `rsh` utility depends on the presence of either `hosts.equiv` or `.rhosts` to allow login, otherwise access is not granted.

5

The rsh utility is not a shell in the sense that it does not interpret commands like the UNIX C Shell or Bourne Shell. Instead, a command entered is sent to the server's standard input and output, executing the command as a local process through the TCP connection. The primary advantage of this is that a shell script that executes on your local machine can be submitted to the remote machine with no modification, where it will run just as if it was local (except using the remote's file system). Unfortunately, any return codes generated by the remote system will not be sent back to your local machine. Also, most screen-oriented applications will not function properly because they have no terminal output to write to.

rcp

The Berkeley rcp (remote copy) command is similar to the UNIX cp command, except that it works across the network. The command syntax and option lists for rcp are the same as those for cp, although a machine name is usually specified as part of the filename by the addition of the machine name followed by a colon (see the following examples). Even recursive copying of directories is supported (which isn't available under FTP or TFTP, a useful and attractive feature of rcp). The rcp program acts as both server and client, initiated when a request arrives.

```
rcp tpci_hpws4:/user/tparker/doc/draft1 .
rcp file2 merlin:/u1/bsmallwood/temp/file2
rcp -r merlin:/u2/tparker/tcp_book tpci_server/tcp_book
rcp merlin:/u1/ychow/iso9000_doc tpci_server:/u1/iso/doc1/iso_doc_from_ychow
rcp file4 tparker@tpci.com:new_info
```

As the examples indicate, the filename at both the local and remote machine is specified, with standard UNIX conventions supported. The third example shows a file being transferred from one machine to another, neither of which is the machine from which the command is initiated. The last example shows the use of a full DNS-style name for the destination address.

The rcp utility is a faster method of transferring files than FTP, although rcp requires access permission through a .rhosts file (not hosts.equiv). Without an entry in this file, access is refused and FTP or TFTP must be used.

rwho

The rwho (remote who) command uses the rwhod daemon to display a list of users on the network. It shows all network users, compiled from a regularly sent packet of information from all running rwhod programs. The frequency of this packet broadcast is system-dependent, but is usually in the order of every one to three minutes. When a rwhod program receives a broadcast from another machine, it places it in a system file for future use. (The file on a UNIX system is called /usr/spool/rwho.)

When a machine has not sent a broadcast message within a time limit (usually 11 minutes), it is assumed that the machine has disconnected from the network and all users listed as active on that machine in the system file are ignored. The rwhod program will drop a user ID from its broadcast if nothing has been entered at the user's terminal in the past hour.

The output from an rwho request is shown in the following example. For each user, it shows his or her login name, machine and terminal name, and the time and date of the user's login.

```
bsmallwood merlin:tty2p      Feb 29 09:01
etreijs    tpci_hpws2:tty01  Feb 29 12:12
rmaclean   goofus:tty02      Feb 28 23:52
tparker    merlin:tty01      Feb 29 11:43
ychow      prudie:tty2a      Feb 28 11:37
```

The rcp program has one major problem on large networks: the continuous sending of update packets by each machine creates a considerable amount of network traffic. For this reason, some implementations directly request the user names only when an rwho request is received.

ruptime

The ruptime utility displays a list of all machines on the network, their status, the number of active users, current load, and elapsed time since the system was booted. The program uses the same information as the rwho command.

A sample output from a ruptime command follows:

```
merlin     up     3:15,12 users, load 0.90, 0.50, 0.09
prudie     down   9:12
tpci_hpws1 up    11:05, 3 users, load 0.10, 0.10, 0.00
tpci_hpws2 up    23:59, 5 users, load 0.30, 0.25, 0.08
tpci_hpws3 down   6:45
tpci_hpws4 up     9:05, 1 user,  load 0.12, 0.05, 0.01
```

rexec

The rexec (remote execution) program is a holdover from earlier versions of the UNIX operating system. It was designed to enable remote execution of a command through a server process called rexecd. The utility uses the dedicated TCP port number 512.

The protocol used by rexec is very similar to rsh, except that an encrypted password is sent with the request and there is a full login process. The rexec utility is seldom used because rsh is a faster and more convenient method for executing a command remotely.

Summary

Today you've looked at the primary protocols that use TCP/IP, as well as the Berkeley utilities. Now that you can see how protocols work on top of the TCP and IP protocols, the layered structure of TCP/IP becomes more pronounced. Future days' texts will build on this information.

Q&A

Q What are the purposes of Telnet and FTP?

A Telnet provides a remote login capability, and FTP enables you to transfer files across the network.

Q What channels (port numbers) are used by Telnet, FTP, and SMTP?

A Telnet uses port number 23. FTP uses port number 21 for the control information and port number 20 for data. SMTP uses port number 25.

Q When you issue a get command in FTP, is it moving a file from the local to remote, or vice versa?

A FTP commands are relative to the remote, so a get command will move a file from the local to the remote.

Q How does TFTP differ from FTP?

A TFTP does not require logging in. It sends a request over UDP. With FTP, you must log in to the destination either directly or through a third-party device.

Q Does rlogin differ from Telnet?

A The rlogin program was developed earlier and for most users has no difference. There are some version dependencies with some releases of rlogin, reflecting its earlier (and less full-featured) origin.

Workshop

The Workshop provides quiz questions to help you solidify your understanding of the material covered. Some Workshop sections of this book also contain exercises to provide you with experience in using what you've learned. Try to understand the quiz and exercise answers before continuing on to the next chapter. Answers are provided in Appendix F, "Answers."

Quiz

1. Explain what a network virtual terminal is.

2. Draw diagrams showing two- and three-party FTP sessions, indicating the port numbers used by each machine.

3. Why would you want to allow anonymous FTP access? Are there any reasons for not allowing it?

4. TFTP enables files to be transferred without logging in. What problems can this cause?

5. What are the Berkeley Utilities?

Exercises

Assuming you have access to a Telnet or FTP session, try logging in to a remote machine and transfer files back and forth. Try to recognize that Telnet does everything relative to the local machine, whereas FTP is relative to the remote.

TCP/IP
Administration
Programs

Although TCP/IP works transparently for the user, there will be occasions when communications seem to be slow and TCP/IP is suspected as the cause. Most users are impatient and expect things to happen right away, so delays for any reason lead to frustration. Rather than sit and wait, most users like to be able to verify that a connection to a remote machine is active and that a delay is caused by network traffic instead of a system failure; or at the least, most users would like to understand why a session is progressing slowly.

TCP/IP has several utility programs that provide status information and performance statistics. Also available are several debugging programs and options to enable a developer or knowledgeable user to trace a problem. This chapter examines the basic set of these tools.

Although TCP/IP is a standard, there are many different implementations of the protocol family. Most versions will have the basic tool set discussed today, although some may alter names and output to their own liking. As examples throughout this chapter, both the Santa Cruz Operation SCO UNIX and Hewlett-Packard's HP-UX implementations of TCP/IP are used for illustration. Both adhere to the System V UNIX standard, and the two are representative of most UNIX implementations.

> **Note:** All network addresses and machine names in this chapter are chosen at random and do not represent any particular network. Because the network addresses used may correspond to a real network, you should not use them in any experimentation, or you may incur the wrath of a system administrator!

Not all the commands shown in this chapter are available to users on most systems, although some system administrators do allow some access to the utilities for checking connection and TCP/IP status. The commands are presented here to show the debugging and diagnostic capabilities available to the TCP/IP user and administrator. The commands are not covered in exhaustive detail but are intended to complete the TCP/IP picture for you. Many of these programs and utilities are shown again later in this book.

Configuration Files

Several files are involved in the complete specification of network addresses and configuration for TCP/IP. For illustration purposes, a UNIX system is used here. Other operating systems will use different filenames, but the purpose of the files is usually the same. You may have to check with your operating system documentation to identify the files used.

UNIX allows comments on every line of these configuration files, as long as they are prefaced by a pound sign (#). If you see this character in your own system's configuration files, you should note that it is not part of an entry. With many operating systems, the default configuration files have many entries, most of which are commented out until the system administrator removes the comments.

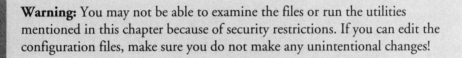

Warning: You may not be able to examine the files or run the utilities mentioned in this chapter because of security restrictions. If you can edit the configuration files, make sure you do not make any unintentional changes!

Symbolic Machine Names: /etc/hosts

Whenever a symbolic name is used as a target address by an application, there must be some method to resolve that name into a network address. An ASCII file is commonly used with the symbolic names matched to network addresses. This does not apply when the Yellow Pages (YP), Network Information Services (NIS), or the Domain Name Server (DNS) are used; they use their own configuration files.

On UNIX systems, the file /etc/hosts is used to hold the network addresses, as well as one special connection called the *loopback* (which is examined later today in the section titled "Loopback Drivers"). The loopback connection address is usually listed as the machine name *loopback* or *localhost*.

6

The file /etc/hosts consists of the network address in one column separated from the symbolic name in another. The network addresses can be specified in decimal, octal, or hexadecimal format (although decimal is the most common). More than one symbolic name can be specified on a line by separating the names with either space characters or tabs. The /etc/hosts file can be as long as necessary to contain all the symbolic names used on the local machine and does not need to be presented in any order. A sample UNIX /etc/hosts file is as follows:

```
# network host addresses
127.0.0.1              localhost local tpci_server
157.40.40.1            tpci_sco1
157.40.40.2            tpci_sco2
157.40.40.3            tpci_hpws1
157.40.40.0            tpci_server tpci_main tpci
47.80.157.36           bnr.ca BNR bnr
191.13.123.4           kitty_cat
210.24.47.128          bobs_machine
```

A system or network administrator can update this file at any time. Whenever a symbolic name is specified by a user or an application, the /etc/hosts file is searched for a matching name, and then the proper address is read from the same line.

Network Names: */etc/networks*

Networks can be addressed by a symbolic name, just as machines are. To resolve the network names, another file is used that contains the corresponding network address. Typically, this file isn't often accessed. The file's most common use is to specify the local network's name.

UNIX systems usually use the file /etc/networks to specify symbolic network names. The format of the file provides a network symbolic name, its network address, and any alias that might be used. A sample /etc/networks file is shown here:

```
# local network names
tpci      146.1        tpci_network  tpci_local
bnr       47.80          BNR bnr.ca
tmn       123.2.21
unique    89.12323       UNIQUE
sco       132.147        SCO
loopback  127            localhost
```

The last entry in the file gives the loopback name. The first entry specifies the local machine name, its network address, and any name variants.

Network Protocols: */etc/protocols*

Protocol numbers are used to identify the transport protocol to the receiving machine to enable proper decoding of the information within the datagram. With TCP/IP, the protocol number is embedded in the Internet Protocol header. A configuration file identifies all the transport protocols available on the system and their respective protocol numbers.

UNIX systems use the /etc/protocols file for this purpose. Usually, this file is not modified by the administrator but is maintained by the system and updated automatically as part of the installation procedure when new software is added. The file contains the protocol name, number, and any alias that may be used for that protocol. A sample /etc/protocols file is shown here:

```
# Internet protocols (IP)
ip      0    IP
icmp    1    ICMP
ggp     3    GGP
tcp     6    TCP
egp     8    EGP
pup     12   PUP
udp     17   UDP
hello   63   HELLO
```

Network Services: */etc/services*

The last configuration file used on most systems identifies the existing network services. This file is not usually modified by an administrator but is maintained by software as it is installed or configured.

The UNIX network services file is /etc/services. The file is in ASCII format consisting of the service name, a port number, and the protocol type. The port number and protocol type are separated by a slash. The port numbers for TCP/IP usually follow the conventions mentioned in the previous chapters. Any optional service alias names follow after the port numbers. A short extract from a sample /etc/services file (the file is usually quite lengthy) is shown here:

```
# network services
echo      7/tcp
echo      7/udp
discard   9/tcp    sink  null
discard   9/udp    sink  null
ftp       21/tcp
telnet    23/tcp
smtp      25/tcp    mail mailx
tftp      69/udp
# specific services
login     513/tcp
who       513/udp   whod
```

hostname

Most systems have a simple program that identifies the name of the local machine. UNIX systems have the utility hostname for this purpose, as well as the uname program, which can give the node name with the command uname -n. The uname utility is usually supported only in System V and compatible operating systems.

The hostname is sometimes saved in a separate file that is read when the operating system starts up, or it can be read from one of the configuration files mentioned previously. The hostname is used by most protocols on the system and many applications, so it is important for proper system operation. The hostname can be changed by editing the system file and rebooting the machine, although many operating systems provide a utility program to ensure this process is performed correctly.

When issued, the hostname and uname commands echo back the local machine name, as the following sample session shows:

```
$ hostname
tpci_sco4.tpci.com
$ uname -n
tpci_sco4
```

On the SCO UNIX system used in the previous example, the hostname command returns the full network name, whereas the uname command provides the local machine name only. On a Hewlett-Packard workstation running HP-UX, both commands return only the local machine name.

A potential problem can occur when the local machine is *multihomed*, or based in several networks. The single name in the configuration file may not provide enough information to permit proper routing over one of the networks. This problem is seldom encountered, but it does require that the system administrator carefully sets the hostname for each network.

Aside from the simple machine name query shown, the hostname system is a full protocol that enables access to the Network Information Center (NIC) tables to verify addresses and obtain information about the network, gateways, and hosts. It uses TCP port number 101 to connect to the NIC. This type of access is usually restricted to the network administrator.

Loopback Driver

The *loopback driver* is probably the most fundamental and often-used diagnostic tool available to an administrator. A loopback driver acts as a virtual circuit, enabling outgoing information to be immediately rerouted back to an input. This enables testing of the machine's circuits by eliminating any external influences, such as the network itself, gateways, or remote machines.

Note: By using a loopback driver, an administrator can be sure that the local machine is working properly and that any failures are from farther out.

Loopback drivers are usually embedded as part of the operating system kernel, or sometimes as an add-on utility program. Most multiuser systems employ an embedded loopback driver. UNIX is a good example: Within the kernel is a device driver specifically designed to act as a loopback driver.

When the loopback driver is used to reroute the output stream, the network interface card (usually an Ethernet card) is bypassed. The loopback driver is useful for testing TCP/IP software installations because it will immediately show any problems with the configuration. This can be done before the machine is physically connected to the network or even before the networking hardware and software is installed.

TCP/IP requires a destination address in order to assemble datagrams; otherwise the software cannot complete the assembly process and generates an error. To fool TCP/IP when using a loopback driver, a special network address is used. In most cases, the network address of the loopback driver is set to 127 (but any host ID number can be used). As previously mentioned, several configuration files on the system will contain the address of the loopback's connection.

arp

The arp program manages entries in the system's Address Resolution Protocol (ARP) tables. You may recall that ARP provides the link between the IP address and the underlying physical address. For more information, see Day 2. Using arp (or its equivalent in other operating systems), the administrator can create, modify, or delete entries in the ARP table. Typically, this will have to be performed whenever a machine's network address changes (either because of a change in the network hardware or because of a physical move).

The arp program differs between implementations and is seldom used by users, so examples of its use are left to the operating system's configuration and administration documentation.

6

ifconfig

The ifconfig program, or one like it, enables an administrator to activate and deactivate network interfaces, as well as to configure them. Access to the ifconfig program is generally restricted (to a superuser or network administrator on a UNIX system). Changes to the configuration can usually be made only before the system is fully operational (such as in single-user mode on a UNIX system).

Examining all the options available to ifconfig would require several dozen pages. Because this material is rarely used and differs with each implementation, administrators are referred to their operating system documentation. It is worth noting that ifconfig enables a network administrator to perform several useful functions:

Activate or deactivate an interface

Activate or deactivate ARP on an interface

Activate or deactivate debugging mode on an interface

Assign a broadcast address

Assign a subnetwork mask

Assign a routing method

When used with only the name of an interface, ifconfig usually returns information about the current state of the interface, as shown in the following example. In this example, a query of both an Ethernet card and the loopback driver is performed. The status flags of the interface are followed by the Internet address, broadcast address, and optionally provides a network mask, which defines the Internet address used for address comparison when routing.

```
tpci_sco1-12> ifconfig ec0
ec0: flags=807<UP,BROADCAST,DEBUG,ARP>
     inet 146.8.12.15 netmask fffff00 broadcast
146.8.12.15
tpci_sco1-13> ifconfig lo0
lo0: flags=49<UP,LOOPBACK,RUNNING>
     inet 127.0.0.1 netmask ff000000
```

The preceding example shows that the Ethernet connection ec0 is active (UP), able to transmit broadcasts (BROADCAST), and is in debugging mode (DEBUG). Also, the ARP protocol is active (ARP). You may recall that a broadcast message is sent to all machines on the local network by setting the host ID address to all 1s.

inetd

The inetd program is a hold-over from the early days of TCP/IP UNIX development. When a machine was started, it would activate TCP/IP and immediately accept connections at its ports, spawning a process for each. To control the processes better, the inetd program was developed to handle the port connections itself, offloading that task from the server. The primary difference is that inetd creates a process for each connection that is established, whereas the server creates a process for each port (which leads to many unused processes).

On many systems, some of the test programs and status information utilities are run through inetd. Typically, services such as echo, discard, and time use inetd.

The inetd program uses a configuration file/. (On UNIX systems, it is usually /etc/inetd.cfg, /etc/intd.conf, or /etc/inetd.cf.) An extract of a sample /etc/inetd.cfg file is shown in the following code example. The first column shows the service name (which corresponds to an entry in the services file such as /etc/services), the socket type (stream, raw, or datagram), protocol name, whether inetd can accept further connections at the same port immediately (nowait) or must wait for the server to finish (wait), the login that owns the service, the server program name, and any optional parameters needed for the server program.

```
#       @(#)inetd.conf     5.2 Lachman System V STREAMS TCP   source
#
#     System V STREAMS TCP - Release 4.0
ftp       stream    tcp    nowait    NOLUID    /etc/ftpd       ftpd
telnet    stream    tcp    nowait    NOLUID    /etc/telnetd    telnetd
shell     stream    tcp    nowait    NOLUID    /etc/rshd       rshd
login     stream    tcp    nowait    NOLUID    /etc/rlogind    rlogind
exec      stream    tcp    nowait    NOLUID    /etc/rexecd     rexecd
finger    stream    tcp    nowait    nouser    /etc/fingerd    fingerd
comsat    dgram     udp    wait      root      /etc/comsat     comsat
ntalk     dgram     udp    wait      root      /etc/talkd      talkd
echo      stream    tcp    nowait    root      internal
discard   stream    tcp    nowait    root      internal
chargen   stream    tcp    nowait    root      internal
daytime   stream    tcp    nowait    root      internal
time      stream    tcp    nowait    root      internal
echo      dgram     udp    wait      root      internal
discard   dgram     udp    wait      root      internal
chargen   dgram     udp    wait      root      internal
daytime   dgram     udp    wait      root      internal
time      dgram     udp    wait      root      internal
```

6

The configuration file is read when the server is booted and every time a hang-up signal is received from an application. This allows dynamic changes to the file, because any modifications would be read and register on the next file read.

netstat

The netstat program or a similar utility provides comprehensive information about the local system and its TCP/IP implementation. This is the program most commonly used by administrators to quickly diagnose a problem with TCP/IP. The actual information and its format supplied by the netstat utility differs with the operating system implementation, but it usually supplies the following important summaries, each of which is covered in more detail later:

Communications end points

Network interface statistics

Information on the data buffers

Routing table information

Protocol statistics

On some systems, information about the interprocess communications and other protocol stacks may be appended. The information to be displayed can usually be toggled with a command-line option. The output from a typical UNIX installation that uses the netstat command is shown in the next few sections, which discuss netstat and its output in more detail. The output and meaning may be different with other operating systems, but the general purpose of the diagnostic tool remains the same.

Communications End Points

The netstat command with no options provides information on all active communications end points. To display all end points (active and passive), netstat uses the -a option.

The output is formatted into columns showing the protocol (Proto), the amount of data in the receive and send queues (Recv-Q and Send-Q), the local and remote addresses, and the current state of the connection. A truncated sample output is shown here:

```
tpci_sco4-12> netstat -a
Active Internet connections (including servers)
Proto Recv-Q Send-Q  Local Address          Foreign Address        (state)
ip        0      0    *.*                    *.*
tcp       0   2124    tpci.login             merlin.1034            ESTABL.
tcp       0      0    tpci.1034              prudie.login           ESTABL.
tcp   11212      0    tpci.1035              treijs.1036            ESTABL.
tcp       0      0    tpci.1021              reboc.1024             TIME_WAIT
tcp       0      0    *.1028                 *.*                    LISTEN
tcp       0      0    *.*                    *.*                    CLOSED
tcp       0      0    *.6000                 *.*                    LISTEN
tcp       0      0    *.listen               *.*                    LISTEN
```

```
tcp        0      0   *.1024              *.*                    LISTEN
tcp        0      0   *.sunrpc            *.*                    LISTEN
tcp        0      0   *.smtp              *.*                    LISTEN
tcp        0      0   *.time              *.*                    LISTEN
tcp        0      0   *.echo              *.*                    LISTEN
tcp        0      0   *.finger            *.*                    LISTEN
tcp        0      0   *.exec              *.*                    LISTEN
tcp        0      0   *.telnet            *.*                    LISTEN
tcp        0      0   *.ftp               *.*                    LISTEN
tcp        0      0   *.*                 *.*                    CLOSED
udp        0      0   *.60000             *.*
udp        0      0   *.177               *.*
udp        0      0   *.1039              *.*
udp        0      0   *.1038              *.*
udp        0      0   localhost.1036      localhost.syslog
udp        0      0   *.1034              *.*
udp        0      0   *.*                 *.*
udp        0      0   *.1027              *.*
udp        0      0   *.1026              *.*
udp        0      0   *.sunrpc            *.*
udp        0      0   *.1025              *.*
udp        0      0   *.time              *.*
udp        0      0   *.daytime           *.*
udp        0      0   *.chargen           *.*
udp        0      0   *.route             *.*
udp        0      0   *.*                 *.*
```

In the preceding example, there are three active TCP connections, as identified by the state ESTABL. One has data being sent (as shown in the Send-Q column), and another has incoming data in the queue. The network names and port numbers of the connection ends is shown whenever possible. An asterisk (*) means that there is no end point associated with that address yet.

One connection is waiting to be hung up, identified by TIME_WAIT in the state column. After 30 seconds, these sessions are terminated and the connection freed. Any row with LISTEN as the state has no connection at the moment, and is waiting. There is no state column for UDP sessions because they do not have an end-to-end connection (as discussed in Day 5).

Network Interface Statistics

The behavior of the network interface (such as the network interface card) can be determined with the -i option to the netstat command. This information quickly shows an administrator whether there are major problems with the network connection.

The netstat -i command displays the name of the interface, the maximum number of characters a packet can contain (Mtu), the network and host addresses or names, the number of input packets (Ipkts), input errors (Ierrs), output packets (Opkts), output errors (Oerrs), and number of collisions (Collis) experienced in the current sampling session. The collisions column will only have relevance with a networking system that allows packet collisions, such as Ethernet. A sample output from a `netstat -i` command is shown here:

```
tpci_sco4-14> netstat -i
Name  Mtu   Network   Address     Ipkts  Ierrs Opkts  Oerrs Collis
ec0   1500  tpci      merlin         34  0       125  0     0
lan0  1497  47.80     tpci_hpws4  11625  0     11625  0     0
lo0   8232  loopback  localhost     206  0       206  0     0
```

An administrator can obtain more specific information about one interface by using the `-I` option with a device name and a time interval, specified in seconds, such as `netstat -I ec0 30`, to obtain specific information about the behavior of the `ec0` (Ethernet) interface over the last 30 seconds.

Data Buffers

Information about the data buffers can be obtained with the `netstat` command's `-m` option. Monitoring the behavior of the buffers is important, because they directly impact the performance of TCP/IP. The output of the `netstat -m` command differs depending on the version of UNIX in use, reflecting the different implementations of the TCP/IP code.

The `netstat -m` command output from a System V-based UNIX version is shown in the following code example. Entries are provided for the streamhead, queue, message descriptor table (`mblks`), data descriptor table (`dblks`), and the different classes of data descriptor tables. The columns show the number of blocks currently allocated (`alloc`), the number of columns free (`free`), the total number of blocks in use (`total`), the maximum number of blocks that were in use at one time (`max`), and the number of times a block was not available (`fail`).

```
tpci_sco4-23> netstat -m
streams allocation:
                      config  alloc  free  total  max   fail
streams               292     79     213   233    80    0
queues                1424    362    1062  516    368   0
mblks                 5067    196    4871  3957   206   0
dblks                 4054    196    3858  3957   206   0
class 0,    4 bytes   652     50     602   489    53    0
class 1,   16 bytes   652     2      650   408    4     0
class 2,   64 bytes   768     6      762   2720   14    0
class 3,  128 bytes   872     105    767   226    107   0
class 4,  256 bytes   548     21     527   36     22    0
class 5,  512 bytes   324     12     312   32     13    0
class 6, 1024 bytes   107     0      107   1      1     0
class 7, 2048 bytes   90      0      90    7      1     0
class 8, 4096 bytes   41      0      41    38     1     0
```

```
total configured streams memory: 1166.73KB
streams memory in use: 44.78KB
maximum streams memory used: 58.57KB
```

For the administrator, the failure column is important. It should always show 0s. If a larger number appears, that resource has been overtaxed and the number of blocks assigned to that resource should be increased (followed by a kernel rebuild and a reboot of the system to effect the changes).

Routing Table Information

Routing tables are continually updated to reflect connections to other machines. To obtain information about the routing tables, the netstat -r and -rs options are used. (The latter generates statistics about the routing tables.)

The output from netstat -r and netstat -rs commands are shown in the following code example. The columns show the destination machine, the address of the gateway to be used, a flag to show whether the route is active (U) and whether it leads to a gateway (G) or a machine (H for host), a reference counter (Refs) that specifies how many active connections can use that route simultaneously, the number of packets that have been sent over the route (Use), and the interface name.

```
tpci_sco4-56> netstat -r
Routing tables
Destination     Gateway          Flags    Refs     Use  Interface
localhost       localhost        UH          4      10  lo0
merlin          localhost        UH          2       2  ec0
treijs          hoytgate         UG          0       0  ec0
47.80           bcarh736         U          12   21029  lan0
tpci sco4-57> netstat -rs
routing:
            0 bad routing redirects
            0 dynamically created routes
            0 new gateways found unreachable
            2 destinations found unreachable
          122 uses of a wildcard route
            0 routes marked doubtful
            0 routes cleared of being doubtful
            0 routes deleted
```

Protocol Statistics

Statistics about the overall behavior of network protocols can be obtained with the netstat -s command. This usually provides summaries for IP, ICMP, TCP, and UDP. The output from this command is useful for determining where an error in a received packet was located, which then leads the user to isolate whether that error was caused by a software or network problem.

Issuing the `netstat -s` command provides a verbose output. A sample output is shown in the following code. The entries are self-explanatory.

```
tpci_sco4-67> netstat -s
ip:
     183309 total packets received
     0 bad header checksums
     0 with size smaller than minimum
     0 with data size < data length
     0 with header length < data size
     0 with data length < header length
     0 with unknown protocol
     13477 fragments received
     0 fragments dropped (dup or out of space)
     0 fragments dropped after timeout
     0 packets reassembled
     0 packets forwarded
     0 packets not forwardable
     75 no routes
     0 redirects sent
     0 system errors during input
     309 packets delivered
     309 total packets sent
     0 system errors during output
     0 packets fragmented
     0 packets not fragmentable
     0 fragments created
icmp:
     1768 calls to icmp_error
     0 errors not generated because old message was icmp
     Output histogram:
         destination unreachable: 136
     0 messages with bad code fields
     0 messages < minimum length
     0 bad checksums
     0 messages with bad length
     Input histogram:
         destination unreachable: 68
     0 message responses generated
     68 messages received
     68 messages sent
     0 system errors during output
tcp:
     9019 packets sent
             6464 data packets (1137192 bytes)
         4 data packets (4218 bytes) retransmitted
         1670 ack-only packets (918 delayed)
         0 URG only packets
         0 window probe packets
         163 window update packets
         718 control packets
             24 resets
     9693 packets received
         4927 acks (for 74637 bytes)
         37 duplicate acks
         0 acks for unsent data
```

```
        5333 packets (1405271 bytes) received in-sequence
        23 completely duplicate packets (28534 bytes)
        0 packets with some dup. data (0 bytes duped)
        38 out-of-order packets (5876 bytes)
        0 packets (0 bytes) of data after window
        0 window probes
        134 window update packets
        0 packets received after close
        0 discarded for bad checksums
        0 discarded for bad header offset fields
        0 discarded because packet too short
        0 system errors encountered during processing
    224 connection requests
    130 connection accepts
    687 connections established (including accepts)
    655 connections closed (including 0 drops)
    24 embryonic connections dropped
    0 failed connect and accept requests
    0 resets received while established
    5519 segments updated rtt (of 5624 attempts)
    5 retransmit timeouts
        0 connections dropped by rexmit timeout
    0 persist timeouts
    0 keepalive timeouts
        0 keepalive probes sent
        0 connections dropped by keepalive
    0 connections lingered
        0 linger timers expired
        0 linger timers cancelled
        0 linger timers aborted by signal
udp:
    0 incomplete headers
    0 bad data length fields
    0 bad checksums
    68 bad ports
    125 input packets delivered
    0 system errors during input
    268 packets sent
```

6

ping

The ping (Packet Internet Groper) utility is used to query another system to ensure a connection is still active. (You may recall the ruptime utility from the last chapter, which does this too. However, ruptime waits five minutes before trying the remote, and you may want to know right away if the connection is active.) The ping command is available on most operating systems that implement TCP/IP.

The ping program operates by sending out an Internet Control Message Protocol (ICMP) echo request. If the destination machine's IP software receives the ICMP request, it will issue an echo-reply immediately. The sending machine will continue to send an echo request until the ping program is terminated with a break sequence (Ctrl+C or the delete key, labelled Del, in UNIX). After termination, ping displays a set of statistics. A sample ping session is shown here:

```
tpci_sco1-45> ping merlin
PING merlin: 64 data bytes
64 bytes from 142.12.130.12: icmp_seq=0.  time=20.  ms
64 bytes from 142.12.130.12: icmp_seq=1.  time=10.  ms
64 bytes from 142.12.130.12: icmp_seq=2.  time=10.  ms
64 bytes from 142.12.130.12: icmp_seq=3.  time=20.  ms
64 bytes from 142.12.130.12: icmp_seq=4.  time=10.  ms
64 bytes from 142.12.130.12: icmp_seq=5.  time=10.  ms
64 bytes from 142.12.130.12: icmp_seq=6.  time=10.  ms
— merling PING Statistics —
7 packets transmitted, 7 packets received, 0% packet loss
round-trip (ms) min/avg/max = 10/12/20
```

An alternate method to invoke ping is to provide the number of times you want it to query the remote. Also, you could provide a packet length as a test. The following example instructs ping to use 256 data byte packets and try five times. Using ping to send large packets is one method of determining the network's behavior with large packet sizes, especially when fragmentation must occur. The ping program is also useful for monitoring response times of the network, by observing the reply time on packets sent as the network load (or the machine load) changes. This information can be very useful in optimization of TCP/IP.

```
tpci_sco1-45> ping merlin 256 5
PING merlin: 256 data bytes
256 bytes from 142.12.130.12: icmp_seq=0.  time=20.  ms
256 bytes from 142.12.130.12: icmp_seq=1.  time=10.  ms
256 bytes from 142.12.130.12: icmp_seq=2.  time=10.  ms
256 bytes from 142.12.130.12: icmp_seq=3.  time=20.  ms
256 bytes from 142.12.130.12: icmp_seq=4.  time=10.  ms
— merling PING Statistics —
5 packets transmitted, 5 packets received, 0% packet loss
round-trip (ms) min/avg/max = 10/13/20
```

Some older implementations of ping simply reply with a message that the system at the other end is active. (The message is of the form X is alive.) To obtain the verbose messages shown previously, the -s option must be used.

The ping program is useful for diagnostics because it provides four important pieces of information: whether the TCP/IP software is functioning correctly, whether a local network device can be addressed (validating its address), whether a remote machine can be accessed (again validating the address and testing the routing), and verifying the software on the remote machine.

trpt

There is a tracing option built into TCP/IP. When simpler methods have failed, this option can be used to trace a problem. To activate the trace, a system call is sent to the end point that turns on a flag. Most TCP/IP implementations enable the tracing option to be turned on from the command line using the -d (debug) option. When tracing is turned on, all activities are echoed to a buffer or to the screen, depending on the system configuration.

The output from the TCP/IP tracing option is examined using the program trpt (trace report). A specific connection can be specified, or all behavior passing through TCP/IP can be displayed. The output from trpt is verbose and of little interest to most users.

Summary

Today, you learned about the basic administration programs used with TCP/IP, as well as the configuration files that are necessary in order to use symbolic names. Although this information is not likely to be used by most users, knowing the available tools and the type of diagnostics that can be produced is useful in better understanding TCP/IP.

Q&A

Q All the TCP/IP protocols available to you are listed in a system configuration file. Which file is this?

A All TCP/IP protocols are listed in /etc/protocols. The file lists the protocol name and the corresponding protocol number.

Q What command would give you overall statistics about the network protocols running on your system?

A One of the best summaries is obtained with the netstat -s command.

6

Workshop

The Workshop provides quiz questions to help you solidify your understanding of the material covered. Some Workshop sections of this book also contain exercises to provide you with experience in using what you've learned. Try to understand the quiz and exercise answers before continuing on to the next chapter. Answers are provided in Appendix F, "Answers."

Quiz

1. What is a loopback driver used for?

2. What does the following excerpt from a `netstat -a` command tell you?

```
Proto Recv-Q Send-Q Local Address        Foreign Address        (state)
ip       0      0    *.*                  *.*
tcp      0    1024   tpci.login           merlin.1034            ESTABL.
tcp    8756     0    tpci.1035            treijs.1036            ESTABL.
tcp      0      0    tpci.1021            reboc.1024             TIME_WAIT
tcp      0      0    *.1028               *.*                    LISTEN
tcp      0      0    *.6000               *.*                    LISTEN
```

2. What is the utility `ping` used for?

7

Gateway Protocols

TCP/IP functions perfectly well on a local area network, but its development was spurred by internetworks (more specifically, by the Internet itself), so it seems logical that TCP/IP has an architecture that works well with internetwork operations. Today you'll examine internetwork specifics in more detail by looking at the manner in which gateways transfer routing information between themselves. You have been introduced to some of this material (notably on Day 3), so its role in the overall structure of TCP/IP should be understood.

The routing method used to send a message from its origin to destination is important, but the method by which the routing information is transferred depends on the role of the network gateways. There are special protocols developed specifically for different kinds of gateways, all of which function with TCP.

Gateways, Bridges, and Routers

To forward messages through networks, a machine's networking software compares the destination address of the message (contained in the Protocol Data Unit, or PDU) to the local machine's address. If the message is not for the local machine, the message is passed on to the next machine. Moving messages around small networks is quite easy, but large networks and internetworks add to the complexity, requiring gateways, bridges, and routers, which try to establish the best method of moving the message to its destination.

Defining the meaning of these terms is relatively easy:

- A gateway is a device that performs routing functions, usually as a stand-alone device, that also can perform protocol translation from one network to another.

- A bridge is a network device that connects two or more networks that use the same protocol.

- A router is a network node that forwards datagrams around the network.

The gateway's protocol conversion capability is important (otherwise, the machine would be no different from a bridge). Protocol conversion usually takes place in the lower layers, sometimes including the transport layer. Conversion can occur in several forms, such as when moving from a local area network format to Ethernet (in which case the format of the packet is changed) or from a proprietary file convention to another (in which case the file specifications are converted).

Bridges act as links between networks, which often have a bridge at either end of a dedicated communications line (such as a leased line) or through a packet system such as Internet. There may be a conversion applied between bridges in order to increase the transmission speed. This, of course, requires both ends of the connection to understand a common protocol.

Routers operate at the network level, forwarding packets to their destination. Sometimes a protocol change can be performed by the router that has several delivery options available, such as Ethernet or serial lines.

A term in common use when dealing with routes is *packet-switching*. A packet-switched network is one in which all transfers are based on a self-contained packet of data (like that of TCP/IP's datagrams). There are also message-switched (self-contained, complete messages as with UNIX's UUCP system) and line-switched (fixed or dedicated connections) networks, but these are rarely used with TCP/IP. Packet-switched networks tend to be faster overall than message-switched networks, but they are considerably more complex, too.

Gateway Protocols

Gateway protocols are used to exchange information with other gateways in a fast, reliable manner. Using gateway protocols, transmission time over large internetworks has been shown to increase, although there is considerable support for the idea of having only one protocol across the entire Internet (which would eliminate gateway protocols in favor of TCP/IP throughout).

The Internet provides for two types of gateways: core and non-core. All core gateways are administered by the Internet Network Operations Center (INOC). Non-core gateways are not administered by this central authority, but by groups outside the Internet hierarchy (who may still be connected to the Internet but administer their own machines). Typically, corporations and educational institutions are non-core gateways.

The origin of the core gateways arose from the ARPAnet, wherein each node was under the control of the governing agency. ARPAnet called them *stub gateways*, while any gateway not under direct control (non-core in Internet terms) was called a *nonrouting gateway*. The move to the Internet and its proliferation of gateways required the implementation of the Gateway-to-Gateway Protocol (GGP), which was used between core gateways. The GGP was usually used to spread information about the non-core gateways attached to each core gateway, enabling routing tables to be built.

As the Internet grew, it became impossible for any one gateway to hold a complete map of the entire internetwork. This was solved by having each gateway handle only a specific section of the internetwork, relying on neighboring gateways to know more about their

7

own attached networks when a message was passed. One problem that frequently occurred was a lack of information for complete routing decisions, so default routes were used.

Earlier in this book, the term *autonomous system* was introduced. An autonomous system is one in which the structure of the network it is attached to is not visible to the rest of the internetwork. Usually, a gateway leads into the network, so all traffic for that network must go through the gateway that hides the internal structure of the local network to the rest of the internetwork.

If there is more than one gateway within the local network and they can talk to each other, they are considered interior neighbors. (The term interior neighbor is sometimes applied to the machines within the network, too, not just the gateways.) If the gateways belong to different autonomous systems, they are exterior gateways. Thus, when default routes are required, it is up to the exterior gateways to route messages between autonomous systems. Interior gateways are used to transfer messages into an autonomous system.

Within a network, the method of transferring routing information between interior gateways is usually the Routing Information Protocol (RIP) or the less-common HELLO protocol, both of which are Interior Gateway Protocols (IGP). These protocols are designed specifically for interior neighbors. On the Internet, messages between two exterior gateways are through the Exterior Gateway Protocol (EGP). RIP, HELLO, and EGP all rely on a frequent (every 30 seconds) transfer of information between gateways to update routing tables.

Note: The three gateway protocols are intertwined: EGP is used between gateways of autonomous systems, whereas the IGP's RIP and HELLO are used within the network itself. GGP is used between core gateways.

Why not use GGP for all internetwork communications, dropping the need for EGPs? The answer lies in the fact that core gateways that use GGP know about all the other core gateways on the internetwork. This simplifies their messaging and provides complete routing tables. However, core gateways usually lead into many complex networks of more autonomous networks, most of which the core gateways don't know about. However, the exterior gateways must know about all the networks directly connected to it, but not all the networks on the entire internetwork, so the routing tables and routing algorithms for a core and non-core gateway are different. This also means messages will have different formats, as routing information for a non-core gateway will have some connections that are "hidden" to other gateways.

It is possible for a large autonomous system to be composed of several subnetworks or areas, each of which communicates with the other areas through an IGP. Each subnetwork or area will have a designated gateway, called a *border gateway*, or *border router*, to indicate it is within an area. Border routers communicate with each other using IGP. A commonly encountered term is *boundary gateway*, which is the same as an exterior gateway or a path to another autonomous network. This is illustrated in Figure 7.1, which shows three subnetworks or areas that communicate with each other through boundary gateways or routers using IGP, and two exterior gateways (also called boundary gateways) that communicate with the rest of the internetwork using EGP.

Figure 7.1. *Interior and exterior gateways.*

Routing Daemons

To handle the routing tables, most UNIX systems use a daemon called *routed*. A few systems run a daemon called *gated*. Both routed and gated can exchange RIP messages with other machines, updating their route tables as necessary. The gated program also can handle EGP and HELLO messages, updating tables for the internetwork. Both routed and gated can be managed by the system administrator to select favorable routes, or to tag a route as not reliable.

The configuration information for gated and routed is usually stored as files named gated.cfg, gated.conf, or gated.cf. Some systems specify gated information files for each protocol, resulting in the files gated.egp, gated.hello, and gated.rip. A sample configuration file for EGP used by the gated process is shown here:

```
#    @(#)gated.egp 4.1 Lachman System V STREAMS TCP  source
#   sample EGP config file

traceoptions general kernel icmp egp protocol ;
autonomoussystem 519 ;
rip no;
egp yes {
    group ASin 519 {
        neighbor  128.212.64.1 ;
    } ;
} ;
static {
    default gateway 128.212.64.1 pref 100 ;
} ;
propagate proto egp as 519 {
    proto rip gateway 128.212.64.1 {
        announce 128.212 metric 2 ;
    } ;
    proto direct {
        announce 128.212 metric 2 ;
    } ;
} ;
propagate proto rip {
    proto default {
        announce 0.0.0.0 metric 1 ;
    } ;
    proto rip {
        noannounce all ;
    } ;
} ;
```

The UNIX system administrator also has a program called *route* that enables direct entry of routing table information. The information on a UNIX system regarding routing is usually stored in the file /etc/gateways.

It has become common practice to allow a default network Internet address of 0.0.0.0, which refers to a gateway on the network that hopefully is capable of resolving an unknown address. (This is included in the previous sample configuration file as *proto default*.) The default route is used when the local machine cannot resolve the address properly. As the routing tables on a gateway are usually more complete than those on a local machine, this does help send packets to their intended destination. If the default address gateway cannot resolve the address, an Internet Control Message Protocol (ICMP) error message is returned to the sender.

Routing

Routing refers to the transmission of a packet of information from one machine through another. Each machine that the packet enters will analyze the contents of the packet header and decide its action based on the information within the header. If the destination address of the packet matches the machine's address, the packet should be retained and processed by higher-level protocols. If the destination address doesn't match the machine's, the packet is forwarded further around the network. Forwarding may be to the destination machine itself, or to a gateway or bridge if the packet is to leave the local network.

Routing is a primary contributor to the complexity of packet-switched networks. It is necessary to account for an optimal path from source to destination machines, as well as handle problems such as a heavy load on an intervening machine or the loss of a connection. The route details are contained in a routing table, while several sophisticated algorithms work with the routing table to develop an optimal route for a packet.

Creating a routing table and maintaining it with valid entries is an important aspect of a protocol. There are a few common methods of building a routing table:

☐ A fixed table is created with a map of the network, which must be modified and reread every time there is a physical change anywhere on the network.

☐ A dynamic table is used that evaluates traffic load and messages from other nodes to refine an internal table.

☐ A fixed central routing table is used that is loaded from the central repository by the network nodes at regular intervals or when needed.

Each method has advantages and disadvantages. The fixed table approach, whether located on each network node or downloaded at regular intervals from a centrally maintained fixed table, is inflexible and can't react to changes in the network topology quickly. The central table is better than the first option, simply because it is possible for an administrator to maintain the single table much more easily than a table on each node.

The dynamic table is the best for reacting to changes, although it does require better control, more complex software, and more network traffic. However, the advantages usually outweigh the disadvantages, and a dynamic table is the method most frequently used on the Internet.

7

Fewest-Hops Routing

Most networks and gateways to internetworks work on the assumption that the shortest route (in terms of machines traveled through) is the best way to route messages. Each machine that a message passes through is called a *hop*, so this routing method is known as *fewest hops*. Although experimentation has shown that fewest hops is not necessarily the fastest method (because it doesn't take into account transmission speed between machines), it is one of the easiest routing methods to implement.

To provide fewest-hops routing, a table of the distance between any two machines is developed, or an algorithm is available to help calculate the number of hops required to reach a target machine. This is shown using the sample internetwork of gateways in Figure 7.2 and its corresponding table of distances between the gateways in the Figure, which is shown in Table 7.1.

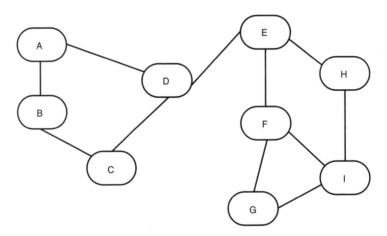

Figure 7.2. *An internetwork of gateways.*

Table 7.1. Table of fewest hops from Figure 7.2.

	AA	BB	CC	DD	EE	FF	GG	HH	II
AA	—	11	22	21	32	33	44	33	44
BB	11	—	11	22	33	44	55	44	55
CC	22	11	—	11	22	33	44	33	44
DD	11	22	11	—	11	22	33	22	33

	AA	BB	CC	DD	EE	FF	GG	HH	II
EE	22	33	22	11	—	11	22	11	22
FF	33	44	33	32	11	—	11	22	11
GG	44	55	44	33	22	11	—	22	11
HH	33	44	33	22	11	22	22	—	11
II	44	55	34	33	22	11	11	11	—

When a message is to be routed using the fewest-hops approach, the table of distances is consulted and the route with the least number of hops is selected. The message is then routed to the gateway that is closest to the destination network. When intermediate gateways receive the message, they too perform the same type of table lookup and forward to the next gateway on the route.

There are several problems with the fewest-hops approach. If the tables of the gateways through which a message travels to its destination have different route information, it is conceivable that a message that left the source machine on the shortest route could end up following a more circuitous path because of differing tables in the intervening gateways. The fewest hops method also doesn't account for transfer speed, line failures, or other factors that could affect the overall time to travel to the destination, because it is merely concerned with the shortest apparent distance, assuming all connections are equal. To accommodate these factors, another routing method must be used.

Type of Service Routing

This type of routing depends on the type of routing service available from gateway to gateway. This is called *type of service* (TOS) routing. It is also more formally called *quality of service* (QOS) by OSI. TOS includes consideration for the speed and reliability of connections, as well as security and route-specific factors.

To effect TOS routing, most systems use dynamic updating of tables that reflect traffic and link conditions. They also take into account current queue lengths at each gateway, because the fastest theoretical route may not matter if the message is backlogged in a queue. This information is obtained through the frequent transfer of status messages between gateways, especially when conditions deteriorate.

Dynamic updating of tables can have a disadvantage in that if tables are updated too frequently, a message may circulate through a section of the internetwork without proper routing to its destination, or proceed through a long and convoluted path. For this reason, dynamic updating occurs at regular but not-too-frequent intervals. To prevent stray datagrams from circulating on the internetwork too long, the Time-to-Live information in the IP message header is important.

> **Note:** The IP header's Time-to-Live (TTL) field is very important to dynamic gateway routing protocols, which is why it is a mandatory field. Without it, datagrams could circulate throughout the network indefinitely.

The dynamic nature of TOS routing can sometimes cause a message's fragments to be routed in different ways to a destination. For example, if a long message of 10 datagrams is being sent by one route but the routing tables are changed during transmission to reflect a backlog, the remainder of the datagrams may be sent via an alternate route. This doesn't matter, of course, because the receiving machine will reassemble the message in the proper order as the datagrams are received.

Updating Gateway Routing Information

A somewhat simplified example of a dynamic update is useful at this stage. The exact communications protocols between gateways will be examined in more detail later today.

Assume that two autonomous networks are connected to each other at two locations, as shown in Figure 7.3, with connections to different autonomous networks at other locations. The A–C connection and the B–D connection may both be used for routing from within the networks, depending on which is the optimal path. Gateway C will have a copy of gateway A's routing table, and vice versa. Gateways B and D will have copies of the other's routing tables, too. These copies are transmitted at intervals so the gateways can maintain an up-to-date picture of the connections available through the other gateway. The gateways use EGP to send the messages. (They would use GGP if they were core gateways.)

Suppose that a gateway link within one of the networks was broken due to a machine or connection failure, such as that between gateway C and machine X, shown in Figure 7.3. Gateway C would find out about the problem through an IGP message and update its routing table to reflect the break, usually by putting the largest legal value for routing length in that entry. (Remember that IGP is a general term for any internal network protocol for gateway communications, such as RIP or HELLO.) Gateway C will transfer its new copy of the routing table to gateway A.

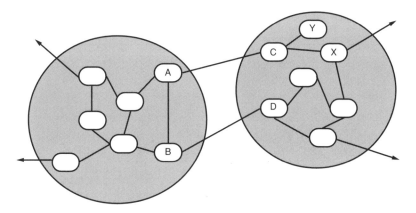

Figure 7.3. *Two interconnected networks.*

Routing a message to machine Y would now be impossible through the C–X connection. However, because gateway A has the routing information from C, and it exchanges routing information with gateway B, which also exchanges with gateway D, any message passing through either D or B for machine Y could be rerouted up through gateway A, then C, and finally to Y. An EGP message between B–D and A–C would indicate that the new route costs less than the maximum value assigned going through C–X (which is broken), so the round-about transfer through the four gateways can be used.

EGP messages between gateways are usually sent whenever a connection problem exists and the routing information is set to its maximum (worst) value, or when a better connection alternative has been discovered for some reason. This can be because of an update from a remote gateway's routing table, or the addition of new connections, machines, or networks to the system. Whichever happens, an EGP message informs all the connected gateways of the changes.

Gateway-to-Gateway Protocol (GGP)

The GGP protocol is used for communications between core gateways. A recent improvement of the protocol, called SPREAD, is starting to be used but is not yet as common as GGP. Even if GGP is phased out in favor of SPREAD, examining GGP is a useful illustration of gateway-to-gateway protocols.

GGP is a vector-distance protocol, meaning that messages tend to specify a destination (vector) and the distance to that destination. Vector-distance protocols are also called Bellman-Ford protocols, after the researchers who first published the idea. For a vector-distance protocol to be effective, a gateway must have complete information about all the gateways on the internetwork, otherwise computing a distance with a fewest-hops type of protocol will not succeed.

> **Note:** You may recall from earlier today that core gateways have complete information about all other core gateways, so a vector-distance protocol will work. Non-core gateways don't have a complete internetwork map, so GGP-type messages will not be useful.

A gateway establishes its connections to other gateways by sending out messages, waiting for replies, and then building a table. This is initially accomplished when a gateway is installed and has no routing information at all. This aspect of communications is not defined within GGP, but relies on network-specific messages. Once the initial table has been defined, though, GGP is used for all messages.

Connectivity with another gateway on the Internet is determined using the K-out-of-N method. In this procedure, a gateway sends an echo message to another gateway and waits for a reply. It repeats this every 15 seconds. According to the Internet standards, if the gateway does not receive three (K) replies out of four (N) requests, the other gateway is considered down, or unusable, and routing messages are not sent to that gateway. This process may be repeated at regular intervals.

If a down gateway becomes active, or up, again, the Internet standards require two out of four echo messages to be acknowledged. This is called J-out-of-M, where J is two and M is four. The Internet-assigned values for J, K, M, and N can be changed for autonomous networks, but the standard defines the values for use on the Internet itself.

Each message between gateways has a sequence number that is incremented with each transmitted message. Each gateway will track its own sequence number for sending to every other gateway it is connected to, as well as the incoming sequence numbers from that gateway. They are not necessarily the same, because more messages may flow one way than the other; although usually each message should have an acknowledgment or reply of some type.

Sequence numbers have important meanings for the messages and are not just for the sake of keeping an incremental count of the traffic volume. When a gateway receives a message from another gateway, it compares the sequence number in that message to the last received sequence number in its internal tables. If the latest message has a higher sequence number than the last message received, the gateway will accept the message and update its sequence number to the latest-received value. If the number was less than the last-received sequence number, the message is considered old and is ignored, with an error message containing the just-received message sent back. This process is shown in Figure 7.4.

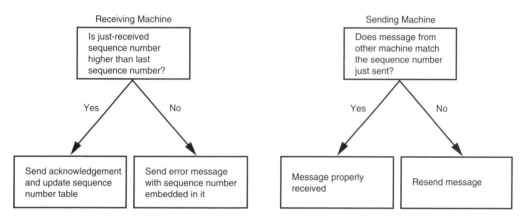

Figure 7.4. *Processing sequence numbers in GGP.*

The receiving gateway acknowledges the received message by sending a return message that contains the sequence number of the just-received message. The other gateway will compare that number with the number of its last sent message, and if they are the same, the gateway knows that the message was properly received. If the numbers do not match, the gateway will know an error occurred and transmit the message again.

In the case where a message was ignored by the recipient gateway, the sending gateway will receive a message with the sequence number of the ignored message. It can then determine which messages were skipped and adjust itself accordingly, resending messages that need to be sent.

The GGP message format is shown in Figure 7.5. After it is constructed, it is encapsulated into an IP datagram that includes source and target addresses. The first field is a message type, which is set to a value of 12 for routing information. The sequence number was discussed earlier and provides an incremental counter for each message. The Update field is set to a value of 0 unless the sending gateway wants a routing update for the provided destination address, in which case it is set to a value of 1. The number of distances field holds the number of groups of addresses contained in the current message.

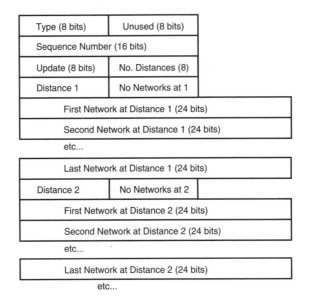

Figure 7.5. *The GGP message format.*

For each distance group in the message, a distance value and the number of networks that can be reached at that distance is provided, followed by all the network address identifications. According to the GGP standard, not all the distances need to be reported, but the more information supplied, the more useful the message is to each gateway.

GGP does not deal with full Internet addresses specifically, so the host portion of the address does not necessarily have to be included in the address, although the network address will always be provided. This can result in different lengths of addresses in the identification filed (either 8, 16, or 24 bits, depending on the type of address).

There are three other formats used with GGP messages, as shown in Figure 7.6. The acknowledgment message uses the type field to indicate whether the message is a positive acknowledgment (type is set to 2) or a negative acknowledgment (type is set to 10) . The sequence number, as mentioned earlier today, is used to identify the message to which the acknowledgment applies.

Type (8 bits)	Unused (8 bits)
Sequence Number (16 bits)	

GGP Acknowledgement

Type (8 bits)
Unused (24 bits)

GGP Echo Request and Echo Reply

Type (8 bits)
Unused (24 bits)

GGP Network Interface Status

Figure 7.6. *Other GGP message formats.*

The echo request and echo reply formats are passed between gateways to inform of status changes and to ensure that the gateway is up. An echo request has the type field set to the value eight, while an echo reply has the type field set to a value of 0. Because the address of the sending gateway is embedded in the IP header, it is not duplicated in the GGP message. The remaining 24 bits of the message are unused.

The network interface status message is used by a gateway to ensure it is able to send and receive messages properly. This type of message can be sent to the originating gateway itself, with the type field set to a value of 9 and the IP address in the header set to the network interface's address.

The External Gateway Protocol (EGP)

The External Gateway Protocol was examined in some detail on Day 3, but will be expanded on here. As mentioned earlier, an EGP is used to transfer information between non-core neighboring gateways. Non-core gateways contain complete details about their immediate neighbors and the machines attached to them, but lack information about the rest of the network. Core gateways know about all the other core gateway but often lack the details of the machines beyond a gateway.

EGP is usually restricted to information within the gateway's autonomous system. This prevents too much information from passing through the networks, especially when most of the information that relates to external autonomous systems would be unusable to another gateway. EGP therefore imposes restrictions on the gateways of the machines it passes routing information about.

Core gateways use GGP and non-core gateways use EGP, so there must be some method for the two to communicate with each other to find out about "hidden" machines and networks that lie beyond their routing tables. This can be shown by Figure 7.7, where gateway A is a core gateway leading from the internetwork to a network that has non-core gateways leading to two other networks. Another gateway on the internetwork will not have information about the networks and gateways past the core gateway, unless specifically updated about them through a request. The Internet uses a method by which any autonomous (non-core) gateway can send "reachability" information to other systems, which must also go to at least one core gateway. If there is a larger autonomous network, one gateway will usually assume the responsibility for handling this reachability information. In Figure 7.7, Gateway A would be responsible for sending information about the three networks that lead from it, as well as the two non-core gateways.

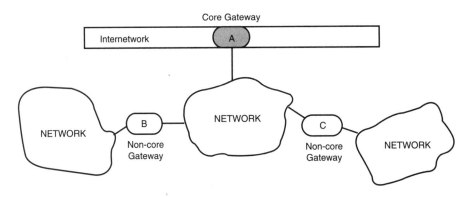

Figure 7.7. *Core and non-core gateways.*

External gateway protocols use a polling process to keep themselves aware of their neighbors as they become active or go down, and to exchange routing and status information with all of their neighbors. EGP is also a state-driven protocol, meaning it depends on a state table containing values that reflect gateway conditions and a set of operations that must be performed when a state table entry changes. There are five states, as shown in Table 7.2.

Table 7.2. EGP states.

State	Description
0	Idle
1	Acquisition
2	Down
3	Up
4	Cease

The meaning of each of these EGP states are as follows:

☐ An idle state means the gateway is not involved in any activity and has no resources allocated to it. It will usually respond to a message to initialize itself but ignores all other messages unless it switches to either the down or acquisition states.

☐ An acquisition state enables a gateway to transmit messages but not act as a full messaging gateway. It can receive messages and change to either down or idle states.

☐ The down state is when the gateway is not operational, as far as polling operations are concerned. Messages are neither received nor generated.

☐ The up state is used whenever a gateway is processing and responding to all EGP messages it receives and can transmit messages.

☐ A gateway is in cease state when the gateway ceases all updating operations but can still send and receive cease and cease acknowledgment messages.

All EGP messages fall into one of three categories: commands, responses, or indications. A command usually requires an action to be performed, whereas a response is a reply to a command to perform some action. An indication shows current status. Command-response signals are shown in Table 7.3.

7

Table 7.3. EGP commands and their responses.

Command	Response
Request	Confirm
Refuse	
Error	
Cease	Cease Ack
Error	
Hello	IHU (I Heard You)
Error	
Poll	Update
Error	

The layout of EGP messages is shown in Figure 7.8. All EGP messages use the same layout, although some append information to the basic header shown in Figure 7.8. The different messages and their field values will be examined in more detail in the next section. The different fields in the basic header include the following:

☐ The Version field holds the EGP version number of the sending machine (the current version is 2).

☐ The Type field identifies the type of EGP messages. There are 10 message types in EGP, as shown in Table 7.4.

☐ The Code field contains a value that identifies the subtype of the message.

☐ The Status field is used with the Type and Code fields to reflect the current status of the gateway's state.

☐ The checksum is calculated for the EGP message in the same manner as other TCP/IP headers.

☐ The System Number is an identification of the autonomous system that the sending gateway belongs to.

☐ The Sequence Number of the message is an incremental counter for each message, also used to identify a reply to a previous message.

Version (8 bits)	Message Type (8 bits)
Code (8 bits)	Status (8 bits)
Checksum (16 bits)	
System Number (16 bits)	
Sequence Number (16 bits)	

Basic EGP Message Layout

Version (8 bits)	Message Type (8 bits)
Code (8 bits)	Status (8 bits)
Checksum (16 bits)	
System Number (16 bits)	
Sequence Number (16 bits)	
Hello Interval (16 bits)	
Poll Interval (16 bits)	

EGP Neighbor Acquisition Message Layout

Version (8 bits)	Message Type (8 bits)
Code (8 bits)	Status (8 bits)
Checksum (16 bits)	
System Number (16 bits)	
Sequence Number (16 bits)	
Reserved (16 bits)	
IP Source Network Address (16 bits)	

EGP Poll Message

Figure 7.8. *The EGP message layout.*

Table 7.4. EGP message types.

Message	Type/Code Numbers	Description
Request acquisition	3/0	Requests the acquisition of a neighbor. Also can initialize polling variables.
Confirm acquisition	3/1	Confirms the acquisition of the neighbor. Also can initialize polling variables.
Refuse acquisition	3/2	Denies the acquisition of a neighbor.
Cease request	3/3	Requests the deacquisition of a neighbor.
Cease Ack response	3/4	Acknowledges the deacquisition of a neighbor.
Hello	3/0	Checks to see whether the neighbor is reachable.

continues

Table 7.4. continued

Message	Type/Code Numbers	Description
IHU (I Heard You)	3/1	Confirms that the neighbor is reachable.
Poll	2/0	Requests reachability update.
Update	1/0	Reachability update information.
Error		Error response.

EGP State Variables and Timers

As mentioned, EGP is state-driven, which means that the current state of the system depends on the last message received, or the condition of one of the software timers. EGP maintains a state table with several parameters that can be referenced to determine actions. These values usually refer to delays between sending or receiving messages of a specific type. In addition, a set of timers are maintained for ensuring intervals between events are reasonable. The EGP parameters and timers are shown in Table 7.5, using the names employed in the RFC that defines EGP.

Table 7.5. EGP parameters and timers.

Name	Description
M	Hello polling mode.
P1	Minimum interval acceptable between successive received Hello commands. The default is 30 seconds.
P2	Minimum interval acceptable between successive received Poll commands. The default is 120 seconds.
P3	Interval between Request or Cease command retransmissions. The default is 30 seconds.
P4	Interval during which the state variables are maintained without receiving an incoming message when in the up or down state. The default is one hour.

Name	Description
P5	Interval during which the state variables are maintained without receiving an incoming message when in the cease or acquisition state. The default is two minutes.
R	Receives sequence number.
S	Sends sequence number.
T1	Interval between `Hello` command retransmissions.
T2	Interval between `Poll` command retransmissions.
T3	Interval during which reachability attempts are counted.
t1	Retransmission timer for request, hello, and cease messages.
t2	Retransmission timer for Poll messages.
t3	Aborts timer.

Many of the state parameters are set during the initial establishment of a connection between neighbors. The exceptions are the P1 through P5 values, which are established by the host system and not modified by the neighbors. The send sequence number is determined only after a message has been received from the other gateway.

A full discussion of the changes between EGP states and the events that occur when a state change happens would be longer than this book and is not of relevance to the level of discussion. Therefore, the original RFC should be consulted for full state condition information. It is useful at this point simply to be aware of the state-driven nature of EGP and that the state can be changed by a message reception, lack of a reply to a message, or expiration of a timer.

EGP Messages

The different types of messages used by EGP have already been defined, but each has a slightly different layout. These can now be examined in more detail. Refer to Figure 7.8 for the formats of these messages.

Neighbor Acquisition

A Neighbor Acquisition message (Request, Confirm, and Refuse Acquisition message types) is sent when a neighbor is being checked for acquisition. The same message format is used whether the particular message is a request, a confirmation, or a refusal.

The type is set to a value of 3 to indicate the message is a neighbor acquisition, while the code field provides the details as to the type of acquisition message, as shown in Table 7.6.

Table 7.6. EGP acquisition message codes.

Code	Description
0	Request Acquisition
1	Confirm Acquisition
2	Refuse Acquisition
3	Cease
4	Cease Acknowledgment

The status field in the acquisition message header is set to one of eight possible values and is used to provide further information about the request. The valid status field values are shown in Table 7.7.

Table 7.7. EGP acquisition message status values.

Status	Description
0	Unspecified—used when no other code is applicable
1	Active—indicates an active status mode
2	Passive—indicates a passive status mode
3	Insufficient resources available
4	Administratively prohibited
5	Going down either because of operator intervention or expiry of the t3 timer

Status	Description
6	Parameter error with incoming message
7	Protocol violation in incoming message or response message is incompatible with current machine state

The EGP Neighbor Acquisition message adds two new fields to the basic EGP message header. The 16-bit Hello Interval field specifies the minimum interval between Hello command pollings, in seconds. The 16-bit Poll Interval field specifies the minimum interval between Poll command pollings, again in seconds.

Neighbor Reachability

The Neighbor Reachability messages are used to ensure a neighbor that was previously acquired is still active and communicating. No extra fields are added to the basic EGP message format shown in Figure 7.8.

The type field is set to a value of 3, but the code field has a value of either 0 for a Hello message or one for an IHU (I Heard You) response. The status field can have one of three values, shown in Table 7.8.

Table 7.8. EGP neighbor reachability status field values.

Status	Description
0	Indeterminate—used when no other code is applicable
1	Neighbor is in an up state
2	Neighbor is in a down state

Poll

The Poll messages are used to request network reachability information. An extra two fields are added to the basic EGP message format, which are a 16-bit field reserved for future use and a 32-bit IP Source Network field.

The Poll messages have the type field set to a value of 2 and the code field set to a value of 0. The status field is set to one of the same three values used in the Reachability message, shown in Table 7.8.

The 16-bit Reserved field attached to the end of the basic EGP message format is ignored in the current versions of EGP. A 32-bit IP Source Network field is used to specify the IP Address of the network about which the gateway is requesting reachability information.

Update

Update messages are sent as a reply to a Poll message and provide information about network reachability. The format of the update message is shown in Figure 7.9 and will be seen to be similar to the GGP format discussed earlier.

Figure 7.9. *EGP Update message format.*

The type of an Update message is set to 1 and the code is set to 0. The status field is set to one of the values shown in Table 7.9. (The values are the same as those for Reachability and Poll messages except for the addition of one value.)

Table 7.9. EGP Update Message status field values.

Status	Description
0	Indeterminate—used when no other code is applicable
1	Neighbor is in an up state
2	Neighbor is in a down state
128	Unsolicited message

After the familiar EGP header information are three new fields. The number of internal gateways and number of external gateways fields specify the number of interior and exterior gateways that are reported in the message, respectively. The IP Source Network Address field contains the IP Address of the network to which the information relates.

Following the three gateway summaries and the usual header are one or more sets of information that each gateway on the current system is sending information about. These are called "gateway blocks" because each set of fields refer to one gateway. The first field is the gateway's IP address. The Number of Distances field provides the number of distances that are reported in the gateway block and the number of networks that lie at that distance. Then, for each distance that is specified, the IP network addresses of each network are provided. There can be many blocks of gateway information provided in an update message.

Errors

The final EGP message is the Error message, which has the same format as the basic EGP message with two fields attached. The 16-bit first field is reserved. Following this is a 96-bit field that contains the first 96 bits of the message that generated the error.

Interior Gateway Protocols (IGP)

There are several interior gateway protocols in use, none of which have proven themselves dominant. Usually, the choice of an IGP is made on the basis of network architecture and suitability to the network's software requirements. Earlier today, RIP and HELLO were mentioned. Both are examples of IGPs. Together with a third protocol, called Open Shortest Path First (OSPF), these IGPs can now be examined in more detail.

Both RIP and HELLO calculate distances to a destination, and their messages contain both a machine identifier and the distance to that machine. In general, messages tend to be long because they contain many entries for a routing table. Both protocols are constantly connecting between neighbors to ensure the machines are active and communicating, which can cause network traffic to build.

The Routing Information Protocol (RIP)

The Routing Information Protocol found wide use as part of the University of California at Berkeley's local area network software installations. Originally developed from two routing protocols created at Xerox Palo Alto Research Center (PARC), RIP became part of UCB's BSD UNIX release, from which it became widely accepted. Since then, many versions of RIP have been produced, to the point that most UNIX vendors have their own enhanced RIP products. The basics are now defined by an Internet RFC.

RIP uses a broadcast technology (showing its LAN heritage). This means that the gateways broadcast their routing tables to other gateways on the network at regular intervals. This is also one of RIP's downfalls, because the increased network traffic and inefficient messaging can slow down networks compared to other IGPs. RIP tends to obtain information about all destinations in the autonomous system the gateways belong to. Like GGP, RIP is a vector-distance system, sending a network address and distance to the address in its messages.

A machine in a RIP-based network can be either active or passive. If it is active, it sends its routing tables to other machines. Most gateways are active devices. A passive machine does not send its routing tables, but can send and receive messages that do affect its own routing table. Most user-oriented machines (such as PCs and workstations) are passive devices. RIP employs the User Datagram Protocol (UDP) for messaging, employing port number 520 to identify messages as originating with RIP.

The format of the RIP messages is shown in Figure 7.10. The message header is composed of three fields for the command (set to one if a request and two if a response), the version number of the RIP protocol, and an unused reserved field. The rest of the message contains address information. Each set begins with an identifier of the family protocol used (RIP is not specifically for the Internet's protocols, but if used on the Internet, this value is set to 2) and a set of network IDs. There are 96 bits available for the network address, of which only 32 maximum are necessary for an Internet address. The last field is a "metric" value that usually identifies the number of hops to the network.

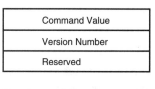

etc...

Figure 7.10. *RIP message format.*

A request message is usually sent to another gateway when a routing update is needed. When a request is received, the system examines the message to check each network address provided. If its routing table has a distance to that network address, it is placed in the corresponding metric field in the response. If there is no entry in the local routing table, no value is returned. One convention in common use is to code the family as one and the metric field as 16. When this is received, the message is interpreted as a request for the entire routing table.

Each RIP-based machine in the network maintains a routing table, with an entry for each machine that it can communicate with. The table has entries for the target's IP address, its distance, the IP address of the next gateway in the path to the target, a flag to show whether the route has recently been updated, and a set of timers that control the route. The distance is expressed as a number of hops required to reach the target, and have a value from 1 to 15. If the target is unreachable, a value of 16 is set.

The timers involved with RIP are devoted to each possible route in the routing table. A time-out timer is set when the route is initialized and each time the route is updated. If the timer expires (the default setting is 180 seconds) before another update, the route is considered unreachable. A second timer, called the garbage-collection timer, takes over after the time-out timer and marks when the route is completely expunged from the routing table. The garbage-collection timer has a default value of 120 seconds. If a request for a routing update is received after the time-out timer has expired but before the garbage-collection timer has expired, the entry for that gateway is sent but with the maximum value for the route value. After the garbage-collection timer has expired, the route would not be sent at all.

A response timer triggers a set of messages every 30 seconds to all neighboring machines, in an attempt to update routing tables. These messages are composed of the machine's IP address and the distance to the recipient machine.

The HELLO Protocol

The HELLO protocol is often used, especially when TCP/IP installations are involved. It is different from RIP in that HELLO uses time instead of distance as a routing factor. This, of course, requires the network of machines to have reasonably accurate timing, which is synchronized with each machine. For this reason, the HELLO protocol depends on clock synchronization messages.

The format of a HELLO message is shown in Figure 7.11. The primary header fields are

☐ A checksum of the entire message

☐ The current date of the sending machine

☐ The current time of the sending machine

☐ A timestamp used to calculate round-trip delays

☐ An offset that points to the following entries

☐ The number of hosts that follow as a list

Checksum
Date
Time
Timestamp
Offset
Number of hosts

Delay for Host 1
Offset for Host 1

etc...

Figure 7.11. *HELLO message format.*

Following the header are a number of entries with a delay estimate to the machine and an offset, which is an estimate of the difference between the sending and receiving clocks. The offsets are important because HELLO is a time-critical protocol, so the offset enables correction between times on different machines.

The timestamp on messages is used by machines that the message passes through to calculate delays in the network. In this manner, a routing table based on realistic delivery times can be constructed.

The Open Shortest Path First (OSPF) Protocol

The Open Shortest Path First protocol was developed by the Internet Engineering Task Force, with the hope that it would become the dominant protocol within the Internet. In many ways, the name "shortest path" is inaccurate in describing this protocol's routing process (both RIP and HELLO use a shortest path method, RIP based on distance and HELLO on time). A better description for the system would be "optimum path," in which a number of criteria are evaluated to determine the best route to a destination.

The HELLO protocol is used for passing state information between gateways and for passing basic messages, while the Internet Protocol (IP) is used for the network layer.

OSPF uses the destination address and type of service (TOS) information in an IP datagram header to develop a route. From a routing table that contains information about the topology of the network, an OSPF gateway (formally called a *router* in the RFC, although both terms are interchangeable) determines the shortest path using cost metrics, which factor in route speed, traffic, reliability, security, and several other aspects of the connection. Whenever communications must leave an autonomous network, OSPF calls this external routing. The information required for an external route can be derived from both OSPF and EGP.

There are two types of external routing with OSPF. A Type 1 route involves the same calculations for the external route as for the internal. In other words, the OSPF algorithms are applied to both the external and internal routes. A Type 2 route only uses the OSPF system to calculate a route to the gateway of the destination system, ignoring any routes of the remote autonomous system. This has an advantage in that it can be independent of the protocol used in the destination network and eliminates a need to convert metrics therein.

OSPF enables a large autonomous network to be divided into smaller areas, each with its own gateway and routing algorithms. Movement between the areas is over a backbone, or the parts of the network that route messages between areas. Care must be taken to avoid confusing OSPF's areas and backbone terminology with those of the Internet, which are similar but do not mean precisely the same thing. OSPF defines several types of routers or gateways:

☐ An Internal Router is one in which all connections belong to the same area, or one in which only backbone connections are made.

☐ A Border Router is a router that does not satisfy the description of an Internal Router (it has connections outside an area).

☐ A Backbone Router has an interface to the backbone.

☐ A Boundary Router is a gateway that has a connection to another autonomous system.

OSPF is designed to enable gateways to send messages to each other about internetwork connections. These routing messages are called *advertisements*, which are sent through HELLO update messages. There are four types of advertisements used in OSPF:

☐ A Router Links advertisement provides information on a local router's (gateway) connections in an area. These messages are broadcast throughout the network.

☐ A Network Links advertisement provides a list of routers that are connected to a network. It is broadcast throughout the network, too.

☐ A Summary Links advertisement contains information about routes outside the area. It is sent by border routers to their entire area.

☐ An Autonomous System Extended Links advertisement contains information on routes in external autonomous systems. It is used by boundary routers, but covers the entire system.

OSPF maintains several tables for determining routes, including the protocol data table (the high-level protocol in use in the autonomous system), the area data table or backbone data table (which describes the area), the interface data table (information on the router-to-network connections), the neighbor data table (information on the router-to-router connections), and a routing data table (which contains the route information for messages). Each table has a structure of its own, the details of which are not needed for this level of discussion. Interested readers can refer to the RFC for complete specifications.

OSPF Packets

As mentioned earlier, OSPF uses IP for the network layer. The OSPF specification provide for two reserved multicast addresses, one for all routers that support OSPF (224.0.0.5) and one for a designated router and a backup router (224.0.0.6). The IP protocol number 89 is reserved for OSPF. When IP sends an OSPF message, it uses the protocol number and a Type of Service (TOS) field value of 0. Usually, the IP precedence field is set higher than normal IP messages, too.

There are two header formats used by OSPF. The primary OSPF message header format is shown in Figure 7.12. Note that the fields are not shown in their scale lengths in this figure for illustrative purposes. The version number field identifies the version of the OSPF protocol in use (currently version 1). The Type field identifies the type of message and may contain a value from those shown in Table 7.10.

Table 7.10. OSPF header type values.

Type	Description
1	Hello
2	Database description
3	Link state request

Type	Description
4	Link state update
5	Link state acknowledgment

| Version (8 bits) |
| Type (8 bits) |
| Packet Length (16 bits) |
| Router ID (32 bits) |
| Area ID (32 bits) |
| Checksum (16 bits) |
| Authentication Type (16 bits) |
| Authentication (64 bits) |

Note: Fields are not to scale!

Figure 7.12. *OSPF message header format.*

The Packet Length field contains the length of the message, including the header. The Router ID is the identification of the sending machine, while the Area ID identifies the area the sending machine is in. The Checksum field uses the same algorithm as IP to verify the entire message, including the header.

The Authentication Type (AUType) field identifies the type of authentication to be used. There are currently only two values for this field: 0 for no authentication, and 1 for a password. The Authentication field contains the value that is used to authenticate the message, if applicable.

The second header format used by OSPF is for link state advertisements only, and is shown in Figure 7.13. All link state advertisements use this format, which identifies each advertisement to all routers. This header mirrors the topological table.

The Link State Age field contains the number of seconds since the link state advertisement originated. The Options field contains any IP Type of Service (TOS) features supported by the sending machine. The Link State Type identifies the type of link advertisement using one of the values shown in Table 7.11. The value in the Link State Type field further defines the format of the advertisement.

Link State Age (16 bits)
Options (8 bits)
Link StateType (8 bits)
Link State ID (32 bits)
Advertising Router (32 bits)
Link State Sequence Number (32 bits)
Link State Checksum (16 bits)
Length (16 bits)

Note: Fields are not to scale!

Figure 7.13. *OSPF link state advertisement header format.*

Table 7.11. Link state advertisement header type values.

Value	Description
1	Router links (router to area)
2	Network links (router to network)
3	Summary link (information on the IP network)
4	Summary link (information on autonomous system border router)
5	AS external link (external to autonomous system)

The Link State ID field identifies which portion of the internetwork is described in the advertisement. The value depends on the Link State Type field and can contain IP addresses for networks or router IDs. The Advertising Router field identifies the originating router. The Link State Sequence Number is an incrementing number used to prevent old or duplicate packets from being interpreted. The Checksum field uses an IP algorithm for the entire message, including the header. Finally, the Length field contains the size of the advertisement, including the header.

HELLO Packets

Either types of the OSPF headers are further encapsulated by the HELLO protocol, which is used for messaging between neighboring routers. The information in the HELLO header sets the parameters for the connection. The entire HELLO packet format is shown in Figure 7.14.

Note: Fields are not to scale!

Figure 7.14. *OSPF HELLO packet format.*

After the OSPF header is the Network Mask field, which is dependent on the interface. The Hello Interval is the number of seconds between subsequent Hello packets from the same router. The Options field is for IP's Type of Service supported values. The Router Priority field defines whether the router can be designated as a backup. If the field has a value of 0, the router cannot be defined as a backup. The Dead Interval is the number of seconds before a router is declared to be down and unavailable. The Designated and Backup Router fields hold the addresses of the designated and backup routers, if there are any. Finally, there is a set of fields for each neighbor, which contains the address of each router that has recently (within the time specified by Dead Interval) sent Hello packets over the network.

When this type of message is received by another router and has been validated as containing no errors, the neighbor information can be processed into the neighbor data table.

Another message that is used to initialize the database of a router is the database description packet. It contains information about the topology of the network (either in whole or in part). To provide database description packet service, one router is set as the master while the other is the slave. The master sends the database description packets, while the slave acknowledges them with database description responses.

The format of the database description packet is shown in Figure 7.15. After the OSPF header is a set of unused bits followed by three 1-bit flags. When the I (initial) bit is set to 0, it indicates that this packet is the first in a series of packets. The M (more) bit, when

7

set to 1, means that more database description packets follow this one. The MS (master/slave) bit indicates the master-slave relationship. When it has a value of 1 it means that the router that sent the packet is the master. A 0 indicates the sending machine is the slave. The Data Descriptor Sequence Number is an incremental counter. The rest of the packet contains Link State Advertisements, seen earlier in Figure 7.13.

Figure 7.15. *The Database Description packet layout.*

Link State Request and Update Packets

The link state request packet asks for information about a topological table from a database, where as the update can provide topological information of the types shown in Table 7.10, seen earlier. The request packet is usually sent when an entry in the router's topological table is corrupted, missing, or out of date. The format of the Link State Request packet is shown in Figure 7.16. The Link State Request packet contains the OSPF header and a block of three repeating fields for the Link State Type, Link State ID, and Advertising Router.

Figure 7.16. *OSPF Link state request packet format.*

The Link State Update packet has four formats, depending on the link state type: router links, network links, summary links, or autonomous systems external links. The router links advertisement packet is sent to neighbors periodically and contains fields for each router link and the type of service provided in each link, as shown in Figure 7.17.

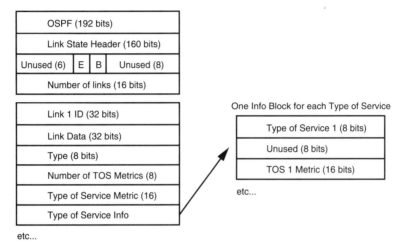

Figure 7.17. *OSPF router links advertisement packet format.*

After the OSPF header and the link state advertisement header are two single-bit flags surrounded by a 6- and 8-bit unused field. The E (external) flag, when set to 1, indicates that the router is an autonomous systems (AS) boundary router. The B (border) flag, when set to 1, indicates that the router is an area border router. Following the unused 8-bit area is a field for the number of links (advertisements) in the message. Following this, the links are provided in sequence, one link to a block.

Each link state advertisement block in the router links advertisement packet (whew!) has a field for the Link ID (the type of router, although the value is dependent in the Type field later in the block), the Link Data (whose value is an IP address or a network mask depending on the Type field's setting), the Type field (a value of 1 indicates a connection to another router, 2 a connection to a transit network, and 3 a connection to a stub network), and the Number of TOS field that shows the number of metrics for the link (at least one must be provided, which is called TOS 0). Then, a repeating block is appended for each TOS, providing the type and the metric.

The other three formats available are the Network Links advertisement, Summary Links advertisement, and Autonomous Systems (AS) External Links advertisement. The formats of these advertisements are shown in Figure 7.18. The fields have all been described earlier in this section.

Figure 7.18. *OSPF Network, Summary, and AS links advertisement layouts.*

The last packet involved in OSPF is the link state acknowledgment packet, which is required when a link state advertisement has been received correctly. The layout of the acknowledgment packet is shown in Figure 7.19. The fields following the OSPF header are for the Link State Type, Link ID, the Advertising Router ID, Link State Sequence Number, Link State Checksum value, and Link State Age, all of which have been mentioned.

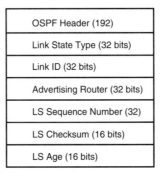

Figure 7.19. *Link state acknowledgment packet layout.*

Summary

Today, you looked at the gateway protocols used within the TCP/IP family specifically, as well as in general use on the Internet and most networks. Gateways are critical components for forwarding information from one network to another. Without gateways, each machine on the network would require a full map of every other machine on the internetwork.

There are several protocols of importance, depending on the role of the gateway. Today, you also looked at the use of bridges, routers, and brouters in a network, and the role that each of these can play. With this material, you can leave the subject of gateways. Except for some message passing and administration material, you know know all you need about gateway protocols used with TCP/IP.

Q&A

Q What is a boundary gateway?

A A boundary gateway sits between two networks within a larger internetwork, as would be found in a large corporation. The boundary gateways mark the edges (or boundaries) of each local area network, passing messages to other LANs within the larger internetwork. Boundary gateways do not communicate with the networks outside of the organization. This task is performed by exterior gateways.

Q How are sequence numbers used to control status messages within GGP? Explain for both the sending and receiving gateways.

A The sending gateway sends packets with an incrementing sequence number. The destination gateway receives each packet and echoes back the sequence number in a message. If the destination gateway receives the next packet with a sequence number that does not follow the last one received, an error message is returned to the sender with the sequence number of the last packet in it. If the sequence number is correct, an acknowledgment is sent. As the sending gateway receives packets from the destination, it compares the sequence number in the packet to its own internal counter. If the sequence number in the destination machine's packet does not match, the packet that would have been next in sequence from the last correctly received packet is resent.

Q What is a core gateway?

A A core gateway is one that resides as an interface between a network and the internetwork. A non-core gateway is between two LANs that are not connected to the larger internetwork.

Q Protocol conversion takes place in which of the following: gateways, routers, bridges, and brouters?

A Gateways perform protocol conversion. They have to because they may join two dissimilar network types. Some recent routers and brouters are capable of protocol conversion.

Q What are the three types of routing tables?

A Routing tables can be fixed (a table that is modified manually every time there is a change), dynamic (one that modifies itself based on network traffic), or fixed central (one downloaded at intervals from a central repository, which may be dynamic).

Workshop

The Workshop provides quiz questions to help you solidify your understanding of the material covered. Some Workshop sections of this book also contain exercises to provide you with experience in using what you've learned. Try to understand the quiz and exercise answers before continuing on to the next chapter. Answers are provided in Appendix F, "Answers."

Quiz

1. Define the roles of gateways, routers, bridges, and brouters.

2. What is a packet-switched network?

3. What is the difference between interior and exterior neighbor gateways?

4. What are the advantages and disadvantages of the three types of routing tables?

5. What is the HELLO protocol used for?

Domain Name
Service

TCP/IP uses a 32-bit address to route a datagram to a destination. It is useful to forget these 32-bit addresses and use common names instead because names are much easier to remember. There are several methods used for this. One employs an ASCII file on the sending machine that has names and corresponding addresses. One major limitation to this system is that the machine will only be able to route to others that have an entry in this file, which can be impossible to maintain when there are many target machines.

Another approach is to off-load the address resolution to another process that acts like a directory service. There are two such schemes in common use today: Domain Name Service (DNS) and Network Information Service (NIS), which is now part of NFS. Today, you will look at DNS in more detail. On Day 9, "Network File System," you will examine NFS.

Also today, you will look at the BOOTP protocol, a system that is becoming widely adopted as diskless workstations and client/server systems become more common. BOOTP relies on TCP/IP. Anyone working with TCP/IP can eventually expect to run across the BOOTP protocol, so an explanation of it is useful at this stage.

Finally, the day closes with a quick look at the Network Time Protocol (NTP), which is used to ensure synchronization of timestamps between machines.

Domain Name Service (DNS)

A symbolic name is a character string that is used to identify a machine. A symbolic name can be straightforward (`bills_machine` and `tpci_server1`) or more complex, as is often the case in large organizations where the name identifies the type of machine and its location (such as `hpws510`, where `hpws` identifies an HP workstation on the fifth floor, room 10). When sending information to remote machines, IP addresses or Internet address must be used. Instead of requiring the user to memorize the remote machine's numbers, it is common to use a symbolic name. After all, a simple name is much easier to remember than a 32-bit Internet address. As seen earlier in this book, the conversion from a symbolic name to an actual IP address is usually performed within the sending machine, using a file such as UNIX's `/etc/hosts`. This type of approach works well within a small network, where a limited number of destination machines are involved. When dealing with the entire Internet, though, it is unreasonable to expect an ASCII file to contain all possible symbolic names and their addresses.

The sheer size of a file required to hold all possible symbolic domain names and their corresponding unique network addresses is not the only problem. Large networks tend to change constantly, especially on an internetwork the size of the Internet. Hundreds of additions and modifications to existing entries must be performed daily. The time required to update each machine (or even selected gateways to autonomous networks) on the internetwork would be huge.

The solution to the problem is to offer a method of moving the management of the lookup tables away from the Network Information Center (NIC), which governs the Internet, and toward the participants and their autonomous networks in such a manner that the load on the network is small but flexibility is not compromised. This is what the Domain Name Service (DNS) does. DNS is sometimes also called the Internet directory service, although the name is somewhat of a misnomer.

UNIX implements DNS through a daemon called *named*, which runs on a *name server,* a machine that handles the resolution of symbolic names using DNS methods. Part of the system is a library of functions that can be used in applications to perform queries on the name server. This query routine is called the *resolver* or *name resolver* and may reside on another machine. The name server and resolver are examined in more detail shortly.

DNS Structure

The Domain Name Service, as its name implies, works by dividing the internetwork into a set of *domains* or networks, which can be further divided into subdomains. This structure resembles a tree, as shown in Figure 8.1, using some arbitrarily chosen domain names. The first set of domains are called the *top-level domains.* There are six top-level domains in regular use:

- ☐ arpa for Internet-specific organizations

- ☐ com for commercial enterprises

- ☐ edu for educational organizations

- ☐ gov for governmental bodies

- ☐ mil for military organizations

- ☐ org for noncommercial organizations

In addition to these top-level domains, there are dedicated top-level domains for each country that is connected. These are usually identified by a short form of the country's name, such as .ca for Canada and .uk for the United Kingdom. These country top-level domains are usually left off diagrams of the Internet structure for convenience (otherwise, there would be hundreds of top-level domains). The domain breakdown is sometimes repeated beneath the country domain, so there could be a .com extension coupled with .ca to show a Canadian commercial domain, or .edu with .uk for a British university.

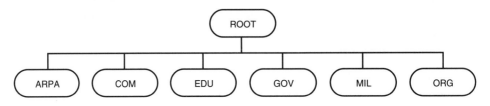

Figure 8.1. *The Internet domain structure.*

Beneath the top-level domains is another level for the individual organizations within each top-level domain. The domain names are all registered with the Network Information Center (NIC) and are unique to the network. Usually the names are representative of the company or organization, but a few "cute" names do work their way in (usually because of historical reasons).

There are two ways to name a target. If the target is on the internetwork, the *absolute name* is used. The absolute name is unique and unambiguous, specifying the domain of the target machine. A *relative name* can be used either within the local domain, where the name server will know the target is within the domain and hence doesn't need to route the datagram onto the internetwork, or when the relative name is known by the name server and can be expanded and routed correctly.

The Name Server

Each DNS Name Server manages a distinct area of a network (or an entire domain, if the network is small). The set of machines managed by the name server is called a *zone*. There may be several zones managed by one name server. Within each zone, there is almost always a designated secondary or backup name server, with the two (primary and secondary) name servers holding duplicate information. The name servers within a zone communicate using a *zone transfer protocol.*

DNS operates by having a set of nested zones. Each name server communicates with the one above it (and, if there is one, the name server below it). Each zone has at least one name server responsible for knowing the address information for each machine within that zone. Each name server also knows the address of at least one other name server. Messages between name servers usually use the User Datagram Protocol (UDP) because its connectionless method provides for better performance. However, TCP is used for database updates because of its reliability.

When a user application needs to resolve a symbolic name into a network address, a query is sent by the application to the resolver process, which then communicates the query to the name server. (You will examine the resolver in more detail in "Resource Records," later today.) The name server checks its own tables and returns the network address corresponding to the symbolic name. If the name server doesn't have the information it requires, it can send a request to another name server. This process is shown in Figure 8.2. Both the name servers and the resolvers use database tables and caches to maintain information about the machines in the local zone, as well as recently requested information from outside the zone.

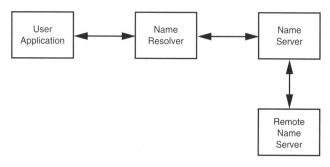

Figure 8.2. *Resolving symbolic names.*

When a name server receives a query from a resolver, there are several types of operations that the name server can perform. Name resolver operations fall into two categories: *recursive* and *nonrecursive*. A recursive operation is one in which the name server must access another name server for information.

Nonrecursive operations performed by the name server include a full answer to the resolver's request, a referral to another name server (which the resolver must send a query to), or an error message. When a recursive operation is necessary, the name server contacts another name server with the resolver's request. The remote name server will reply to the request with either a network address or a negative message indicating failure. DNS rules prohibit a remote name server from sending a referral to yet another name server.

Resource Records

The information required to resolve symbolic names is maintained by the name server in a set of *resource records,* which are entries in a database. Resource records (often abbreviated *RR*) contain information in ASCII format. Because ASCII is used, it is easy to update the records. The format of resource records is shown in Figure 8.3.

| Name (Variable length) |
| Type (16 bits) |
| Class (16 bits) |
| TTL (32 bits) |
| Data Length (16 bits) |
| Data (Variable length) |

Figure 8.3. *The resource record format.*

The Name field is the domain name of the machine the record refers to. If there is no name specified, the previously used name is substituted. The Type field identifies the type of resource record. Resource records are used for several different purposes, such as mapping names to addresses and defining zones. The Type of resource record is identified by a mnemonic code or a number. These codes and their meanings are shown in Table 8.1. Some of the resource record types are now obsolete (3 and 4), whereas others are considered experimental at this time (13 and 17–21).

Table 8.1. Resource record types.

Number	Code	Description
1	A	Network address
2	NS	Authoritative name server
3	MD	Mail destination; now replaced by MX.
4	MF	Mail forwarder; now replaced by MX.
5	CNAME	Canonical alias name
6	SOA	Start of zone authority
7	MB	Mailbox domain name
8	MG	Mailbox member
9	MR	Mail rename domain
10	NULL	Null resource record

Number	Code	Description
11	WKS	Well-known service
12	PTR	Pointer to a domain name
13	HINFO	Host information
14	MINFO	Mailbox information
15	MX	Mail exchange
16	TXT	Text strings
17	RP	Responsible person
18	AFSDB	AFS-type services
19	X.25	X.25 address
20	ISDN	ISDN address
21	RT	Route through

The Class field in the resource record layout contains a value for the class of record. If there is no value specified, the last class used is substituted. Internet name servers usually have the code IN. The Time-to-Live (TTL) field specifies the amount of time in seconds that the resource record is valid in the cache. If a value of 0 is used, the record should not be added to the cache. If the Time-to-Live (TTL) field is omitted, a default value is used. Usually, this field tells the name server how long the entry is valid before it has to ask for an update.

The data section of the resource record contains two parts, consisting of the length of the record and the data itself. The Data Length field specifies the length of the data section. The data is a variable-length field (hence the need for a length value) that describes the entry somehow. The use of this field differs with the different types of resource records.

Some resource record types have a single piece of information in the data area, such as an address, or at most three pieces of information. The only exception is the Start of Authority resource record. The contents of the resource record data areas (except SOAs) are given in Table 8.2.

Table 8.2. The contents of the resource record data area.

RR Type	Fields in data area
A	Address: A network address
NS	NSDNAME: The domain name of host
MG	MGNAME: The domain name of mailbox
CNAME	CNAME: An alias for the machine
HINFO	CPU: A string identifying CPU type OS: A string identifying operating system
MINFO	RMAILBX: A mailbox responsible for mailing lists EMAILBOX: A mailbox for error messages
MD	
MF	
MB	MADNAME: Now obsolete
MR	NEWNAME: Renames the address of a specific mailbox
MX	PREFERENCE: Specifies the precedence for delivery EXCHANGE: The domain name of host that will act as mail exchange
NULL	Anything can be placed in the data field
PTR	PTRDNAME: A domain name that acts as a pointer to a location
TXT	TXTDATA: Any kind of descriptive text
WKS	Address: A network address Protocol:. The protocol used Bitmap: Used to identify ports and protocols

The Start of Authority (SOA) resource record format is used to identify the machines that are within a zone. There is only one SOA record in each zone. The format of the SOA data field is shown in Figure 8.4. The fields in the SOA resource record are mostly used for administration and maintenance of the name server.

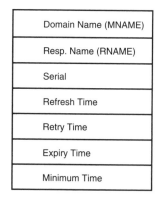

Figure 8.4. *The SOA resource record format.*

The MNAME field is the domain name of the source of data for the zone. The RNAME (responsible person name) field is the domain name of the mailbox of the administrator of the zone. The Serial field contains a version number for the zone. It is incremented when the zone is changed; otherwise, it is maintained as the same value for all such messages.

The Refresh Time is the number of seconds between data refreshes for the zone. The Retry Time is the number of seconds to wait between unsuccessful refresh requests. The Expiry Time is the number of seconds after which the zone information is no longer valid. Finally, the Minimum Time is the number of seconds to be used in the Time-to-Live field of resource records within the zone.

Some sample resource records will show the simple format used. Address resource records consist of the machine name, the type of resource record indicator (A for address RRs, for example), and the network address. A sample address resource record would look like this:

```
TPCI_SCO_4     IN    A    143.23.25.7
```

IN tags the resource record as an Internet class. This format makes it easy to locate a name and derive its address. (The reverse, going from address to name, is not as easy and requires a special format called *IN-ADDR-ARPA,* which is examined in the section titled, "IN-ADDR-ARPA," later today.)

For Well-Known Service resource records (WKS or Type 11), the data field of the record contains three fields used to describe the services supported at the address the record refers to. A sample WKS resource record might look like this:

```
TPCI_SCO.TPCI.COM     IN    WKS    143.23.1.34.
                                   FTP  TCP  SMTP  TELNET
```

The full domain name and Internet address are shown, as is the IN, to show the Internet class of resource records. The type of record is indicated with the WKS. The protocols supported by the machine at that address are listed after the address. In reality, these are bitmaps that correspond to ports. When the port bit is set to a value of 1, the service is supported. The list of ports and services are defined by an Internet RFC.

IN-ADDR-ARPA

The address fields, such as in the Address resource record type, use a special format called *IN-ADDR-ARPA*. This allows reverse mapping from the address to the host name as well as host to address mapping. To understand IN-ADDR-ARPA, it is useful to begin with a standard-format resource record. Earlier, it was mentioned that resource records are maintained in ASCII format. One of the simplest types of resource records is for the address (type A), as seen earlier. An extract from an address file is shown here:

```
TPCI_HPWS1     IN    A     143.12.2.50
TPCI_HPWS2     IN    A     143.12.2.51
TPCI_HPWS3     IN    A     143.12.2.52
TPCI_GATEWAY   IN    A     143.12.2.100
               IN    A     144.23.56.2
MERLIN         IN    A     145.23.24.1
SMALLWOOD      IN    A     134.2.12.75
```

Each line of the file represents one resource record. In this case, they are all simple entries that have the machine's symbolic name (alias), the class of machine (IN for Internet), A to show it is an address resource record, and the Internet address. The entry for the machine TPCI_GATEWAY has two corresponding addresses because it is a gateway between two networks. The gateway will have a different address on each of the networks, hence two resource records in the same file. (As with most other code fragments in this book, these sample addresses are hypothetical.)

This type of file makes name-to-address mapping easy. The name server simply searches for a line that has the symbolic name requested by the application and returns the Internet address at the end of that line. The databases are indexed on the name, so these searches proceed very quickly.

Searching from the address to the name is not quite as easy. If the resource record files were small, time delays for a manual search would not be appreciable; but with large zones there can be thousands or tens of thousands of entries. The index is on the name, so searching for an addresses would be a slow process. To solve this reverse-mapping problem, IN-ADDR-ARPA was developed. IN-ADDR-ARPA uses the host address as an index to the host's resource record information. When the proper resource record is located, the symbolic name can be extracted.

IN-ADDR-ARPA uses the PTR resource record type (see Table 8.1) to point from the address to the name. There may be one of these pointer indexes maintained on each name server. An example of a number-to-name file follows:

```
23.1.45.143.IN-ADDR-ARPA.    PTR    TPCI_HPWS_4.TPCI.COM
1.23.64.147.IN-ADDR-ARPA.    PTR    TPCI_SERVER.MERLIN.COM
3.12.6.123.IN-ADDR-ARPA.     PTR    BEAST.BEAST.COM
143.23.IN-ADDR-ARPA          PTR    MERLINGATEWAY.MERLIN.COM
```

The Internet addresses are reversed in the IN-ADDR-ARPA file for ease of use. As shown in the sample file, it is not necessary to specify the complete address for a gateway because the domain name will provide enough routing information.

Messages

DNS Messages are transferred between name servers to update their resource records. The fields of these messages are quite similar to those of the records themselves. The format of the DNS message is shown in Figure 8.5. The header has several subfields that contain information about the type of question or answer being sent. The rest of the message consists of four variable-length fields, which are further subdivided:

☐ *Question:* The information required

☐ *Answer:* The answer to the query (from the RR)

☐ *Authority:* The name of other name servers that may have the information requested, if it is not readily available on the targeted name server

☐ *Additional information:* Information that may be provided to answer the query or the addresses of name servers, if the authority field was used

Header
Question
Answer
Authority
Additional

Figure 8.5. *The DNS message format.*

The DNS Message header has several different fields itself, as shown in Figure 8.6. The header is present in all DNS messages. The header ID field is 16 bits long and is used to match queries and answers to each other. The single-bit QR field is set to a value of 0 to indicate a query, or a value of 1 to show a response. The OpCode field is 4 bits long and can have one of the values shown in Table 8.3.

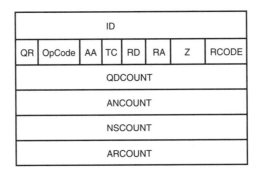

Figure 8.6. *The DNS message header format.*

Table 8.3. The DNS message header OpCode values.

OpCode	Description
0	Standard query
1	Inverse query
2	Server status request
3–15	Not used

The AA field is the authoritative answer bit. A value of 1 in a response message indicates that the name server is the recognized authority for the queried domain name. The TC (truncation) bit is set to a value of 1 when the message is truncated because of excessive length. Otherwise, the TC bit is set to 0. The RD (recursion desired) bit is set to 1 when the name server is requested to perform a recursive query. The RA (recursion available) bit is set to 1 in a response when the name server can perform recursions.

The Z field is 3 bits long and is not used. The RCODE field is 4 bits long and can be set to one of the values shown in Table 8.4. The QDCOUNT field is a 16-bit field for the number of entries in the question section. The ANCOUNT is another 16-bit field for the number of replies in the answer section (the number of resource records in the answer).

Table 8.4. The DNS message header RCODE values.

RCODE value	Description
0	No errors
1	Format error; name server unable to interpret the query
2	Name server problems have occurred
3	The name server could not find the domain reference in the query
4	Name server does not support this type of query
5	Name server will not perform the requested operation because of administrative reasons
6–15	Not used

The NSCOUNT field is 16 bits and specifies the number of server resource records in the authority section of the message. The ARCOUNT 16-bit field specifies the number of resource records in the additional record section.

The Question section of the message has three fields of its own, as shown in Figure 8.7. The Question field carries the query, which is identified by these fields. The QNAME field is the domain name requested. The QTYPE is the type of query, using one of the values given earlier. (See Table 8.1.) The QCLASS is the class of query.

Figure 8.7. *The DNS message question field format.*

Each of the last three fields in the DNS message (reply, authority, and additional information) have the same format, as shown in Figure 8.8. The Name field holds the domain name of the resource record. The Type field has any of the valid resource record type values. (See Table 8.1.) The Class is the class of data in the data field. The Time-to-Live (TTL) field is the number of seconds the information is valid without an update. The RDLENGTH field is the length of the information in the data field. Finally, the

RDATA field is the resource record information or other data, depending on the class and type of the query and reply. There may be many such records in the reply, authority, and additional information sections of the DNS message.

Name
Type
Class
Time to Live (TTL)
Data Length (RDLENGTH)
Data (RDATA)

Figure 8.8. *The DNS message reply, authority, and additional information field format.*

Name Resolver

As far as user applications are concerned, resolving symbolic names into actual network addresses is easy. The process has already been mentioned. The application sends a query to a process called the *name resolver,* or *resolver* (which sometimes resides on another machine). The name resolver may be able to resolve the name directly, in which case it sends a return message to the application. If the resolver cannot determine the network address, the resolver communicates with the name server (which may contact another name server).

The resolver is intended to replace existing name resolution systems on a machine, such as UNIX's /etc/hosts file. The replacement of these common mechanisms is transparent to the user, although the administrator must know whether the native name resolution system or DNS is to be used on each machine so the correct tables can be maintained.

When the resolver acquires information from a name server, it stores the entries in its own cache to reduce the need for more network traffic if the same symbolic name is used again (as is often the case with applications that work across networks). The amount of time the name resolver stores these records is dependent on the Time-to-Live field in the resource records sent, or on a default value set by the system.

When a name server cannot resolve a name, it may send back a message to the resolver with the address of another name server in the authority field of the message. The resolver must then address a message to the other name server in the hopes of resolving the name. The resolver can ask the name server to conduct the query itself by setting the RD (recursive) bit in the message. The name server can refuse or accept the request.

The resolver uses both UDP and TCP in its query process, although UDP is the most common, due to its speed. However, iterative queries or transfers of large amounts of information may resort to TCP because of its higher reliability.

Under the UNIX operating system, there are several different implementations of the name resolver in use. The resolver supplied with the BSD versions of UNIX was particularly limited, offering neither a cache or iterative query capabilities. To solve these limitations, the Berkeley Internet Name Domain (BIND) server was added. BIND provides both caching and iterative query capabilities in three different modes: as a primary server, as a secondary server, or as a caching-only server (which doesn't have a database of its own, only a cache). The use of BIND on BSD systems allowed another process to take over the workload of name resolution, a process that may be on another machine entirely.

BOOTP Protocol

TCP/IP needs to know an Internet address before it can communicate with other machines. This can cause a problem when a machine is initially loaded or has no dedicated disk drive of its own. Reverse Address Resolution Protocol (RARP) can be used to determine an IP address, but there is an alternative that is in common use: the *bootstrap protocol,* or BOOTP. BOOTP uses User Datagram Protocol (UDP) to enable a diskless machine to determine its IP address without using RARP.

Diskless machines usually contain startup information in their PROMs. Because these must be kept small and consistent between many models of diskless workstations to reduce costs, it is impossible to pack a complete protocol such as TCP/IP into a chip. It is also impossible to embed an IP address, because the chip may be used in many different machines on the same network. This forces a newly booted diskless workstation to determine its own IP address from the other machines on the network. (In practice, the diskless machine also must determine the IP address of the network server it will use, as well as the address of the nearest IP gateway.)

BOOTP overcomes a few problems with RARP. RARP requires direct access to the network hardware, which can cause problems when dealing with servers. Also, RARP supplies only an IP address. When large packets must be sent, this wastes a lot of space that could be used for useful information. BOOTP was developed to use UDP and can be implemented within an application program. BOOTP also requires only a single packet of information to provide all the information a new diskless workstation requires to begin operation. So, BOOTP is more efficient and easier to develop applications for, making it popular.

To determine a diskless workstation's IP address, BOOTP uses the broadcast capabilities of IP. (You may recall that IP enables several special network addresses that are broadcast to all machines on the network.) This lets the workstation send a message even when it doesn't know the destination machine's address or even its own.

Note: IP broadcast addresses such as 255.255.255.255 enable a message to be sent to all machines on a network despite having no source or destination network address.

BOOTP puts all the communications tasks on the diskless workstation. It specifies that all UDP messages sent over the network use checksums and that the do-not-fragment bit be set. This tends to reduce the number of lost, misinterpreted, or duplicated datagrams.

To handle the loss of a message, BOOTP uses a simple set of timers. When a message has been sent, a timer starts. If no reply has been received when the timer runs out, the message is resent. The protocol stipulates that the timer is set to a random value, which increases each time the timer expires until it reaches a maximum value, after which it is randomized again. This prevents massive traffic if several machines fail at once and try to broadcast BOOTP messages at the same time.

BOOTP uses the terms *client* and *server* to refer to machines. The client is the machine that initiates a query, and the server is the machine that replies to that query. From these definitions, it is easy to see that client and server have no physical relation to any workstation, because the role of each workstation can change with message traffic. Because most systems can handle multiple traffic threads at a time, it is possible for a machine to be both a client and a server simultaneously.

Note: When considering client/server roles in BOOTP, remember that the machine that sends the first message is the client and the machine that replies is the server. There is no relationship to client/server architecture terms.

BOOTP Messages

BOOTP messages are kept in fixed formats for simplicity and to enable the BOOTP software to fit in a small space within a PROM. The format of BOOTP messages is shown in Figure 8.9. The OpCode is used to signal either a request (set to a value of 1) or a reply (set to a value of 2). The HTYPE field indicates the network hardware type. The HLEN field indicates the length of a hardware address. (These two fields are the same as in ARP.)

Figure 8.9. *The BOOTP message format.*

The HOPS field keeps track of the number of times the message is forwarded. When the client sends the request message, a value of 0 is put in the HOPS field. If the server decides to forward the message to another machine, it increments the HOPS count. (Forwarding is necessary when bootstrapping a machine across more than one gateway.)

The Transaction Number field is an integer assigned by the client to the message and is unchanged from request to reply. This enables matching the replies to the correct request. The Seconds field is the number of seconds the client has been booted, assigned by the client when the message is sent.

The Client IP Address field is filled in as much as possible by the client. This may result in a partial network address or no information at all, depending on the client's knowledge of the network it is in. Any information that is unknown is set to 0 (so the field may be `0.0.0.0` if nothing is known about the network address). If the client wants information from a particular server, it can put the address of the server in the Server IP Address field. Similarly, if the client knows the server's name, it will put it in the Server Host Name field. The same applies for the other address fields. If the fields are set to 0, any server can respond. If a specific server or gateway is given, only that machine will respond to the message.

The Vendor-specific field is used, as the name suggests, for implementation information that is specific to each vendor. This field is optional. The first 32 bits define the format of the remaining information. These first bits are known as the *magic cookie,* and have a standard value of 99.120.83.99. Following the magic cookie are sets of information in a three-field format: a type, a length, and a value. There are several types identified by the Internet RFC, as shown in Table 8.5. The length field is not used for types 0 and 255, but it must be present for types 1 and 2. The length can vary, depending on the number of entries in the other types of messages.

Table 8.5. BOOTP vendor-specific types.

Type	Code	Length	Description
Padding	0	—	Used only for padding messages
Subnet Mask	1	4	Subnet mask for local network
Time of Day	2	4	Time of Day
Gateways	3	Number of entries	IP addresses of gateways
Time Servers	4	Number of entries	IP addresses of time servers
IEN116 Server	5	Number of entries	IP addresses of IEN116 servers
DomainName Server	6	Number of entries	IP addresses of Domain Name Servers
Log Server	7	Number of entries	IP addresses of log servers
Quote Server	8	Number of entries	IP addresses of quote servers

Type	Code	Length	Description
LPR Servers	9	Number of entries	IP addresses of lpr servers
Impress	10	Number of entries	IP addresses of impress servers
RLP Server	11	Number of entries	IP addresses of RLP servers
Hostname	12	Number of bytes	Client host name in host name
Boot size	13	2	Integer size of boot file
Unused	128-254	—	Not used
End	255	—	End of list

You may remember that a machine can obtain the subnet mask from an ICMP message, but BOOTP is the recommended method of obtaining this value.

The Boot Filename field can specify a filename from which to obtain a memory image that enables the diskless workstation to boot properly. This may be vendor-set or supplied by the server. This enables the memory image to be obtained from one machine while the actual addresses are obtained from another. If this field is set to 0, the server selects the memory image to send.

The process of booting follows two steps. The first is to use BOOTP to obtain information about the network addresses of the client and at least one other machine (a gateway or server). The second step uses a different protocol to obtain a memory image for the client.

> **Note:** A two-step process using two different protocols is used to separate the configuration and operating system load of the machine. The use of two protocols enables optimization for each task. Two steps are also used because the machine that replies to the BOOTP client message may not be the machine that downloads the memory image.

Network Time Protocol (NTP)

Timing is very important to networks, not only to ensure that internal timers are maintained properly, but also for synchronization of clocks for sending messages and timestamps within those messages. Some systems rely on time for routing (as you saw yesterday). Ensuring that time clocks are consistent and accurate is a task often overlooked, but remains important enough to have a formal procedure defined by an Internet RFC. The protocol that maintains time standards is called the Network Time Protocol, or NTP. NTP can use either TCP or UDP; port 37 is dedicated to it.

The operation of NTP relies on obtaining an accurate time from a query to a primary time server, which itself gets its timing information from a standard time source (such as the National Institute of Standards and Technology in the U.S.). The time server queries the standard clock (also called a *master clocking source*) and sets its own times to the standard.

Once the primary time server has an accurate time, it sends NTP messages to secondary time servers further out on the internetwork. Secondary time servers can communicate with more secondary time servers using NTP, although accuracy is lost with each communication due to latency in the networks. Eventually, these time messages can be sent to gateways and individual machines within a network, if the administrator so decides. Usually each network will have at least one primary time server and one secondary server, although large networks may have several of each.

The format of NTP messages is simple, as shown in Figure 8.10. There are several control fields that are used for synchronization and updating procedures, but the details of these fields are not important to this discussion. The Sync Distance to Primary is an estimate of the round trip delay incurred to the primary clock. The ID of the Primary time server is the address of the primary.

Control Fields
Sync Distance to Primary
Network ID of Primary
Time local clock updated
Originating timestamp
Receiving timestamp
Transmit timestamp
Authentication

Figure 8.10. *The NTP message format.*

There are several timestamps in the NTP message. The Time Local Clock Updated is the time the message originator's local clock was updated. The Originate timestamp is the time the message was sent. The Receive timestamp is the time it was received. The Transmit timestamp is the time the message was transmitted after reception.

All timestamps are calculated from an offset of the number of seconds since January 1, 1900. The timestamp fields are 64 bits, the first 32 bits for a whole number and the last 32 for a fraction. The final Authentication field is optional and can be used to authenticate the message.

Summary

You have now seen how the Domain Name Service works. DNS is an integral and important part of most TCP/IP installations, allowing symbolic names to be resolved properly across networks. The use of name servers was explained, as well as the manner in which records are stored within the servers. Associated with DNS is the ARP and IN-ADDR-ARPA name resolution process.

Today, you also looked at the BOOTP protocol, which is necessary to allow many diskless terminals and workstations to connect to the network and load their operating systems. Without BOOTP, we would all need full-featured computers or workstations.

Q&A

Q What are the top-level domain names and what are their purposes?

A The top level domains are .arpa (Internet-specific), .com (commercial), .edu (educational institutions), .gov (governmental), .mil (military), and .org (non-commercial organizations).

Q What does a DNS name server do?

A The DNS name server manages a zone of machines and provides name resolution for all machines within that zone.

Q If a name server cannot resolve a name using its own tables, what happens?

A Queries can be sent from the machine receiving the query to other name servers to search for a resolution. If another machine does have the answer, it is not returned to the inquiring machine, though. Only the address of the name resolver with the answer is returned. The inquiring machine must then send a specific query to the resolver with the answer.

Q What is the advantage of the IN-ADDR-ARPA format?

A IN-ADDR-ARPA enables a mapping from the IP address to the symbolic host name. Sometimes, this is a fast way to obtain the symbolic name of a destination machine.

Q Why does BOOTP use UDP?

A Simply because it is smaller to code. To embed TCP code in a PROM would take much more room than the simple code needed for UDP.

Workshop

The Workshop provides quiz questions to help you solidify your understanding of the material covered. Some Workshop sections of this book also contain exercises to provide you with experience in using what you've learned. Try to understand the quiz and exercise answers before continuing on to the next chapter. Answers are provided in Appendix F, "Answers."

Quiz

1. What protocol is used by DNS name servers? Why is that a good choice?

2. What is a DNS resource record?

3. Show a sample entry in an IN-ADDR-ARPA file and explain what the fields mean.

4. BOOTP helps a diskless workstation boot. How does it get a message to the network looking for its IP address and the location of its operating system boot files?

5. What is the Network Time Protocol? Why is it used?

9

Network File System

Today you'll look at the Network File System (NFS), a set of protocols and products that are in wide use with TCP/IP-based networks. NFS is especially popular with UNIX networks but is now available for many platforms. You'll also look at several protocols that are closely associated with NFS, such as Yellow Pages (YP), Network Information Service (NIS), and the Remote Execution Service (REX).

Today's text will concentrate on UNIX versions of these protocols, simply because they serve as an excellent illustration. For other operating systems, names of files and procedures may change, but the fundamentals will be compatible.

Network File System (NFS)

The move to distributed processing and client/server architectures has meant that many users have small, powerful machines on their desks that communicate with a larger server somewhere on a network. The applications the user needs are often located in places other than on their desktop, so some method of accessing remote files (applications and data) is required. Although both Telnet and `rlogin` enable a user to use a remote machine, neither system takes advantage of the user's desktop machine. Peripheral sharing also became important as local area networks grew. To help integrate workstations into local area networks, as well as to simplify remote file access and peripheral sharing, Sun Microsystems introduced the Network File System (NFS).

Sun designed NFS so that it would allow machines from different vendors to work together, even if they used different operating systems. Sun published the NFS specifications, enabling other vendors to adopt their own hardware and software to work smoothly with NFS. This results in a completely homogeneous network. Since Sun's introduction, NFS has become a *de facto* standard among UNIX environments, with strong support in other operating systems, too.

NFS actually refers to both a product and a protocol. There is an NFS product that consists of a set of protocols for different tasks (which are examined in the section titled "NFS Protocols"). The NFS protocol is the one protocol of the NFS product that deals with file access. To avoid confusion, you should think of the NFS protocol specifically (instead of the entire product set) when NFS is mentioned today.

NFS is now intimately tied with UNIX, and it is shipped as part of the System V Release 4 software version. It is also tied to TCP/IP, which remains the communications protocol of choice for UNIX networks. For other operating systems, NFS is usually an extension that is added at the system administrator's option. UNIX systems use the process `nfsd` to manage NFS access.

NFS enables an application to read and write files that reside on NFS servers, with the access to the NFS server completely transparent to the application and the user. For developers, NFS requires no extra coding or special handling, which makes it especially attractive. This transparent access to another machine's file structure is achieved by logically attaching the NFS server to the client, a process called *mounting*. The NFS server's file system can be attached as a whole, or just a portion of it can be mounted. The directory at which the mount occurs is called the *mount point*. The concept of shared files is similar to that encountered with NFS and is sometimes called a *distributed file system,* although this is a misnomer with NFS.

Note: UNIX has had the capability to mount or attach another file system for a long time. This type of mounting can occur across networks and is transparent to the application and user, as long as filenames take into account the full pathname of the mounted file system. The NFS mount is similar to the UNIX mount process.

NFS uses the term *client* to represent any machine that requests a file from another machine, which is the *server*. Multitasking operating systems can act as both client and server simultaneously, with processes on the machine accessing files on another machine while others on the network access its own hard disk. Usually, there are restrictions imposed for the files or portions of a file system that can be shared, both for security and speed considerations. Typical NFS installations will use personal computers or diskless workstations as clients accessing a powerful server system. Because personal computer operating systems such as MS-DOS are single-tasking, PCs usually act only as clients unless they run a multitasking operating system such as Windows NT or OS/2. It is possible to have an entire network of multitasking computers sharing their drives with each other, although in practice this works well only for small networks.

Because of the need to transfer files quickly, the network speed becomes vitally important. When it was designed, the original goal for an NFS-mounted file system was to provide performance equivalent to 80 percent of the performance expected from a locally mounted hard disk. This puts the performance emphasis on both the NFS disk drive and the network system. Typically, NFS disk drives are among the fastest available, to reduce bottlenecks at the drive end. The network hardware and software must be chosen to allow the fastest possible throughput.

Because NFS is UNIX-based, the security offered is rudimentary. For this reason, Sun has introduced Secure NFS, which implements an encrypted messaging protocol for added protection against unauthorized access to NFS-mounted file systems.

NFS Protocols

The NFS product comprises several protocols, only one of which is called the NFS protocol. The NFS product protocols are designed as a set of layers, similar to the OSI model. The layers of the NFS product are compared to the OSI layers in Figure 9.1. Each protocol in the NFS product has an Internet RFC dedicated to its specification.

Figure 9.1. *NFS protocol layers.*

The NFS product is based on the OSI layered model, resulting in protocols that are independent (in theory, at least). The design philosophy is that any single-layer protocol could be replaced with any other one, assuming the functionality of the protocol was the same. To date there are no common alternatives for the two lower-layer products, RPC and XDR, although there are several for the top layer.

Note: The source code for both the Remote Procedure Call (RPC) and External Data Representation (XDR) protocols is available free of charge from Sun Microsystems.

Remote Procedure Call (RPC)

The Remote Procedure Call (RPC) protocol acts as the session layer and as the message exchanger for all NFS-based applications. RPC is composed of a set of procedures that can be incorporated into high-level applications to handle any required network access. The remote procedures are no more complicated to use than local procedures.

> **Note:** RPC was specially developed for NFS but has since found use in other protocol suites. The principles covered here apply to those RPC products, too.

Application developers can create their own RPC procedures between a client (the one that issues the request) and the server (the one that process the request). A group of procedures is called a *service*. Each server can use only one service, so each service is assigned a *program number* to identify itself to both the client and the server.

RPC functions over the network between a client and a server. The process followed by an RPC is shown in Figure 9.2. It begins with the activation of the procedure by the client, from which a request message is sent to the server. After receiving the message and extracting the request, the server executes the requested procedure and assembles a response message with the results. Upon receipt of the reply, the client disassembles the message and continues with the application's normal execution. Every step of the procedure is controlled by routines within the RPC library (which is linked in to the applications).

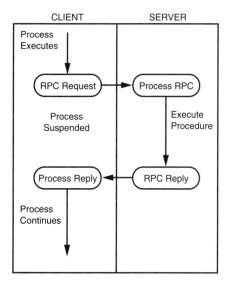

Figure 9.2. *The execution of an RPC.*

RPC messages can be sent using either TCP or UDP (or, for that matter, any other protocol that provides the same functionality). Typically, RPC is used with UDP because a connection-based protocol is not necessary. UDP is usually faster. However, UDP does impose a maximum packet size, which may cause some problems with procedures. Also, UDP does not guarantee delivery, so an application that uses UDP must handle reliability issues (usually with a retransmission timer).

The use of TCP offers the capability not only to ignore reliability concerns (leaving that to the TCP software) but also to batch requests. With a batch connection, the client and server agree that the client can send a number of RPC requests one after another without waiting for acknowledgment or a reply to each. This can be a useful feature with some applications.

The RPC protocol is used to send requests and replies. The format of the RPC protocol packet header is shown in Figure 9.3, with all fields coded in the Extended Data Representation (XDR) format (see "External Data Representation," later today). The Transaction ID is used to match requests and replies, and is changed (usually incremented) by the client with each new request. The Direction Indicator shows whether the message originated with the client (a value of 0) or with the server (a value of 1). The Version Number is the version of RPC used. The Program Number identifies the service (set of procedures) to use, as mentioned earlier. The Procedure Number identifies the particular procedure in the service.

Figure 9.3. *The RPC protocol header.*

Some procedures may require a client to authenticate itself to the server, both for identification purposes and for security reasons. The RPC protocol header contains two fields for authentication. The Authorization Information field is for information itself, while the Authorization Verification field is used for the validation. The RPC RFC does not define how authentication is to be performed, leaving it up to the application developer, but it does specify two fields with a maximum size of 400 bytes each. There are currently four types of authentication predefined for use:

- [ ] *None:* No authentication is used. Both authentication fields have zero length.

- [ ] *UNIX:* Uses UNIX permissions (group and user IDs). This type of authentication is used by the NFS protocol. There is no authentication information.

- [ ] *Short:* Short authentication process. The client generates an authentication sequence, which is returned by the server (usually a reference to a previous RPC request for convenience).

- [ ] *DES:* Authentication is a character string with a Data Encryption Standard (DES) encoded time stamp used as the verification. The DES authentication is used by the secure NFS product.

The only authentication system that is really secure is the DES method. The other three systems can be readily broken by a developer.

Each service that uses RPC has a program number that uniquely identifies it to the protocol. RPC keeps track of connections using a program number for each, which can be mapped to a program name. In UNIX, this mapping is performed in the file /etc/rpc. A sample /etc/rpc file follows:

```
portmapper     100000  portmap sunrpc
rstat_svc      100001  rstatd rstat rup perfmeter
rusersd        100002  rusers
nfs            100003  nfsprog
ypserv         100004  ypprog
mountd         100005  mount showmount
ypbind         100007
walld          100008  rwall shutdown
yppasswdd      100009  yppasswd
etherstatd     100010  etherstat
rquotad        100011  rquotaprog quota rquota
sprayd         100012  spray
3270_mapper    100013
rje_mapper     100014
selection_svc  100015  selnsvc
database_svc   100016
rexd           100017  rex
alis           100018
sched          100019
llockmgr       100020
```

```
nlockmgr     100021
x25.inr      100022
statmon      100023
status       100024
bootparam    100026
ypupdated    100028   ypupdate
keyserv      100029   keyserver
ypxfrd       100069   ypxfr
pcnfsd       150001   pcnfsd
```

This file shows the program name and its corresponding program number. The third column, when present, shows a program name that corresponds to the process name in the first column. The program numbers shown in this file are assigned by the RPC RFC and should be consistent across all implementations of RPC.

Port Mapper

Connections between a client and server are over ports, each with its own number (port numbers are used in TCP/IP to define a connection). To prevent problems with port allocation using RPC, a *port mapper* was developed. Without the port mapper, a server could easily run out of available ports with only a few RPC connections active.

The port mapper controls a table of ports and RPC programs using those ports. The port mapper itself has a dedicated port number (port 111 with both UDP and TCP). The ports available to RPC connections are assigned when the RPC program is initiated, at which time these port numbers are sent to the port mapper.

When a client wants to use RPC, it sends a request to the server. This request follows the RPC header format, shown in Figure 9.3, and includes the version number of RPC, the service number, and the protocol to be used. The port mapper can then allocate a suitable port number and return that number in a reply message to the client. Once a port number has been assigned for that client, it is maintained, so that all procedure requests come over that port until the application terminates. The port numbers may be maintained over several processes, so the port inquiry need only be conducted once between system power cycles.

This procedure does have a drawback: The client must know the server's address. It cannot simply send out a generic request for a server with the services it is looking for. This has been overcome with some newly developed network file systems, although not with NFS.

External Data Representation (XDR)

The External Data Representation (XDR) is the method by which data is encoded within an RPC message (or other protocol systems, as well). There is no formal message header or protocol system for XDR, although the XDR RFC does define the method of encoding data.

XDR is used to ensure that data from one system is compatible with others. It may seem that no formal definition is required, but consider the case of an EBCDIC-based machine communicating with an ASCII-based machine. XDR enables both ends to convert their local data representation to a common format, removing any doubts about the meaning of the data. (EBCDIC–ASCII is not the major conversion problem. Some systems use high bits as significant, while other use low bits. Also, formats for defining types of numbers differ considerably.)

The XDR format uses sequential bits written into a buffer, and then is formatted into a message and sent to the lower protocol layers. XDR relies on an 8-bit byte, with the lower bytes the most significant. The RFC defines that all integer data types are converted to 4-byte integers, with an extended 64-bit *hyperinteger* format available. IEEE 32-bit formats are used for floating-point numbers, where the mantissa is the lower 23 bits, the exponent takes eight bits, and the sign of the number is 1 bit. When data takes less than 4 bytes for any type, padding is added to ensure 4-byte lengths.

> **Note:** A special C-like language called XDR has been developed to simplify the handling of XDR-format data. It can be used within other programming languages.

Network File System Protocol

The NFS protocol is composed of a set of RPC procedures. It is not a protocol in the conventional sense of defining a complex handshaking process between two machines. Instead, it is a method of communicating information about a procedure to be run. NFS uses UDP and has a port number of 2049 assigned. This port number is nonsense; it arises from an error in the original implementation that could not be corrected subsequently because of compatibility issues. Because the port numbers are assigned by the port mapper, this number has no real meaning.

NFS was designed to be a *stateless* protocol, meaning that the machines using NFS would not have to maintain state tables to use the protocol. Also, it was designed to be robust, meaning that after failures (of a connection or a machine) the system could recover quickly and easily.

The NFS protocol is difficult to describe without introducing some programming, because the system is described in terms of the XDR language. This type of discussion is beyond the scope of this book; for more information, refer to the RFCs. However, it is possible to convey a sense of the protocol's contents through an overview of its capabilities and features.

To understand the NFS procedures that comprise the protocol, it is necessary to examine the data structures and objects in the protocol. NFS defines a set of constants that are used to establish various parameters, such as the number of bytes in a pathname, the maximum number of bytes in a read or write request, or the size of an NFS pointer. These are called *protocol constants* and should be the same for all implementations of NFS.

> **Note:** A *data object* is a set of variables or values that are combined in one entity, much as an entry in a telephone book is actually composed of a name, address, and telephone number. All three variables or values combine to form a single entry or object.

Several data objects are used by NFS to define files and their attributes. Because NFS deals specifically with files, these objects are important to the protocol. One data object is the file handle (or *fhandle*), which uniquely identifies a file on the server. File handles are provided in all NFS messages that refer to the file. As with most NFS data types, the file handle is a 32-byte field of free format, which is understandable by the server. For example, a UNIX file is uniquely defined by its device major and minor numbers and its inode number. The filename itself is not used.

A data object is used for the file type (called *ftype*), which defines all the kinds of files known by NFS. These mimic the UNIX file types, including a regular file (any kind of data), a directory (which is a file entry in UNIX), links (which are several pointers under different names to the same file), and both block and character mode files.

Also used is a data structure for the file attributes, called *fattr*. This defines the permissions of the file, the times of access, the owner, and several other parameters. This is necessary whenever a file read or write is performed, because the attributes must be correct to enable the procedure to continue. (The attributes can be changed by another NFS procedure called *set attributes*, or *sattr*.)

These data objects can be combined into a larger entity using a discriminating union. A *discriminating union* is a combination of several data objects that are given a single label. These discriminating unions can be thought of as a label followed by data, which may differ, depending on the outcome of a procedure. For example, after a procedure has been executed, a discriminating union may be a label followed by either an error message or the result of the procedure, if it executes properly. The union, though, is referred to by the label and doesn't care about the contents in the data area. This type of structure is used to simplify programming.

There are 17 procedures defined within the NFS protocol. These procedures are summarized in Table 9.1. This book doesn't go into detail about the procedures, because they are not relevant to the level of discussion. The RFC covers them all in exhaustive detail.

Table 9.1. NFS procedures.

Name	Description
Null	Null procedure
Fetch file attributes	Returns the attributes of a file
Set file attributes	Sets the attributes of a file
Read file system root	Not used; now obsolete
Lookup filename	Returns the file handle corresponding to a filename
Read contents of link	Returns details of symbolic links to a file
Read file	Reads a file
Write to cache	Not used
Write to file	Writes a file
Create file	Creates a new file and returns the new file's handle
Delete file	Deletes a file
Rename file	Renames a file
Generate link	Creates a link to a file (same file system)
Generate symbolic link	Generates a symbolic link (across file systems)
Create directory	Creates a new directory
Delete directory	Removes a directory
Read directory	Returns a list of files in the directory
Read file system attributes	Returns information about the file system

Programmers may have noticed the lack of any open and close file functions within NFS. This arises from the stateless nature of the protocol. When a file must be opened, it is the local NFS process that handles it, not the remote process. This allows for better control of files and ports after failure of a machine or a connection.

Mount Protocol

In today's introduction, I mentioned that NFS works by mounting an NFS server file system onto a client file system. As you have just seen, though, the NFS protocol is actually about file access and information, not connecting file systems. This file system mounting procedure is dealt with as a separate issue by the NFS product, using the Mount protocol. Mount uses UDP.

The Mount protocol is involved in returning a file handle from the server to the client, enabling the client to access an area on the server file system. The protocol returns not only the file handle but also the name of the file system in which the requested file resides. Mount consists of a number of procedures that facilitate communications between the client and server, designed especially for dealing with files.

A process called mountd takes care of handling the mount protocol at both ends of a connection. The mountd process maintains a list of machines and pathnames that are involved in a mount operation. Once a mount has been performed, NFS can continue operating without referring back to mount at all. This lets mount continue to modify its internal tables without affecting ongoing sessions. This can cause a problem if a client crashes and reconnects. The server will still have the original connections listed in its internal mount tables. To correct this problem, most NFS clients send a command (called UMNTALL, or unmount all) to all NFS servers when they boot.

> **Note:** The mount protocol is involved only during the original connection between a client and a server. The mountd process keeps track of connections, but once the connection is established the mount protocol relinquishes all control to NFS. All NFS needs for accessing a file system is a valid file handle (which mount provides when the connection is made).

As mentioned earlier, the mount protocol consists of a set of procedures. These are summarized in Table 9.2 and are self-explanatory.

Table 9.2. Mount protocol procedures.

Name	Description
NULL	Null
MNT	Mounts a file system and returns the file handle and file system name
UMNT	Unmounts a server file system, deleting the entry from the mount table
UMNTALL	Unmounts all server file systems used by the client and updates the mount table
EXPORT	Provides a list of exported file systems
DUMP	Provides a list of the file systems on the server that are currently mounted on the client

Some versions of NFS enable an automount capability, in which the remote file systems are mounted only when required. This prevents them from being attached for extended periods of time and simplifies administration. The process of automounting is completely transparent to the user.

The automount capability is built upon NFS's procedures but performs a few clever tricks. The automounter is not part of NFS but is an application that sits on top of it. Symbolic links are the key to the automounter's operation.

File Locking

There are occasions when a system administrator will want to prevent access to an NFS-available file system. Such instances occur regularly during maintenance, software updates, or to protect data during a particular process. UNIX has the capability to lock a particular file by changing permissions and the same can be done for file systems to some extent, but it would seem intuitive that locking a file system is more involved than simply locking a file or two. The capability to lock file systems from access was not developed with the original NFS product but was implemented as a parallel service after NFS became more widely available.

> **Note:** Separating functionality (such as file locking) into separate protocols or procedures is consistent with both the OSI and NFS philosophy. This also enables better portability and compatibility across platforms.

File system locking is handled by several protocols and procedures, involving a few daemon processes. In the original file locking system developed by Sun Microsystems, a lock daemon called lockd was used. This requires that every RPC activity that involves a lock communicates with the process, even when it is on another machine. The communications between RPC and lockd uses a protocol called Kernel Lock Manager (KLM), which rides on UDP.

Whenever a lock procedure was called, lockd decided whether it could handle the task on the local machine or whether messages had to be sent to remote lockd processes (on other machines). Communications between different lockd processes is through another protocol called the Network Lock Manager (NLM). There are several versions of both KLM and NLM in use, with implementations available for most hardware platforms.

A process called statd (status monitor) monitors the state of locks and handles queries against a locked file system. This is necessary so that a new query against a locked file system can be queued (if its locked is for a short time) or rejected (if the file system is locked for a while).

There are several built-in protection systems for file locking, such as automatic timers to prevent infinite locking after a machine crash, conflicting requests for locks, and a short period for completion of existing procedures before a lock is completed. These are all defined and explained in the RFC.

Remote Execution Service (REX)

The Remote Execution Service (REX) is designed to enable a user to run commands on another machine with full environment variables, without incurring the overhead of processes such as Telnet, rlogin, or rsh. REX uses a daemon called rexd that runs on the server and which employs NFS' services. (Remember that each machine can be both client and server, so most multitasking machines on a network will run rexd.) REX is commonly used when some applications are installed on only a few machines but should be available to all users.

REX has an important advantage over the other UNIX utilities for this type of service. It enables access to the local machine's data while executing the command on the remote.

This enables a user to run an application on another machine while accessing data files on the local machine. It also enables another machine's resources to be used without starting a user shell process or logging in to the remote machine.

To run an application or execute a command on a remote machine, the REX on command is used. The syntax adds the name of the machine on which the command is to be executed and the command to run. For example:

```
$ hostname
tpci_hpws4
$ cat file1
This is the file "file1" on "tpci_hpws4".
This is the client machine.
$ on merlin hostname
merlin
$ rsh merlin cat file1
cat: cannot open file1
$ on merlin cat file1
This is the file "file1" on "tpci_hpws4".
This is the client machine.
```

This example shows the remote machine executing a cat command on a local file. When the remote machine runs commands using on, an identical environment to the client is established on the remote, including user and group IDs and environment variables. So, if the remote machine in the previous example had a file called file1, but it was not in the search path of the process running the command, the system would still refer back to the client for the file.

rusers and *spray*

Two utilities available to NFS users are simple examples of RPC programs. They are also useful to the user who wants to check the status of connections and the load on a remote machine.

The spray program is similar to ping, in that it sends a batch of messages across the network and waits for replies. There are several supported options that can configure the use of spray. When the spray command is issued with the -c option, it sends a supplied number of datagrams to the remote machine and times the results. A typical use is

```
$ spray -c 200 beast
sending 200 packets of length 86 to beast...
    in 18.3 seconds elapsed time,
    4 packets (2.00%) dropped by beast
Sent:  10 packets/sec, 912 bytes/sec
Recd:   9 packets/sec, 862 bytes/sec
```

The rusers program gives you an idea of who is logged into remote machines. A typical output is the following:

```
$ rusers
beast.tpci.com        tparker  bsmallwood  rmaclean
merlin.tpci.com       ychow  etreijs  tgrace
tpci_hpws3.tpci.com   tparker  sysadm
tpci_hpws4.tpci.com   pepper
```

As shown, the output from the `rusers` program includes the machine name and the list of users on that machine. Some implementations support options for `rusers`, while some have slightly differing output.

Network Information Service (NIS) and Yellow Pages (YP)

The Yellow Pages (YP) protocol is an RPC application layer service (such as NFS) that provides a versatile directory service. Because of copyright restrictions, Yellow Pages was renamed to Network Information Service (NIS), although both terms are in common use. YP was developed for several reasons, but the one that affects users the most is access permissions. The affect these permissions have on users is generally transparent except for one major advantage.

If you are a user on a large network and you tend to connect to other machines frequently (either through Telnet or FTP, for example), you must maintain accounts on each machine you connect to. Thus, you would need user accounts on every machine you could conceivably want to access. Maintaining the passwords on a large number of machines is awkward, because you must log into each one and perform password changes. Yellow Pages was developed to enable one single, central user file to be shared over the network, requiring only a single entry to enable access to all machines (unless specific restrictions are imposed) and simplifying a password change on all machines to one step.

In RPC terms, this combination of user ID and password works on the RPC authentication procedures. RPC uses the user and group IDs to grant access to files, so it is necessary for the client and server's user and group IDs match. Without NIS, this could be very difficult to implement because each machine's user file may have to same names, but their user IDs may not coincide. Worse, another user with a matching user ID on another machine could access files on your machine as though he or she were logged in as you.

NIS is a distributed access system in that each machine on the network that uses NIS accesses a central server, called the *NIS master* or *ypmaster* (depending on the version), for access information. On larger networks to spread the load, and for all networks as a backup contingency, a number of other machines are designated as *slaves* or *ypslaves,* which maintain up-to-date access information. In case of a failure of the master server, a slave will take up the functions. NIS uses both TCP and UDP for communications.

> **Note:** There are two versions of YP or NIS in general use. The first release (version 1) had serious problems under certain circumstances, so version 2 was quickly released. However, some systems still use the older version.

The YP or NIS protocol (both names are valid, although NIS should properly be used now) has a set of procedures defined within the RFC. These allow a search for master servers, access to the user files, and system management functions. Another procedure is used to transfer copies of the master files. A number of machines are grouped together into one NFS subnetwork, called a *domain* (not to be confused with the Internet domain). Each domain has master and slave machines.

NIS keeps the access information in a set of *maps,* each map corresponding to a particular area or domain of a network. This allows for several groups to use the same NIS master but have different access permissions. The NIS maps do not have to correspond to DNS domains, allowing more versatility in configuration. Maps consist of a set of records in ASCII format, each with an *index key* for fast lookup. The index key is usually the user name. The records have the same structure as normal user files (such as UNIX's /etc/passwd), both for compatibility and for simplicity.

> **Note:** The use of NIS or YP does not negate the need for a complete set of access files on each machine, because NIS or YP is loaded after the machine has been booted (and these files read). The stand-alone files should have access for a system administrator at least, although it is good practice to also include the most frequent users in case of a network crash preventing access to the NIS directories.

NIS is not restricted to the users of a system. Any file can be set up to use NIS, such as the list of machines on a network (UNIX's /etc/hosts file). Thus, only one change needs to be made to these files on any network. A set of aliases also can be managed by NIS or YP.

Several YP/NIS specific commands are involved with the protocol, although most system administrators set up aliases to minimize the impact on users. For most users, only one command is necessary on a regular basis. For UNIX systems, this is the command yppasswd to change a user's password. This is usually aliased to passwd, the normal password change command. Application developers may have to examine the NIS protocol in more detail when writing client/server code that will run on an NIS-based system, but the effects of the distributed system are usually transparent.

RPC and NFS Administration

RPC and NFS have two primary administration tools available for providing status updates and indications of trouble within the system. Usually these tools are not available to end users, although it is useful to know of their existence and their roles in monitoring NFS and RPC.

Running any single tool is usually not sufficient to isolate a problem. Often, one tool will report a problem with a port, but upon closer examination it is found that the port is functioning and the process at the other end died. Therefore, these tools are designed to be used to complement each other until an accurate diagnosis can be produced.

rpcinfo

The rpcinfo program monitors the port mapper of the machine on which it is running, and through the network, the port mappers of servers. Because the port mapper is the program that controls access to RPCs, this type of information is important in tracking problems. The rpcinfo program can display the contents of the mapping tables, showing the port and program numbers for each connection, and is able to activate remote servers for testing a connection.

Typically, rpcinfo is called with the -p option to show the list of RPC programs that are currently tracked by the port mapper. An optional machine name can be added to display only connections with one machine. A typical output from the rpcinfo program is shown here:

```
$ rpcinfo -p
  program vers proto   port
   100000    2   tcp    111  portmapper
   100000    2   udp    111  portmapper
   100008    1   udp   1026  walld
   150001    1   udp   1027  pcnfsd
   150001    2   udp   1027  pcnfsd
   100002    1   udp   1028  rusersd
   100002    2   udp   1028  rusersd
   100024    1   udp   1029  status
   100024    1   tcp   1024  status
```

```
100020   1   udp   1034   llockmgr
100020   1   tcp   1025   llockmgr
100021   2   tcp   1026   nlockmgr
100021   1   tcp   1027   nlockmgr
100021   1   udp   1038   nlockmgr
100021   3   tcp   1028   nlockmgr
100021   3   udp   1039   nlockmgr
```

In case of a problem contacting the port mapper, rpcinfo returns an error message. In such a case, the port mapper is not functioning correctly and there may be no contact with other machines. A check using ping will verify this. An example of this kind of fatal error message is shown here:

```
$ rpcinfo -p
rpcinfo: can't contact port mapper:
RFC: Remote system errer -125
```

Specific connections can be tested with rpcinfo by using the machine and process name, as the following example shows:

```
$ rpcinfo -u merlin walld
program 100008 version 1 is ready and waiting
```

Note that the -u option is used for UDP connections, whereas -t must be used with TCP connections. In this example, the client rpcinfo sent a request to the specified program and waited for a reply. A successful reply results in the message shown previously. If a reply is not received before a timer expires, an error message is displayed.

In the previous sample output, there is a process called pcnfsd, which is an RPC server developed for use with MS-DOS based machines. It handles access rights and spooling services for the DOS side, while simplifying the DOS machine's access to NFS services.

nfsstat

The nfsstat program, as its name suggests, provides statistics about the number and types of RPC requests that are made. It is usually called without an option, although several exist (depending on the implementation and version) to show specific statistics or sample only certain parts of the connection.

The output from nfsstat is shown here for a typical small network:

```
Server rpc:
calls      badcalls    nullrecv    badlen      xdrcall
10465      0           0           0           0

Server nfs:
calls      badcalls
10432      0
null       getattr     setattr     root        lookup      readlink     read
```

```
1 0%        24 0%        1 0%        0 0%        10123 0%    0 0%        5 0%
wrcache     write        create      remove      rename      link        symlink
0 0%        2 0%         0 0%        1 0%        0 0%        1 0%        0 0%

Client rpc:
calls       badcalls     retrans     badxid      timeout     wait        newcred
8273        2            0           0           0           0           0

Client nfs:
calls       badcalls
8263        0
null        getattr      setattr     root        lookup      readlink    read
1 0%        24 0%        1 0%        0 0%        10123 0%    0 0%        5 0%
wrcache     write        create      remove      rename      link        symlink
0 0%        2 0%         0 0%        1 0%        0 0%        1 0%        0 0%
```

The output from nfsstat is useful for diagnosing connection problems. The value shown as badcalls shows the number of defective RPC message processed by the system. The values for nullrecv and badlen show the number of empty or incomplete messages. The value for xdrcall shows the number of errors in understanding messages.

For the client side, badxid shows the number of received messages that did not match with a sent request (based on the identification numbers). The timeout and retrans values show the number of times a message had to be resent. If these numbers are high, it usually means the connection is too slow or there is a fault with UDP. The wait value shows the number of times a process had to be delayed because of a lack of available ports.

These types of statistics are useful for configuring RPC properly. System administrators can adjust (tweak) values for the NFS system and monitor effects on performance over time.

Summary

The Network File System has a reputation for being complex and ornery. It is neither. Instead, NFS is an elegant solution to a problem and one in common usage. Today you have examined the concept and basic architecture of NFS, hopefully without getting bogged down in the details.

Q&A

Q In one sentence, tell what does NFS does?

A NFS enables an application to read and write files residing on remote machines as though they were on the local file system.

Q Define client and server as used in NFS.

A Despite complex definitions from the computer industry, this one is really easy. A client issues a request. The server answers it.

Q What is the role of RPC in NFS?

A The Remote Procedure Call protocol handles message exchange between NFS-based systems. It is a set of procedures that can be called by clients.

Q What does a port mapper do?

A The port mapper provides a correlation between the ports on a machine and the applications that use them.

Q What does the Kernel Lock Manager do?

A The Kernel Lock Manager is involved in file locking, preventing access to files or file systems. A file lock request is issued by clients when they want exclusive access to a file. The Kernel Lock Manager handles file lock requests.

Workshop

The Workshop provides quiz questions to help you solidify your understanding of the material covered. Some Workshop sections of this book also contain exercises to provide you with experience in using what you've learned. Try to understand the quiz and exercise answers before continuing on to the next chapter. Answers are provided in Appendix F, "Answers."

Quiz

1. Show how the NFS layers compare to the OSI Reference Model.

2. Explain how a port mapper assigns ports.

3. What is External Data Representation?

4. What does the Mount protocol do?

5. What is REX? What advantage does REX have over similar utilities?

10

TCP/IP and Networks

In the previous nine days, you have seen TCP/IP and its associated protocols covered in considerable depth. It is now time to begin looking at TCP/IP in a broader sense. Today you'll learn how TCP/IP can operate with other protocols in a networked system, as well as protocols that don't use TCP/IP but which are commonly encountered.

It is useful to understand how TCP/IP operates in conjunction with other protocols so the management of TCP/IP is clearer (you'll learn about managing a TCP/IP network in the next few days). You may find that some material today is repeated from earlier days, or rephrased slightly to present a different approach to the subject. In a sense, today acts as a summary, albeit incomplete, of the TCP/IP system as a whole.

To round out today, you'll look at the miscellaneous optional services provided through TCP/IP. Most are dedicated to a simple task, but they do serve their purpose well and use TCP/IP, hence their inclusion here.

TCP/IP and Other Protocols

TCP/IP is not often found as a sole protocol. It is usually one of a number of protocols used in any given network. Therefore, the interactions between TCP/IP (and its associated protocols) and the other protocols that may be working with it must be understood. It is easiest to begin looking at this subject from a local area network point of view, and then expand that view to cover internetworks.

The layers of a TCP/IP protocol, as well as most other OSI-model protocols, are designed to be independent of each other, allowing mixing of protocols. When a message is to be sent over the network to a remote machine, each protocol layer builds on the packet of information sent from the layer above, adding its own header and then passing the packet to the next lower layer. After being received over the network (packaged in whatever network format is required), the receiving machine passes the packet back up the layers, removing the header information one layer at a time.

Replacing any layer in the protocol stack requires that the new protocols can interwork with the other layers, as well as perform all the required functions of that layer (for example, duplicating the services of the replaced protocol). Also, performing duplicate operations in more than one layer (redundant operations) is to be avoided for obvious reasons.

To examine the interworking of the layers and the substitution or addition of others, a simple installation can be used as a starting point. Figure 10.1 shows a simple layered architecture using TCP and IP with the Ethernet network. Figure 10.1 also shows the assembly of Ethernet packets as they pass from layer to layer.

Header or Tail

Figure 10.1. *A simple layered architecture.*

As you saw earlier in this book, the process begins with a message of some form from an upper layer protocol (ULP) that itself is passing a message form an application. As the message is passed to TCP, it adds its own header information and passes to the IP layer, which does the same. When the IP message is passed to the Ethernet layer, Ethernet adds its own information at the front and back of the message and sends the message out over the network.

> **Note:** The operating system itself is not a single layer, but runs throughout the entire layered architecture with connections to each layer. The interfaces between the operating system layer's protocols differ depending on the host machine, but it is convenient to ignore the operating system's influence.

Although this simple model may seem ideal, in practice it has a few problems. Most importantly, it requires IP to interface directly with the Ethernet layer. This interface is not a clean one, but has many connections that break from the ideal layered architecture.

LAN Layers

To expand on the layered system requires a better understanding of the interfaces to the network layer in a local area network. Figure 10.2 shows an expanded layer architecture for a LAN. This type of architecture applies for collision sense multiple access (CSMA) and collision detect (CD) networks such as Ethernet.

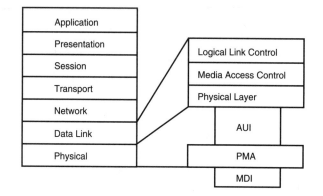

Figure 10.2. *LAN architecture.*

The LAN involves some additional layers. The Logical Link Control (LLC) layer is an interface between the IP layer and the network layers. There are several kinds of LLC configurations, but it is sufficient at this point to know its basic role as a buffer between the network and IP layers, either as a simple system for a connectionless service or as an elaborate system for connection-based service. LLC is usually used with the High-Level Data Link Control (HDLC) link standard. For connectionless service, this uses an *unnumbered information* (UI) message frame, while connection-based services can use the *asynchronous balanced mode* (ABM) message frame, both supported by HDLC. The configuration of LLC with respect to TCP/IP is important.

The Media Access Control (MAC) layer was mentioned briefly on Day 2. MAC is responsible for managing traffic on the network, such as collision detection and transmission times. It also handles timers and retransmission functions. MAC is independent of the network medium but is dependent on the protocol used on the network.

The Physical layer in the LAN architecture is composed of several services. The Attachment Unit Interface (AUI) provides an attachment between the machine's physical layer and the network medium. Typically, the AUI is where the network ports or jacks are located.

The Medium Attachment Unit (MAU) is composed of two parts: the Physical Medium Attachment (PMA) and the Medium Dependent Interface (MDI). The MAU is responsible for managing the connection of the machine to the LAN medium itself, as well as providing basic data integrity checking and network medium monitoring. The MAU has functions that check the signal quality from the network and test routines for verifying the network's correct operation.

When these layers are added to the layered architecture for a protocol stack, the IP-Ethernet layer is separated. This is shown in Figure 10.3. This type of configuration is more common than the one shown in Figure 10.1 and is usually called the IP/802 configuration (because Ethernet is defined by the IEEE 802 specification).

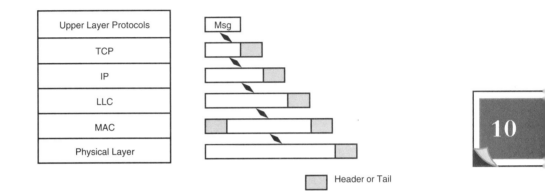

10

Figure 10.3. *TCP/IP with LLC/MAC.*

The IP/802 LAN can be connectionless using a simple form of LLC called LLC Type 1, which supports unnumbered information (UI). The LLC and MAC layers help separate IP from the Physical layer. There are more headers added to the message packet, but these have useful information. The LLC header has both source and destination service access points (SAP) to identify the layers above.

UDP is frequently used instead of TCP in this type of network. UDP is not as complex as TCP, so the entire network's complexity is reduced. However, UDP has no message integrity functionality built in, so a different form of LLC (called LLC Type 2) is used, which implements these functions. LLC Type 2 provides the data integrity functionality that TCP usually provides, such as sequencing, transfer window management, and flow control. The disadvantage is that these functions are now below the IP layer, instead of above it. Fatal problems with the LLC layer can result in problems that must be dealt with in the application layer itself.

> **Note:** The differences between TCP and LLC Type 1, versus UDP and LLC Type 2, must be carefully weighed by a system administrator. The TCP/LLC 1 combination is more complex than UDP/LLC 2 but offers excellent reliability and integrity, while UDP/LLC 2 is better for high-throughput networks. In some cases, UDP/LLC 2 results in duplicated functions, because the LLC versions differ considerably amongst vendors.

NetBIOS and TCP/IP

A popular PC-oriented LAN uses NetBIOS, which can be cleanly integrated with TCP/IP. Figure 10.4 shows the network architecture for this kind of LAN. NetBIOS resides above the TCP or UDP protocol, although it usually has solid links into that layer (so the two layers cannot be cleanly separated). NetBIOS connects applications together in the upper layers, providing messaging and resource allocation.

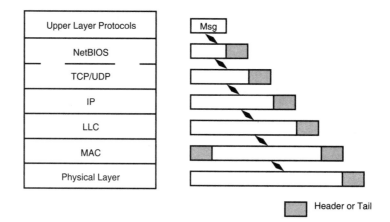

Figure 10.4. *The NetBIOS LAN architecture.*

Three Internet port numbers are allocated for NetBIOS. These are for the NetBIOS name service (port 137), datagram service (port 138), and session service (port 139). There is also the provision for a mapping between Internet's Domain Name Service (DNS) and the NetBIOS Name Server (NBNS). (DNS was covered in detail yesterday.) The NetBIOS Name Server is used to identify PCs that operate in a NetBIOS area. In the interface between NetBIOS and TCP, a mapping between the names is used to produce the DNS name.

IP can be configured to run above NetBIOS, eliminating TCP or UDP entirely and running NetBIOS as a connectionless service. In this case, NetBIOS takes over the functions of the TCP/UDP layer and the upper layer protocols must have the data integrity, packet sequencing, and flow control functions. This is shown in Figure 10.5. In this architecture, NetBIOS encapsulates IP datagrams. It is necessary for strong mappings to exist between IP and NetBIOS so that NetBIOS packets reflect IP addresses. (To do this, NetBIOS codes the names as IP.*nnn.nnn.nnn.nnn*.)

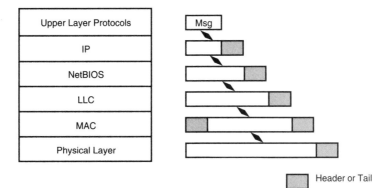

| Upper Layer Protocols |
| IP |
| NetBIOS |
| LLC |
| MAC |
| Physical Layer |

Msg

Header or Tail

Figure 10.5. *Running IP above NetBIOS LAN.*

This type of network requires that the upper layer protocols handle all the necessary features of the TCP protocol, but the advantage is that the network architecture is simple and efficient. For some networks, this type of approach is well-suited, although the development of suitable ULPs can be problematic at times.

XNS and TCP/IP

The Xerox Network System (XNS) was widely used in the past and still retains a reasonable percentage of network use. XNS is popular because Xerox released the code to the public domain, hence making it a cost-effective network system. In most cases, XNS protocols were designed to work with Xerox's Ethernet, too. XNS now appears in several commercial network software packages.

XNS can use IP, as shown in Figure 10.6. The Sequenced Packet Protocol (SPP) is above the IP layer, providing some TCP function, although it is not as complete a protocol. In the ULP layer is the Courier protocol, which provides presentation and session layer services.

XNS uses the term *Internet Transport Protocols* to refer to the set of protocols used, including IP. Among the protocols is the Routing Information Protocol (RIP) and an error protocol similar to the Internet Control Message Protocol (ICMP).

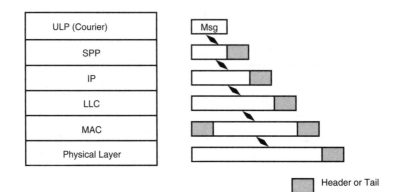

Figure 10.6. *The XNS network architecture.*

IPX and UDP

Novell's Netware networking product has a protocol similar to IP called the Internet Packet Exchange (IPX), which is based on Xerox's XNS. The IPX architecture is shown in Figure 10.7. IPX usually uses UDP for a connectionless protocol, although TCP can be used when combined with LLC Type 1.

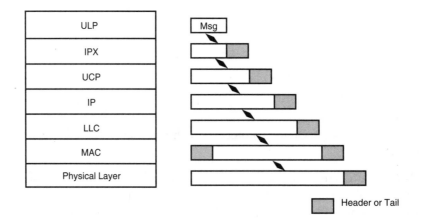

Figure 10.7. *The IPX LAN architecture.*

The stacking of the layers (with IPX above UDP) ensures that the UDP and IP headers are not affected, with the IPX information encapsulated as part of the usual message process. As with other network protocols, a mapping is necessary between the IP Address and the IPX addresses. IPX uses a network and host number of 4 and 6 bytes, respectively. These are converted as they are passed to UDP.

It is possible to reconfigure the network to use IPX networks by using TCP instead of UDP, and substituting the connectionless LLC Type 1 protocol. This results in the architecture shown in Figure 10.8. When using this layer architecture, IP addresses are mapped using ARP.

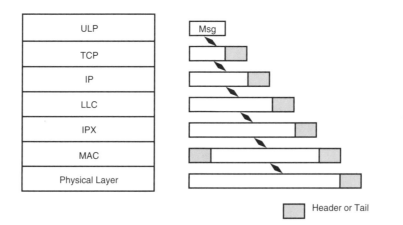

Figure 10.8. *An IPX-based LAN architecture.*

ARCnet and TCP/IP

ARCnet is widely used for LANs and has an Internet RFC for using it with IP. The architecture is similar to that of the IPX-based network except with ARCnet replacing IPX, as shown in Figure 10.9. Messages passed down from IP are encapsulated into ARCnet datagrams.

A special placement of the IP datagram behind the client data area of the ARCnet header ensures that IP compatibility is maintained if the message must pass out of the ARCnet network (through a converter, of course). IP addresses are mapped to ARCnet addresses using ARP. The protocol also supports RARP to some extent.

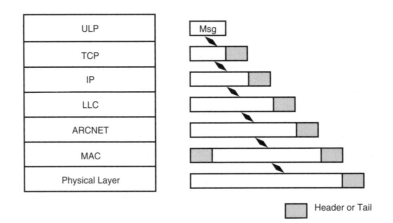

Figure 10.9. *The ARCnet-based LAN architecture.*

FDDI Networks

The Fiber Distributed Data Interface (FDDI) is an ANSI-defined, high-speed network that uses fiber-optic cable as a transport medium. FDDI is gaining string support because of the high throughout that can be achieved. For TCP/IP, FDDI uses a layered architecture like the other networks discussed. FDDI differs slightly from other media in that there are two sublayers for the physical layer.

FDDI's addressing scheme is similar to other Ethernet networks, requiring a simple mapping, as seen with the Ethernet system. IP and ARP can both be used over FDDI. IP is used with the LLC Type 1 connectionless service.

The frame size for FDDI is set to 4,500 bytes, including the header and other framing information. After that is taken in to account, there are 4,470 bytes available for data. (The Internet RFC for FDDI defines 4,096 bytes for data and 256 bytes for header layers above the MAC layer.) This large packet size can cause problems for some gateways, so routing for FDDI packets must be carefully chosen to prevent truncation or corruption of the packet by a gateway that can't handle the large frame size. In case of doubt, FDDI packets should be reduced in size to 576 data bytes.

X.25 and IP

X.25 networks modify the network architecture by using an OSI TP4 layer on top of IP and the X.25 Packet Layer Procedures (PLP) layer below IP. This is shown in Figure

10.10. TP4 is a TCP-like protocol that does not use port identifiers. The destination and source fields in the header are the *transport service access points* (TSAPs). TP4 is more complex than TCP, which sometimes works against it.

Figure 10.10. *The X.25-based LAN architecture.*

X.25 is not often used on a LAN, but it is used as a connection to a packet-switched network. An Internet RFC defines the rules for X.25 IP-based packet switching, including the limits to IP datagram sizes (576 bytes) and virtual circuits.

ISDN and TCP/IP

The Integrated Services Digital Network provides packet-switched TCP/IP networks. The architecture is shown in Figure 10.11. IP is not in the stack because it is usually incorporated into CLNP. (Both TCP and IP can be used with ISDN instead of OSI TP4 and CLNP, but the ISDN versions are optimized for that network.)

ISDN uses a more complex architecture that most networks, replacing gateways and routers with *terminal adapters* and *ISDN nodes*. These perform the equivalent functions but have a more rigidly (and complex) internal architecture. The details are not relevant here, so the interested reader should read a good ISDN book.

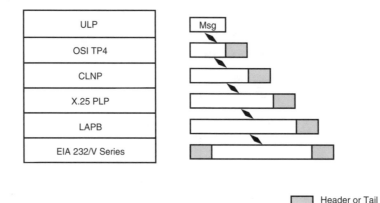

Figure 10.11. *The ISDN-based LAN architecture.*

Switched Multi-Megabit Data Services and IP

The Switched Multi-Megabit Data Services (SMDS) system is a public, packet-switched connectionless service that provides high throughput with large packet sizes (up to 9,188 data bytes). SMDS uses a subscriber-to-network and network-to-subscriber access mechanism for flow control. SMDS works with IP by interfacing the SMDS to the LLC layer.

SMDS using IP supports multiple logical IP subnetworks (LISs), which can be managed separately but are treated as a single unit by SMDS. This method does require all the subnetworks to have to same IP address. The architecture of the SMDS layers are quite complex, so they are not covered in detail here. SMDS uses LLC Type 1 frames.

Asynchronous Transfer Mode (ATM) and BISDN

Two new protocols for high-speed internetworks that are becoming popular are Asynchronous Transfer Mode (ATM) and Broadband ISDN (BISDN). The architecture on the user's machine is similar to the TCP/IP architectures discussed previously, although additional layers can be added to provide new services such as video and sound capabilities.

The router, gateway, or other device that accesses the high-speed network is more complex, too. Called a *terminal adapter* (as with ISDN), it provides a sophisticated interface between user layers and adaptation layers, which are application-specific. From the terminal adapter, traffic is passed to the ATM service, which provides switching and multiplexing services.

Optional TCP/IP Services

TCP/IP networks can offer a number of optional services that users and applications can make use of. All these optional services have strict definitions for their protocols. These optional services and their assigned port numbers are shown in Table 10.1.

Table 10.1. Optional TCP/IP services.

Service	Port	Description
Active Users	11	Returns the names of all users on the remote system
Character Generator	19	Returns all printable ASCII characters
Daytime	13	Returns the date and time, day of the week, and month of the year
Discard	9	Discards all received messages
Echo	7	Returns any messages
Quote of the Day	17	Returns a quotation
Time	37	Returns the time since January 1, 1900 (in seconds)

Active Users

The Active Users service returns a message to the originating user, which contains a list of all users currently active on the remote. The behavior of the TCP and UDP versions is the same. When requested, the Active Users service monitors port 11 and, upon establishment of a connection, responds with a list of the currently active users and then closes the port. UDP sends a datagram, whereas TCP uses the connection itself.

Character Generator

The Character Generator service is designed to send a set of ASCII characters. Upon receipt of a datagram (the contents of which are ignored), the character generator service returns a list of all printable ASCII characters. The behavior of the TCP and UDP versions of the character generator are slightly different.

The TCP character generator monitors port 19, and upon connection ignores all input and sends a stream of characters back until the connection is broken. The order of characters is fixed. The UDP character generator service monitors port 19 for an incoming datagram (remember UDP doesn't create connections) and responds with a datagram containing a random number of characters. Up to 512 characters can be sent.

Although this service may seem useless, it does have diagnostic purposes. It can ensure that a network can transfer all 95 printable ASCII characters properly, and also can be used to test printers for their ability to print all the characters.

Daytime

The Daytime service returns a message with the current date and time. The format it uses is the day of the week, month of the year, day of the month, time, and the year. Time is specified in *HH*:*MM*:*SS* format. Each field is separated by spaces to enable parsing of the contents.

Both TCP and UDP versions monitor port 13 and, upon receipt of a connection of datagram, return the message. The Daytime service can be used for several purposes, including setting system calendars and clocks to minimize variations. It also can be used by applications.

Discard

The Discard service simply discards everything it receives. TCP waits for a connection on port 9, while UDP receives datagrams through that port. Anything incoming is ignored. No responses are sent.

The Discard service may seem pointless, but it can be useful for routing test messages during system setup and configuration. It also can be used by applications in place of a discard service of the operating system (such as `/dev/null` in UNIX).

Echo

The Echo service returns whatever it receives. It is called through port 7. With TCP, it simply returns whatever data comes down the connection, whereas UDP returns an identical datagram (except for the source and destination addresses, of course). The echoes continue until the port connection is broken or no datagrams are received.

The Echo service provides very good diagnostics about the proper functioning of the network and the protocols themselves. The reliability of transmissions can be tested this way, too. Turnaround time from sending to receiving the echo provides useful measurements of response times and latency within the network.

Quote of the Day

The Quote of the Day service does as its name implies. It returns a quotation from a file of quotes, randomly selecting one a day when a request arrives on port 17. If a source file of quotations is not available, the service fails.

Time

The Time service returns the number of seconds that have elapsed since January 1, 1990. Port 37 is used to listed for a request (TCP) or receive an incoming datagram (UDP). When a request is received, the time is sent as a 32-bit binary number. It is up to the receiving application to convert the number to a useful figure.

The Time service is often used for synchronizing network machines, or for setting clocks within an application.

Using the Optional Services

As already mentioned, the optional services can be accessed from an application. Users can directly access the service of choice (assuming it is supported) by using Telnet. A simple example is shown here:

```
$ telnet merlin 7
Trying...
Connected to merlin.tpci.com
Escape character is '^T'.
This is a message
This is a message
Isn't this exciting?
Isn't this exciting?
<Ctrl+T>
$ telnet merlin 13
```

```
Trying...
Connected to merlin.tpci.com
Escape character is '^T'.
Tues Jun 21 10:16:45 1994
Connection closed.
$ telnet merlin 19
!"#$%&'()*+,-./0123456789:;<=>?@ABCDEFGHIJKLMNOPQRSTUVWXYZ[[\]^_abcdefg
"#$%&'()*+,-./0123456789:;<=>?@ABCDEFGHIJKLMNOPQRSTUVWXYZ[[\]^_abcdefgh
#$%&'()*+,-./0123456789:;<=>?@ABCDEFGHIJKLMNOPQRSTUVWXYZ[[\]^_abcdefghi
$%&'()*+,-./0123456789:;<=>?@ABCDEFGHIJKLMNOPQRSTUVWXYZ[[\]^_abcdefghij
%&'()*+,-./0123456789:;<=>?@ABCDEFGHIJKLMNOPQRSTUVWXYZ[[\]^_abcdefghijk
&'()*+,-./0123456789:;<=>?@ABCDEFGHIJKLMNOPQRSTUVWXYZ[[\]^_abcdefghijkl
'()*+,-./0123456789:;<=>?@ABCDEFGHIJKLMNOPQRSTUVWXYZ[[\]^_abcdefghijklm
<Ctrl+T>
$
```

In this example, a connection to port 7 starts an Echo session. Everything typed by the user is echoed back immediately, unchanged. Then a connection to port 13 provides the Daytime service, showing the current date and time. The connection is broken by the service once the data is sent. Finally, the character generator is started. Both the echo and character generator services were terminated with the Telnet break sequence of Ctrl+t.

Summary

Today, you've covered a lot of material, mostly about the way TCP/IP can interact with other networking systems and protocols. By combining TCP/IP with existing networks, the advantages of both can be gained, as well as having compatibility with a wide range of TCP-based devices.

You also have looked at several protocols that round out the TCP/IP family. These are basic services, but they are essential to the proper operation of a TCP/IP-based network.

Q&A

Q What is the role of the Media Access Control (MAC) layer in a network architecture?

A The MAC handles traffic for the network, including collisions and timers. The MAC is independent of the network's physical medium, but its exact role and implementation depend on the network protocols.

Q What is the difference between LLC Type 1 and LLC Type 2?

A Logical Link Control (LLC) Type 1 is a simpler form that supports unnumbered information, designed for TCP. LLC Type 2 is for UDP and offers message integrity functionality.

Q What is XNS?

A XNS is the Xerox Network System, a networking design that Xerox released to the public domain. Since XNS is essentially free, it has gained a lot of support. XNS supports Ethernet.

Q What is ISDN?

A The Integrated Services Digital Network is a packet-switched, high-speed network that supports broadband (many-channel) communications.

10

Q Why is a simple network protocol like the character generator supported?

A As simple as it may be, the character generator protocol (and many others like it) are used for basic tasks and queries that would require much more complex coding and operations when performed as part of a larger protocol. The character generator protocol is useful for testing communications. It is small, fast, easy to implement, and easy to understand.

Workshop

The Workshop provides quiz questions to help you solidify your understanding of the material covered. Some Workshop sections of this book also contain exercises to provide you with experience in using what you've learned. Try to understand the quiz and exercise answers before continuing on to the next chapter. Answers are provided in Appendix F, "Answers."

Quiz

1. What components make up a Medium Attachment Unit (MAU), and what are their roles?

2. What is FDDI? Why is it popular?

3. What is the role of the Discard service?

4. The Time protocol is often used by network devices. What is its role?

5. Does the presence of a second network protocol (like IPX) affect the basic TCP/IP protocol suite's operations?

11

Setting Up A Sample TCP/IP Network: UNIX Hosts

Today's and tomorrow's lessons show how TCP/IP is installed and configured on a sample network. This book uses the Santa Cruz Operation's SCO UNIX as an example of a UNIX implementation. The process will be similar for other UNIX versions, although configuration procedures and information may change. UNIX and TCP/IP are intertwined closely, because the original implementations of TCP/IP were for UNIX systems. TCP/IP was developed for the BSD UNIX version that originated at the University of California at Berkeley, and much of the language of TCP/IP is hooked into the BSD versions. SCO UNIX, though, is an AT&T System V Release 4 version of UNIX that provides some compatibility with BSD UNIX.

Tomorrow, you'll look at two DOS implementations (for DOS and Microsoft Windows) of TCP/IP and see how they communicate to the SCO UNIX servers set up today.

Most of the material covered today will be familiar if you have read through the book in order. Some of it is summarized and shown again for quick reference, as well as for those who read out of order. If you get lost, consult the index for a pointer to more information.

Sample Configuration

For today's text, a dedicated TCP/IP network has been created to show the steps in setting up, configuring, and testing a basic TCP/IP implementation. The network relies on an SCO UNIX server (running SCO's Open Desktop, an X interface to UNIX) connected over an Ethernet network to a second SCO UNIX system and two DOS-based PCs. One PC will run DOS while the other runs Microsoft Windows 3.11. A Hewlett-Packard LaserJet will be treated as a common printing device for the entire network, configured so print requests from any machine can be sent to it.

Each of the four machines has its own name and IP address. For this sample network, the IP address mask has been randomly chosen as 147.120. The names of the machines have been chosen from the author's pets (although any unique name could do, of course). The sample network configuration is shown in Figure 11.1.

The physical setup of the network is undertaken first. It involves installing a network interface card in each machine, ensuring that its jumpers for interrupt vector and memory I/O address do not conflict with any other card in the system. All of the boards used in this system are from different manufacturers, to show the independent nature of the network.

Figure 11.1. *Sample TCP/IP network.*

Cable must be run between all the machines, connecting the network interface cards together. In the case of Ethernet, the cables must be properly terminated. The sample network uses thin Ethernet, which closely resembles television coaxial cable. Thin Ethernet connectors resemble a *T*, with cables attached to both ends of the *T* and the stem connected to the network card. Two of the machines form the ends of the cable and require a terminator as part of their *T*.

To test the physical network, it is easiest to wait until basic software configuration has been completed before sending simple packets. If problems exist, the physical network will be the first to be checked. Some network monitoring devices can supply integrity information prior to installing the network, but these devices are not usually available to system administrators who are just beginning their installation, or who have a small number of machines to maintain.

Configuring TCP/IP Software

This section follows through the configuration of the TCP/IP software. The discussion applies equally to the UNIX and DOS machines on the sample network, as it would to any other type of machine (such as a Macintosh). Filenames may change with some operating systems, but the general approach remains valid.

Most operating systems and TCP/IP software packages include several utilities with menu-driven scripts that help automate the installation process. Some operating systems still require manual configuration of several files using a text editor. To properly configure TCP/IP software, you must know several pieces of information before you start. The necessary information is as follows:

Domain name: The name the entire network will use.

System name: The unique name of each local machine.

IP address: The full address of each machine.

Driver type: Each interface to the network must be associated with a device driver, instructing the operating system how to talk to the device.

Broadcast address: The address used for network-wide broadcasts.

Netmask: The network mask that uniquely identifies the local network.

Hardware network card configuration information: The interrupt vector and memory address of the network card.

The system domain name is necessary if the network is to be connected to other machines outside the local network. Domain names can be invented by the system administrator. If, however, the network is to interface with Internet or one of its service providers, the domain name should be approved by the Network Information Center (NIC). Creating and registering a new domain is as simple as filling in a form. Domain names usually reflect the company name, with the extension identifying the type of organization. The sample network uses the name `tpci.com` (the author's consulting company).

As seen earlier in this book, the machine name is used for symbolic naming of a machine instead of forcing the full IP address to be specified. The system name must be unique on the local network. Other networks may have machines with the same name; but their network masks are different, so there is no possible confusion during packet routing. In most cases, system names are composed of eight characters (or less) and are usually all lowercase characters (in keeping with UNIX tradition for lowercase). The system name can be a mix of characters and numbers. Larger organizations tend to number their machines, and small companies give their machines more familiar names.

The device driver instructs the operating system on how to communicate with the network interface (usually either a network card or a serial port). Each interface has its own specific device driver. Most operating systems have device drivers included in their distribution software, although some require software supplied with the network card. There are generic public domain drivers available for most network cards on bulletin board systems.

With most operating systems, there are limits to the number of similar devices that are supported. SCO UNIX, for example, allows up to four Ethernet cards, two Token Ring adapters, four Serial Line Internet Protocol (SLIP) lines, and four Point to Point Protocol (PPP) lines. These limits should be enough for a machine on any network! The sample network uses dedicated Ethernet network cards from four different manufacturers, purchased off-the-shelf at a local office supply store.

The network card configuration must be known in order to install the device driver properly. Network cards usually have several configuration settings, depending on the system for which they are designed. For the PC-based machines in the sample network, each card must have a unique interrupt vector (called an IRQ) and a unique I/O memory address.

Most network cards come with default settings that may conflict with other cards in the system. Users must carefully check for conflicts, resorting to a diagnostic program, if one is available. UNIX users have several utilities available, depending on the operating system. SCO UNIX and similar systems have the utility hwconfig, which shows the current hardware configuration. The following example shows the hwconfig output and the output from the command with the -h option to provide "long" formatting with headers (making it is easier to read):

```
$ hwconfig
name=fpu vec=13 dma=- type=80387
name=serial base=0x3F8 offset=0x7 vec=4 dma=- unit=0 type=Standard nports=1
name=serial base=0x2F8 offset=0x7 vec=3 dma=- unit=1 type=Standard nports=1
name=floppy base=0x3F2 offset=0x5 vec=6 dma=2 unit=0 type=96ds15
name=floppy vec=- dma=- unit=1 type=135ds18
name=console vec=- dma=- unit=vga type=0 12 screens=68k
name=adapter base=0x2C00 offset=0xFF vec=11 dma=- type=arad ha=0 id=7 fts=st
name=nat base=0x300 offset=0x20 vec=7 dma=- type=NE2000 addr=00:00:6e:24:1e:3e
name=tape vec=- dma=- type=S ha=0 id=4 lun=0 ht=arad
name=disk vec=- dma=- type=S ha=0 id=0 lun=0 ht=arad fts=stdb
name=Sdsk vec=- dma=- cyls=1002 hds=64 secs=32
$
$ hwconfig -h
device          address       vec  dma  comment
======          =======       ===  ===  =======
fpu                -           13    -   type=80387
serial          0x3f8-0x3ff    4    -   unit=0 type=Standard nports=1
serial          0x2f8-0x2ff    3    -   unit=1 type=Standard nports=1
floppy          0x3f2-0x3f7    6    2   unit=0 type=96ds15
floppy             -           -    -   unit=1 type=135ds18
console            -           -    -   unit=vga type=0 12 screens=68k
adapter         0x2c00-0x2cff 11    -   type=arad ha=0 id=7 fts=st
nat             0x300-0x320    7    -   type=NE2000 addr=00:00:6e:24:1e:3e
tape               -           -    -   type=S ha=0 id=4 lun=0 ht=arad
disk               -           -    -   type=S ha=0 id=0 lun=0 ht=arad fts=stdb
Sdsk               -           -    -   cyls=1002 hds=64 secs=32
```

This output is from one of the SCO UNIX servers set up for the sample network. It has the network Ethernet card already configured as device nat, which uses IRQ 7 (shown under the vec or interrupt vector column). The nat line also shows the memory address as 300-320 (hexadecimal) and the device driver as NE2000 (a Novell NetWare-compatible driver). The address and vec column show no conflicts between the settings used for the Ethernet card and other devices on the system. (The adapter entry is for a high-speed SCSI-2 card, which controls both the tape and the Sdsk devices. The latter is the primary SCSI hard drive. All other entries should be self-explanatory.)

DOS users can use the Microsoft Diagnostic utility, MSD.EXE, or one of several third-party tools such as Central Point PC Tools or The Norton Utilities to display IRQ vectors and memory addresses in use by the system. Some software will even indicate which vectors and addresses are available for use.

There is no need to have the same IRQ and memory address for each card, because the network itself doesn't care about these settings. The IRQ and memory addresses are required for the machine to communicate with the network interface card only. The sample network used a different IRQ and memory address on each machine.

IRQ and memory addresses are usually set on the network interface card itself using either jumpers on pins or a DIP-switch block. The documentation accompanying the card should provide all the information necessary for setting these values. Some recently introduced network interface cards can be configured through software, allowing its settings to be changed without removing the card from the system. This can be very handy when a user is unsure of the best settings for the card.

The IP address is a 32-bit number that must be unique for each machine. If the network is to be connected to the Internet, the IP address must be assigned by the NIC (when you register your domain name). Even if no access to the Internet is expected, problems with arbitrarily assigning an IP address can occur when messages are passed with other networks. If the network will not be connected to the outside world, a system administrator can ignore the NIC's numbering system and adopt any IP address. It is worthwhile, though, to consider future expansion and connection to other networks.

The NIC has set four classes of IP addresses in use, depending on the size of the network. Each class has some addresses that are restricted. These are shown in Table 11.1. Most networks are Class B, although a few large corporations require Class A networks.

Table 11.1. The NIC IP address classes.

Class	Network Mask Bytes	Number of hosts per network	Valid addresses
A	1	16,777,216	1.0.0.1 to 126.255.255.254
B	2	65,534	128.0.0.1 to 191.255.255.254
C	3	254	224.0.0.0 to 255.255.255.254
D	reserved		

The network mask is the IP address stripped of its network identifiers, leaving only the local machine address. For a Class A network, this will strip 1 byte, whereas a Class B network will strip 2 bytes (leaving 2). The small Class C network will strip 3 bytes as the network mask, leaving 1 byte to identify the local machine (hence the limit of 254 machines on the network). The sample network is configured as a Class B machine with the randomly chosen IP address network mask of 147.120 (not NIC-assigned).

The broadcast address identifies packets that are to be sent to all machines on the local network. Because most network cards ignore any incoming packets that don't have a specific IP address in them, a special broadcast address can be set that the card will intercept in addition to locally destined messages. The broadcast address has the host portion (the local machine identifiers) set to either all 0s or all 1s, depending on the convention followed. For convenience, the broadcast address' network mask is usually the same as the local network mask.

Broadcast addresses may seem simple because there are only two possible settings. Such addresses, however, commonly cause problems because conflicting settings are used on a network. BSD UNIX used the convention of all 0s for releases 4.1 and 4.2, and 4.3BSD and AT&T UNIX moved to all 1s for the broadcast address. The Internet standard specifies all 1s as the broadcast address. If problems are encountered on the network with broadcasts, check all the configurations to ensure they are using the same setting. The sample network uses an all 1s mask for its broadcast address.

The steps followed for configuring TCP/IP are straightforward, generally following the information required. The configuration steps are as follows:

Link drivers: TCP/IP must be linked to the operating system's kernel to enable TCP/IP to be run when the system boots.

Add host information: Provides a list of all hosts on the network (used for name resolution).

Establish routing tables: Provides the information for routing packets properly if name resolution isn't sufficient.

Set user access: Configures the system to allow access in and out of the network, as well as establishing permissions.

Remote device access: Configures the system for access to remote printers, scanners, CD-ROM jukeboxes, and other shared network devices.

Configure the name domain server: If using a distributed address lookup system such as Berkeley Internet Name Domain Server (BIND) or NIS, complete the name server files. (This step is necessary only if using BIND or a similar service.)

Tune system for performance: Since a system running TCP/IP has different behavior than one without TCP/IP, some system tuning is usually required.

Configure NFS: If the network file system (NFS) is to be used, configure both the file system and the user access.

Anonymous FTP: If the system is to allow anonymous FTP access, configure the system and public directories for the service.

You will use these steps (not necessarily in the sequence given) as the individual machines on the network are configured. The processes are different with each operating system, but the overall approach remains the same.

UNIX TCP/IP Configuration

SCO UNIX provides several configuration utilities to help provide information for TCP/IP and to link the driver into the kernel correctly. This does not eliminate the need to manually edit the many configuration files and supply information about the other machines on the network. Most of the information in this section, although specific to SCO UNIX, is generally applicable to most operating systems.

Most UNIX systems have a main server machine that starts the network processes. The machine is sometimes called a *super server,* because any machine that runs network processes and accepts requests from other machines is a server. UNIX uses the process `inetd` (Internet daemon) as the master server for all network processes listed in the configuration files. Hardware configuration requires linking information about the network card and protocol to the operating system kernel. The configuration is sometimes called a *chain*. The process is usually automated by a script file, requiring users to provide the interrupt vector number, the I/O memory address, and the type of card. The device driver for that network card will then be rebuilt into the kernel so the driver is active whenever the system boots.

On SCO UNIX systems, a utility called `netconfig` is used, prompting the user for the three pieces of information and then rebuilding the kernel. The process is repeated for each network card on a machine. (The sample network has only one card each.) When started, `netconfig` presents the user with this screen:

```
$ netconfig
Currently configured chains:
  1. nfs->sco_tcp
     nfs         SCO NFS Runtime System for SCO Unix
     sco_tcp     SCO TCP/IP for UNIX
  2. sco_tcp->lo0
     sco_tcp     SCO TCP/IP for UNIX
     lo0         SCO TCP/IP Loopback driver
Available options:
  1. Add a chain
  2. Remove a chain
  3. Reconfigure an element in a chain
  q. Quit
Select option: Please enter a value between 1 and 3 ('q' to quit):
```

Since a TCP/IP device driver is being added, option 1 is selected. Some users confuse the first configured chain in the list with a TCP/IP driver for the network and attempt to reconfigure it. The first driver listed in the previous output is a default value for NFS and should be left alone.

After indicating that a new chain is to be added, the system asks for the type of chain:

```
Num    Name       Description
  1.   lmxc       SCO LAN Manager Client
  2.   nfs        SCO NFS Runtime System for SCO UNIX
  3.   sco_ipx    SCO IPX/SPX for UNIX
  4.   sco_tcp    SCO TCP/IP for UNIX
Select top level of chain to Add or 'q' to quit:
```

Option 4 is chosen since you are installing TCP/IP. (LAN Manager and IPX/SPX are used for integration with DOS-based networks. The NFS Runtime System is added later if NFS is to be used on the network.)

The `netconfig` utility then presents a list of several dozen network interface cards for which the system has default values. If the card installed in the system is shown, the entry for the card is chosen. If the card is not on the list, a compatible entry must be found. This sometimes requires digging through the network interface card's documentation for emulation or compatible values, or contacting the manufacturer. Drivers are usually available for Ethernet cards.

11

The system then prompts for the IRQ the card is set for, followed by the memory address. After these are entered, the operating system creates the necessary entries in its internal configuration files to include the device driver for the network card. As a final step, the system asks if the user wants to rebuild and relink the kernel. This must be done if the new drivers are to be effective. After a system reboot, the drivers are active and can be tested with the `ping` command.

The UNIX TCP/IP networking software relies on several files for configuration. These are summarized in Table 11.2. Remember that filenames may change with different implementations of the UNIX operating system, but the configuration information will be consistent.

Table 11.2. TCP/IP UNIX configuration files.

File	Description
/etc/hosts	Host names
/etc/networks	Network names
/etc/services	List of known services
/etc/protocols	Supported protocols
/etc/hosts.equiv	List of "trusted" hosts
/etc/ftpusers	List of "unwelcome" FTP users
/etc/inetd.conf	List of servers started by `inetd`

For the sample network, modifying these files is quite easy. All the sample files in this section are shown relative to the primary server machine called freya.

The `/etc/hosts` file contains the names of the four machines and their network addresses. The file looks like this:

```
#      @(#)hosts    1.2 Lachman System V STREAMS TCP   source
#      SCCS IDENTIFICATION
147.120.0.1        localhost tpci
147.120.0.1        freya freya.tpci.com
147.120.0.2        merlin merlin.tpci.com
147.120.0.3        pepper pepper.tpci.com
147.120.0.4        sinbad sinbad.tpci.com_
```

Each line contains the local machine name and its full name with the domain listed. This helps resolve any variation in specifying the name. As new machines are added to the network, new lines are added to the file. The local machine has two entries in the file, one for the official name and one for localhost. Either name can be used, although localhost is usually used for testing through the loopback driver.

The /etc/networks file holds a list of network names. This lets you name networks in the same way as machines. Most small networks don't modify this file unless they are communicating with other networks on a regular basis. The following example shows some of the SCO network machines. The sample network has no subnetworks that need specifying, but another two networks that make up part of tpci.com are added. (The sample network's subnetwork address—the third number—is 0, and the other two subnetworks specified in this file have the values 2 and 3.)

```
#       @(#)networks 1.2 Lachman System V STREAMS TCP   source
#       SCCS IDENTIFICATION
loopback        127
sco             132.147
sco-hq          132.147.128
sco-mfg         132.147.64
sco-engr        132.147.192
sco-slip        132.147.32
sco-tcplab      132.147.160
sco-odtlab      132.147.1
tpci-dev        147.120.2
tpci-acct       147.120.3
```

The /etc/services file includes information about all the TCP and UDP services supported by the system. For the sample network and most small networks, the default values are acceptable. These entries are changed only if a service is being removed from TCP/IP, such as to prevent Telnet access. The file looks like this:

```
#       @(#)services 5.1 Lachman System V STREAMS TCP   source
#
#    System V STREAMS TCP - Release 4.0
# Network services, Internet style
#
echo            7/tcp
echo            7/udp
discard         9/tcp           sink null
discard         9/udp           sink null
systat          11/tcp          users
daytime         13/tcp
daytime         13/udp
netstat         15/tcp
qotd            17/tcp          quote
chargen         19/tcp          ttytst source
chargen         19/udp          ttytst source
ftp             21/tcp
telnet          23/tcp
smtp            25/tcp          mail
time            37/tcp          timserver
time            37/udp          timserver
rlp             39/udp          resource        # resource location
nameserver      42/tcp          name            # IEN 116
whois           43/tcp          nicname
```

```
domain          53/tcp      nameserver     # name-domain server
domain          53/udp      nameserver
mtp             57/tcp                     # deprecated
bootps          67/udp      bootps         # bootp server
bootpc          68/udp      bootpc         # bootp client
tftp            69/udp
rje             77/tcp      netrjs
finger          79/tcp
link            87/tcp      ttylink
supdup          95/tcp
hostnames      101/tcp      hostname       # usually from sri-nic
tsap           102/tcp      osi-tp0 tp0
#csnet-cs      105/?
pop            109/tcp      postoffice
sunrpc         111/tcp
sunrpc         111/udp
auth           113/tcp      authentication
sftp           115/tcp
uucp-path      117/tcp
nntp           119/tcp      readnews untp  # USENET News Transfer Protocol
ntp            123/tcp
ntp            123/udp
nb-ns          137/udp        nbns netbios-nameservice
nb-ns          137/tcp        nbns netbios-nameservice
nb-dgm         138/udp        nbdgm netbios-datagram
nb-dgm         138/tcp        nbdgm netbios-datagram
nb-ssn         139/tcp        nbssn netbios-session
snmp           161/udp
snmp-trap      162/udp
bgp            179/tcp
#
# UNIX specific services
#
exec           512/tcp
biff           512/udp      comsat
login          513/tcp
who            513/udp      whod
shell          514/tcp      cmd            # no passwords used
syslog         514/udp
printer        515/tcp      spooler        # line printer spooler
talk           517/udp
ntalk          518/udp
efs            520/tcp                     # for LucasFilm
route          520/udp      router routed  # 521 also
timed          525/udp      timeserver
tempo          526/tcp      newdate
courier        530/tcp      rpc
conference     531/tcp      chat
netnews        532/tcp      readnews
netwall        533/udp                     # -for emergency broadcasts
uucp           540/tcp      uucpd          # uucp daemon
remotefs       556/tcp      rfs_server rfs # Brunhoff remote filesystem
pppmsg         911/tcp                     # PPP daemon
listen        1025/tcp      listener RFS remote_file_sharing
nterm         1026/tcp      remote_login network_terminal
ingreslock    1524/tcp
```

The `/etc/hosts.equiv` file controls access from other machines. The `/etc/ftpusers` file prevents unauthorized logins with specific user names. Both files are examined in more detail in the sections titled "User Equivalence" and "Anonymous FTP," later today.

The `/etc/inetd.conf` file, mentioned earlier, controls the processes started by the `inetd` daemon when the system boots. The default `inetd.conf` file is fine for the sample system and seldom requires modification. The file appears as follows:

```
#       @(#)inetd.conf    5.2 Lachman System V STREAMS TCP   source
#
#     System V STREAMS TCP - Release 4.0
#
#       SCCS IDENTIFICATION
ftp         stream   tcp  nowait   NOLUID   /etc/ftpd        ftpd
telnet      stream   tcp  nowait   NOLUID   /etc/telnetd     telnetd
shell       stream   tcp  nowait   NOLUID   /etc/rshd        rshd
login       stream   tcp  nowait   NOLUID   /etc/rlogind     rlogind
exec        stream   tcp  nowait   NOLUID   /etc/rexecd      rexecd
finger      stream   tcp  nowait   nouser   /etc/fingerd     fingerd
#uucp       stream   tcp  nowait   NOLUID   /etc/uucpd       uucpd
# Enabling this allows public read files to be accessed via TFTP.
#tftp       dgram    udp  wait     nouser   /etc/tftpd       tftpd
comsat      dgram    udp  wait     root     /etc/comsat      comsat
ntalk       dgram    udp  wait     root     /etc/talkd       talkd
#bootps     dgram    udp  wait     root     /etc/bootpd      bootpd
echo        stream   tcp  nowait   root     internal
discard     stream   tcp  nowait   root     internal
chargen     stream   tcp  nowait   root     internal
daytime     stream   tcp  nowait   root     internal
time        stream   tcp  nowait   root     internal
echo        dgram    udp  wait     root     internal
discard     dgram    udp  wait     root     internal
chargen     dgram    udp  wait     root     internal
daytime     dgram    udp  wait     root     internal
time        dgram    udp  wait     root     internal
smtp        stream   tcp  nowait   mmdf     /usr/mmdf/chans/smtpd smtpd /usr/mmdf/
                                            chans/smtpsrvr smtp
```

With the files set up as shown and the daemons properly loading, TCP/IP and UDP should both be active and available. Most operating systems require a reboot after any changes to the kernel or some configuration files, so modifications to the TCP/IP files should be followed by system resets.

When the system boots, the TCP/IP daemons should be listed in the startup messages shown on the console. Any errors in the daemon startups are shown on the display or mailed to the system administrator. Usually, these error messages are cryptic but at least indicate the presence of a problem (which is better than you worrying about configuration information when the daemon is at fault).

Testing the TCP/IP configuration is straightforward. Begin by using ping on each machine to ensure that the software is talking to the network hardware. Unfortunately, a successful ping of the local machine does not always mean the network is being accessed properly; it simply means the network software is processing the request. To test the network interface itself, ping the other machines on the network. In this example, freya is the local host and pepper is a DOS machine running FTP Software's PC/TCP:

```
$ ping freya
PING localhost (147.120.0.1): 56 data bytes
64 bytes from localhost (147.120.0.1): icmp_seq=0 ttl=255 time=0 ms
64 bytes from localhost (147.120.0.1): icmp_seq=1 ttl=255 time=0 ms
64 bytes from localhost (147.120.0.1): icmp_seq=2 ttl=255 time=0 ms
64 bytes from localhost (147.120.0.1): icmp_seq=3 ttl=255 time=0 ms
64 bytes from localhost (147.120.0.1): icmp_seq=4 ttl=255 time=0 ms
— localhost ping statistics —
5 packets transmitted, 5 packets received, 0% packet loss
round-trip min/avg/max = 0/0/0 ms
$ ping pepper
PING pepper (147.120.0.3): 56 data bytes
64 bytes from localhost (147.120.0.1): icmp_seq=0 ttl=255 time=20 ms
64 bytes from localhost (147.120.0.1): icmp_seq=1 ttl=255 time=20 ms
64 bytes from localhost (147.120.0.1): icmp_seq=2 ttl=255 time=50 ms
64 bytes from localhost (147.120.0.1): icmp_seq=3 ttl=255 time=30 ms
64 bytes from localhost (147.120.0.1): icmp_seq=4 ttl=255 time=40 ms
— pepper ping statistics —
5 packets transmitted, 5 packets received, 0% packet loss
round-trip min/avg/max = 20/32/50 ms
```

The first test shows that the software is configured properly. The command to ping freya resulted in a conversion within the /etc/hosts file to recognize the instruction as the localhost entry. After verifying the local connection, the remote machine is tried. The successful round trip of the packets indicates that the remote is working properly, too, and that the network is functional.

If the localhost ping command failed, the software was probably incorrectly configured, or the hardware was not accessed properly. First check the connectors on the network cards, because they have an annoying habit of working loose. Next check the network configuration (IRQ, address, and type of adapter), followed by the configuration files, as shown earlier. If everything looks correct and the remote machine answers its own ping command properly, there is a problem with software compatibility.

The netstat network status command is useful for monitoring the network's performance and detecting problems. TCP/IP system administrators frequently use the options -i, -m, and -s are. See Day 13 for more troubleshooting information.

A common problem is the lack of enough STREAMS buffers, which causes a process to hang or a connection to terminate for no apparent reason. The size of the STREAMS buffer and its current status can be checked with the command netstat -m.

```
$ netstat -m
streams allocation:
                        config   alloc    free   total     max    fail
streams                    292      78     214     145      79       0
queues                    1424     360    1064     327     364       0
mblks                     5077     197    4880    3189     206       0
dblks                     4062     197    3865    3167     205       0
class 0,    4 bytes        652      51     601     357      53       0
class 1,   16 bytes        652       1     651     284       3       0
class 2,   64 bytes        768       8     760    2158      15       0
class 3,  128 bytes        872     104     768     237     106       0
class 4,  256 bytes        548      21     527      90      22       0
class 5,  512 bytes        324      12     312      13      13       0
class 6, 1024 bytes        107       0     107       1       1       0
class 7, 2048 bytes         98       0      98       1       1       0
class 8, 4096 bytes         41       0      41      26       1       0
total configured streams memory: 1183.09KB
streams memory in use: 44.66KB
maximum streams memory used: 58.28KB_
```

The number under the `fail` column should be 0 in each row, otherwise there is a problem with the amount of buffers allocated. To change the number of STREAMS buffers allocated, kernel variables must be changed and the kernel relinked. As a general rule, if there are problems with the existing STREAMS buffer sizes, increase the number by 50 percent. If that doesn't solve the problem, increase by another 50 percent.

To fully test the TCP/IP system use Telnet or FTP to log in, and transfer files from machine to machine. Because these two utilities are the most common users of TCP/IP (unless NIS or NFS are active), they will help show any problems with the port assignments, services provided, or name mapping.

Pseudo ttys

UNIX uses pseudo ttys (false terminals) to allow external machines to use Telnet and `rlogin` for access to the local machine. Without a pseudo tty, the remote machine will not be able to establish a session.

The SCO UNIX system configures 32 pseudo ttys by default, which should be plenty for small and moderate sized networks. (Remember that 32 pseudo ttys allows 32 sessions from remote users.) Adding or deleting pseudo ttys can be done through a configuration utility or with the `mkdev ptty` command. There is no useful advantage gained by drastically reducing the number of pseudo ttys on small networks. Pseudo ttys should be reconfigured after TCP/IP has been installed and is working correctly.

User Equivalence

User equivalence lets a user `rlogin` to another machine with the same account information, without entering a password. This is helpful when a user must log in to another machine frequently, avoiding the login process for speed and reducing the number of processes running on the remote.

To permit user equivalence, UNIX requires that the user exists on both machines and that entries in two configuration files match. The `/etc/passwd` file, which controls overall access to the machine, must have an entry for the user's login name on both machines. One of two configuration files also must have information about the user.

If the file `.rhosts` were used, user equivalence would be established only for accounts specifically named in the file. The `.rhosts` file usually resides in the root directory and has one entry per line, specifying the remote machine name and the user ID. A `.rhosts` file looks like this:

```
# .rhosts file for tpci.com
merlin tparker
merlin ychow
merlin bsmallwood
pepper etreijs
pepper tparker
freya rmaclean
```

With this configuration, the user `tparker`, on remote machine `merlin`, could log in to the local machine as `tparker` only. A user can allow access to an account by other by creating a `.rhosts` file in his or her home directory.

If the file `hosts.equiv` were used (which usually resides in the `/etc` directory), user equivalence would be valid for any account on both machines except root. If the file `hosts.equiv` contained only a machine name, any valid user on that machine would be allowed user equivalence (except root). The machine is called a *trusted* host.

Unfortunately, this type of access poses considerable security problems, so it should be used only under stringently controlled or very reliable conditions. A major problem is that a user can log in as any other valid user on the remote system without using a password. A sample `hosts.equiv` file looks like this:

```
# hosts.equiv for tpci.com
merlin tparker
pepper
freya rmaclean
```

In this example, any user on the remote system (`pepper`) could log in as any valid user (except root) on the local machine, without using a password. Only the user `tparker`, on the remote machine `merlin`, could log in as any valid system user (except root) on the local machine. The potential for misuse of user equivalence with this type of access is high, although it can be handy for access to specific utilities or applications.

If both `.rhosts` and `hosts.equiv` exist with entries for the same machine or machine and user IDs, the entry from the `hosts.equiv` file would be used for determining the user's equivalence. Remember that for both the `.rhosts` and `hosts.equiv`, matching user entries must exist in the `/etc/passwd` file.

User equivalence configuration can cause problems for system administrators, which are frequently blamed on the network software. Also, some users may want to allow specific entries by a user on a remote system, without having the system administrator grant open privileges.

To illustrate the entries more clearly, a concrete example may help. Assume user `ychow`, on the machine `pepper`, wants to access machine `merlin` as both `ychow` and `shortie` without using passwords. (In other words, `ychow` on `pepper` is equivalent to `ychow` and `shortie` on `merlin`.) There are several methods of configuring the system to allow this. The system administrator can create an `.rhosts` file in the root directory that has the following entries:

```
pepper ychow
pepper shortie
```

This only allows `ychow` (on `pepper`) to log in as `ychow`, though, with no access as `shortie` unless `shortie` is logged in to `pepper`, too. This isn't what is required. An entry in the `hosts.equiv` file like this:

```
pepper ychow
```

doesn't solve the problem either because `ychow` can now log in as any valid user on `merlin`. Solving this requires that each user that wants to allow `ychow` to access his or her directories place an `.rhosts` file in their home directories. On the sample network, both `ychow`'s and `shortie`'s home directories on `merlin` would have the same entries.

User `ychow` can now log in to `merlin` using one of the following commands:

```
rlogin merlin
rlogin merlin -l shortie
```

The latter command logs `ychow` in as the user equivalent `shortie`. The first retains the same login ID. Note that the `.rhosts` file resides in the home directories of the users who want to allow remote user access.

11

Anonymous FTP

Anonymous FTP enables users from other locations to access a system without logging on. They obtain the FTP prompt as usual but enter **anonymous** as the user name. In most systems, a password can be anything, although convention dictates that the user's login name be supplied for tracking purposes. There is no check of the names, however. Once logged in to anonymous FTP, users can browse through public directories are retrieve files that reside there. Anonymous FTP is excellent for distributing information to the general public, but its open access has accompanying security concerns.

When a user logs into the anonymous FTP account, UNIX invokes a process called chroot, which restricts the user from moving out of the home directory. The dependence on chroot requires that some system configuration files (including a copy of the /etc/passwd and /etc/group files) reside in the anonymous FTP directories.

Configuring a UNIX system for anonymous FTP involves establishing a public directory system and changing file permissions to prevent unwanted access to other parts of the file system. Also, an anonymous account is created using the user name ftp. Anonymous FTP usually uses the user ftp home directory created when the user is generated.

To set up anonymous FTP access, create a user called ftp. With UNIX systems, this is usually performed with a script called mkuser or a system utility. Alternatively, the user can be added to the /etc/passwd file. A group called ftp should exist or be created. Once the home directory for the user ftp exists, change its user and group identifies to ftp (using the chown and chgrp commands).

Assuming the user ID ftp has been created and the home directory is /usr/ftp, the steps to follow are shown here. (Comments shown after the pound sign (#) are for description purposes only and need not be entered.)

```
$ cd /usr/ftp    # change to the home directory
$ chmod 555 .    # set file permissions to r-x
$ chown ftp .    # change the owner to ftp
$ chgrp ftp .    # change the group to ftp
$ mkdir pub      # create public directory (see below)
$ chmod 777 pub  # set pub dir permissions as rwx
$ mkdir bin      # create bin dir for executables
$ cd bin
$ chmod 555 bin  # set bin dir to r-x
$ cp /bin/sh /bin/ls .
$ cd ..
$ mkdir etc      # create etc dir for passwd file
$ chmod 555 etc  # set etc dir to r-x
$ cd etc
$ cp /etc/passwd /etc/group .
$ chmod 444 passwd group
$ cd ..
```

If you want to create subdirectories beneath the home directory for the anonymous user to access, ensure that the user has the correct ownership, too. It is common practice to create a directory called ftp/pub for uploading files to the system. Set file permissions so that the user cannot exit the home directory structure. In the previous example, all the directories except pub were set to read and execute only. The example copied the shell and listing utilities into the FTP directory structure so the anonymous user could access them. Other utilities can be copied if desired.

The /etc/passwd and /etc/group files must be copied into a directory called etc (below the FTP user home directory) to allow chroot to function properly. It is strongly recommended that these files be edited to remove any other user information; it is conceivable that an anonymous user could access and analyze the files for information about the local system, leading to an unwelcome break-in. Remove all users from the /etc/passwd file except for root, daemon, uucp, and the ftp entries. Similarly, prune the /etc/group file to remove all but these entries.

To help prevent unwanted access, the file etc/ftpusers can be created that contains user names that result in immediate disconnection. This file should have entries for root and uucp as a minimum.

SLIP and PPP

Serial Line Internet Protocol (SLIP) and Point-to-Point Protocol (PPP) operate over serial lines and require some additional information. Since SLIP and PPP connections are between two machines, the source and destination IP addresses are needed. Also, the serial port identifier is needed, including the interrupt vector it uses. Serial lines must be properly configured with their baud rates. This is usually set within another file on the system. SLIP connections also require a netmask setting, although this is not needed for PPP.

PPP is more versatile than SLIP. SLIP supports asynchronous communications only, whereas PPP allows synchronous and asynchronous communications. SLIP must have a dedicated line that is always tied up, whereas PPP can share the line with other programs like UUCP and free the line on command. SLIP lacks any error detection, and PPP implements it. Given the choice, PPP is the better serial-line TCP protocol, although it is not available with all operating system implementations.

SLIP and PPP connections are established in the same manner as the TCP/IP kernel. SCO UNIX uses the netconfig utility, mentioned previously. When adding a SLIP or PPP chain, the system prompts for the serial line to be used, the baud rate, the addresses of the local and destination machines, and the remote machine's name. It then configures the system to use that serial port. After relinking the kernel and rebooting, the serial line is available for either SLIP or PPP (depending on the way it was configured).

BIND

The Berkeley Internet Name Domain (BIND) system is supported by SCO UNIX. Like DNS, BIND answers queries about clients, providing names and IP addresses. BIND has the same types of servers as DNS (discussed in Day 9):

> *Primary master server:* Loads data from its filesystem; can delegate authority to other servers

> *Secondary master server:* Gets data and authorization from the primary master server

> *Cache-only server:* Caches information it receives; can answer queries if it has information, otherwise defers to master servers

> *Remote server:* A workstation or small machine with a limited amount of memory; doesn't function as a primary server

> *Slave server:* Forwards queries it cannot handle to a master server; may maintain a small database

In a typical network with Internet access, there may be one master server. Depending on the size of the network, secondary servers may be added. Slave servers are usually found only on very large networks or those with subnetworks.

When it boots, the master server loads several configuration files and the main database. The BIND process, called *named*, reads the boot file usually called /etc/named.boot, which contains information about the type of server the system is, the location of the initial data, and the zones it has authority over. A primary server has a line in the boot file that looks like this:

```
directory    /usr/local/lib/named
```

The first field on the line indicates that the machine is the primary server, the second is the zone over which it has control, and the last field is the name of the file that contains host information.

A secondary server starts up in the same way, except it waits for permission from the primary server to start handling BIND requests. The configuration file is similar, and looks like this:

```
secondary  tpci.com   147.120.0.1
```

The first and second fields indicate that the machine is a secondary server with control over the specified domain. The rest of the line specifies the address of the primary server for the zone. There may be more than one primary server, in which case all the addresses are listed on the line. With multiple primary servers available, each one is tried in order for data.

Cache-only servers have a line in the configuration file that specifies its type, domain, and the name of the cache file it uses:

```
cache   .   root.cache
```

In this case, it handles the local system with a file called `root.cache` as the database.

There are three files involved in BIND name resolution. The file `named.local` gives addresses for the local loopback interface (localhost). The `named.hosts` file contains information about all the machines in the zone. The `named.rev` file is used for address-to-name resolution using IN-ADDR-ARPA. The file gives the domain in that format.

BIND uses standard resource records, such as DNS. (See Day 9.) The full details of these records are beyond the scope of this discussion, so interested readers should refer to the system documentation.

Remote Printing

Remote printing is a useful feature that enables a user on one machine to send print jobs to other machines that have attached printers. The system is called Remote Line Printing (RLP) and is commonly used to share printers in a workgroup. It also is useful for allowing access to specialty printers such as color lasers and plotters. RLP does not support printer classes, and some operating systems impose restrictions on supported print-command-line options. Remote administration of printers is not supported.

RLP functions differently than normal UNIX printing. When a print request is issued, the system consults the printer configuration file (usually `/etc/printcap`) to determine whether the printer is local or remote. If the print request is for a local printer, the usual process applies. If the request is for a remote printer, the local system spools the print request and invokes the `lpd` daemon, which packages the print request and sends it to the remote machine where it is spooled for the printer. A user can set a remote printer as the default destination, as is commonly done in workgroups that share a single printer.

There are several versions of RLP available with support for different operating systems on a network. SCO UNIX, for example, supports two kinds of clients: SCO-based systems and 4.3BSD systems. This enables workstations running Berkeley's 4.3BSD to queue print requests to SCO print servers. SCO clients use RLP with the same commands as a local printer would (`lp` and `cancel`), but 4.3BSD clients have special versions of the commands (`lpr` and `lprm`).

Assuming RLP is available with your operating system (some versions of UNIX do not support it), it is usually installed and activated with a script or utility program. With SCO UNIX, a `mkdev rlp` command will initiate the installation script. Other operating systems use a similar utility. During the installation process, a number of directories are created to handle the spooling, and modifications are made to the printer configuration files. The old printing commands are archived to a directory, and new versions that support RLP are copied into their place.

Remote printing requires a special entry in the printer configuration file (`/etc/printcap`). Some operating systems (such as SCO UNIX) have a script that will edit the file for you, prompting for the configuration information. A sample line in the file for a remote printer would look like this:

```
hplaser::lp=:rm=main_hplaser:rp=hplaser:sd=/usr/spool/lpd/hplaser
```

The first field is the name used by the local machine to refer to the printer. The second field is usually empty. It defines the name of an error log file but is not used on most systems. The third field is the device name for a local printer. Remote printers leave the field as `lp=` with no specified printer. The fourth field is the network name for the printer. It can be the same as the local name. The fifth field is the name the print server uses for the printer (usually the same as the local name). Finally, the sixth field is the name of the spooling directory for the printer. This is where print requests are spooled before being sent to the remote printer.

In order for machines on the network to access the Hewlett-Packard LaserJet that is attached to the main machine on the sample network, the three remote machines should have entries for the printer in their `/etc/printcap` files. The main machine will also have an entry for it, but as a local printer.

Administering a remote printer is done either by logging in to the console of the machine to which the printer is attached, or using a number of RLP utilities from another machine. The utilities differ with each operating system.

Configuring SNMP

Most TCP/IP networks use the Simple Network Management Protocol (SNMP) to monitor the network for problems. It enables a system to examine and alter networking information maintained by other machines on the network. SNMP is a simple protocol that uses UDP as a transport.

Many UNIX operating systems use a daemon to run SNMP. When the system is running, SNMP listens on its dedicated port for incoming requests. There are usually three configuration files involved.

The file /etc/snmpd.conf contains basic information required by SNMP. The file contains identifiers for the types of SNMP and TCP/IP software, as well as the contact name of the system administrator and the location of the system. A sample file looks like this:

```
# snmpd.conf configuration file for tpci.com
# the first two fields are default value
descr=SNMPD Version 4.0 for SCO UNIX
objid=SCO.1.0
contact=Tim Parker x53153
location=Network Room
```

If SNMP is set to send trap messages (asynchronous event messages), it will send introductory packets (called *cold-start* traps) to other systems that are functioning. It reads the names of the systems to send cold-start traps to from the file /etc/snmpd.trap, which lists names, IP addresses, and port numbers:

```
# sample snmpd.trap file for tpci.com
# lists symbolic name, IP address, and port
test1    128.212.64.99    162
merlin   147.120.0.2      162
```

The file snmpd.comm is a list of community and IP address pairs that specifies from whom the agent can accept queries. Each line in the file has the name of the community (sometimes called a session), the IP address of the site (a value of 0.0.0.0 allows any address to communicate), and the privileges that site allows. If the privilege is set to READ, only read operations are permitted. WRITE allows read and write operations, and NONE restricts all access.

```
# Copyrighted as an unpublished work.
# (c) Copyright 1989 INTERACTIVE Systems Corporation
# All rights reserved.
#       @(#)snmpd.comm    3.1 INTERACTIVE SNMP  source
test1 128.212.64.99 READ
test2 128.212.64.15 WRITE
test3 128.212.64.15 READ
public 0.0.0.0 read
beast 0.0.0.0 read
excaliber 0.0.0.0 read
```

Configuration of SNMP is usually through an interactive shell script. During the script, the user is prompted for all the information needed for the three configuration files. SCO UNIX uses the command mkdev snmp to install the system.

Configuring NFS

The Network File System (NFS) enables directories to be shared. A client can mount a directory from another server onto his or her own file system and work as though it were an integral part of the structure. NFS is often used when a large server holds software that should be available to many users, or with workstations that have only a small file system of their own.

NFS uses two daemons. The `mountd` daemon handles requests for mounting local file systems. The `nfsd` daemon handles the actual transfer of information between the mounted file system. Both NFS daemons use the Remote Procedure Call (RPC) feature of TCP/IP. Another daemon commonly found is `pcnfsd`, which is used by DOS machines that want to access NFS.

For a file system to be shared with other machines, it must be listed in the host's `/etc/exports` file. The file also includes the name or IP address of each machine that is allowed to mount the file system. A file to allow all machines on the sample network to mount `/usr/tpci_apps` and only one machine to mount `/usr/debuggers` would look like this:

```
# sample /etc/exports file for tpci.com
# no machine names means all have access
/usr/tpci_apps
/usr/debuggers      -access=merlin
```

A client can mount a file system during a session or have it mounted automatically when the system boots. To mount for a session only, the user mounts the server file system with the mount command. Upon reception of the request, the server checks the `/etc/exports` file to ensure that the client is allowed access to the file system, and if access is allowed, the mount is completed. Each client machine maintains a list of mounted file systems in a file usually called `/etc/mnttab`. When the file system is removed from the client file system using the unmount command, the corresponding entry in `/etc/mnttab` is removed.

To mount a file system automatically, the name of the remote file system is added to the file `/etc/default/filesys`. The format of this file is more complex than a simple mount command. A sample entry is as follows:

```
bdev=merlin:/usr/app_dir mountdir=/usr/mnt \
    fsck=no rcfsck=no rcmount=yes \
    mount=no fstype=NFS \
    nfsopts="soft,bg,intr"
```

The entry next to `bdev` specifies the remote file system to mount (in this case, `merlin:/usr/app_dir`). The `mountdir` entry indicates where to mount it on the local file system. The rest of the entry handles the way the machine mounts the file system. If `fsck` or rcfsck is set to yes, the file system is checked when the client mounts the file system or when the system enters multiuser mode, respectively. The rcmount entry indicates whether the mount is to be performed automatically when the system enters multiuser mode.

The mount entry indicates whether users can manually mount and unmount the file system. The fstype specifies the type of file system and usually must be set to NFS. The nfsopts line gives the options to use when mounting the system. The keyword soft means to attempt recovery after a server failure, bg means to allow repeated attempts to remount in the background if the mount didn't succeed immediately, and intr means to allow interrupts to function across the network. Some network cards require that sizes of transmission packets be specified in the mount command, too.

To allow client users to manually mount and unmount a file system, the /etc/default/filesys file must have mount=yes. NFS does not allow a mounted file system from a remote machine to be shared in turn by the local (that is, daisy-chained). It is advisable to ensure that users know how NFS works. They should not keep a file system mounted if they are not going to use it (because it ties up system resources and increases network traffic).

NFS requires that each user of NFS have a unique user ID across the network. Group IDs also must be unique across the entire network. The user ID and group ID numbers must be the same on all networked machines. This is the same approach used for user equivalence with rlogin, mentioned earlier in this section. The need for identical names and numbers can sometimes mean changing user ID and group IDs when NFS is added to an existing system. (This is also a good reason to use a network-wide password system such as NIS or Yellow Pages.)

Configuring NFS is relatively easy. The daemons that control NFS must be running, and the configuration files must allow access. Other than that, there is nothing special to be done. Starting the mountd daemon is usually contingent on the startup scripts finding the file /etc/exports. If the file exists, mountd is started; otherwise it is not started to save memory. The startup file for NFS is usually /etc/nfs.

The startup file also specifies the number of nfsd processes that should be started. One nfsd daemon should exist for each client request the machine is expected to handle. A final step is to start the exportfs process to export the file /etc/exports. The code for the mountd and nfsd daemons in the sample network's /etc/nfs file looks like this:

```
# start mountd and nfsd if /etc/exports exists
if [ -x /etc/exports ]
then
   echo " starting mountd\c"
     mountd
```

```
      echo " starting nfsd\c"
      nfsd 6
        /etc/exportfs -a
fi
```

This script starts six `nfsd` daemons. In most configuration files, these two steps already exist, most commonly as two different steps.

Configuring NIS

The Network Information Service (NIS) is used to allow access files to be shared across all machines on the network. It is very useful to have NIS implemented when NFS is active. The sample network implements a simple NIS system, requiring only one master server and no slaves. There is no complex NIS domain specification needed because of the small size of the network (but the domain name is still set in a configuration file).

NIS requires four daemons to be active. They are usually started as the machine enters multiuser mode. The daemons are as follows:

> `ypserv`: Handles requests for NIS information
>
> `ypbind`: Listens for NIS requests and sends them to `ypserv`
>
> `ypxfrd`: Handles requests from slaves
>
> `yppasswddd`: Handles password change requests

NIS divides users into two categories: local and distributed. Local users are maintained in the local password files (`/etc/passwd`) and can access only the local machine. Distributed users can access any machine on the NIS network and use the same user ID throughout (which is needed for NFS). Password information is maintained in three files under NIS:

> `/etc/passwd.yp`: Contains distributed user accounts
>
> `/etc/passwd.local`: Contains local user accounts
>
> `/etc/passwd`: Contains all active accounts (of both types)

The master NIS server will have an `/etc/passwd` file that has all the entries of the other two files. Slave servers would have the local file and a copy of the distributed accounts file from the master server. If a user is in both the local and distributed file, the information in the local file would take precedence (which may control startup shells or home directories, depending on where the user logged in).

Configuring NIS requires that the NIS files are in the search path and that the configuration files are set properly. A script is available with most operating systems to ensure that the information is correctly added and that the daemons are started properly. Several utilities are supplied for managing the NIS files.

SCO UNIX uses the command `mkdev nis` to configure the NIS server. When run, the script asks whether the machine is a master or a slave and then proceeds to set up the kernel drivers and NIS files. After ensuring that all the names of the domain and associated machines are correct, the kernel is rebuilt and, after a system reboot, NIS is active. Managing an NIS system requires some knowledge about NIS and the users of the local system (and is beyond the scope of today's text.)

Summary

Today you learned to install and configure SCO UNIX machines with TCP/IP. These methods have been tested and work correctly. In the process, today's text mentioned several alternate services such as anonymous FTP and remote printing. Whether these are available on your network is up to you (or the system administrator). Tomorrow, you'll learn about two DOS-based machines that you can add to your network.

Q&A

Q What information is necessary to configure a machine's TCP/IP software?

A For a complete configuration, TCP/IP requires the domain name, system name, IP address, driver type, broadcast address, netmask, and hardware network card settings. Some systems allow configuration with only some of this information.

Q What does the network mask do?

A The network mask removes the network identifier from an IP address, leaving only the local machine's address. For example, an IP address of `146.120.94.4` can have the network mask `146.120` applied to leave the local machine address `94.4`.

Q What role does the `/etc/inetd.conf` file play?

A The file `/etc/inetd.conf` indicates the processes started by the inetd daemon when a system boots.

Q Explain user equivalence.

A User equivalence lets a user access another machine without a password during the login process. It is controlled by a set of files controlled by the system or individual users.

Q Which two daemons does NFS require?

A NFS needs both `mountd` (to handle mounting requests for the local file system) and `nfsd` (to handle the transfer of information).

Workshop

The Workshop provides quiz questions to help you solidify your understanding of the material covered. Some Workshop sections of this book also contain exercises to provide you with experience in using what you've learned. Try to understand the quiz and exercise answers before continuing on to the next chapter. Answers are provided in Appendix F, "Answers."

Quiz

1. How many devices are allowed on a Class B network (the most common)?

2. What is the difference between the BSD UNIX TCP/IP broadcast address setting and the one normally used?

3. What is a pseudo tty?

4. What does the following `.rhosts` file do?

   ```
   # .rhosts
   artemis tparker
   artemis goof
   artemis aarmenakis
   mig rmaclean
   ```

5. What is anonymous FTP, and why would you use it?

Setting Up a
Sample TCP/IP
Network: DOS
Clients

Yesterday, the two UNIX machines on the sample network were configured. Both followed the same procedure and had similar configuration files. In this chapter, two DOS-based PCs are added. One machine runs DOS alone and will be configured using ftp Software's PC/TCP. The other runs Microsoft's Windows for Workgroups 3.11 and will use NetManage's Chameleon NFS.

Configuring DOS machines is different than the UNIX systems because of the change in file system, operating system architecture, and individual software vendor's approaches. However, the same basic information is required and the steps to adding DOS machines are analogous to those for a UNIX system.

Although this chapter specifically uses two commercial packages, the process will be similar with other vendors' TCP/IP products. The names of files and the exact configuration information may differ, but the same general principles will apply.

DOS-Based TCP/IP: ftp Software's PC/TCP

PC/TCP from ftp Software has been available for several years and has become a *de facto* standard for DOS machines that want to connect with a TCP/IP network. PC/TCP runs under both DOS and Windows. It lets a user perform all the TCP/IP functions, such as ftp and telnet, and includes software for several of the TCP family of protocols, including SNMP. Other machines can also access a PC running PC/TCP, copying its files.

PC/TCP can be run as a dedicated network, or it can piggyback on top of other networks, such as Windows for Workgroups or Novell NetWare. The system administrator will decide the nature of the network. For example, if a large Windows for Workgroups network already exists but a user wants access to a TCP/IP UNIX server, it may not make sense to convert the entire network to TCP/IP. In that case, either a second network card can be added specifically for the TCP/IP network, or TCP/IP can coexist with the Windows for Workgroups system. (Remember that TCP/IP isn't really particular about the network transport type.)

The sample network is TCP/IP-based, so PC/TCP will be installed to run on that network protocol. However, since it would be useful to be able to run Windows for Workgroups over the network between the two PC machines, the installation will take that possibility into consideration as well. TCP/IP and Windows for Workgroups can reside simultaneously on the network with one of two different setups.

The system can be set to enable Windows for Workgroups and TCP/IP packets to reside on the same network. With this approach TCP/IP sends out IP packets while Windows for Workgroups sends out NetBEUI (the default type). Both use NDIS (Network Device

Interface Specification) device drivers to communicate with the network card. The problem with this approach is that other machines receiving the packets may get confused because of two different packet types, and the system will not work well if an external network is to be accessed (such as Internet) because routers do not handle NetBEUI packets.

The alternative is to configure Windows for Workgroups to encapsulate its message within IP packets, which can then be sent across the internetwork and the local network between TCP/IP machines with no problems. This has a couple of useful advantages. The network is completely IP-based so routers can handle the traffic through internetworks, and also a Windows for Workgroups computer on another network can communicate through the router—making the Windows for Workgroups services more widely available. A receiving Windows for Workgroups machine would have to extract the information from the IP packet, but otherwise the systems works well.

The sample network is configured to enable both PC/TCP and Windows for Workgroups to coexist using NDIS drivers (the second alternative previously mentioned). This results in two software stacks—one for PC/TCP and one for Windows for Workgroups—coexisting and communicating with the NDIS driver. This structure is shown in Figure 12.1.

Figure 12.1. *PC/TCP and Windows for Workgroups stacks using NDIS.*

PC/TCP uses a kernel that is loaded into memory when DOS boots. (It is a Terminate and Stay Resident (TSR) program.) To ensure the network is available at all times, the kernel is usually added to the AUTOEXEC.BAT file. The sample network will use a kernel called ETHDRV.EXE, which is the Ethernet driver supplied with PC/TCP. (A different kernel must be used if the network is IEEE 802.3 Ethernet, which differs from the normal DIX Ethernet.) In addition, an NDIS Converter must be loaded as a device driver to provide NDIS-format packets to the protocol manager.

Installing PC/TCP

PC/TCP includes an automated installation procedure that copies the distribution media to the hard disk and sets up some of the configuration files. In this chapter, most of the system will be configured manually to show the necessary steps and to allow users to verify the changes made to system files by the installation program.

Installation of PC/TCP requires the same basic information as TCP/IP under UNIX: the device driver, the system's name and IP address, and the names and IP addresses of other systems that are to be accessed. The process begins with a properly installed network card. The IRQ and memory address of the card must be known and a device driver for it present for inclusion in the CONFIG.SYS file. Device drivers are usually supplied by the network card vendor, but generic drivers are also included with the PC/TCP software disks. They include drivers for the most popular types of network systems but may not include all possible cards and drivers.

After copying all the distribution files to the hard drive, the configuration can begin. The sample machine is running DOS 6.2 and Windows for Workgroups 3.11. Changes in either software release may affect the following details presented, but the PC/TCP installation instructions should be updated for new releases. When installing PC/TCP with Windows for Workgroups, the Windows network must be installed, configured, and running properly first.

During the installation process, PC/TCP requires a lengthy serial number and authentication key. These verify the software and prevent a network from using many copies of the same software when only one license has been purchased.

There are four files involved in the initial configuration:

CONFIG.SYS: Starts the device drivers for the network and PC/TCP

AUTOEXEC.BAT: Starts the PC/TCP kernel

PROTOCOL.INI: Defines the type of network and drivers

PCTCP.INI: Kernel parameters for PC/TCP

Yesterday, UNIX kernel parameter configuration was mentioned for fine-tuning the behavior of the operating system with TCP/IP. In some cases, this is necessary with the DOS PC/TCP system, too. A utility program called KAPPCONF enables the kernel parameters to be altered. The settings for the kernel are saved in a configuration file called PCTCP.INI.

AUTOEXEC.BAT Commands

The `AUTOEXEC.BAT` file requires environment variables to be set and two instructions added. One instruction starts the network while the other loads the Ethernet driver. The sample machine already had Windows for Workgroups installed, so there was a line that read

```
C:\WINDOWS\NET START
```

which started the network. (The drive assignments for all the examples in this chapter may be different on other systems, of course, as might the installation directories. Installation defaults were used throughout this chapter for both PC/TCP and Windows for Workgroups. Change their values as needed.) The `NET START` command can remain in place, or be replaced with a PC/TCP command called `netbind`, which accomplishes the same thing for NDIS drivers. If both commands are in the `AUTOEXEC.BAT` file, an error message will result when the second network startup command is executed.

The following line must be added to the `AUTOEXEC.BAT` file:

```
C:\PCTCP\ETHDRV
```

which starts the PC/TCP Ethernet driver. If another network system is being used, this would be replaced with the device driver for that network (such as IEEEDRV for IEEE 802.3 Ethernet or SLPDRV for SLIP).

It is useful to define two environment variables in the `AUTOEXEC.BAT` file for the PC/TCP software to use when searching for file. One is a simple addition to the `PATH` command, adding the PCTCP installation directory to the search path. The second is an environment variable that points to the `PCTCP.INI` file. The two declarations look like this:

```
SET PCTCP=C:\PCTCP\PCTCP.INI
SET PATH=C:\PCTCP;%PATH%
```

The latter change to the `PATH` command adds C:\PCTCP to an already defined `PATH`. An alternative would be to edit the `PATH` command to include the directory on the same line as the rest of the declaration. The PC/TCP software can be run without these environment variables defined, but problems with file locations may result if commands are not executed from the installation directory.

Therefore, the completed `AUTOEXEC.BAT` file should have either of the following four-line combinations in them:

```
SET PCTCP=C:\PCTCP\PCTCP.INI
SET PATH=C:\PCTCP;%PATH%
C:\WINDOWS\NET START
C:\PCTCP\ETHDRV
```

or

```
SET PCTCP=C:\PCTCP\PCTCP.INI
SET PATH=C:\PCTCP;%PATH%
C:\PCTCP\NETBIND
C:\PCTCP\ETHDRV
```

When these lines are executed, the system will display status messages. The NETBIND command displays this message if it loads successfully:

```
MS-DOS LAN Manager v2.1 Netbind
Microsoft Netbind version 2.1
```

A third line may display a status message about the interrupt vector used by the system. If NETBIND couldn't load correctly, it generates a message like this:

```
MS-DOS LAN Manager v2.1 Netbind
Error: Making PROTMAN IOCTL call.
```

This usually is generated when the network is already running (such as from a NET START command issued before the NETBIND command).

The ETHDRV command displays a message with status information when it loads successfully. It looks like this:

```
MAC/DIS converterFTP Software PC/TCP Resident Module 2.31    01/07/94 12:38
Copyright (c) 1986-1993 by FTP Software, Inc.  All rights reserved.
Patch level 17637
Patch time: Fri Jan 07 14:25:09 1994
Kernel interrupt vector is 0x61
Code Segment occupies 49.0K of conventional memory
Data Segment occupies 19.5K of conventional memory
Packet Driver found at vector 0x60
      name:
      version: 30, class: 1, type: 57, functionality: 6
ifcust (PC/TCP Class 1 packet driver - DIX Ethernet) initialized
5 free packets of length 1514, 5 free packets of length 160
The Resident Module occupies 68.7K of conventional memory
```

If there is an error when the ETHDRV program loads, it generates an error message (or varying utility). A sample error is shown here:

```
FTP Software PC/TCP Resident Module 2.31    01/07/94 12:38
Copyright (c) 1986-1993 by FTP Software, Inc.  All rights reserved.
Patch level 17637
Patch time: Fri Jan 07 14:25:09 1994
PC/TCP is already loaded (interrupt 0x61). Use 'inet unload' to unload it.
```

This error occurred because a PC/TCP driver had been loaded prior to the ETHDRV command.

Some users like to leave these commands out of the AUTOEXEC.BAT file and issue them manually. This has the advantage of reducing the amount of memory chewed up when the machine boots and the network is not required. A useful compromise is to create a small batch file that has these two commands and then run the batch file only if the network is used. Both NETBIND and ETHDRV do not seem to be critical when they are loaded (some software insists on being loaded first or last).

CONFIG.SYS Commands

The CONFIG.SYS file has to have drivers loaded for the protocol manager, the NDIS packet converter, and the network card driver. Systems running Windows for Workgroups may require additional drivers. The CONFIG.SYS file must have an entry setting the number of files open at one time to at least 20. If this doesn't exist, PC/TCP will crash. Add the line

```
FILES=20
```

to the CONFIG.SYS file. Depending on the amount of memory available, the number could be readily increased. With 8MB RAM, a value of 40 is satisfactory.

The protocol manager is supplied as part of Windows for Workgroups, and there is one included with the PC/TCP software package. The choice is the system administrator's. If Windows for Workgroups 3.1 (not 3.11) was already loaded and functional, CONFIG.SYS will have a line similar to this:

```
DEVICE=C:\WINDOWS\PROTMAN.DOS /I:C:\WINDOWS
```

The protocol manager is not always used with the Windows for Workgroups 3.11 release because it is included with other drivers within the CONFIG.SYS file (such as IFSHLP.SYS). If there is no protocol manager started at boot time, one should be added from the PC/TCP software. The entry within the CONFIG.SYS file is

```
DEVICE=C:\PCTCP\PROTMAN.DOS \I:C:\PCTCP
```

which loads the PC/TCP protocol manager. The \I at the end of the command tells the driver where to look for files (in this case the PC/TCP installation directory).

A network card driver should appear next in the CONFIG.SYS. This will differ for each network card, but for the sample network's Intel EtherExpress 16 network card, the line is

```
DEVICE=C:\WINDOWS\EXP16.DOS
```

This loads the EXP16 driver for the Intel network card. This was included with the Windows for Workgroups software but is also available as a generic driver. Some machines with Windows for Workgroups already installed may have this command already in the CONFIG.SYS file.

The final step is to load the PC/TCP NDIS Packet Converter. The current release of PC/TCP uses a packet converter called DIS_PKT.GUP. The line looks like this:

```
DEVICE=C:\PCTCP\DIS_PKT.GUP
```

Some systems running Windows for Workgroups 3.1 (and a few that have upgraded to 3.11) will have the line

```
DEVICE=C:\WINDOWS\WORKGRP.SYS
```

in the CONFIG.SYS file. This is for Windows for Workgroups and is not necessary if the PC/TCP is to be used as a DOS-based system only. If the file was not installed by Windows for Workgroups (and the system worked properly without it), there is no need to add it.

When the system boots, the device drivers will be loaded in turn. Each displays a short message showing its version number. Any errors that occur will also be displayed. Usually the device drivers don't cause any problems.

The properly configured CONFIG.SYS file should have these lines in it:

```
DEVICE=C:\WINDOWS\PROTMAN.DOS /I:\C:\WINDOWS
DEVICE=C:\WINDOWS\EXP16.DOS
DEVICE=C:\PCTCP\DIS_PKT.GUP
```

if it is using the Windows for Workgroups protocol manager, or these lines if using the PC/TCP protocol manager:

```
DEVICE=C:\PCTCP\PROTMAN.DOS /I:\C:\PCTCP
DEVICE=C:\WINDOWS\EXP16.DOS
DEVICE=C:\PCTCP\DIS_PKT.GUP
```

As noted earlier, the network interface driver (EXP16) will be different if the machine does not use the Intel EtherExpress 16 board.

The position within the CONFIG.SYS file of the device drivers isn't critical, although there may be problems if they are loaded into high memory with other drivers. Experimentation is the only way to find the most memory-efficient sequence.

PROTOCOL.INI File

Windows for Workgroups has a PROTOCOL.INI file as part of its setup. The file tells the system about the network cards and drivers in use. The PC/TCP PROTOCOL.INI file does the same, but it resides in the PCTCP directory.

The contents of the PROTOCOL.INI file will be different for each network card and driver configuration. There must be a section labeled [PKTDRV] (all in uppercase) that defines the driver name, the binding to the network card, and any configuration information needed. The sample network's PROTOCOL.INI file looks like this:

```
[PKTDRV]
drivername=PKTDRV$
bindings=MS$EE16
intvec=0x60

[MS$EE16]
DriverName=EXP16$
IOADDRESS=0x360
IRQ=11
IOCHRDY=Late
TRANSCEIVER=Thin Net (BNC/COAX)
```

This PROTOCOL.INI file defines the packet driver as PKTDRV$, the default driver with PC/TCP. The binding to the Intel EtherExpress 16 card used refers to another section in the file that lists the address, IRQ, and some specifics of the EtherExpress card. These lines could have been included in the [PKTDRV] section but were separated for compatibility with the Windows for Workgroups PROTOCOL.INI, which is similar. The EtherExpress 16 card is set to use IRQ 16, memory address 360, and use the Thin Ethernet cable connector. The intvec line in the [PKTDRV] section does not define the IRQ for the network card. It is an interrupt for the driver.

A PROTOCOL.INI file for a system using a simpler network card than the EtherExpress can be shorter. A sample PROTOCOL.INI file for such as card might look like this:

```
[PKTDRV]
drivername=PKTDRV$
binding=MS$ELNKII
intvec=0x65
chainvec=0x67
```

Finding the settings for the variables in the PROTOCOL.INI file can be harrowing. If Windows for Workgroups is installed and running, the Windows PROTOCOL.INI file can be a good source of information and can sometimes be copied without modification. Otherwise, the network card documentation can sometimes help.

PCTCP.INI File

The PCTCP.INI file holds the kernel configuration information for PCTCP. In most cases, it can be left as supplied with the software. Tweaking the kernel parameters should be performed only after the network is installed and operating properly. The file is quite lengthy and care should be taken to avoid accidental changes (which can render the system inoperative).

If the installation script is not used to install PC/TCP, a minimum `PCTCP.INI` file must be created. Examples are included with the distribution media, usually under the name `TEMPLATE.INI`. There are two ways to create the `PCTCP.INI` file and configure it properly. The first is to use an editor and modify the template file. The alternative is to run the kernel configuration utility `kappconf`.

A minimum `PCTCP.INI` file needs to have the software serial number and activation key, the IP address, broadcast address, router address, a subnet mask, and information about the system in general. The minimum `PCTCP.INI` file would look like this:

```
[pctcp general]
domain                = tpci.com
host-name             = merlin
time-zone             = EST
time-zone-offset      = 600
user                  = tparker

[pctcp kernel]
serial-number         = 1234-5678-9012
authentication-key    = 1234-5678-9012
interface             = ifcust 0
low-window            = 0
window                = 2048

[pctcp ifcust 0]
broadcast-address     = 255.255.255.255
ip-address            = 147.120.0.2
router                = 147.120.0.1
subnet-mask           = 255.255.0.0

[pctcp addresses]
domain-name-server    = 147.120.0.1
mail-relay            = 147.120.0.1
```

This configuration assumes that the SCO UNIX server (147.120.0.1) is the primary server for the network. As different features of PC/TCP are enabled (such as SNMP and Kerberos), new sections are added to the `PCTCP.INI` file.

Windows *SYSTEM.INI* File

If Windows for Workgroups is to be active at the same time and use the PC/TCP drivers, the `SYSTEM.INI` file requires modification. The Windows for Workgroups file must be set to use the Windows for Workgroups driver instead of the PC/TCP driver.

When the PC/TCP installation detects a copy of Windows, it makes changes to the `SYSTEM.INI`. Some of these must be modified to enable Windows to boot properly. One of the most important changes is the commenting out of the Windows for Workgroups network driver and its replacement with the PC/TCP driver:

```
network.drv=C:\PCTCP\PCTCPNET.DRV
```

For Windows for Workgroups 3.1, confirm that the SYSTEM.INI file has these three sections, with the commands shown:

```
[boot]
network.drv=wfwnet.drv

[boot.description]
network.drv=Microsoft Windows for Workgroups (version 3.1)

[386Enh]
device=c:\pctcp\vpctcp.386
device=c:\pctcp\wfwftp.386
```

Windows for Workgroups 3.11 has a slightly different SYSTEM.INI. It should look like this:

```
[boot]
network.drv=wfwnet.drv

[boot.description]
network.drv=Microsoft Windows Network (version 3.11)

[386Enh]
device=c:\pctcp\vpctcp.386
```

At the bottom of the Windows for Workgroups' SYSTEM.INI file, PC/TCP sometimes adds a block of information that looks like this:

```
[vpctcp]

; These option settings may be added to SYSTEM.INI, in a
;   new section "[vpctcp]".

; The next line tells VPCTCP how much copy space memory to request.
;   It is in units of kilobytes (x1024).  This value is only a bid,
;   as Windows may choose to reduce your allocation arbitrarily.
;   This value should be increased if using Windows applications which
;   call the PC/TCP DLL from another DLL; suggested value in such
;   instances is at least 28.
MinimumCopySpace=12

; The next line tells VPCTCP the segment (paragraph) number of the
;   beginning of memory reserved for devices, BIOS, and upper-
;   memory blocks (which could contain TSRs).  All calls below the
;   PSP of Windows or above this parameter are not processed by
;   the VxD but rather are passed-thru to the kernel untouched.
HiTSRFenceSegment=A000h

; eof
```

For most installations, this block can be left as it is. The comment lines (those beginning with a semicolon) are ignored by Windows, whereas the two variables established are used by PC/TCP. There is no need to delete this information. However, as the first note indicates, users of PC/TCP may have to increase the value to account for heavy usage.

If the target system is running Windows 3.1 (not Windows for Workgroups), there are more changes to be made because the SYSTEM.INI file and network-dependent initialization files will not have the proper format yet. To configure a Windows system, changes must be made to the PROGMAN.INI and SYSTEM.INI files.

PROGMAN.INI controls the startup of Windows Program Manager. Normally, this is modified by the PC/TCP installation script; but if a manual installation has been performed, changes must be made with a text editor. The PROGMAN.INI file must have the following lines added:

```
[Groups]
GROUP16 = C:\PCTCP\PCTCPDOS.GRP
GROUP17 = C:\PCTCP\PCTCPWIN.GRP
```

The numbers next to GROUP should be higher than any existing number, usually sequential. In this example, the list of groups ran to number 15.

Changes to the SYSTEM.INI file must be made in a few sections. In the [386Enh] section, add a line for the PC/TCP device driver:

```
device=c:\pctcp\vpctcp.386
```

A [vpctcp] section must be added with the following entries:

```
[vpctcp]
MinimumCopySpace=12
HiTSRFenceSegment=A000h
```

See the discussion of Windows for Workgroups' SYSTEM.INI file for more information on these variables.

Some additional entries may be necessary if the network driver is located in high memory, there is a conflict with the default serial port IRQs, and if a Token Ring network is used. See the PC/TCP installation manual for complete change information.

Windows for Workgroups Using NetBIOS

As mentioned earlier, Windows for Workgroups can be set to use IP packets. This requires a NetBIOS driver for both Windows for Workgroups and PC/TCP. The architecture of such as system is shown in Figure 12.2. The Windows for Workgroups packets are sent through PC/TCP's NetBIOS and then into the normal PC/TCP stack.

Figure 12.2. *Windows for Workgroups with NetBIOS.*

To install Windows for Workgroups in this manner, Windows must first be set up to use the Microsoft LAN Manager option. This is usually a matter of selecting the LAN Manager option from the network window if it is not already the default setting. (Consult the Windows for Workgroups documentation for more information.)

The configuration files must also be changed to reflect the new architecture. The AUTOEXEC.BAT file has the network initiation command, the network kernel driver, and a NETBIOS command:

```
C:\WINDOWS\NET START
C:\PCTCP\ETHDRV
C:\PCTCP\NETBIOS.COM
```

A NETBIND can be performed instead of a NET START command, although the latter is preferable. The NETBIOS command must come after the NETBIND or NET START command.

The CONFIG.SYS file is similar to that seen earlier, with the same drivers. A sample CONFIG.SYS file for this type of architecture is like this:

```
DEVICE=C:\WINDOWS\PROTMAN.DOS /I:\C:\WINDOWS
DEVICE=C:\WINDOWS\EXP16.DOS
DEVICE=C:\PCTCP\DIS_PKT.GUP
```

This starts the protocol manager, the card driver, and the NDIS packet converter. This example uses the Intel EtherExpress 16 card driver.

The PROTOCOL.INI file is the same as the previous example. A sample PROTOCOL.INI file for the Intel EtherExpress 16 card is like this:

```
[PKTDRV]
drivername=PKTDRV$
bindings=MS$EE16
intvec=0x60
```

```
[MS$EE16]
DriverName=EXP16$
IOADDRESS=0x360
IRQ=11
IOCHRDY=Late
TRANSCEIVER=Thin Net (BNC/COAX)
```

Finally, the SYSTEM.INI file requires that the Windows for Workgroups network driver be used (not the PC/TCP network driver). This may require editing the SYSTEM.INI file, as noted earlier. The SYSTEM.INI file should contain the following lines:

```
[boot]
network.drv=wfwnet.drv

[boot.description]
network.drv=Microsoft Windows for Workgroups (version 3.1)

[386Enh]
device=c:\pctcp\vpctcp.386
device=c:\pctcp\wfwftp.386
TimerCriticialSection=50000
```

The last line in the [386Enh] section may have to be added manually. The version number in the [boot.description] section will change to (version 3.11) with the latest version of Windows for Workgroups.

Testing PC/TCP

After making all the changes previously mentioned, the machine is rebooted. If no error messages are displayed when the new commands are executed, the system is ready for testing. The simplest test is to use PING to ensure that the TCP/IP software is talking to the local machine, and then ist to test the remote machines.

There hasn't yet been machine name information for other machines added to the system, so the IP addresses must be used with PING. (These were specified when the system was installed and reside in the PCTCP.INI file.) The following is an example of a PING command for the local machine (147.120.0.3), one of the two SCO UNIX servers (147.120.0.1), and the fourth machine (147.120.0.4) on the sample network that has not yet been installed—and hence should not communicate:

```
C:\> ping 147.120.0.3
host responding, time = 25 ms

Debugging information for interface ifcust  Addr(6): 00 aa 00 20 18 bf
interrupts: 0 (2 receive, 0 transmit)
packets received: 2, transmitted: 3
receive errors: 0, unknown types: 0
    runts: 0, aligns: 0, CRC: 0, parity: 0, overflow: 0
```

```
       too big: 0, out of buffers: 0, rcv timeout: 0, rcv reset: 0
transmit errors: 0
       collisions: 0, underflows: 0, timeouts: 0, resets: 0
       lost crs: 0, heartbeat failed: 0
ARP statistics:
arps received: 1 (0 requests, 1 replies)
       bad: opcodes: 0, hardware type: 0, protocol type: 0
arps transmitted: 2 (2 requests, 0 replies)
5 large buffers; 4 free now; minimum of 3 free
5 small buffers; 5 free now; minimum of 4 free
C:\>
C:\> ping 147.120.0.1
host responding, time = 25 ms

Debugging information for interface ifcust  Addr(6): 00 aa 00 20 18 bf
interrupts: 0 (5 receive, 0 transmit)
packets received: 5, transmitted: 6
receive errors: 0, unknown types: 0
       runts: 0, aligns: 0, CRC: 0, parity: 0, overflow: 0
       too big: 0, out of buffers: 0, rcv timeout: 0, rcv reset: 0
transmit errors: 0
       collisions: 0, underflows: 0, timeouts: 0, resets: 0
       lost crs: 0, heartbeat failed: 0
ARP statistics:
arps received: 2 (0 requests, 2 replies)
       bad: opcodes: 0, hardware type: 0, protocol type: 0
arps transmitted: 3 (3 requests, 0 replies)
5 large buffers; 4 free now; minimum of 3 free
5 small buffers; 5 free now; minimum of 4 free
C:\>
C:\> ping 147.120.0.4
ping failed: Host unreachable: ARP failed

Debugging information for interface ifcust  Addr(6): 00 aa 00 20 18 bf
interrupts: 0 (5 receive, 0 transmit)
packets received: 5, transmitted: 7
receive errors: 0, unknown types: 0
       runts: 0, aligns: 0, CRC: 0, parity: 0, overflow: 0
       too big: 0, out of buffers: 0, rcv timeout: 0, rcv reset: 0
transmit errors: 0
       collisions: 0, underflows: 0, timeouts: 0, resets: 0
       lost crs: 0, heartbeat failed: 0
ARP statistics:
arps received: 2 (0 requests, 2 replies)
       bad: opcodes: 0, hardware type: 0, protocol type: 0
arps transmitted: 4 (4 requests, 0 replies)
5 large buffers; 4 free now; minimum of 3 free
5 small buffers; 5 free now; minimum of 4 free
```

12

The message ping failed: Host unreachable for the last attempt is expected. PC/TCP provides the user with diagnostic messages with each PING command. To suppress these messages and simply get a success or fail message, the -z option can be used:

```
C:\> ping -z 147.120.0.3
host responding, time = 25 ms
C:\>
```

```
C:\> ping -z 147.120.0.1
host responding, time = 25 ms
C:\>
C:\> ping -z 147.120.0.4
ping failed: Host unreachable: ARP failed
```

If the ping command is not successful with the local address, either the network interface card is configured incorrectly or the software installation has incorrect parameters. Check the network card for the correct IRQ and memory settings and then check the cable to ensure it is connected properly and network terminators are in place. The software must have the correct drivers loaded, the machine name, IP address, and similar information.

If the local machine responds but the remotes do not, check the network connections. Try ping from one of the remotes to ensure it can reach the other machines. Experience has shown that PC-based TCP/IP implementations can be quirky when booting. It is not unusual to have a ping command fail four or five times and then start working properly. Repeat the commands several times, waiting a few seconds between each.

Once the machines can successfully respond to a ping request, try ftp or telnet from the DOS based machine. An ftp attempt to log on to the SCO UNIX machine is shown:

```
FTP Software PC/TCP File Transfer Program 2.31    01/07/94 12:38
Copyright (c) 1986-1993 by FTP Software, Inc.  All rights reserved.
FTP Trying....Open
220 tpci.tpci.com FTP Server (Version 5.60 #1) ready.
Userid for logging in on 147.120.0.1? tparker
331 Password required for tparker.
Password for logging in as tparker on 147.120.0.1? abcdefg
230 User tparker logged in.
ftp:147.120.0.1> ls
.profile
.lastlogin
.odtpref
trash
Initial.dt
XDesktop3
mailfolders
xdesk.jul
mbox
xdesk.doc
insight.doc
Transferred 265 bytes in 0 seconds
226 Transfer complete.
ftp:147.120.0.1> exit
```

This session, which displayed the listing of files on the SCO UNIX server, shows that the ftp command worked properly. The ftp session was closed with the command exit.

Following the DOS-based test, start Windows (if it was installed) and ensure that the applications within the PC/TCP Applications program group are available and working. If problems are encountered with Windows starting, it is likely that an error was made in the SYSTEM.INI file. Check the previous instructions for the correct configuration.

After all that, the ftp Software PC/TCP system is installed and configured properly. The DOS machine can now be used for TCP/IP applications such as ftp and telnet. If some of the more powerful protocol features were installed, they are also usable. The DOS-based machine installation is now completed. The PC/TCP documentation contains instructions for using the system, as well as fine-tuning the kernel. It also helps users create gateways, routers, mail servers, and several other TCP/IP-related features.

Windows-Based TCP/IP: NetManage's Chameleon

NetManage produces a line of TCP/IP-based software specifically for Windows and Windows for Workgroups. These applications are designed to provide full access to TCP/IP utilities through the Windows environment. NetManage's line of products includes a basic TCP/IP stack (called Newt), as well as full TCP/IP application packages in several forms, all called Chameleon. The system is also available for Windows NT.

Chameleon uses the standard NDIS (Network Device Interface Specification) or the ODI (Open-Data Link Interface) for communicating with the network interface card. This allows any card that uses either NDIS or ODI to be used with Chameleon.

Prior to installation of Chameleon, the same steps are performed as for the DOS-based TCP/IP package. The network interface card must be installed with suitable IRQ and memory address settings. If Chameleon is being added to an existing Windows for Workgroups system, the network card should already be installed and properly configured.

The same information is required as for all TCP/IP installations: the host name, IP address, broadcast mask, subnetwork mask, and any information about gateways or routers that needs to be included.

The version of ChameleonNFS used for the sample network had its installation information slightly jumbled because of updates to both Chameleon and Windows for Workgroups. The information supplied in this chapter applies to Windows for Workgroups 3.1 and 3.11 and ChameleonNFS version 4.0.

Installing Chameleon

Chameleon should be installed over a fully functional Windows or Windows for Workgroups system. If Windows for Workgroups is used, ensure that the network performs properly (if possible). The installation procedure for Chameleon is simple. From the Program Manager's File menu, select Run; then execute the SETUP.EXE program from the first Chameleon disk. As with most Windows applications, this will start the installation program.

> **Warning:** The changes made to the system files may cause problems affecting Windows capability to boot. Before installing the Chameleon software, make copies of the AUTOEXEC.BAT, CONFIG.SYS, PROTOCOL.INI, WIN.INI, and SYSTEM.INI files. If problems are encountered, these files can return the system to its original state.

The Chameleon installation programs requires a lengthy serial number and an activation key to ensure that there is only one such version on a network (This locks out multiple installations using the same serial number and activation key.) The installation script will prompt for the distribution diskettes in order and copy all the necessary files.

Following the installation process, Chameleon will build the program group with the Chameleon applications included. The program group is shown in Figure 12.3. After creating the program group, Chameleon starts a customization screen that lets you specify your IP address, host name, network mask, and broadcast address. Save this information, and then exit out of Windows to the DOS prompt to complete the check of the installation.

Figure 12.3. *Chameleon program group.*

Because of the different installation variables encountered with different network drivers, it is advisable to manually check the following configuration files:

```
AUTOEXEC.BAT
CONFIG.SYS
PROTOCOL.INI
SYSTEM.INI
```

The following sections discuss each of these files. If the files do not have the information specified in them, add them with a text editor. Failure to check the files properly may result in Windows being unable to boot properly. If this happens, copy the backup files, restart Windows, and reinstall or reconfigure as necessary.

AUTOEXEC.BAT

The changes to the AUTOEXEC.BAT file necessary to enable Chameleon to run are the inclusion of the installation directory in the PATH environment variable and a network startup command. If Chameleon is installed on a Windows for Workgroups system, the network startup command should already exist.

The PATH environment variable must be modified to include the Chameleon installation directory, which by default is C:\NETMANAG. An existing PATH statement can be altered, or a new line added below the existing PATH statement which looks like this:

```
PATH=C:\NETMANAG;%PATH%
```

Of course, the correct drive and subdirectory should be substituted. This chapter assumes default values throughout.

The command

```
C:\WINDOWS\NET START
```

will already be in the AUTOEXEC.BAT file if a Windows for Workgroups system is used (either version 3.1 or 3.11). If Chameleon is installed on a Windows system, the NETBIND command included with the distribution software should be called:

```
C:\NETMANAG\NETBIND
```

Chameleon may install a SHARE command in the AUTOEXEC.BAT if one does not exist. If one doesn't exist, it is advisable to add it if others can access the machine. SHARE is a DOS utility that activates file-sharing and record-locking. SHARE is necessary in order to prevent error messages and potential system freezes if other machines will be accessing the machine the software is installed on.

The completed AUTOEXEC.BAT file will look like this for a Windows for Workgroups 3.1 or 3.11 installation:

```
PATH=C:\NETMANAG;%PATH%
C:\WINDOWS\NET START
SHARE
```

and like this for a Windows installation:

```
PATH=C:\NETMANAG;%PATH%
C:\NETMANAG\NETBIND
SHARE
```

If the NET START or NETBIND command is not executed properly, Windows will display an error message when it loads. In some cases, Windows can lock up while it tries to access the network drivers.

CONFIG.SYS

The CONFIG.SYS file may be considerably different for each installation. The HIMEM memory device driver is required, and the SMARTDRIVE caching system is recommended. All installations should have adequate values for the FILES and BUFFERS settings, which are normally set by Windows when it is installed. The CONFIG.SYS should have these values as a minimum:

```
BUFFERS=30
FILES=30
LASTDRIVE=Z
STACKS=9,256
```

This creates enough file and buffer settings to enable multiple files to be open at once. Higher values are better, although there is a trade-off of efficiency once the values exceed a certain value (different for the amount of RAM in a system). The LASTDRIVE setting enables more drives to be open than are physically connected to the system. This is necessary when remote drives are mounted, either through Windows for Workgroups or Chameleon.

For a Windows and Windows for Workgroups 3.1 system, Chameleon will add the following commands to the CONFIG.SYS file:

```
DEVICE=C:\NETMANAG\PROTMAN.DOS /I:C:\NETMANAG
DEVICE=C:\NETMANAG\EXP16.DOS
DEVICE=C:\NETMANAG\NETMANAG.DOS
```

These load the device drivers for the protocol manager, the network interface card, and the specific protocol for Chameleon. The protocol manager and network interface card device drivers were discussed in the DOS section earlier in this chapter.

Windows for Workgroups 3.11 usually has a command in the CONFIG.SYS file that looks like this:

```
DEVICE=C:\WINDOWS\IFSHLP.SYS
```

This automatically loads all the necessary drivers. In some cases, Chameleon will add the command for the Windows for Workgroups 3.1 device drivers to the end of the CONFIG.SYS file, even if the IFSHLP.SYS driver exists. Comment out the added device drivers and try the system without them. The IFSHLP.SYS device driver should be sufficient.

SYSTEM.INI

The Windows SYSTEM.INI file requires a few changes to ensure that Chameleon is loaded properly. These should be affected by the installation script, but check the lines carefully anyway.

The [boot] section of the SYSTEM.INI file should have the two lines (following the [boot] section):

```
[boot]
shell=progman.exe
network.drv=C:\NETMANAG\MULT400.DRV
```

The shell line may be different if the system uses a replacement program manager (such as Central Point PC Tools for Windows Desktop Manager). The MULT400 driver supports several networks at a time. The order of these lines in the SYSTEM.INI file is not important, as long as they appear in the proper section. The MULT400 driver takes care of loading all the necessary drivers for each network. Windows for Workgroups should have the line:

```
network.drv=wfwnet.drv
```

either commented out with a semicolon at the start of the line or removed entirely. The WFWNET driver is the Windows for Workgroups network driver, which must be replaced by MULT400.

The [boot.description] section of the SYSTEM.INI file will be changed to this:

```
[boot.description]
network.drv=NetManage ChameleonNFS
```

or a similar line if another NetManage product is installed.

The [386Enh] section will have several changes made. These are as follows:

```
[386Enh]
device=C:\netmanag\nmredir.386
network=*vnetbios,*vwc,vnetsup.386,vredir.386,vserver.386
netmisc=ndis.386,ndis2sup.386
netcard=
transport=nwlink.386,nwnblink.386,netbeui.386
InDOSPolling=FALSE
```

The order of lines in the section doesn't matter. They load the correct network device drivers into the Windows kernel.

Finally, the [network drivers] section should have these lines:

```
[network drivers]
netcard=elnk3.dos
devdir=C:\WINDOWS
LoadRMDrivers=YES
transport=ndishlp.sys,c:\netmanag\netmanag.dos,*netbeui
```

The netcard line will change depending on the network interface card used. The LoadRMDrivers line should be changed from the Windows for Workgroups default value of NO to YES.

PROTOCOL.INI

The PROTOCOL.INI file for a Windows for Workgroups installation doesn't require many changes. The driver information should already exist. There is a new section added by Chameleon that should look like this:

```
[NETMANAGE]
DRIVERNAME=netmng$
BINDINGS=MS$ELNK3
```

The BINDINGS line will change depending on the network interface card. It is easiest to copy the line from another section of the PROTOCOL.INI file.

Testing Chameleon

After the changes to the four configuration files are completed, reboot the system and start Windows. Watch for error messages as the Chameleon lines in the CONFIG.SYS and AUTOEXEC.BAT files are executed. If Windows for Workgroups was installed and working prior to installing Chameleon, there should not be any errors.

The easiest way to test the new TCP/IP system is to use the PING utility within the Chameleon program group. When selected, it displays a small dialog box. Select the Start option, which displays another dialog box waiting for a machine name. Enter the name of the local machine (as provided during the customization of the system). This is shown in Figure 12.4.

Figure 12.4. *Using* PING *to test the local host.*

The PING window should show a successful result. This is indicated by a message showing the number of bytes received, as well as time information. A sample output from a successful attempt to ping the local machine is shown in Figure 12.5.

Figure 12.5. PING *diagnostic messages.*

If the ping attempt was not successful, Chameleon will display a message about the network drivers not installed. Upon receipt of such as message, check the network card settings and all the configuration information.

To try sending a ping attempt across the network, a host table must be created first. This is done through the Chameleon CUSTOM application. It displays a status screen, as shown in Figure 12.6.

Figure 12.6. *The Chameleon custom screen.*

Select the Service's menu Host Table option to display the Host Table dialog box. To add the other machines on the sample network, enter a name in the top window labeled Official Name and click the Add button. This will show a window for the IP address, which should be filled in completely. Then click OK. The IP address and the machine name are now entered into the host table. This window is shown in Figure 12.7, with the address for the machine pepper added. If a machine has more than one name, those names can be added as aliases through this screen, too.

Figure 12.7. *Chameleon's Host Table IP Address dialog box.*

The next step is to use ping to send to another machine on the network. Figure 12.8 shows the output from a ping attempt on freya, the sample network's SCO UNIX server and to pepper, which is not booted (and hence should fail). The system timed out on the pepper attempt.

```
Ping - PING.CFG
File  Start  Settings  Help
    64 bytes received, icmp_seq=1, time=0 ms
--- Round-trip (ms)  min/avg/max = 0/0/0 ---
    64 bytes received, icmp_seq=1, time=0 ms
--- Round-trip (ms)  min/avg/max = 0/0/0 ---
    0 bytes received, icmp_seq=1, time=5822 ms
--- Round-trip (ms)  min/avg/max = 5822/5822/5822 ---

Host: pepper [147.120.0.3]    1 transmitted    0 received    100% los
```

Figure 12.8. PING *across a network.*

If the ping attempts across the network failed on all machines, the problem is likely with the configuration. Check all the configuration information (as previously noted), as well as the network cables and cards. Make sure the machines to be pinged are up and running TCP/IP.

If the network is operating properly, try the FTP and Telnet applications from the Chameleon program group. Full instructions for these utilities are in the documentation. As long as a host table entry has been created and `ping` succeeded, the other utilities should function properly. Both provide a graphical interface that Windows users will find familiar, instead of a character-based line interface found with DOS. To configure more elaborate functions within Chameleon (such as SNMP, mail, and Gateway routing), consult the Chameleon documentation.

Summary

Today you learned how to install and configure two PC-based systems: one for DOS and one specifically for Windows. They are now connected to the sample network, and files can be transferred between the machines quickly and easily. The DOS machines also can run Windows for Workgroups piggy-backed on the TCP/IP network.

Adding other machines usually follows the same procedure. For example, to add a Macintosh running Mac TCP/IP, follow the installation guide to install and configure the software, and then use `ping` to verify everything is working correctly.

Q&A

Q How do TCP/IP and Windows for Workgroups manage to interwork when the transmission packets are of different formats?

A There are two ways to solve the problem. Encapsulate Windows for Workgroups information into IP packets, or vice versa, with IP packets encapsulated by Windows for Workgroups. Either approach requires a conversion in the lower layers of the devices receiving the packets.

Q Why must a DOS TCP/IP driver be loaded as a terminate-and-stay-resident program?

A If a TSR wasn't used, the TCP/IP driver would be loaded and then unloaded when the program terminated, making it unavailable to any other applications. As a TSR, it is readily available for any application that requires the TCP/IP kernel.

Q What is NDIS?

A NDIS is the Network Device Interface Specification, a device driver for DOS applications to communicate with a network card.

Workshop

The Workshop provides quiz questions to help you solidify your understanding of the material covered. Some Workshop sections of this book also contain exercises to provide you with experience in using what you've learned. Try to understand the quiz and exercise answers before continuing on to the next chapter. Quiz answers are provided in Appendix F, "Answers."

Quiz

1. Why is it preferable to have Windows for Workgroups packets encapsulated by IP, rather than the reverse?

2. Why is the SHARE command necessary when using TCP/IP on a DOS network?

3. Use a diagram to show how Windows for Workgroups and TCP/IP co-reside on a layered architecture for DOS.

Managing and Troubleshooting TCP/IP

Today you will not learn how to install, configure, and manage a network. Network management and configuration is a complex issue, and there are many good books available if you are interested. Today's text does present an overview of network topologies and configuration issues, as well as examine the basic steps in troubleshooting faulty TCP/IP systems. Remember that this is an overview only, intended to provide you with the background to the process.

Traditionally, network management usually means two different tasks: monitoring and controlling. *Monitoring* means watching the network's behavior to ensure it is functioning smoothly. *Controlling* is changing the network while it is running, altering the configuration in some manner to improve performance or affect parts that are not functioning correctly.

ISO goes further than this, dividing network management into five parts defined within the Open Systems Interconnection Reference Model (OSI-RM). These five parts are called Specific Management Functional Areas (SMFAs) in the standard. The five aspects are

- [ ] *Accounting management:* Providing information on costs and account usage
- [ ] *Configuration management:* Managing the actual configuration of the network
- [ ] *Fault management:* Detecting, isolating, and correcting faults, including maintaining error logs and diagnostics
- [ ] *Performance management:* Maintaining maximum efficiency and performance, including gathering statistics and maintaining logs
- [ ] *Security management:* Maintaining a secure system and managing access

The five groups have some overlap, especially between performance and fault management. However, the division of the network management tasks can help account for all the necessary aspects. In some cases, large organizations have dedicated people for each group.

Network Management Standards

The Internet Advisory Board (IAB) has developed, or adopted, a number of standards for network management. These have been, for the most part, specifically designed to fit TCP/IP requirements, although whenever possible, they do meet the OSI architecture. An Internet working group responsible for the network management standards adopted a two-stage approach to provide for current and future needs.

The first step involves the use of the Simple Network Management Protocol (SNMP), which was designed and implemented by the working group. SNMP is currently used on many Internet networks, and it is integrated into many commercially available products. As technology has improved, SNMP has evolved and become more encompassing.

The second step involves OSI network management standards called the Common Management Information Services (CMIS) and Common Management Information Protocol (CMIP), both to be used in future implementations of TCP/IP. The IAB has published the *Common Management Information Services and Protocol over TCP/IP* (*CMOT*) as a standard for TCP/IP and OSI management.

Both SNMP and CMOT use the concept of network managers exchanging information with processes within network devices such as workstations, bridges, routers, and multiplexers. The primary management station communicates with the different management processes, building information about the status of the network. The architecture of both SNMP and CMOT is such that the information that is collected is stored in a manner that enables other protocols to read them.

The SNMP manager handles the overall software and communications between the devices using the SNMP communications protocol. Support software provides a user interface, allowing a network manager to observe the condition of the overall system, individual components, and monitor any specific network device.

SNMP-managed devices all contain the SNMP agent software and a database called the Management Information Base (MIB). The MIB currently has 126 fields of information about the device status, performance of the device, its connections to different devices, and its configuration. The SNMP manager queries the MIB through the agent software and can specify changes to the configuration. Most SNMP managers query agents at a regular interval, such as every 15 minutes, unless instructed otherwise by the user.

The SNMP agent software is usually quite small (typically less than 64KB) because the SNMP protocol is simple. SNMP is designed to be a polling protocol, meaning that the manager will issue messages to the agent. For efficiency and small size of executable programs, SNMP messages are enclosed within a UDP datagram and routed via IP (although many other protocols could be used). There are only five message types available in SNMP:

- □ *Get request:* Used to query an MIB

- □ *Get next request:* Used to read sequentially through an MIB

- □ *Get response:* Used for a response to a get-request message

☐ *Set request:* Used to set a value in the MIB

☐ *Trap:* Used to report events

UDP port 161 is used for all messages except traps, which arrive on UDP port 162. Agents receive their messages from the manager through the agent's UDP port 161.

Despite its widespread use, SNMP has some disadvantages. The most important may also be an advantage, depending on your point of view: the reliance on UDP. Because UDP is connectionless, there is no reliability inherent in the message sending. Another problem is that SNMP provides only a simple messaging protocol, so filtering messages cannot be performed. This increases the load on the receiving software. Finally, SNMP uses polling, which consumes a considerable amount of bandwidth. The tradeoffs between SNMP and its more recent successor, CMIP, will make the decision of a management protocol more difficult in the future.

SNMP enables proxy management, which means that a device with an SNMP agent and MIB can communicate with other devices that do not have the full SNMP agent software. This proxy management lets other devices be controlled through a connected machine by placing the device's MIB in the agent's memory. For example, a printer can be controlled through proxy management from a workstation acting as an SNMP agent, which also runs the proxy agent and MIB for the printer.

Proxy management can be useful to offload some devices that are under heavy load. For example, it is common under SNMP to use proxy to handle authentication processes—which can consume considerable resources—by passing this function to a less heavily used machine. Proxy systems also can affect the processing that needs to be performed at a bridge, for example, by having a proxy reformat the datagrams arriving, again to offload the bridge from that time-consuming task.

Network Topologies

You briefly examined local area network topologies on Day 1, looking at bus and ring networks, so that material should be familiar to you. You can now extend your attention from the local area network topology to the larger internetworked topology by using TCP/IP. As you do that, you must tie in the role of routers, bridges, and similar devices into the network topology, and show their role in a TCP/IP system.

One useful concept to keep in mind is the 80/20 rule, which states that 80 percent of most network traffic is for local machines, while 20 percent will need to move off the LAN. In reality, the ratio of local traffic is usually much higher, but planning for an 80/20 split helps establish workable limits for connections to network backbones.

Local area networks (LANs) are tied to a larger network backbone (either a wide area network, WAN, or an internetwork such as the Internet) through a device that handles the passage of datagrams between the LAN and backbone. In a simple setup, a router performs this function. This is shown in Figure 13.1. Routers connect networks that use different link layer protocols or Media Access Control (MAC) protocols. Routers only examine the headers of datagrams that are specifically sent to them, or are broadcast messages, but there is a lot of processing involved within the router.

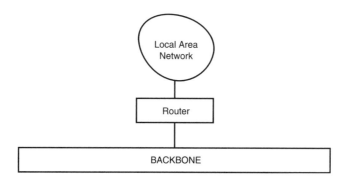

Figure 13.1. *A router connects a LAN to the backbone.*

If two or more LANs are involved in one organization and there is the possibility of a lot of traffic between them, it is better to connect the two LANs directly with a bridge instead of loading the backbone with the cross-traffic. This is shown in Figure 13.2. Bridges also can connect two wide area networks using a high-speed line, as shown in Figure 13.3.

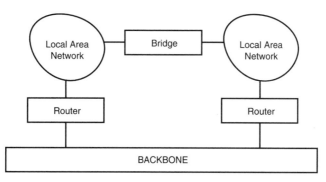

Figure 13.2. *Using a bridge to connect two LANs.*

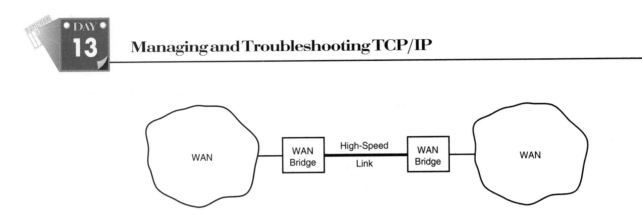

Figure 13.3. *Bridges connect two WANs.*

You may recall that bridges are used when the same network protocol is on both LANs, although the bridge does not care which physical media is used. Bridges can connect twisted-pair LANs to coaxial LANs, for example, or act as an interface to a fiber-optic network. As long as the Media Access Control (MAC) protocol is the same, the bridge will function properly.

Many high-end bridges available today will automatically configure themselves to the networks they connect and learn the physical addresses of equipment on each LAN by monitoring traffic. One problem with bridges is that they examine each datagram that passes through them, checking the addresses of the source and destination. This adds overhead and slows the routing through the bridge. (As mentioned earlier, routers don't examine each datagram.)

In a configuration using bridges between LANs or WANs, traffic from one LAN to another can be sent through the bridge instead of onto the backbone, providing better performance. For services such as Telnet and FTP, the speed difference between using a bridge or going through a router onto a heavily used backbone can be appreciable. If the backbone is not under the direct administration of the LAN's administrators (as with the Internet), having a bridge also provides a method for the corporation or organization to control the connection.

The use of a bridge has one other advantage: If the backbone fails, intercommunications between the two LANs is not lost. The same applies, of course, if the bridge fails, because the backbone can be used as a rerouting path. For critical networks, backbones are usually duplicated for redundancy. In the same manner, most organizations will have duplicate routers and bridges in case of failure.

Bridges can be used when splitting a large LAN into smaller networks. This is often necessary when a LAN continues to expand as new equipment is added. Eventually the network traffic becomes bottlenecked. A useful and relatively easy solution is to divide the larger LAN into smaller LANs connected over a backbone. This helps conform more to the 80/20 rule, while simplifying the traffic and administration overhead. This is shown in Figure 13.4. If the backbone is carefully chosen with lots of excess capacity, this type of topology can account for sizable future growth.

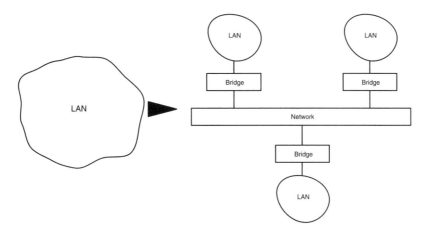

Figure 13.4. *Dividing a large LAN into several smaller LANs.*

Routers, too, can be used to control large networks. This is an advantage when broadcasts are frequently used, because the router can filter out broadcasts that apply only to a specific LAN. (Most bridges propagate broadcasts across the network.) The use of a single *switching router,* or *hub router,* is becoming popular for joining different LANs within an organization, too, as shown as in Figure 13.5.

When large networks are necessary, several routers can be used to split the load. Intelligent network routers can optimize the routing of datagrams, as well as monitor and control network traffic and bottlenecks at any location.

There are many occasions when the advantages of a bridge and a router together are ideal. These combined devices, called *brouters,* are now making an appearance. Brouters can perform routing with some messages and bridging with others by examining incoming datagrams and using a filter mask to decide which function is performed. Brouters have the capability to handle multiple protocols, much like routers.

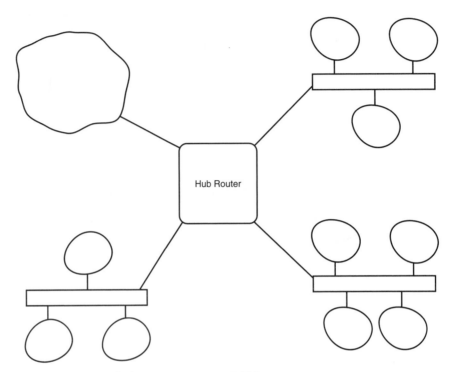

Figure 13.5. *Using a hub router to connect LANs.*

Configuring a Network

Equipment available today is much more capable than it was when TCP/IP began its development cycle. In some ways, this has simplified the task of adding to or configuring a network, but it has also posed some problems of its own. Most equipment can be added to a network by simply attaching the network medium (such as a coaxial or twisted-pair cable) and configuring the interface with the IP address and domain name.

Of course, the more complicated the network, the more work must be done. Configuring a bridge, for example, can be as simple as connecting it to the networks it serves. Most bridges can autoconfigure themselves and watch the network traffic to build a table of network address. However, adding filters to restrict traffic or limiting access through blocking ports all require more detailed configuration processes.

Configuring a network and TCP/IP is not difficult, but it can be time-consuming. Different operating systems approach the task in a variety of ways. UNIX, for example, uses a large number of small configuration files scattered throughout the file system. IBM mainframes use a single large file. Configuration on some systems uses a menu-driven interface that practically guides the user through all the necessary steps, ensuring no errors are made.

For most networks and their interface cards, the following information is required:

- [ ] *Physical address:* Usually provided by the interface manufacturer
- [ ] *IP address:* Optional with serial-line interfaces
- [ ] *Subnet mask:* Specifies the network address
- [ ] *Protocol:* IP, if TCP/IP or UDP is used
- [ ] *Routing protocols:* Whether ARP and/or RARP are used
- [ ] *Broadcast address:* Format to use for broadcasts, usually all 1s

Secondary IP addresses may be used for devices such as routers that can handle two logical networks. As noted, serial interfaces do not need an IP address, although one can be supplied. Serial interfaces also require a setting to indicate whether the device is configured to act as Data Terminal Equipment (DTE) or Data Communications Equipment (DCE), the serial port's baud rate and parity, and settings for the maximum size of a transmission.

Whatever equipment is used on a network, they all have a physical connection to the network transport medium. Typically this is a network card in a workstation, desktop PC, or printer. Software supplied with the device controls the interface, eliminating most of the worries of matching hardware, software, and protocols. After deciding on an IP address, the setting can be programmed either by switches or software and the device is ready to talk to the network.

IP addresses can be chosen at random by the system administrator, but this can cause problems when the datagrams are released to a larger internetwork such as Internet. Ideally, a network mask is assigned by the Network Information Center (NIC). This is then combined with the administrator's own numbering scheme in the LAN to produce the full IP address.

The IP addresses are assigned by the NIC based on the *class* of network, which reflects the size of the organization and the number of local equipment addresses required. As shown in Figure 13.6, there are four NIC-approved IP address structures. Class A addresses are for very large networks that need 24 bits available for local addresses,

13

reducing the network address to 7 bits. Class B assigns 16 bits locally and 14 bits for the network address, while Class C allows only 8 bits for local addresses and 21 bits for the network address. Class C networks are for small companies only, as only 256 local addresses can be created. (Class D addresses are used for special systems not usually encountered by users.)

Figure 13.6. *The four IP address class structures.*

Numbering schemes within a network are left to the administrator's whim, although a convention of assigning low numbers to routers and bridges is usually followed. It is also useful to use Address Resolution Protocol (ARP) on local servers or routers to provide for faster startup when machines query for their IP addresses. This prevents system-wide broadcasts. The manner in which user equipment starts up (whether it use BOOTP, ARP, or RARP) can affect the configuration of the local servers and routers.

Physical addresses of network connectors seldom have to be changed over their default settings. Most vendors guarantee a unique physical setting for their hardware, so these can usually be maintained with no change. For the conversion of IP address to physical address, this information must be stored in a routing table.

Routing tables for small networks are often created and maintained by hand. Larger networks may involve too many changes for the manual approach to be effective, so a routing protocol, such as Routing Information Protocol (RIP), is used. There are several routing protocols available, including RIP and Open Shortest Path First (OSPF). The choice of the routing protocol can be important and usually depends on the size of the network and the connections between subnetworks and external systems. Routing protocols should be started automatically when the network is booted.

Configuring the network includes setting the domain name and network IP mask, following the formats approved by the NIC. Many operating systems have utilities that help configure the domain name and network IP mask. The *Domain Administrator's Guide,* which describes the process of forming a domain name, is available from the NIC (RFC 1032). Of course, these steps apply only if the network is to connect to the Internet or similar internetwork. If the network is autonomous with no outside connections, the administrator can choose any network IP mask and domain name (although future connections may force a complete reconfiguration of the network if an NIC-consistent scheme is not used).

Connections to the Internet require an Autonomous System (AS) number from the NIC, which provides other systems with your border router address. Gateway protocols such as the Exterior Gateway Protocol (EGP) or newer Border Gateway Protocol (BGP) must be installed and configured to provide Internet routing.

Also involved in naming are the name-to-address resolution tables, which convert a symbolic name to an IP address. These are usually configured manually, although some automated formatting tools are offered with different operating systems. If the Domain Name System (DNS) is to be implemented, that adds another level of complexity to the name configuration—the details of which are best left to more specialized texts.

Some routers can be configured to filter message traffic. In these cases, the masks used to restrict or allow datagrams must be added to the router tables, as well as any limitations or exceptions to requests for socket services (such as Telnet). Setting ARP tables in routers can help bring up newly started machines more quickly than when a broadcast is sent networkwide to the primary ARP server. A number of routers can be configured for priority routing, allowing priority based on the protocol, type of service, or a selected criteria such as an IP address or socket.

Router software can be accessed either locally through a dedicated terminal or over the network. The latter enables a system administrator to log in using Telnet from a machine on the network and then to run configuration or maintenance utilities. It is advisable to make access to these utilities extremely limited.

After the network addresses have been established, TCP can be configured. This is normally performed on a per-machine basis using an interface utility. In the TCP software configuration are settings for default window sizes and maximum segment size. If changes over the standard TCP port assignments are required, the configuration files must be edited. Processes that start TCP and monitor ports for connections (such as `inetd`, described on Day 6) must be added to the system startup files. Other services such as electronic mail (which may use a dedicated protocol such as SNMP) must be installed and properly configured.

13

Monitoring and Basic Troubleshooting Utilities

On Day 6 you looked as TCP/IP network utilities such as `ping`, `finger`, `ruptime`, and `netstat`, which help determine the status of connections and interfaces. I mention them here again briefly, as well as introduce some new commands. Several software vendors now offer talented network monitoring products that provide excellent information about the network, its connections, and the traffic it carries. Many of these products also enable dynamic configuration of the system.

The `ping` (Packet Internet Groper) command is the easiest method to check a machine's connection to the network. It uses the Internet Control Message Protocol (ICMP) to send a request for response. The `ping` command is useful with routers, because it can check each interface. Different versions of `ping` are available, some with different options.

A similar utility is `spray`, which uses a Remote Procedure Call (RPC, discussed on Day 9) to send a constant stream of datagrams or ICMP messages. The difference between `ping` and `spray` is that `spray` sends the datagrams constantly, whereas `ping` has an interval between datagrams. This can be useful for checking burst-mode capabilities of the network. The output of a `spray` command on a BSD UNIX system follows:

```
$ spray -c 5 tpci_sun2
sending 5 packets of lnth 86 to tpci_sun2 ...
    in 0.3 seconds elapsed time,
    1 packets (20.00%) dropped by tpci_sun2
Sent: 19 packets/sec, 1.8K bytes/sec
Rcvd: 16 packets/sec, 1.6K bytes/sec
```

Day 6 covered the `netstat` command in some detail. It is useful for checking the status of the network. The implementations of `netstat` vary widely, depending on the operating system version.

Some systems have a utility called `traceroute` (available as public-domain software), which sends a series of UDP datagrams to the target. The datagrams are constructed slightly differently, depending on their location in the stream. The first three datagrams have the Time-to-Live (TTL) field set to 1, meaning the first time a router encounters the message it is returned with an expired message. The next three messages have the TTL field set to 2, and so on, until the destination is reached.

The `traceroute` output shows the round-trip time of each message (which is useful for identifying bottlenecks in the network) and the efficiency of the routing algorithms (through a number of routers that may not be the best route). A sample output from a `traceroute` command (all machine names and IP address are invented) is as follows:

```
$ traceroute black.cat.com
1  TPCI.COM (127.01.13.12)    51ms  3ms  4ms
2  BEAST.COM (143.23.1.23)    60ms  5ms  7ms
3  bills_machine.com (121.22.56.1)   121ms  12ms  12ms
4  SuperGateway.com (130.12.14.2)    75ms  13ms  10ms
5  black.cat.com  (122.13.2.12)    45ms  4ms  6ms
```

While dealing with RPC, there is a utility called rpcinfo that can determine which RPC services are currently active on the local or any remote system that supports RPC. The options supported by rpcinfo vary with the implementation, but all enable flags to decide which type of service to check. For example, the -p option displays the local portmapper. The following example shows the options supported on the SCO UNIX version of rpcinfo, as well as the output for the portmapper:

```
$ rpcinfo
Usage: rpcinfo [ -n portnum ] -u host prognum [ versnum ]
       rpcinfo [ -n portnum ] -t host prognum [ versnum ]
       rpcinfo -p [ host ]
       rpcinfo -b prognum versnum
$ rpcinfo -p
   program vers proto   port
    100000    2   tcp    111   portmapper
    100000    2   udp    111   portmapper
    150001    1   udp   1026   pcnfsd
    150001    2   udp   1026   pcnfsd
    100008    1   udp   1027   walld
    100002    1   udp   1028   rusersd
    100002    2   udp   1028   rusersd
    100024    1   udp   1029   status
    100024    1   tcp   1024   status
    100020    1   udp   1034   llockmgr
    100020    1   tcp   1025   llockmgr
    100021    2   tcp   1026   nlockmgr
    100021    1   tcp   1027   nlockmgr
    100021    1   udp   1038   nlockmgr
    100021    3   tcp   1028   nlockmgr
    100021    3   udp   1039   nlockmgr
```

Monitoring NFS (an RPC service) can be more complicated. A few utility programs are available. The nfsstat command displays information about recent calls:

```
$ nfsstat
Server rpc:
calls      badcalls    nullrecv    badlen      xdrcall
458        0           1           2           0

Server nfs:
calls      badcalls
412        2
null       getattr     setattr     root        lookup      readlink    read
0 0%       200 49%     0 0%        0 0%        120 29%     75 18%      126 31%
wrcache    write       create      remove      rename      link        symlink
0 0%       0 0%        0 0%        0 0%        0 0%        0 0%        0 0%
mkdir      rmdir       readdir     fsstat
0 0%       0 0%        52 13%      12 3%
```

13

```
Client rpc:
calls      badcalls   retrans    badxid     timeout    wait       newcred
1206       1          0          0          3          0          0
peekeers   badresps
0          1

Client nfs:
calls      badcalls   nclget     nclsleep
1231       0          1231       0
null       getattr    setattr    root       lookup     readlink   read
0 0%       0 0%       0 0%       0 0%       562 46%    134 11%    137 11%
wrcache    write      create     remove     rename     link       symlink
0 0%       0 0%       0 0%       0 0%       0 0%       0 0%       0 0%
mkdir      rmdir      readdir    fsstat
0 0%       0 0%       239 19%    98 8%
```

The mount program shows which directories are currently mounted, while the command showmount shows the current NFS servers on the system:

```
$ mount
pepper:/                /server              nfs ro,bg,intr
pepper:/apps            /server/apps         nfs ro,bg,intr
pepper:/usr             /server/usr          nfs rw,bg,intr
pepper:/u1              /server/u1           nfs rw,bg,intr
$ showmount
m_server.tpci.com
merlin.tpci.com
sco_gate.tpci.com
tpti.tpci.com
```

The mount output shows the directories on the machine named pepper that were mounted onto the local /server directory when the system booted. The permissions for each mounted directory are shown at the end of each line, where ro means *read-only* and rw means *read-write*. The bg in the status lines means *background,* indicating that if the mount fails the system will try again periodically. The intr option means keyboard interrupts can be used to halt the reconnection attempts.

Also available as public domain software are nfswatch and nhfsstone. The nfswatch utility monitors all NFS traffic on a server and updates status information at predetermined intervals. This can be useful for watching the load change during the day. The nhfsstone utility is for benchmarking, generating an artificial load and measuring the results.

A fast method to verify a port's proper functioning is to connect to it with Telnet or FTP. Both programs enable the user to specify the port to use instead of the default. In the following example, port 25 (usually used for mail) is tested:

```
$ telnet tpci_hpws4 25
Trying 127.12.12.126 ...
Connected to tpci_hpws4.
Escape shcracter is '^]'.
```

```
220 tpci_hpws4 Sendmail 3.1 ready at Sat, 2 July 94 12:16:54 EST
HELO TPCI_SERVER_1
250 tpci_hpws4 This is garbage typed to force a closed connections as it doesn't
understand this stuff
QUIT
221 tpci_hpws4 closing connection
Connection closed by foreign host.
```

In this example, port 25 received the connection request properly and waited for the mail protocol messages. Because it didn't get any, it closed the connection. This short session does establish that port 25 is functioning properly as far as connections are concerned. It doesn't convey any information about the integrity of the mail transfer protocol, though.

All these utilities can be combined to provide a troubleshooting checklist for basic problems. These at least tell you where the problem is, if not more. A diagnostic procedure is assembled from the utilities, such as

- ☐ If DNS is on the system, use a DNS utility such as nslookup to ensure DNS is active.

- ☐ If NFS is used, check it with the mount utility.

- ☐ Use ping to check a remote machine is alive.

- ☐ Use traceroute to ensure a routing problem is not occurring. Check all ports of the routers if traceroute fails (use the Telnet login process shown previously).

- ☐ Use netstat to examine ICMP messages recently generated.

- ☐ Try logging in to the remote directly with FTP or Telnet.

- ☐ If RPCs appear to be the problem, use rpcinfo.

Of course, if better tools are available from commercial sources, use them to their full advantage. It is important to know that you don't have to spend thousands of dollars on a network monitoring tool, though, because the utilities supplied with the operating system are often quite capable (if not as fancy or graphically oriented).

Troubleshooting the Network Interface

The physical connection to the network is a suitable starting point for troubleshooting when a problem is not obvious. Because there are many popular network interfaces, each of which must be dealt with in a slightly different manner, some generalizations must be made. The overall approach remains the same, though.

Assuming the network itself is functional, the most common problems with the network interface is a faulty network card or a bad connector. Checking each is easily done by simple replacement. If the problem persists, the fault is most likely higher up in the architecture.

Faulty network transport media (usually cables) are not uncommon. If a device at the end of a cable is not functioning, it is worthwhile to check the cable itself to ensure that a communication path exists. This can be done with a portable computer or terminal, or in some cases a conductivity tester, depending on the network. A systematic testing process can narrow down a network cabling problem to a specific segment.

One overlooked problem arises not because of a real fault with the network interface or the network itself, but because one device on the network is transmitting a different protocol. This can foul up the entire network and grind it to a halt. (For example, an Ethernet network may have one or more devices set to transmit IEEE 802.3 frames, which are not the same as Ethernet.)

If there is a conversion from one protocol to another, that can be suspect. For example, it is common to find AppleTalk networks running TCP/IP. The IP messages are encapsulated in AppleTalk frames. If the conversion between the two formats (which can occur at a gateway or router) is not clean, some faulty packets may be passed. This can cause network problems, too.

If the network connections and network interface cards appear to be working (which can be verified with a network analyzer or board swapping), the problem is in a higher layer.

Troubleshooting the Network (IP) Layer

The network layer (where IP resides) can be the most trouble-prone aspect of the network if configuration rules are not followed scrupulously. Because this layer handles routing, any mistakes can cause lost packets making it appear that a machine on the network is not communicating with others. ICMP can be a useful tool for troubleshooting this layer.

One of the most common mistakes, especially with large networks, is the duplication of IP addresses. This can be an accident as a new address is programmed, or a user can move his or her machine and in the process jumble the IP address. It is not uncommon for users to change the IP address by mistake when "investigating" the software. The network mask must also be correct, of course.

Addressing of packets within the IP layer (where the source and destination IP addresses are encapsulated in the IP header) is a source of problems. Determining destination IP addresses require communications with another machine, which hopefully holds the necessary information. If the Domain Name System (DNS) is active, it can contribute to the confusion the server has faulty tables.

It is necessary for IP address to be mapped to the physical address. Both ARP and RARP require this table to direct packets over the network. If a network card is changed for any reason, the unique physical address on the board will no longer correspond to the IP address, so messages will be rerouted elsewhere. Network administrators must keep track of any changes to the network hardware in all devices.

Problems also can occur with devices that handle intermediary routing, such as bridges, routers, and brouters. These devices must be aware of all changes to the network, as well as physical and logical addresses for the devices to which they are connected. Specialized protocols such as Routing Information Protocol (RIP) and Open Shortest Path First (OSPF) handle much of this maintenance, but somewhere in the network a manual notation of changes must be made.

There are many potential sources of problems with the network layer. Even processes that should work without trouble, such as packet fragmentation and reassembly, can cause problems.

Connectivity between machines at both the transport and network levels can be tested using utilities such as `ping`. A systematic check of machines along a network and out over an internetwork can help isolate problems, not just in the source and destination machines but also in intermediate processors such as routers. The `traceroute` utility can be used for this, too, if it is available.

Troubleshooting TCP and UDP

13

Assuming the network layer is functioning correctly, the host-to-host software may be a problem. If the software is correctly installed and started (which may sound obvious but is a common cause of failure), a process to isolate the problem must be followed. There are many files involved with both TCP and UDP—differing with each operating system version—so the documentation accompanying the TCP or UDP software should be consulted.

The protocol in use must be determined first: Is the machine using TCP or UDP, and if both, are both failing? Problems such as too many retransmissions or no timeout values may make UDP appear as if it is failing, but TCP would not be affected (unless it uses the same port or too many processes are active).

Port addresses can be problematic, especially with TCP. Each port on a machine can be sent a `ping` message from a remote to verify it is communicating properly. If a port request fails, it may indicate an improper or missing entry in a configuration file. The `finger` utility may also be useful. If messages are passing correctly from one machine to another, the problem is in the configuration of the software, or a higher-level application.

Incorrect configuration parameters can cause TCP or UDP failures. For example, if the send and receive window values for TCP are set to low levels, there may be no opportunity for applications to pass enough information. In this case, it may appear that TCP is at fault. Carefully check all configuration files and settings.

Troubleshooting the Application Layer

Assuming both IP and TCP or UDP are functioning properly, the application layer is suspect. It is in this layer that higher-level protocols such as the File Transfer Protocol (FTP), Telnet, and SMTP are based. It can be difficult to find problems within the application layer, although a few simple tests will help eliminate obvious solutions. Several commercial utilities are available to monitor reception within the application layer.

Assuming data is getting to the right application (which can be checked with some diagnostic tools or simple programming routines), the problem may be in interpretation. Verify that the communications between two applications are both the same format. More than one application has expected ASCII and received EBCDIC. Diagnostics will show the messages moving into the application properly, but they are total gibberish to the application when it tries to interpret them.

Assuming that is not the problem, there may be a fault with the applications at either end. Although you might assume that a Telnet program from one vendor would talk to one from another vendor, this is not true (in an unfortunately large number of cases). If there are no identical software packages, or versions known to work with the other package, this can be difficult to troubleshoot. This kind of cross-application problem is particularly prevalent with mixed-platform systems, such as a PC-based FTP or a TCP/IP software package trying to access services on a UNIX host.

Some readily available utilities can be used to monitor the application layer. Some of these utilities are distributed with operating systems, and others are distributed as public domain software. The utility `snmpwatch` is a network monitoring program that reports on any SNMP variables that change their values. This can be helpful when diagnosing communications problems within SNMP.

The Internet Rover is a network monitor program that enables testing of several protocols, including Telnet, FTP, and SMTP. Unfortunately, it doesn't work with all operating system variants. Another tool for SMTP testing is `mconnect`, which verifies connections.

Security

This is not the place for a long discourse on computer security. Instead, I'll touch on the impact security has on TCP/IP-based networks. Security is an important issue and is often overlooked, usually to the administrator's rue. Taking the steps to set up a proper security policy and protecting the system as well as possible should be a mandatory task for every system administrator.

Routers can be significant in a network's security plan. Most routers enable the system administrator to restrict traffic through the router in some manner, either in one direction or both. A router can be set, for example, to prohibit Telnet or `rlogin` requests from outside the network, but enable through file transfer requests such as FTP. Routers also can prevent traffic into a local network through the router from anywhere outside the network, cutting down on access into (and through) a network.

Routers usually perform this type of traffic filtering by simply looking at the datagram headers for the requested port. If one of the restricted ports is requested, the datagram can be returned to the sender or discarded. Setting the proper access filters from a network router can be an effective and simply a manner of restricting outside access.

Unfortunately, the Internet and most networks were simply not designed to prevent unauthorized access or monitoring. These features were usually added as an afterthought, and as such have some problems. Watching network traffic and trapping addresses, user IDs, and passwords is ridiculously easy, so MIT developed Kerberos security protocols to help.

Kerberos (named after the three-headed dog guarding the gates of Hades) uses an encryption key and server introduction method to enable access. Kerberos is slowly being adopted as a standard among Internet users (despite some governmental protests), and it works well with the TCP/IP family of protocols. For more information on Kerberos, connect to `ATHENA.MIT.EDU` over the Internet or send electronic mail requesting information.

Summary

You've taken a brief look at the network management and troubleshooting tools available with TCP/IP. As mentioned in the introduction, both subjects are complex, potentially demanding, and still considered by many to be an art. There are many excellent books on network management, so you are encouraged to scour your library or bookstore for ones that interest you if you wish to know more about this subject.

The tools provided within the TCP/IP family give you enough diagnostic resources to isolate the source of practically any software and hardware problem. Sometimes the solution to a problem is simple and can be easily managed through a configuration change. Often, though, a problem is outside the bounds of TCP/IP's protocol, requiring more powerful diagnostic procedures. It is useful to follow the steps outlined first, though, and resort to other systems only when the TCP/IP diagnostics have been unable to help.

System administration and network troubleshooting are both curious tasks. They require a lot of work at times, but there is an undeniable sense of accomplishment when a network runs smoothly or when you have tracked down and fixed a problem. Although only a few users in every group will be called upon to perform either task, those that do are in for quite an adventure!

Q&A

Q According to the OSI Reference Model, what is the role of fault management?

A Fault management is the detection, isolation, and correction of faults. It also includes the maintenance and checking of error and diagnostic logs. Fault management is one of the five different Specific Management Functional Areas defined by the ISO as part of the OSI-RM.

Q What are CMIP and CMIS? How do they relate to SNMP?

A CMIP is the Common Management Information Protocol. CMIS is the Common Management Information Service. Both are part of the OSI network management proposal for use as a replacement for SNMP.

Q With SNMP, what is proxy management?

A Proxy management is when a device that cannot hold the full SNMP agent software and management information base (MIB) has that information controlled by another machine (its proxy). The proxy communicates with the device being managed. A typical example is a printer attached to a workstation. The workstation acts as the printer's proxy because the printer has no controlling software with it.

Q What four utilities provide the basic TCP/IP troubleshooting information?

A The four utilities most commonly used for troubleshooting a TCP/IP network are `ping`, `finger`, `ruptime`, and `netstat`.

Q When would you use the utility `traceroute`?

A The `traceroute` utility is used to send UDP datagrams to a target machine, one hop at a time. The output from `traceroute` will show each machine that forwards the message, allowing you to step along the route to isolate a problem.

Workshop

The Workshop provides quiz questions to help you solidify your understanding of the material covered. Some Workshop sections of this book also contain exercises to provide you with experience in using what you've learned. Try to understand the quiz and exercise answers before continuing on to the next chapter. Answers are provided in Appendix F, "Answers."

Quiz

1. What are the five parts of the OSI Reference Model dealing with network management (called the Specific Management Functional Areas)?

2. What is a Management Information Base (MIB)?

3. What is `ping`?

4. Assume a LAN has some machines using Ethernet and others using IEEE 802.3. Will they be able to communicate?

5. What is Kerberos?

The Socket
Programming
Interface

Today you'll look at the last aspect of TCP/IP this course will cover: the socket interface for programming. This information is intended to convey the process needed to integrate an application with TCP/IP and, as such, involves some basic programming functions. It is not necessary to understand programming to understand this information. The functions will help you understand the steps TCP/IP goes through when creating connections and sending data.

Understanding the socket interface is helpful even if you never intend to write a line of TCP/IP code, because all the applications you will work with use these principles and procedures. Debugging or troubleshooting a problem is much easier when you understand what is going on behind the user interface. Today I don't attempt to show the complete socket interface. Instead I deal only with the primary functions necessary to create and maintain a connection. It is not intended to be a programming guide, either.

Since the original socket interface was developed for UNIX systems, today's text has a decidedly UNIX-based orientation. However, the same principles apply to most other operating systems that support TCP/IP.

TCP/IP is fortunate in that it has a well-defined application programming interface (API), which dictates how an application will use TCP/IP. This solves a basic problem that has occurred on many other communications protocols: there are several approaches to the same problem, each incompatible with the other. The TCP/IP API is portable (it works across all operating systems and hardware that support TCP/IP), language-independent (it doesn't matter which language you use to write the application), and relatively uncomplicated.

The Socket API was developed at the University of California at Berkeley as part of their BSD 4.1c UNIX version. Since then the API has been modified and enhanced, but still retains its BSD flavor. Not to be outdone, AT&T (BSD's rival in the UNIX market) introduced the Transport Layer Interface (TLI) for TCP and several other protocols. One of the strengths of the Socket API and TLI is that they were not developed exclusively for TCP/IP, but are intended for use with a number of communications protocols. The Socket interface remains the most widespread API in current use, although there are several newer interfaces being developed.

The basic structure of all socket programming commands lies with the unique structure of UNIX I/O. With UNIX, both input and output are treated as simple pipelines, where the input can be from anything and the output can go anywhere. The UNIX I/O system is sometimes referred to as the *open-read-write-close* system, because those are the steps that are performed for each I/O operation, whether it involves a file, a device, or a communications port.

Whenever a file is involved, the UNIX operating system gives the file a *file descriptor,* a small number that uniquely identifies the file. A program can use this file descriptor to identify the file at any time. (The same holds true for a device; the process is the same.) A file operation uses an open function to return the file descriptor, which is used for the read (transfer data to the user's process) or write (transfer data from the user process to the file), followed by a close to terminate the file operation. The open function takes a filename as an argument. The read and write use the file descriptor number, the address of the buffer in which to read or write the information, and the number of bytes involved. The close uses the file descriptor. The system is easy to use and simple to work with.

TCP/IP uses the same idea, relying on numbers to uniquely identify an end point for communications (a socket). Whenever the socket number is used, the operating system can resolve the socket number to the physical connector. An essential difference between a file descriptor and a socket number is that the socket requires some functions to be performed prior to the establishment of the socket (such as initialization). In techno-speak, "a file descriptor binds to a specific file or device when the open function is called, but the socket can be created without binding them to a specific destination at all (necessary for UDP), or bind them later (for TCP when the remote address is provided)." The same open-read-write-close procedure is used with sockets.

The process was actually used literally with the first versions of TCP/IP. A special file called /dev/tcp was used as the device driver. The complexity added by networking made this approach awkward, though, so a library of special functions (the API) was developed. The essential steps of open, read, write, and close are still followed in the protocol API, though.

Socket Services

There are three types of socket interfaces defined in the TCP/IP API. A socket can be used for TCP *stream communications,* in which a connection between two machines is created. It can be used for *UDP datagram communications,* a connectionless method of passing information between machines using packets of a predefined format. Or it can be used as a *raw* datagram process in which the datagram bypass the TCP/UDP layer and go straight to IP. The latter type arises from the fact that the socket API was not developed exclusively for TCP/IP.

The presence of all three types of interfaces can lead to problems with some parameters that depend exclusively on the type of interface. You must always bear in mind whether TCP or UDP is used.

14

There are six basic communications commands that the socket API addresses through the TCP layer:

☐ open: Establishes a socket

☐ send: Sends data to the socket

☐ receive: Receives data from a socket

☐ status: Obtains status information about a socket

☐ close: Terminates a connection

☐ abort: Cancels an operation and terminates the connection

All six operations are logical and used as you would expect. The details for each step may be quite involved, but the basic operation remains the same. Many of the functions have been seen in previous days when dealing with specific protocols in some detail. Some of the functions (such as open) comprise several other functions that are available if necessary (such as establishing each end of the connection instead of both ends at once).

Despite the formal definition of the functions within the API specifications, there is no formal method given for how to implement them. There are two logical choices: synchronous, or *blocking*, in which the application waits for the command to complete before continuing execution—and asynchronous, or *nonblocking*, in which the application continues executing while the API function is processed. In the latter case, a function call further in the application's execution can check the API functions' success and return codes.

The problem with the synchronous or blocking method is that the application must wait for the function call to complete. If timeouts are involved, this can be a noticeable delay for the user.

Transmission Control Block

The Transmission Control Block (TCB) is a complex data structure that contains details about a connection. The full TCB has more than 50 fields in it. The exact layout and contents of the TCB are not necessary for today's material, but the existence of the TCB and the nature of the information it holds are key to the behavior of the socket interface.

Creating a Socket

The API lets a user create a socket whenever necessary with a simple function call. The function requires the family of protocol to be used with the socket (so the operating system knows which type of socket to assign and how to decode information), the type of communication required, and the specific protocol. Such a function call is written as follows:

```
socket(family, type, protocol)
```

The *family* of protocol actually specifies how the addresses will be interpreted. Examples of families are TCP/IP (coded as AF_INET), Apple's Appletalk (AF_APPLETALK), and UNIX filesystems (AF_UNIX). The exact protocol within the family is specified as the protocol parameter. When used, it specifically indicates the type of service that is to be used.

The *type* parameter indicates the type of communications that is used. It may be a connectionless datagram service (coded as SOCK_DGRAM), a stream delivery service (SOCK_STREAM), or a raw type (SOCK_RAW). The result from the function call will be an integer that can be assigned to a variable for further checking.

Binding the Socket

Because a socket can be created without any binding to an address, there must be a function call to complete this process and establish the full connection. With the TCP/IP protocol, the socket function does not supply the local port number, the destination port, or the IP address of the destination. The bind function is called to establish the local port address for the connection.

Some applications (especially on a server) will want to use a specific port for a connection. Other applications are content to let the protocol software assign a port. A specific port can be requested in the bind function. If it is available, the software will allocate it and return the port information. If the port cannot be allocated (it may be in use), a return code indicates an error in port assignment.

The bind function has the format

```
bind(socket, local_address, address_length)
```

where *socket* is the integer number of the socket to which the bind is completed, *local_address* is the local address to which the bind is performed, and *address_length* is an integer that gives the length of the address in bytes. The address is not returned as a simple number but has the structure shown in Figure 14.1.

14

Address Family	Address (Bytes 0 and 1)
Address (Bytes 2 through 5)	
Address (Bytes 6 through 9)	
Address (Bytes 10 through 13)	

Figure 14.1. *Address structure used by the socket API.*

The address data structure (which is called usually called sockaddr for *socket address*) has a 16-bit Address Family field that identifies the protocol family of the address. The entry in this field determines the format of the address in the following field (which may contain other information than the address depending on how the protocol has defined the field). The address field can be up to 14 bytes in length, although most protocols do not need this amount of space.

Note: The use of a data structure instead of a simple address has its roots in the UNIX operating system and the closely allied C programming language. The formal structure of the socket address enables C programs to use a union of structures for all possible address families. This saves a considerable amount of coding in applications.

TCP/IP has a family address of 2, following which the address field contains both a protocol port number (16 bits) and the IP address (32 bits). The remaining 8 bytes are unused. This is shown in Figure 14.2. Because the address family defines how the address field is decoded, there should be no problem with TCP/IP applications understanding the two pieces of information in the address field.

Address Family (value = 2)	Protocol (16 bits)
IP Address (32 bits)	
Unused	
Unused	

Figure 14.2. *The address structure for TCP/IP.*

Connecting to the Destination

After a local socket address and port number have been assigned, the destination socket can be connected. A one-ended connection is referred to as being in an *unconnected state,* whereas a two-ended (complete) connection is in a *connected state.* After a bind function, an unconnected state exists. To become connected, the destination socket must be added to complete the connection.

> **Note:** Connectionless protocols such as UDP do not require a connected state to function. They can, however, be connected to enable transfer between the two sockets without having to specify the destination address each time. Connection-based protocols such as TCP require both ends of the connection to be specified.

To establish a connection to a remote socket, the connect function is used. The connect function's format is

```
connect(socket, destination_address, address_length)
```

where *socket* is the integer number of the socket to which to connect, the *destination_address* is the socket address data structure for the destination address (using the same format as shown in Figure 14.1), and the *address_length* is the length of the destination address in bytes.

The manner in which connect functions is protocol-dependent. For TCP, connect establishes the connection between the two endpoints and returns the information about the remote socket to the application. If a connection can't be established an error message is generated. For a connectionless protocol such as UDP, the connect function is still necessary but stores only the destination address for the application.

The *open* Command

The open command prepares a communications port for communications. This is an alternative to the combination of the functions shown previously, used by applications for specific purposes. There are really three kinds of open commands, two of which set a server to receive incoming requests and the third used by a client to initiate a request. With every open command, a TCB is created for that connection.

The three open commands are an unspecified passive open (which enables a server to wait for a connection request from any client), a fully specified passive open (which enables a server to wait for a connection request from only a specific client), and an active open (which initiates a connection with a server). The input and output expected from each command is shown in Table 14.1.

Table 14.1. open command parameters.

Type	Input	Output
Unspecified passive open	local port optional: timeout, precedence, security, maximum segment size	local connection name local connection name
Fully specified passive open	local port, remote IP address, remote port optional: timeout, precedence, security, maximum segment size	local connection name
Active open	local port, destination IP address, destination port optional: timeout, precedence, security, maximum segment size	local connection name

When an open command is issued by an application, a set of functions within the socket interface are executed to set up the TCB, initiate the socket number, and establish preliminary values for the variables used in the TCB and the application.

The passive open command is issued by a server to wait for incoming requests. With the TCP (connection-based) protocol, the passive open issues the following function calls:

☐ socket: Creates the sockets and identifies the type of communications

☐ bind: Establishes the server socket for the connection

☐ `listen`: Establishes a client queue

    ☐ `accept`: Waits for incoming connection requests on the socket

The active `open` command is issued by a client. For TCP, it issues two functions:

    ☐ `socket`: Creates the socket and identifies the communications type

    ☐ `connect`: Identifies the server's IP address and port; attempts to establish communications

If the exact port to use is specified as part of the `open` command, a `bind` function call replaces the `connect` function.

Sending Data

There are five functions within the Socket API for sending data through a socket. These are send, `sendto`, `sendmsg`, `write`, and `writev`. Not surprisingly, all these functions send data from the application to TCP. They do this through a buffer created by the application (for example, it may be a memory address or a character string), passing the entire buffer to TCP. The send, `write`, and `writev` functions only work with a connected socket because they have no provision to specify a destination address within their function call.

The format of the send function is simple. It takes the local socket connection number, the buffer address for the message to be sent, the length of the message in bytes, a Push flag, and an Urgent flag as parameters. An optional timeout may be specified. Nothing is returned as output from the send function. The format is

```
send(socket, buffer_address, length, flags)
```

The `sendto` and `sendmsg` functions are similar, except they enable an application to send a message through an unconnected socket. They both require the destination address as part of their function call. The `sendmsg` function is simpler in format than the `sendto` function, primarily because another data structure is used to hold information. The `sendmsg` function is often used when the format of the `sendto` function would be awkward and inefficient in the application's code. Their formats are

```
sendto(socket, buffer_address, length, flags, destination, address_length)
sendmsg(socket, message_structure, flags)
```

The last two parameters in the sendto function are the destination address and the length of the destination address. The address is specified using the format shown in Figure 14.1. The `message_structure` of the sendmsg function contains the information left out of the sendto function call. The format of the message structure is shown in Figure 14.3.

14

Pointer to Socket Address
Size of Socket Address (in bytes)
Pointer to iovector List (Message)
Length of iovector list
Destination Address
Length of Destination Address

Figure 14.3. *The message structure used by* sendmsg.

The fields in the sendmsg message structure give the socket address, size of the socket address, a pointer to the iovector, which contains information about the message to be sent, the length of the iovector, the destination address, and the length of the destination address.

Note: The sendmsg function uses the message structure to simplify the function call. It also has another advantage: the recvmsg function uses the same structure, simplifying an application's code.

The iovector is an address for an array that points to the message to be sent. The array is a set of pointers to the bytes that comprise the message. The format of the iovector is simple. For each 32-bit address to a memory location with a chunk of the message, there is a corresponding 32-bit field that holds the length of the message in that memory location. This format is repeated until the entire message is specified. This is shown in Figure 14.4. The iovector format enables a message to be sent that is noncontiguous. In other words, the first part of the message may be in one location in memory, while the rest is separated by other information. This can be useful, because it saves the application from copying long messages into a contiguous location.

The write function takes three arguments for the socket number, the buffer address of the message to be sent, and the length of the message to send. The format of the function call is

```
write(socket, buffer_address, length)
```

The writev function is similar to write except it uses the iovector to hold the message. This lets it send a message without copying it into another memory address. The format of writev is

```
writev(socket, iovector, length)
```

where `length` is the number of entries in iovector.

The type of function chosen to send data through a socket depends on the type of connection used and the level of complexity of the application. To a considerable degree, the choice is also a personal one of the programmer.

Pointer to Message Block 1 (32 bits)
Length of Message in Block 1 (32 bits)
Pointer to Message Block 2 (32 bits)
Length of Message in block 2 (32 bits)

. . .

Pointer to Message in Block n (32 bits)
Length of Message in Block n (32 bits)

Figure 14.4. *The* iovector *format.*

Receiving Data

Not surprisingly, since there are five functions to send data through a socket, there are five corresponding functions to receive data: `read`, `readv`, `recv`, `recvfrom`, and `recvmsg`. They all accept incoming data from a socket into a reception buffer. The receive buffer can then be transferred from TCP to the application.

The `read` function is the simplest and can only be used when a socket is connected. Its format is

```
read(socket, buffer, length)
```

where the number of the socket or a file descriptor from which to read the data is the first parameter, followed by the memory address in which to store the incoming data, and the maximum number of bytes to be read.

As with `writev`, the `readv` command enables incoming message to be placed in noncontiguous memory locations through the use of an iovector. The format of `readv` is

```
readv(socket, iovector, length)
```

14

where *length* is the number of entries in the iovector. The format of the iovector is the same as mentioned previously and shown in Figure 14.4.

The recv function also can be used with connected sockets. It has the format

recv(*socket*, *buffer_address*, *length*, *flags*)

which corresponds to the send function's arguments.

The recvfrom and recvmsg functions enable data to be read from an unconnected socket. Their formats include the sender's address:

recvfrom(*socket*, *buffer_address*, *length*, *flags*, *source_address*, *address_length*)

recvmsg(*socket*, *message_structure*, *flags*)

The message structure in the recvmsg function corresponds to the structure in sendmsg. (See Figure 14.3.)

Server Listening

A server application that expects clients to call in to it has to create a socket (using socket), bind it to a port (with bind), and then wait for incoming requests for data. The listen function handles problems that could occur with this type of behavior by establishing a queue for incoming connection requests. The queue prevents bottlenecks and collisions, such as when a new request arrives before a previous one has been completely handled, or when two requests arrive simultaneously.

The listen function establishes a buffer to queue incoming requests, thereby avoiding losses. The function lets the socket accept incoming connection requests, which are all sent to the queue for future processing. The function's format is

listen(*socket*, *queue_length*)

where *queue_length* is the size of the incoming buffer. If the buffer has room, incoming requests for connections are added to the buffer and the application can deal with them in the order of reception. If the buffer is full, the connection request is rejected.

After the server has used listen to set up the incoming connection request queue, the accept function is used to actually wait for a connection. The format of the function is

accept(*socket*, *address*, *length*)

where *socket* is the socket on which to accept requests, *address* is a pointer to a structure similar to Figure 14.1, and *length* is a pointer to an integer showing the length of the address.

When a connection request is received, the protocol places the address of the client in the memory location indicated by the address parameter and the length of that address in the length location. It then creates a new socket that has the client and server connected together, sending back the socket description to the client. The socket on which the request was received remains open for other connection requests. This enables multiple requests for a connection to be processed, so that if that socket were closed down with each connection request, only one client-server process could be handled at a time.

One possible special occurrence must be handled on UNIX systems. It is possible for a single process to wait for a connection request on multiple sockets. This reduces the number of processes that monitor sockets, thereby lowering the amount of overhead the machine uses. To provide for this type of process, the `select` function is used. The format of the function is

```
select(num_desc, in_desc, out_desc, excep_desc, timeout)
```

where *num_desc* is the number of sockets or descriptors that are monitored, *in_desc* and *out_desc* are pointers to a bit mask that indicates the sockets or file descriptors to monitor for input and output respectively, *excep_desc* is a pointer to a bit mask that specifies the sockets or file descriptors to check for exception conditions, and *timeout* is a pointer to an integer that indicates how long to wait (a value of 0 indicates forever). To use the `select` function, a server creates all the necessary sockets first and then calls `select` to determine which ones are for input, output, and exceptions.

Getting Status Information

There are several status functions that are used to obtain information about a connection. They can be used at any time, although they are typically used to establish the integrity of a connection in case of problems or to control the behavior of the socket.

The status functions require the name of the local connection, and return a set of information, which may include the local and remote socket names, local connection name, receive and send window states, number of buffers waiting for an acknowledgment, number of buffers waiting for data, and current values for the urgent state, precedence, security, and timeout variables. Most of this information is read from the Transmission Control Block. The format of the information and the exact contents vary slightly, depending on the implementation.

The function `getsockopt` enables an application to query the socket for information. The function format is

```
getsockopt(socket, level, option_id, option_result, length)
```

14

where *socket* is the number of the socket, *level* indicates whether the function refers to the socket itself or the protocol that uses it, *option_id* is a single integer that identifies the type of information requested, *option_result* is a pointer to a memory location where the function should place the result of the query, and *length* is the length of the result.

The corresponding setsockopt function lets the application set a value for the socket. The function's format is the same as getsockopt, except *option_result* points to the value that is to be set and *length* is the length of the value.

Two functions provide information about the local address of a socket. The getpeername function returns the address of the remote end. The getsockname function returns the local address of a socket. They have the formats

```
getpeername(socket, destination_address, address_length)
getsockname(socket, local_address, address_length)
```

The addresses in both functions are pointers to a structure of the format shown in Figure 14.1.

Two hostname functions for BSD UNIX are gethostname and sethostname, which enable an application to obtain the name of the host and set the hostname (if permissions allow). Their formats are as follows:

```
sethostname(name, length)
gethostname(name, length)
```

name is the address of an array that holds the name, and *length* is an integer that gives the name's length.

A similar set of functions provides for domain names. The functions setdomainname and getdomainname enable an application to obtain or set the domain names. Their formats are

```
setdomainname(name, length)
getdomainname(name, length)
```

The parameters are the same as with the sethostname and gethostname functions, except for the format of the name (which reflects domain name format).

Closing a Connection

The close function closes a connection. It requires only the local connection name to complete the process. It also takes care of the TCB and releases any variable created by the connection. No output is generated.

The close function is initiated with the following call:

```
close(socket)
```

where the socket name is required. If an application terminates abnormally, the operating system closes all sockets that were open prior to the termination.

Aborting a Connection

The abort function instructs TCP to discard all data that currently resides in send and receive buffers and closes the connection. It takes the local connection name as input. No output is generated. This function can be used in case of emergency shutdown routines, or in case of a fatal failure of the connection or associated software.

The abort function is usually implemented by the close() call, although some special instructions may be available with different implementations.

UNIX Forks

UNIX has two system calls that can affect sockets: fork and exec. Both are frequently used by UNIX developers because of their power. (In fact, forks are one of the most powerful tools UNIX offers and are tools that most other operating systems lack.) For simplicity, I will deal with the two functions as though they perform the same task.

A fork call creates a copy of the existing application as a new process and starts executing it. The new process has all the original's file descriptors and socket information. This can cause a problem if the application programmer didn't take into account the fact that two (or more) processes will try to use the same socket (or file) simultaneously. Therefore, applications that may fork have to take into account potential conflicts, so code around them by checking the status of shared sockets.

The operating system itself keeps a table of each socket and how many processes have access to it. An internal counter is incremented or decremented with each process's open or close function call for the socket. When the last process using a socket is terminated, the socket is permanently closed. This prevents one forked process from closing a socket when its original is still using it.

Summary

Today you've seen the basic functions that are performed by the socket API during establishment of a TCP or UDP call. You've also seen the functions that are available to application programmers. Although the treatment has been at a high level, you should be able to see that working with sockets is not a complex, confusing task. Indeed, socket programming is surprisingly easy once you've tried it.

14

Not everyone will want to write TCP or UDP applications, of course. However, understanding the basics of the socket API will help in understanding the protocol and troubleshooting. If you are interested in programming sockets, one of the best books on the subject is *UNIX Network Programming* by W. Richard Stevens (Macmillan).

Q&A

Q What is the socket interface used for?

A The socket interface enables you to write applications that make optimal use of the TCP/IP family of protocols. Without it, you would need another layer of application to translate your program's calls to TCP/IP calls.

Q What is the difference between a blocking and nonblocking function?

A A blocking function waits for the function to terminate before enabling the application to continue. A nonblocking function enables the application to continue executing while the function is performed. Both have important uses in applications.

Q What does binding do?

A Binding makes a logical connection between a socket and the application. Without it, the application couldn't access the socket.

Q What happens when an active open command is executed?

A An active open command creates a socket and binds it, and then issues a connect call to identify the IP address and port. The active open command then tries to establish communications.

Q What is the difference between an abort and a close operation?

A A close operation closes a connection. An abort abandons whatever communications are currently underway and closes the connection. With an abort, any information in receive buffers is discarded.

Workshop

The Workshop provides quiz questions to help you solidify your understanding of the material covered. Some Workshop sections of this book also contain exercises to provide you with experience in using what you've learned. Try to understand the quiz and exercise answers before continuing on to the next chapter. Quiz answers are provided in Appendix F, "Answers."

Quiz

1. What are the six basic socket commands?

2. A Transmission Control Block performs what function?

3. What is the difference between an unspecified passive open and a fully specified passive open?

4. What command will display status information about a socket?

5. What is a fork?

14

Abbreviations

ACB	Access Control Block
ACK	Acknowledgment
AF	Address Family
ANSI	American National Standard Institute
API	Application Programming Interface
ARP	Address Resolution Protocol
ARPA	Advanced Research Projects Agency
AS	Autonomous System
ASA	American Standards Association
ASCII	American National Standard Code for Information Interchange
ASN.1	Abstract Syntax Notation One
BBN	Bolt, Beranek, and Newman, Incorporated
BER	Basic Encoding Rules
BGP	Border Gateway Protocol
BSD	Berkeley Software Distribution
CMIP	Common Management Information Protocol
CMIS	Common Management Information Services
CMOT	Common Management Information Services and Protocol over TCP/IP
CRC	Cyclic Redundancy Check
CSMA/CD	Carrier Sense Multiple Access with Collision Detection
DARPA	Defense Advanced Research Projects Agency
DCA	Defense Communications Agency
DCE	Distributed Computing Environment
DCE	Data Circuit-terminating Equipment (also called Data Communications Equipment)
DDN	Defense Data Network

DES	Data Encryption Standard
DFS	Distributed File Service
DISA	Defense Information Systems Agency
DIX	Digital, Intel, and Xerox Ethernet Protocol
DME	Distributed Management Environment
DNS	Domain Name System
DSA	Directory System Agent
DSAP	Destination Service Access Point
DTE	Data Terminal Equipment
DUA	Directory User Agent
EBCDIC	Extended Binary Coded Decimal Interchange Code
EGP	Exterior Gateway Protocol
EOF	End of File
EOR	End of Record
FCS	Frame Check Sequence
FDDI	Fiber Distributed Data Interface
FIN	Final Segment
FTAM	File Transfer, Access, and Management
FTP	File Transfer Protocol
GGP	Gateway to Gateway Protocol
GOSIP	Government Open Systems Interconnection Profile
GTF	Generalized Trace Facility
HDLC	High-level Data Link Control Protocol
IAB	Internet Architecture Board
IAB	Internet Activities Board
IAC	Interpret as Command
IANA	Internet Assigned Numbers Authority

ICMP	Internet Control Message Protocol
ID	Identifier
IEEE	Institute of Electrical and Electronic Engineers
IEN	Internet Engineering Notes
IESG	Internet Engineering Steering Group
IETF	Internet Engineering Task Force
IGMP	Internet Group Management Protocol
IGP	Interior Gateway Protocol
IP	Internet Protocol
IRTF	Internet Research Task Force
ISDN	Integrated Services Digital Network
ISN	Initial Sequence Number
ISO	International Organization for Standardization
ISODE	ISO Development Environment
LAN	Local Area Network
LAPB	Link Access Procedures Balanced
LAPD	Link Access Procedures on the D-channel
LLC	Logical Link Control
MAC	Media Access Control
MAN	Metropolitan Area Network
MIB	Management Information Base
MSS	Maximum Segment Size
MTA	Message Transfer Agent
MTU	Message Transfer Unit
MTU	Maximum Transmission Unit
MX	Mail Exchanger
NETBIOS	Network Basic Input/Output System

NFS	Network File System
NIC	Network Interface Card
NIS	Network Information System
NREN	National Research and Education Network
NSAP	Network Service Access Point
NSFNET	National Science Foundation Network
NVT	Network Virtual Terminal
OSF	Open Software Foundation
OSI	Open Systems Interconnect
OSPF	Open Shortest Path First
PAD	Packet Assembly/Disassembly
PDU	Protocol Data Unit
PI	Protocol Interpreter
PING	Packet Internet Groper
POP	Post Office Protocol
PPP	Point-to-Point Protocol
RARP	Reverse Address Resolution Protocol
RFC	Request For Comment
RIP	Routing Information Protocol
RMON	Remote Network Monitor
RPC	Remote Procedure Call
RST	Reset
RTT	Round Trip Time
SDLC	Synchronous Data Link Communication
SLIP	Serial Line Interface Protocol
SMDS	Switched Multimegabit Data Service
SMTP	Simple Mail Transfer Protocol

SNA	Systems Network Architecture
SNMP	Simple Network Management Protocol
SONET	Synchronous Optical Network
SPF	Shortest Path First
SSAP	Source Service Access Point
SSCP	System Services Control Point
SYN	Synchronizing Segment
TCB	Transmission Control Block
TCP	Transmission Control Protocol
TCU	Trunk Coupling Unit
TELNET	Terminal Networking
TFTP	Trivial File Transfer Protocol
TLI	Transport Layer Interface
TP4	OSI Transport Class 4
TSAP	Transport Service Access Point
TTL	Time-to-Live
UA	User Agent
UDP	User Datagram Protocol
ULP	Upper Layer Protocol
WAN	Wide Area Network
XDR	External Data Representation
XNS	Xerox Network Systems

B

Glossary

10Base2   An Ethernet term referring to a maximum transfer rate of 10 megabits per second, which uses baseband signaling with a contiguous cable segment length of 100 meters and a maximum of two segments.

10Base5   An Ethernet term referring to a maximum transfer rate of 10 megabits per second, which uses baseband signaling with 5 continuous segments not exceeding 100 meters per segment.

10BaseT   An Ethernet term referring to a maximum transfer rate of 10 megabits per second, which uses baseband signaling and twisted-pair cabling.

Abstract Syntax Notation One (ASN.1)   An OSI language used to define datatypes for networks. It is used within TCP/IP to provide conformance with the OSI model.

Access control   A process that defines each user's privileges on a system.

Acknowledgment (ACK)   A positive response returned from a receiver to the sender, indicating success. TCP uses acknowledgments to indicate the successful reception of a packet.

Active Open   An operation performed by a client to establish a TCP connection with a server.

Address   A memory location in a particular machine's RAM, a numeric identifier or symbolic name that specifies the location of a particular machine or device on a network, and a means of identifying a complete network, subnetwork, or a node within a network.

Address mask (also called the subnet mask)   A set of rules for omitting parts of a complete IP address in order to reach the target destination without using a broadcast message. The mask can, for example, indicate a subnetwork portion of a larger network. In TCP/IP, the address mask uses the 32-bit IP address.

Address resolution   Mapping of an IP address to a machine's physical address. TCP/IP uses the Address Resolution Protocol (ARP) for this function.

Address Resolution Protocol (ARP)   See Address Resolution.

Address space   A range of memory addresses available to an application program.

Advanced Research Project Agency (ARPA)   DARPA's former name. ARPA was an agency funded by the federal government.

Agent   In TCP/IP, an agent is an SNMP process that responds to *get* and *set* requests. Agents also can send *trap* messages.

American National Standards Institute (ANSI)   The U.S. organization responsible for setting standards.

Application Programming Interface (API)   A set of routines that are available to developers and applications to provide specific services used by the system, usually specific to the application's purpose. They act as access methods into the application.

Application layer   The highest layer in the OSF model. It establishes communications rights and can initiate a connection between two applications.

ARPANET (Advanced Research Projects Agency Network)   A packet switched network that later became known as the Internet.

ASCII (American National Standard Code for Information Interchange)   An 8-bit character set defining alphanumeric characters.

Assigned numbers   Used in Request For Comment (RFC) documents to specify values used by TCP/IP.

Asynchronous   Communications without a regular time basis allowing transmission at unequal rates.

Autonomous system   A collection of routers that are under the control of a single management body. The system usually uses a common Interior Gateway Protocol.

Backbone   A set of nodes and links connected together comprising a network, or the upper layer protocols used in a network. Sometimes the term is used to refer to a network's physical media.

Bandwidth   The range of frequencies transmitted on a channel, or the difference between the highest and lowest frequencies transmitted across a channel.

Baseband   A type of channel in which data transmission is carried across only one communications channel, supporting only one signal transmission at a time. Ethernet is a baseband system.

Baseband signaling   A type of transmission that has a continuous encoded signal. Only one node at a time may send data over this type of transmission technology. Used in local area networks.

Basic Encoding Rules (BER)   The rules for encoding datatypes using ASN.1.

Baud   The number of times a signal changes state in one second.

Berkeley Software Distribution (BSD)   A version of the UNIX operating system that first included TCP/IP support. The UNIX operating systems that included TCP/IP are referred to as 4.2BSD or 4.3BSD.

Bit Error Rate (BER)   The number of errors expected in a transmission.

BITNET (Because It's Time Network)   An electronic mail network connecting more than 200 universities. It merged with the CSNET network to produce CREN.

Bit rate   The rate that bits are transmitted, usually expressed in seconds.

Block mode   A string of data recorded or transmitted as a unit. Block-mode transmission is usually used for high-speed transmissions and in large, high-speed networks.

Border Gateway Protocol (BGP)   A protocol that provides information about the devices that can be reached through a router (into an autonomous network). BGP is newer than EGP.

Bridge   A network device capable of connecting networks that use similar protocols.

Broadband (also known as wideband)   A range of frequencies divided into several narrower bands. Each band can be used for different purposes.

Broadband signaling   The type of signaling used in local area networks that enables multiplexing of more than one transmission at a time.

Broadcast   The simultaneous transmission of the same data to all nodes connected to the network.

Brouter   A network device that is a combination of the functions of a bridge and a router. It can function as a bridge while filtering protocols and packets destined for nodes on different networks.

BSD   See Berkeley Software Distribution.

Buffer   A memory area used for handling input and output.

Burst mode   A transmission mode in which data is transmitted in bursts rather than in continuous streams.

Bus   In network topology, a linear configuration. This term is also used to refer to part of the electronic layout of network devices.

Cache   A memory location that keeps frequently requested material ready. Usually the cache is faster than using a storage device. It is used to speed data and instruction transfer.

Carrier Sense   A signal generated by the physical network layer to inform the data link layer that one or more nodes are transmitting on the network medium.

Carrier Sense Multiple Access with Collision Detection (CSMA/CD)   A network media access control protocol wherein a device listens to the medium to monitor traffic. If there is no signal, the device is allowed to send data.

B

Cheapernet   A reduced-cost Ethernet variant in which the maximum length of the network is 200 feet. It uses inexpensive 75-ohm coaxial cable, simple connectors, and no transceivers.

Client   A program that tries to connect to another program (usually on another machine) called a *server*. The client calls the server. The server listens for calls.

Client/server architecture   A catch-all term used to refer to a distributed environment wherein one program can initiate a session and another program answers its requests. The origin of client/server designs is closely allied with the TCP/IP protocol suite.

CMOT   The TCP/IP implementation of CMIP.

Collision   An event that occurs when two or more nodes broadcast packets at the same time. The packets "collide."

Collision detection   A device's capability to determine whether a collision has occurred.

Common Management Information Protocol (CMIP)   A network management protocol usually associated with OSI. When used with TCP/IP, CMIP is called CMOT.

Common Management Information Service (CMIS)   Management services provided by CMIP.

Connection   A link between two or more processes, applications, machines, network, and so on. Connections may be logical, physical, or both.

Connectionless   A type of network service that does not send acknowledgments upon receipt of data to the sender. UDP is a connectionless protocol.

Connection oriented   A type of network service wherein the transport layer protocol sends acknowledgments to the sender regarding incoming data. This type of service usually provides for retransmission of corrupted or lost data.

Consortium for Research and Education Network (CREN)   The name for the body arising from the combination of CSNET and BITNET.

Contention   A condition occurring in some LANs wherein the Media Access Control (MAC) sublayer enables more than one node to transmit at the same time, risking collisions.

Core Gateway   A router operated by the Internet Network Operations Center to distribute routing information.

Crosstalk   Signals that interfere with another signal.

CSNET (Computer Science Network) An electronic mail network that merged with BITNET to form CREN.

Cyclic Redundancy Check (CRC) A mathematical function performed on the contents of an entity that is then included to enable a receiving system to recalculate the value and compare it to the original. If the values are different, corruption of the contents has occurred.

Daemon A UNIX process that operates continuously and unattended to perform a service. TCP/IP uses several daemons to establish communications processes and provide server facilities.

DARPA (Defense Advanced Research Project Agency) The governmental body that created the DARPANET for widespread communications. DARPANET eventually became the Internet.

Data Circuit-terminating Equipment (DCE) Required equipment to attach Data Terminal Equipment (DTE) to a network or serial line. A modem is a DCE device. Also called Data Communications Equipment and Data Circuit Equipment.

Data Encryption Standard (DES) An encryption standard officially sanctioned in the United States.

Datagram A basic unit of data used with TCP/IP.

Data link The part of a node controlled by a data link protocol. It is the logical connection between two nodes.

Data Link Protocol (DLP) A method of handling the establishment, maintenance, and termination of a logical link between nodes. Ethernet is a DLP.

Data Terminal Equipment (DTE) The source or destination of data, usually attached to a network by DEC devices. A terminal or computer acting as a node on a network is usually a DTE device.

Defense Communications Agency (DCA) The governmental agency responsible for the Defense Data Network (DDN).

Defense Data Network (DDN) Refers to military networks such as MILNET, ARPANET, and the communications protocols (including TCP/IP) that they employ.

Destination address The destination device's address.

Directory System Agent (DSA) A program that accepts queries from a directory user agent (DUA).

Directory User Agent (DUA) A program that helps a user send a query to a directory server.

Distributed Computing Environment (DCE) A set of technologies developed by the Open Software Foundation (OSF) supporting distributed computing.

Distributed File Service (DFS) An Open Software Foundation (OSF) file server technology sometimes used with TCP/IP.

Distributed Management Environment (DME) A system and network management technology developed by the Open Software Foundation (OSF).

Distributed processing When a process is spread over two or more devices, it is distributed. It is usually used to spread CPU loads among a network of machines.

Domain Name System (DNS) A service that converts symbolic node names to IP addresses. DNS is frequently used with TCP/IP. DNS uses a distributed database.

Dotted decimal notation A representation of IP addresses. Also called *dotted quad notation* because it uses four sets of numbers separated by decimals (such as `255.255.255.255`).

Double-byte character set A character set wherein alphanumeric characters are represented by two bytes, instead of one byte, as with ASCII. Double-byte characters are often necessary for oriental languages that have more than 255 symbols.

Drop cable In Ethernet networks, this refers to the cable connecting the device to the network, sometimes through a transceiver.

Dumb terminal A terminal with no significant processing capability of its own, usually with no graphics capabilities beyond the ASCII set.

Emulation A program that simulates another device. For example, a 3270 emulator emulates an IBM 3270 terminal, sending the same codes as the real device would.

Encapsulation To include an incoming message into a larger message by adding information at the front, back, or both. Encapsulation is used by layered network protocols. With each layer, new headers and trailers are added.

Enterprise network A generic term usually referring to a wide area network providing services to all of a corporation's sites.

Ethernet A data link level protocol comprising the OSI model's bottom two layers. It is a broadcast networking technology that can use several different physical media, including twisted-pair cable and coaxial cable. Ethernet usually uses CSMA/CD. TCP/IP is commonly used with Ethernet networks.

Ethernet address   A 48-bit address commonly referred to as a *physical* or *hard* address, which uniquely identifies the Ethernet Network Interface Card (NIC) and hence the device in which the card resides.

Ethernet meltdown   A slang term for a situation wherein an Ethernet network becomes saturated. The condition usually persists only for a short time and is usually caused by a misrouted or invalid packet.

Extended Binary Coded Decimal Interchange Code (EBCDIC)   An alternative to ASCII, used extensively in IBM machinery. Some other vendors use it for mainframes. EBCDIC and ASCII are not compatible but are easy to convert between.

Exterior Gateway Protocol (EGP)   A protocol used by gateways to transfer information about devices that can be reached within their autonomous systems.

Fiber Distributed Data Interface (FDDI)   An ANSI-defined standard for high-speed data transfer over fiber-optic cabling.

File Server   A process that provides access to a file from remote devices.

File Transfer Access Method (FTAM)   A file transfer program and protocol developed by the OSI. It includes some basic management functions.

File Transfer Protocol (FTP)   A TCP/IP application used for transferring files from one system to another.

Fragmentation   The breaking of a datagram into several smaller pieces, usually because the original datagram was too large for the network or software.

Frame   Usually refers to the completed Ethernet packet, which includes the original data and all the TCP/IP layers' headers and trailers (including the Ethernet's).

Frame Check Sequence (FCS)   A mathematical function used to verify the integrity of bits in a frame, similar to the Cyclic Redundancy Check (CRC).

Frame relay   A network switching mechanism for routing frames as quickly as possible.

Gateway   In Internet terms, a gateway is a device that routes datagrams. More recently, this term was used to refer to any networking device that translates protocols of one type of network into those of another network.

Gateway-to-Gateway Protocol (GGP)   A protocol used to exchange routing information between core routers.

Gigabyte   One billion bytes corresponding to decimal 1,073,741,824 (as a kilobyte is 1,024 decimal).

Government Open System Interconnection Profile (GOSIP)   A government standard that uses the OSI reference model.

Hardware Address   The low-level address associated with each device on a network, usually corresponding to the unique identifier of the network interface card (NIC). Ethernet addresses are 48 bits.

High Level Data Link Control (HDLC)   An international data communication standard.

Hop count   The number of bridges that data crosses in a Token Ring network.

IEEE 802.2   An IEEE-approved data link standard used with the 802.3, 802.4, and 802.5 protocol standards.

IEEE 802.3   An IEEE-approved physical layer standard that uses CSMA/CD on a bus network topology.

IEEE 802.4   An IEEE-approved physical layer standard that uses token passing on a bus network topology.

IEEE 802.5   An IEEE-approved physical layer standard using a token passing technology on a ring network topology.

Initial sequence number (ISN)   A number defined during the startup of a connection using TCP used to number datagrams.

Initiate   In TCP/IP, to send a request for something (usually a connection).

Institute of Electrical and Electronic Engineers (IEEE)   A professional organization for engineers that proposes and approves standards.

Integrated Service Digital Network (ISDN)   A set of standards for integrating multiple services (such as voice, data, and video).

Interface   A shared point between two software applications or two hardware devices.

Interior Gateway Protocol (IGP)   A protocol used by gateways in an autonomous system to transfer routing information.

International Organization for Standardization (ISO)   An international body composed of individual country's standards groups. ISO focuses on international standards.

Internet   A collection of networks connected together that span the world using the NFSNET as their backbone. The Internet is the specific term for a more general internetwork or collection of networks.

Internet Activities Board (IAB)   The Internet group that coordinates the development of the TCP/IP protocol suite.

Internet Address   A 32-bit address used to identify hosts and networks on the Internet.

Internet Control Message Protocol (ICMP)   A control and error message protocol that works in conjunction with the Internet Protocol (IP).

Internet Engineering Notes (IEN)   Documents that discuss TCP/IP, available through the Network Information Center (NIC).

Internet Engineering Steering Group (IESG)   The executive party of the IETF.

Internet Engineering Task Force (IETF)   Part of the IAB responsible for short-term engineering needs related to the TCP/IP protocol suite.

Internet Protocol (IP)   The part of TCP/IP that handles routing.

Internet Research Task Force (IRTF)   A part of the IAB that concentrates on research and development of the TCP/IP protocol suite.

IP address   A 32-bit identity that is unique to each network device.

IP datagram   The basic unit of information passed through a TCP/IP network. The datagram header contains source and destination IP addresses.

IS-IS (Intermediate System to Intermediate System Protocol)   A routing protocol that performs routing functions with IP and OSI data.

ISODE (ISO Development Environment)   An attempt to develop software that enables OSI protocols to run on TCP/IP.

ISO Reference Model   The seven-layer ISO networking model. It isolates specific functions within each layer.

Jam   An Ethernet term for communicating to all devices on a network on which a collision has occurred.

Jitter   A term used with 10BaseT (twisted-pair Ethernet) networks where signals are out of phase with one another.

Kerberos   An authentication scheme developed at MIT, used to prevent unauthorized monitoring of logins and passwords.

LAN (local area network)   A collection of devices connected to enable communications between themselves on a single physical medium.

Learning bridge   A network bridge device that has the function of a bridge and the capability to monitor the network in order to determine which nodes are connected to it, and adjust routing data accordingly.

Leased line   A dedicated communication line between two points. It's usually used by organizations to connect computers over a dedicated telephone circuit.

Link   A generic term referring to a connection between two end points.

Logical   Conveys an abstract concept in a simpler manner, such as using a logical machine name instead of its physical address.

Logical Link Control (LLC)   The upper part of the data link sublayer protocol that is responsible for governing the exchange of data between two end points.

Mail Exchanger   A system used to relay mail into a network.

Management Information Base (MIB)   A database used by SNMP containing configuration and statistical information about devices on a network.

Maximum Segment Size   The maximum permissible size for the data part of a packet.

Maximum Transmission Unit (MTU)   The largest datagram that can be handled by a specific network. The MTU may change over different networks, even if the transport is the same (such as Ethernet).

Media Access Control (MAC)   The lower half of the data link sublayer that is responsible for framing data and controlling the physical link between two end points.

Medium Access Unit (MAU)   A device for the central connection of a device operating on a network.

Message Transfer Agent (MTA)   A process that moves messages between devices.

Metropolitan Area Network (MAN)   An IEEE-approved network that supports high speeds over a metropolitan area.

MILNET (Military Network)   A network that originally was part of ARPANET, now designated for exclusive military use in installations that require reliable network services.

Modem (Modulator-Demodulator)   A device that converts digital signals into analog signals, and vice versa. It's used for conversion of signals for transmission over telephone lines.

Modem eliminator   A device that functions as two modems to provide service for data terminal equipment (DTE) and data communication equipment (DCE).

Multihomed host   A device attached to two or more networks.

Multiplex   To simultaneously transmit multiple signals over one channel.

Name resolution   The process of mapping aliases to an address. The Domain Name System (DNS) is one system that does this.

National Institute of Standards and Technology (NIST)   A U.S. standards body, previously called the National Bureau of Standards, that promotes communications-oriented standards.

National Research and Education Network (NREN)   A network backbone supporting large capacities planned for future Internet use.

National Science Foundation Network (NFSNET)   The network that acts as part of the Internet backbone.

NETBIOS (Network Basic Input/Output Operating System)   A network programming interface typically used to connect PCs together.

Network   A number of devices connected to enable a device to communicate with any other device over a physical medium.

Network address   For TCP/IP, the 32-bit IP address of a device.

Network File System (NFS)   A protocol developed by Sun Microsystems that enables clients to mount remote directories onto their own local file systems.

Network Information Center (NIC)   The Internet administration facility that controls the naming of networks accessible over the Internet.

Network Information Service (NIS)   A set of protocols developed by Sun Microsystems used to provide directory services for network information.

Network Interface Card (NIC)   A generic term for a networking interface board used to connect a device to the network. The NIC is where the physical connection to the network occurs.

Network Management   Any aspect of monitoring or controlling a network, including all administration details.

Network Service Access Point   Used to identify an OSI device and point to the transport layer.

Network Virtual Terminal (NVT)   Protocols that govern virtual terminal emulation.

Node   A generic term used to refer to network devices.

Open Shortest Path First (OSPF)   The basic Internet routing protocol for sending data over multiple paths. It uses the network's topology for routing decisions.

Open Software Foundation (OSF)   A consortium of hardware and software vendors collaborating to produce technologies for device-independent operations.

Open Systems Interconnection (OSI)   A family of ISO-developed standards relating to data communications.

Optical Fiber   A plastic or glass cable that uses light as a communications medium.

Packet   In TCP/IP, a term referring to the data passing between the Internet layer and the data link layer. Packet is also a generic term used to refer to data transferred through a network.

Passive Open   An action taken by a server daemon to prepare it to receive requests from clients.

PING (Packet Internet Groper)   A utility program used to test a system's TCP/IP software by sending an ICMP echo request and then waiting for a response.

Point-to-Point   Transmission directly between two points, without any intervening devices.

Point-to-Point Protocol (PPP)   A TCP/IP protocol that provides host-to-network and router-to-router connections. Can be used to provide a serial line connection between two machines.

Port   A number used to identify TCP/IP applications. Generally a port is an entry or exit point.

Protocol   Rules governing the behavior or method of operation of something.

Protocol conversion   The process of changing one protocol to another.

Protocol Data Unit (PDU)   A term used in TCP/IP to refer to a unit of data, headers, and trailers at any layer in a network.

Protocol Interpreter (PI)   A process that carries out FTP functions. FTP uses one PI for the server and one for the user.

Proxy   A mechanism whereby one system functions for another when responding to protocol requests.

Push service   A service provided by TCP to allow an application to specify when data must be transmitted as soon as possible.

B

RARP (See Reverse Address Resolution Protocol)

Receive Window   A range of sequence numbers that a sender may transmit at a given time.

Remote Network Monitor (RMON)   A device (such as a workstation) that collects and maintains information about network traffic.

Remote Procedure Call (RPC)   A TCP/IP protocol that provides a routine that calls a server, which returns output and status (return) codes to the client.

Repeater   A network device that boosts the power of incoming signals to allow the length of a network to be extended.

Requests for Comment (RFCs)   Documents containing specifications for TCP/IP protocols. RFCs are also used to propose new protocols. RFCs are available from the Network Information Center (NIC).

Resolver   Software that enables clients to access the Domain Name System (DNS) database and acquire an address.

Resource   Usually refers to application programs but is also used generally to refer to system capabilities, such as memory and networks.

Retransmission Timeout   Occurs when data has been sent to a destination but no acknowledgment has been received when a timer has expired. When a retransmission timeout occurs, the protocol usually resends to data.

Reverse Address Resolution Protocol (RARP)   A TCP/IP protocol that allows a device to acquire its IP address by performing a broadcast on the network.

RIP (Routing Information Protocol)   A TCP/IP protocol used to exchange information about routing (usually when only a small number of computers are in use).

rlogin   Remote login service that enables a user on one machine to log in as a user on another. It is similar to Telnet.

Round Trip Time   The time for a TCP segment to be sent and its acknowledgment received.

Router   A device that connects LANs into an internetwork and routes traffic between them.

Routing   The process of determining a path to use to send data to its destination.

Routing Information Protocol (RIP)   A protocol used to exchange information between routers.

Routing table   A list of valid paths through which data can be transmitted.

RS232C   A physical layer specification for connecting devices, it's commonly used for serial lines.

SAP (Service Access Point)   The location at which two applications can exchange information.

Segment   A protocol data unit (PDU) that consists of a TCP header and (optional) data. Also used to refer to parts of a network that is divided into smaller parts (segments).

Send Window   A range of sequence numbers that can be received.

Sequence Number   A 32-bit field in the IP header that identifies the datagram.

Serial   A sequence of events occurring one after another.

Serial Line Internet Protocol (SLIP)   A protocol used to utilize TCP/IP over serial lines.

Server   An application that answers requests from other devices (clients). Also used as a generic term for any device that provides services to the rest of the network, such as printing, high-capacity storage, and network access.

Simple Mail Transfer Protocol (SMTP)   In TCP/IP, an application providing electronic mail services.

Socket   In TCP/IP, an addressable point that consists of an IP address and a TCP or UDP port number that provide applications access to TCP/IP protocols.

Socket address   The complete designation of a TCP/IP node consisting of a 32-bit IP address and a 16-bit port number.

Socket descriptor   An integer used by an application to identify the connection.

Source   The originating device.

Source routing   A routing method determined by the source device.

Subnet   In TCP/IP, part of a TCP/IP network identified by a portion of the Internet address.

Subnet address   The part of the IP address that identifies the subnetwork.

Subnet mask   A set of bits that excludes networks from having a system-wide broadcast, instead restricting the broadcast to a subnetwork.

Switched connection   A data link connection that is established on demand (such as a telephone call).

SYN   A segment used in the start of a TCP connection to enable both devices to exchange information defining characteristics about the session. It is also used to synchronize the target and destination devices.

Synchronous data transfer   The transfer of data between two nodes at a timed rate (as opposed to asynchronously).

TCP/IP   Transmission Control Protocol/Internet Protocol.

TELNET   A TCP/IP application that enables a user to log into a remote device.

Terminal Server   A network device that provides physical access for dumb terminals, usually using an abbreviated TCP/IP protocol to enable a dumb terminal to remotely log on.

Terminator   A resistor that must be on both ends of thick and thin Ethernet cable.

Throughput   The amount of data that can be transferred through a medium within a certain time period.

Time-to-Live (TTL)   The amount of time a datagram can remain on the internetwork. It is usually specified as the number of hops to permit.

Token Ring   A lower layer connection-based networking protocol using a token passing method to control data traffic.

Topology   The configuration of network devices.

Traffic   A general term used to describe the amount of data on a network backbone.

Transceiver   A network device required in baseband networks that takes a digital signal and puts it on the analog baseband medium. Transceivers can sense collisions.

Transmission Class 4   An OSI transport layer protocol similar to TCP. It's often referred to as OSI TP4.

Transmission Control Block (TCB)   A data structure that holds information about TCP and UDP connections.

Transmission Control Protocol (TCP)   A transport layer protocol that is part of the TCP/IP protocol suite and provides a connection-based, reliable data stream.

Trivial File Transfer Protocol (TFTP)   A mechanism for remote logons, similar to Telnet, that uses UDP as a transport layer protocol instead of TCP.

UDP (User Datagram Protocol)   A connectionless transport layer protocol. It does not perform retransmission of data.

User Agent   An electronic mail program that helps end users manage messages.

User Service   A service provided by TCP permitting an application to specify that data being transmitted is urgent and should be processed as soon as possible.

Well-Known Port   In TCP/IP, an address for an agreed-upon purpose.

Wide Area Network (WAN)   Usually used to refer to a network spanning large geographic distances.

X.400   A protocol defining standards for electronic mail in an open network.

X.500   A protocol defining standards for directory services in an open network.

Xerox Networking Standard (XNS)   Networking protocols developed by Xerox.

X Series   A collection of widely accepted standards, including data communications.

X Windows   A software protocol developed at MIT for a distributed windowing system. X uses TCP for a transport protocol.

B

Commands

C Commands

The commands associated with the TCP/IP utilities mentioned in this book are summarized in the following list. Refer to the index for their occurrences throughout the text.

arp	View or update the Address Resolution Protocol tables
finger	View the list of users logged on the network
ftp	Invoke the file transfer protocol program
ifconfig	View or configure network interface parameters
mount	Mount a directory or file system onto the local file structure, or view a list of mounted directories or file systems
netstat	Display network statistics
nfsstat	View statistics on NFS usage and configuration
nslookup	Look up IP addresses and associated information through a Domain Name server
ping	Send an ICMP echo message to a remote system to test connectivity
rlogin	Log into a remote host
rpcinfo	Display information about active processes
ruptime	Display the total time a system has been functioning, and its current load
showmount	View all servers currently mounted
spray	Send a batch of UDP datagrams to a remote system to check connectivity and throughput
telnet	Log into a remote host
traceroute	Display messages from routers along the path of a set of test datagrams
ypcat	Display the contents of a Network Information Service database
ypmatch	Look up an entry in a Network Information Service database

Well-Known Port
Numbers

Both TCP and UDP use well-known ports, also known as *service contact ports.* The port names reflect the specific TCP and UDP applications. Ports are the end points of a connection, and they provide a convenient method for accessing and addressing the connection end.

The following list doesn't include all TCP and UDP ports, but it does include all those likely to be encountered. The rest are assigned for historical or experimental reasons.

Port	Name	Description
1	TCPMUX	TCP Port Service Multiplexer
5	RJE	Remote Job Entry
7	ECHO	Echo
9	DISCARD	Discard
11	USERS	Active Users
13	DAYTIME	Daytime
17	QUOTE	Quote of the Day
19	CHARGEN	Character Generator
20	FTP-DATA	File Transfer (Data Channel)
21	FTP	File Transfer (Control Channel)
23	TELNET	Telnet
25	SMTP	Simple Mail Transfer
27	NSW-FE	NSW User System FE
29	MSG-ICP	MSG-ICP
31	MSG-AUTH	MSG Authentication
33	DSP	Display Support Protocol
35		Private Printer Server
37	TIME	Time
39	RLP	Resource Location Protocol
41	GRAPHICS	Graphics
42	NAMESERVER	Host Name Server

Port	Name	Description
43	NICNAME	Who Is
49	LOGIN	Login Host Protocol
53	DOMAIN	Domain Name Server
67	BOOTPS	Bootstrap Protocol Server
68	BOOTPC	Bootstrap Protocol Client
69	TFTP	Trivial File Transfer Protocol
79	FINGER	Finger
101	HOSTNAME	NIC Host Name Server
102	ISO-TSAP	ISO TSAP
103	X400	X.400
104	X400SND	X.400 SND
105	CSNET-NS	CSNET Mailbox Name Server
109	POP2	Post Office Protocol v2
110	POP3	Post Office Protocol v3
111	SUNRPC	SUN RPC Portmap
137	NETBIOS-NS	NETBIOS Name Service
138	NETBIOS-DGM	NETBIOS Datagram Service
139	NETBIOS-SSN	NETBIOS Session Service
146	ISO-TP0	ISO TP0
147	ISO-IP	ISO IP
150	SQL-NET	SQL-NET
153	SGMP	SGMP
156	SQLSRV	SQL Service
160	SGMP-TRAP5	SGMP TRAPS
161	SNMP	SNMP
162	SNMPTRAP	SNMPTRAP

Port	Name	Description
163	CMIP-MANAGE	CMIP/TCP Manager
164	CMIP-AGENT	CMIP/TCP Agent
165	XNS-COURIER	Xerox Network
179	BGP	Border Gateway Protocol

E

RFCs

Most of the information about the TCP/IP protocol family is published as Request for Comments (RFCs). RFCs define the various aspects of the TCP/IP protocol, its use, and management as a set of loosely coordinated notes.

There is a lot of useless information (mostly because it is system-specific or considerably outdated) in the RFCs, but there is also a wealth of detail for those who want to take TCP/IP to its limits. Unexpectedly, there is quite a bit of interesting and humorous reading in the RFCs, including several classic works such as "'Twas the Night Before Start-up" (RFC 968), "ARPAWOCKY" (RFC 527), and "TELNET Randomly-Lose Option" (RFC 748).

This appendix lists the important (or, as just mentioned, interesting or humorous) RFCs that readers may want to refer to. Instructions for accessing the RFCs are also included. This list is not complete. Where possible, old and outdated RFCs have been dropped from the list. However, thinning the list of RFCs is a time-consuming process, involving reading each of the documents in turn. Because there are almost 1,500 RFCs, the author has relied on other user's comments, notes from the NIC, and other reference works for a suitable pruning.

Accessing RFCs

RFCs can be obtained in several ways, the easiest of which is electronically. Paper copies are available upon request. Electronic copies are usually in ASCII format, although some are in PostScript format and require a PostScript interpreter to print them. Most RFCs obtained electronically don't have diagrams, figures, or pictures.

Accessing RFCs Through FTP

RFCs can be obtained using FTP through the Internet Network Information Center (NIC). Use FTP to access the NIC archive NIC.DDN.MIL. Use the user name guest and the password anonymous. RFCs can then be retrieved by using the FTP get command with the following format:

```
<RFC>RFC527.txt
```

Replace the RFC527 portion with the number of the RFC required. You can only FTP into the NIC archive if you have access to a machine with Internet access.

Accessing RFCs Through E-mail

RFCs can be requested through electronic mail. Both the NIC and the NFSNET Network Service Center provide automated responses that return the request's RFC. Both services read incoming electronic mail for keywords that indicate which RFC is required, as well as the sender's e-mail address, and then sends back the RFC requested.

To obtain an RFC from the NIC, send a message with the subject field set to the RFC that you want. Mail it to `service@nic.ddn.mil`. If you want more information on obtaining information through the NIC e-mail system, send mail with the word `help` as the subject.

To obtain RFCs from the NFSNET Network Service Center, send a message with the first two lines like this:

```
REQUEST: RFC
TOPIC: 527
```

where the first line specifies that you want an RFC and the second line gives the RFC number. Send the mail to `info-server@sh.cs.net`. For more information, set the topic to `help`.

Accessing Printed Copies of RFCs

You might not have access to electronic communications, so you must preprinted copy of an RFC. To obtain a printed copy of any RFC, call the Network Information Center at 1-800-235-3155.

It is considered bad manners to make the NIC staff wait while you find which RFCs you want. Make a list first so your telephone conversation is short and succinct. The staff must answer many calls a day.

Useful RFCs Sorted by General Category

General Information

RFC1340 "Assigned Numbers," Reynolds, J.K.; Postel, J.B.; 1992

RFC1360 "IAB Official Protocol Standards," Postel, J.B.; 1992

RFC1208 "Glossary of Networking Terms," Jacobsen, O.J.; Lynch, D.C.; 1991

RFC1180 "TCP/IP Tutorial," Socolofsky, T.J.; Kale, C.J.; 1991

RFC1178 "Choosing a Name For Your Computer", Libes, D.; 1990

RFC1175 "FYI On Where to Start: A Bibliography of Internetworking Information," Bowers, K.L.; LaQuey, T.L.; Reynolds, J.K., Reubicek, K.; Stahl, M.K.; Yuan, A.; 1990

RFC1173 "Responsibilities of Host and Network Managers: A Summary of the "oral tradition" of the Internet," vanBokkelen, J.; 1990

RFC1166 "Internet Numbers," Kirkpatrick, S; Stahl, M.K; Recker, M.; 1990

RFC1127 "Perspective on the Host Requirements RFCs," Braden, R.T.; 1989

RFC1123 "Requirements for Internet Hosts—Application and Support," Braden, R.T., ed; 1989

RFC1122 "Requirements for Internet hosts—Communication Layers," Braden, R.T., ed; 1989

RFC1118 "Hitchhiker's Guide to the Internet," Krol, E., 1989

RFC1011 "Official Internet Protocol," Reynolds, J.R.; Postel, J.B.; 1987

RFC1009 "Requirements for Internet Gateways," Braden, R.T; Postel, J.B.; 1987

RFC980   "Protocol Document Order Information," Jacobsen, O.J.; Postel, J.B.; 1986

TCP and UDP

RFC1072 "TCP Extensions for Long-delay Paths," Jacobson, V.; Braden, R.T.; 1988

RFC896   "Congestion control in IP/TCP Internetworks," Nagle, J.; 1984

RFC879   "TCP Maximum Segment Size and Related Topics," Postel, J.B.; 1983

RFC813   "Window and Acknowledgment Strategy in TCP," Clark, D.D.; 1982

RFC793   "Transmission Control Protocol," Postel, J.B.; 1981

RFC768   "User Datagram Protocol," Postel, J.B.; 1980

IP and ICMP

RFC1219 "On the Assignment of Subnet Numbers," Tsuchiya, P.F.; 1991

RFC1112 "Host Extensions for IP Multicasting," Deering, S.E.; 1989

RFC1088 "Standard for the Transmission of IP Datagrams Over NetBIOS Networks," McLaughlin, L.J.; 1989

RFC950 "Internet Standard Subnetting Procedure," Mogul, J.C.; Postel, J.B.; 1985

RFC932 "Subnetwork Addressing Schema," Clark, D.D.; 1985

RFC922 "Broadcasting Internet Datagrams in the Presence of Subnets," Mogul, J.C.; 1984

RFC919 "Broadcasting Internet Datagrams," Mogul, J.C.; 1984

RFC886 "Proposed Standard for Message Header Munging," Rose, M.T.; 1983

RFC815 "IP Datagram Reassembly Algorithms," Clark, D.D.; 1982

RFC814 "Name, Addresses, Ports, and Routes," Clark, D.D.; 1982

RFC792 "Internet Control Message Protocol," Postel, J.B.; 1981

RFC791 "Internet Protocol," Postel, J.B; 1981

RFC781 "Specification of the Internet Protocol (IP) Timestamp Option," Su, Z.; 1981

E

Lower Layers

RFC1236 "IP to X.121 Address Mapping for DDN IP to X.121 Address Mapping for DDN," Morales, L.F.,Jr.; 1991

RFC1220 "Point-to-Point Protocol Extensions for Bridging," Baker, F.,ed.; 1991

RFC1209 "Transmission of IP Datagrams Over the SMDS Service," Piscitello, D.M.; Lawrence, J.; 1991

RFC1201 "Transmitting IP Traffic Over ARCNET Networks," Provan, D.; 1991

RFC1188 "Proposed Standard for the Transmission of IP Datagrams over FDDI networks," Katz, D.; 1990

RFC1172 "Point-to-Point Protocol Initial Configuration Options," Perkins, D.; Hobby, R; 1990

RFC1171 "Point-to-Point Protocol for the Transmission of Multi-protocol Datagrams over Point-to-Point Links," Perkins, D.; 1990

RFC1149 "Standard for the Transmission of IP Datagrams on Avian Carriers," Waitzman, D.; 1990 (April 1 release!)

RFC1055 "Nonstandard for Transmission of IP Datagrams Over Serial Lines: SLIP," Romkey, J.L.; 1988

RFC1044 "Internet Protocol on Network System's HYPERchannel: Protocol Specification," Hardwick, K.; Lekashman, J.; 1988

RFC1042 "Standard for the Transmission of IP Datagrams over IEEE 802 Networks," Postel, J.B.; Reynolds, J.K.; 1988

RFC1027 "Using ARP to Implement Transparent Subnet Gateways," Carl-Mitchell, S.; Quarterman, J.S.; 1987

RFC903 "Reverse Address Resolution Protocol," Finlayson, R; Mann, T; Mogul, J.C; Theimer, M.; 1984

RFC895 "Standard for the Transmission of IP Datagrams Over Experimental Ethernet Networks," Postel, J.B.; 1984

RFC894 "Standard for the Transmission of IP datagrams Over Ethernet Networks," Hornig, C.; 1984

RFC893 "Trailer Encapsulations," Leffler, S.; Karels, M.J.; 1984

RFC877 "Standard for the Transmission of IP Datagrams Over Public Data Networks," Korb, J.T.; 1983

Bootstrapping

RFC1084 "BOOTP Vendor Information Extensions," Reynolds, J.K.; 1988

RFC951 "Bootstrap Protocol," Croft, W.J.; Gilmore, J; 1985

RFC906 "Bootstrap Loading Using TFTP," Finlayson, R.; 1984

Domain Name System

RFC1035 "Domain Names—Implementation and Specification," Mockapetris, P.V.; 1987

RFC1034 "Domain Names—Concepts and Facilities," Mockapetris, P.V.; 1987

RFC1033 "Domain Administrators Operations Guide," Lottor, M.; 1987

RFC1032 "Domain Administrators Guide," Stahl, M.K.; 1987

RFC1101 "DNS Encoding of Network Names and Other Types," Mockapetris, P.V.; 1989

RFC974 "Mail Routing and the Domain System," Partridge, C.; 1986

RFC920 "Domain Requirements," Postel, J.B.; Reynolds, J.K.; 1984

RFC799 "Internet Name Domains," Mills, D.L.; 1981

File Transfer and File Access

RFC1094 "NFS: Network File System Protocol Specification," Sun Microsystems, Inc.; 1989

RFC1068 "Background File Transfer Program (BFTP)," DeSchon, A.L.; Braden, R. T.; 1988

RFC959 "File Transfer Protocol," Postel, J.B.; Reynolds, J.K.; 1985

RFC949 "FTP Unique-named Store Command," Padlipsky, M.A.; 1985

RFC783 "TFTP Protocol (Revision 2)," Sollins, K.R.; 1981

RFC775 "Directory Oriented FTP Commands," Mankins, D.; Franklin, D.; Owen, A.D.; 1980

Mail

RFC1341 "MIME (Multipurpose Internet Mail Extensions) Mechanisms for Specifying and Describing the Format of Internet Message Bodies," Borenstein, N.; Freed, N.; 1992

RFC1143 "Q Method of Implementing Telnet Option Negotiation," Bernstein, D.J.; 1990

RFC1090 "SMTP on X.25," Ullmann, R.; 1989

RFC1056 "PCMAIL: A Distributed Mail System for Personal Computers," Lambert, M.L.; 1988

RFC974 "Mail Routing and the Domain System," Partridge, C.; 1986

RFC822 "Standard for the Format of ARPA Internet Text Messages," Crocker, D.; 1982

RFC821 "Simple Mail Transfer Protocol," Postel, J.B.; 1982

Routing Protocols

RFC1267 "A Border Gateway Protocol 3 (BGP-3)," Lougheed, K.; Rekhter, Y.; 1991

RFC1247 "OSPF version 2," Moy, J.; 1991

RFC1222 "Advancing the NSFNET routing architecture," Braun, H.W.; Rekhter, Y.; 1991

RFC1195 "Use of OSI IS-IS for Routing in TCP/IP and Dual Environments," Callon, R.W.; 1990

RFC1164 "Application of the Border Gateway Protocol in the Internet," Honig, J.C.; Katz, D.; Mathis, M.; Rekhter, Y.; Yu, J.Y.; 1990

RFC1163 "Border Gateway Protocol (BGP)," Lougheed, K.; Rekhter, Y.; 1990

RFC1074 "NSFNET Backbone SPF-based Interior Gateway Protocol," Rekhter, J.; 1988

RFC1058 "Routing Information Protocol," Hedrick, C.L.; 1988

RFC904 "Exterior Gateway Protocol Formal Specification," Mills, D.L.; 1984

RFC827 "Exterior Gateway Protocol (EGP)," Rosen, E.C.; 1982

RFC823 "DARPA Internet Gateway," Hinden, R.M.; Sheltzer, A.; 1982

RFC1136 "Administrative Domains and Routing Domains: A Model for Routing in the Internet," Hares, S.; Katz, D.; 1989

RFC911 "EGP Gateway under Berkeley UNIX 4.2 EGP Gateway under Berkeley UNIX 4.2," Kirton, P.; 1984

RFC888 "STUB Exterior Gateway Protocol," Seamonson, L.; Rosen, E.C.; 1984

Routing Performance and Policy

RFC1254 "Gateway Congestion Control Survey," Mankin, A.; Ramakrishnan, K.K., eds.; 1991

RFC1246 "Experience with the OSPF Protocol," Moy, J., ed.; 1991

RFC1245 "OSPF Protocol Analysis," Moy, J., ed.; 1991

RFC1125 "Policy Requirements for Inter Administrative Domain routing," Estrin, D.; 1989

RFC1124 "Policy Issues in Interconnecting Networks," Leiner, B.M.; 1989

RFC1104 "Models of Policy Based Routing," Braun, H.W.; 1989

RFC1102 "Policy Routing in Internet Protocols," Clark, D.D.; 1989

Terminal Access

RFC1205 "Telnet 5250 Interface," Chmielewski, P.; 1991

RFC1198 "FYI on the X Window System," Scheifler, R.W.; 1991

RFC1184 "Telnet Linemode Option," Borman, D.A., ed.; 1990

RFC1091 "Telnet Terminal-type Option," VanBokkelen, J.; 1989

RFC1080 "Telnet Remote Flow Control Option," Hedrick, C.L.; 1988

RFC1079 "Telnet Terminal Speed Option," Hedrick, C.L.; 1988

RFC1073 "Telnet Window Size Option," Waitzman, D.; 1988

RFC1053 "Telnet X.3 PAD Option," Levy, S.; Jacobson, T.; 1988

RFC1043 "Telnet Data Entry Terminal Option: DODIIS Implementation," Yasuda, A.; Thompson, T.; 1988

RFC1041 "Telnet 3270 Regime Option," Rekhter, Y.; 1988

RFC1013 "X Window System Protocol, version 11: Alpha Update," Scheifler, R.W.; 1987

RFC946 "Telnet Terminal Location Number Option," Nedved, R.; 1985

RFC933 "Output Marking Telnet Option," Silverman, S.; 1985

RFC885 "Telnet End of Record Option," Postel, J.B.; 1983

RFC861   "Telnet Extended Options: List Option," Postel, J.B.; Reynolds, J.K.; 1983

RFC860   "Telnet Timing Mark Option," Postel, J.B.; Reynolds, J.K.; 1983

RFC859   "Telnet Status Option," Postel, J.B.; Reynolds, JR.; 1983

RFC858   "Telnet Suppress Go Ahead Option," Postel, J.B.; Reynolds, J.K.; 1983

RFC857   "Telnet Echo Option," Postel, J.B.; Reynolds, JR.; 1983

RFC856   "Telnet Binary Transmission," Postel, J.B.; Reynolds, J.K.; 1983

RFC855   "Telnet Option Specifications," Postel, J.B.; Reynolds, J.K.; 1983

RFC854   "Telnet Protocol Specification," Postel, J.B.; Reynolds, J.K.; 1983

RFC779   "Telnet Send-location Option," Killian, E.; 1981

RFC749   "Telnet SUPDUP-Output Option," Greenberg, B.; 1978

RFC736   "Telnet SUPDUP Option," Crispin, M.R.; 1977

RFC732   "Telnet Data Entry Terminal Option," Day, J.D.; 1977

RFC727   "Telnet Logout Option," Crispin, M.R.; 1977

RFC726   "Remote Controlled Transmission and Echoing Telnet Option," Postel, J.B.; Crocker, D.; 1977

RFC698   "Telnet Extended ASCII Option," Mock, T.; 1975

Other Applications

RFC1196 "Finger User Information Protocol," Zimmerman. D.P.; 1990

RFC1179 "Line Printer Daemon Protocol," McLaughlin, L.; 1990

RFC1129 "Internet Time Synchronization: The Network Time Protocol," Mills, D.L.; 1989

RFC1119 "Network Time Protocol (version 2) Specification and Implementation," Mills, D.L.; 1989

RFC1057 "RPC: Remote Procedure Call Protocol Specification: Version 2 Sun Microsystems, Inc.; 1988

RFC1014 "XDR: External Data Representation Standard," Sun Microsystems, Inc.; 1987

RFC954 "NICNAME/WHOIS," Harrenstien, K.; Stahl, M.K.; Feinler, E.J.; 1985

RFC868 "Time Protocol," Postel, J.B.; Harrenstien, K.; 1983

RFC867 "Daytime Protocol," Postel, J.B.; 1983

RFC866 "Active Users," Postel, J.B.; 1983

RFC8GS "Quote of the Day Protocol," Postel, J.B.; 1983

RFC8G4 "Character Generator Protocol," Postel, J.B.; 1983

RFC863 "Discard Protocol," Postel, J.B.; 1983

RFC862 "Echo Protocol," Postel, J.B.; 1983

Network Management

RFC1271 "Remote Network Monitoring Management Information Base," Waldbusser, 5.; 1991

RFC1253 "OSPE version 2: Management Information Base," Baker, P.; Coltun, R.; 1991

RFC1243 "Appletalk Management Information Base," 1991

RFC1239 "Reassignment of Experimental MIBs to Standard MIBs," Reynolds, J.K.; 1991

RFC1238 "CLNS MIB for Use With Connectionless Network Protocol (ISO 8473) and End System to Intermediate System (ISO 9542)," Satz, G.; 1991

RFC1233 "Definitions of Managed Objects for the DS3 Interface Type," Cox, T.A.; Tesink, K., eds.; 1991

RFC1232 "Definitions of Managed Objects for the DS1 Interface Type," Baker, F.; Kolb, C.P. eds.; 1991

RFC1231 "IEEE 802.5 Token Ring MIB," McCloghrie, K.; Fox, R.; Decker, E.; 1991

RFC1230 "IEEE 802.4 Token Bus MIB," McCloghrie, K.; Fox R.; 1991

RFC1229 "Extensions to the Generic-interface MIB," McCloghrie, K., ed.; 1991

E

RFC1228 "SNMP-DPI: Simple Network Management Protocol Distributed Program Interface," Carpenter, G.; Wijnen, B.; 1991

RFC1227 "SNMP MUX protocol and MIB," Rose, M.T.; 1991

RFC1224 "Techniques for Managing Asynchronously Generated Alerts," Steinberg, L.; 1991

RFC1215 "Convention for Defining Traps for Use with the SNMP," Rose, M.T., ed.; 1991

RFC1214 "OSI Internet Management: Management Information Base," LaBarre, L., ed.; 1991

RFC1213 "Management Information Base for Network Management of TCP/IP-based Internets: MiB-II," McCloghrie, K.; Rose, M.T., eds.; 1991

RFC1212 "Concise MIB Definitions," Rose, M.T.; McCloghrie, K., eds.; 1991

RFC1187 "Bulk Table Retrieval with the SNMP," Rose, M.T.; McCloghrie, K.; Davin, J.R.; 1990

RFC1157 "Simple Network Management Protocol (SNMP)," Case, J.D.; Fedor, M.; Schoffstall, M.L; Davin, C.; 1990

RFC1156 "Management Information Base for Network Management of TCP/IP-based internets," McGloghrie, K.; Rose, M.T.; 1990

RFC1155 "Structure and Identification of Management Information for TCP/IP-based Internets," Rose, M.T.; McCloghrie, K.; 1990

RFC1147 "FYI on a Network Management Tool Catalog: Tools for Monitoring and Debugging TCP/IP Internets and Interconnected Devices," Stine, R.H., ed.; 1990

RFC1089 "SNMP over Ethernet," Schoffstall, M.L.; Davin, C.; Fedor, M.; Case, J.D.; 1989

Tunneling

RFC1241 "Scheme for an Internet Encapsulation Protocol: Version 1," 1991

RFC1234 "Tunneling IPX Traffic through IP Networks," Provan, D.; 1991

RFC1088 "Standard for the Transmission of IP Datagrams over NetBIOS Networks," McLaughlin, L.J.; 1989

RFC1002 "Protocol Standard for a NetBIOS Service on a TCP/UDP Transport: Detailed Specifications," NetBIOS Working Group; 1987

RFC1001 "Protocol Standard for a NetBIOS service on a TCP/UDP Transport: Concepts and Methods," NetBIOS Working Group; 1987

OSI

RFC1240 "OSI Connectionless Transport Services on Top of UDP: Version 1," Shue, C.; Haggerty, W.; Dobbins, K.; 1991

RFC1237 "Guidelines for OSI NSAP Allocation in the Internet," Gollela, R.; Gardner, E.P.; Callon, R.W.; 1991

RFC1169 "Explaining the Role of GOSIP," Cerf, V.G.; Mills, K.L.; 1990

Security

RFC1244 "Site Security Handbook"

RFC1115 "Privacy Enhancement for Internet Electronic Mail: Part III— Algorithms, Modes, and Identifiers [Draft]," Linn, J.; 1989

RFC1114 "Privacy Enhancement for Internet Electronic Mail: Part II— Certificate-based Key Management [Draft]," Kent, S.T.; Linn, J.; 1989

RFC1113 "Privacy Enhancement for Internet Electronic Mail: Part I— Message Encipherment and Authentication Procedures [Draft]," Linn, J.; 1989

RFC1108 "Security Options for the Internet Protocol," 1991

Miscellaneous

RFC1251 "Who's Who in the Internet: Biographies of IAB, IESG and IRSG members," Malkin, G.S.; 1991

RFC1207 "FYI on Questions and Answers: Answers to Commonly asked 'Experienced Internet User' Questions," Malkin, G.S.; Marine, A.N.; Reynolds, J.K.; 1991

RFC1206 "FYI on Questions and Answers: Answers to Commonly asked 'New Internet User' questions," Malkin, G.S.; Marine, A.N.; 1991

E

F

Answers

Day 1

1. What does each of the following primitives do?

   Service primitive: Usually refers to data

   Request primitive: One service requesting permission to communicate with another service

   Indication primitive: An indication sent to an application that communications is desired

   Response primitive: Acknowledgment of a communications session

   Confirmation primitive: Sent to indicate that both applications are ready to communicate

2. What is a Service Access Point? How many are there per layer?

   A Service Access Point (SAP) is the point across which communications occurs between layers. There are usually four (two each way) per application.

3. Explain the process followed in adopting a new Internet Standard for TCP/IP.

   The process is shown in Figure 1.7 and explained in the accompanying text.

Day 2

1. Draw the layered architectures of both the OSI Reference Model and TCP/IP. Show how the layers correspond in each diagram.

   The layered architecture of both the OSI-RM and TCP/IP are shown in Figure 2.2.

2. Show the layered Internet architecture, explaining each layer's purpose.

   The Internet layered architecture is shown in Figure 2.5. The applications layer supports user applications. The Service Provider Protocol layer supports TCP, and the Internetworking layer supports IP. (Other protocols can be used, but TCP/IP is the standard for the Internet.) The subnetwork layer holds the physical network.

3. Show how a datagram is transferred from one network, through one of more gateways, to the destination network. In each device, show the layered architecture and how high up the layered structure the datagrams goes.

A diagram that shows this clearly is in Figure 2.6. Note that in the gateways, the datagram resides only in the Physical layer, not moving up any higher until the destination gateway is reached.

4. Draw the IP header and an Ethernet frame, showing the number of bits used for each component. Explain each component's role.

   The Ethernet frame is shown in Figure 2.8. The meaning of each field within the header is explained in the text accompanying the figure.

5. Explain what an ARP Cache is. What is its structure, and why is it used?

   The ARP Cache is a table with a list of IP addresses and their corresponding physical addresses. It is used to help resolve destination addresses.

Day 3

1. Explain why IP is important to the proper transmission of data.

   IP's primary task is the addressing of datagrams. Without IP, routing information would have to be constructed at a higher layer in the architecture.

2. Show the construction of the IP header and the meaning of each element within the header structure.

   The IP header is shown in Figure 3.1. The meaning of each field within the header is explained in the text accompanying the figure.

3. ICMP headers are quite small. Show the structure of a typical message header and the meaning of the bits within it.

   The ICMP header is shown in Figure 3.4. The meaning of fields and their valid values are explained in text accompanying the figure.

4. Explain the different EGP message formats and when they are used.

   There are four EGP message formats in use: neighbor acquisition and neighbor reachability (both of which indicate the presence and status of neighbor devices), poll (to verify that a neighbor is active), and error (for reporting error conditions).

5. Show the EGP message format, and explain the contents of the header and the network reachability information.

   The format of the EGP message headers are shown in Figures 3.6 and 3.7. The text accompanying the figures explains the meanings of the fields within the header.

Day 4

1. Draw a diagram showing the binding of port tables when three machines are sending information to each other.

   This is shown in Figure 4.3.

2. Draw the TCP protocol data unit (PDU) and explain the meaning of each field.

   The TCP PDU is shown in Figure 4.5. The fields are all explained in the accompanying text.

3. Use a diagram to show the signals involved with two machines establishing a TCP connection. Then, show how data is transferred. Finally, show the termination process.

   The diagrams for all three steps are shown in Figures 4.6, 4.7, and 4.8.

4. What is a TCP connection table? How is it used?

   TCP uses a connection table to keep track of all the active connections. Each existing connection has an entry in the table that shows information about the end-to-end connection. The layout of the TCP connection table is shown in Figure 4.9.

5. Draw the UDP header and explain the fields it contains.

   The UDP header is shown in Figure 4.10. The accompanying text explains the purpose of each field.

6. What are the advantages of using UDP over TCP? When would you not want to use UDP?

   UDP is connectionless, hence a little faster. It is not as reliable as TCP, though, so is not useful for applications where a connection must be maintained for long periods or when reliability of transfer is important.

Day 5

1. Explain what a network virtual terminal is.

   A network virtual terminal is used to define both ends of a connection. It has a logical keyboard and a logical printer (display). NVTs are necessary in order to enable a connection to exist.

2. Draw diagrams showing two- and three-party FTP sessions, indicating the port numbers used by each machine.

   These diagrams are shown in Figures 5.4 and 5.5.

3. Why would you want to allow anonymous FTP access? Are there any reasons for disallowing it?

   Anonymous FTP access enables users to upload and download files to your system without having to log in. This can be useful when you want to share information without worrying about user IDs. Anonymous FTP should be disabled if you do not plan on sharing information globally, because there are several possible security concerns with a poorly administered anonymous FTP setup.

4. TFTP enables files to be transferred without logging in. What problems can this cause?

   TFTP's capability to transfer files without a login can enable a remote user to transfer a file to or from your system without your specific knowledge, as long as the security system and file permissions are set to allow this. A well-run system will control TFTP's access considerably.

5. What are the Berkeley utilities?

   The Berkeley Utilities are a set of useful utility programs developed for TCP/IP at the University of California at Berkeley. The tools are known as the Berkeley Utilities in honor of their developers.

Day 6

1. What is a loopback driver used for?

   The loopback driver is a virtual circuit within the host machine, avoiding all contact with the physical network itself. The most common use of a loopback driver is as a diagnostic. By sending data to the loopback driver, you can make sure the protocols are working correctly on your machine. Without this capability, it would be difficult to separate network problems and software configuration problems.

· 2. What does the following excerpt from a `netstat -a` command tell you?

```
Proto Recv-Q Send-Q  Local Address        Foreign Address      (state)
ip        0      0   *.*                  *.*
tcp       0   1024   tpci.login           merlin.1034          ESTABL.
tcp    8756      0   tpci.1035            treijs.1036          ESTABL.
tcp       0      0   tpci.1021            reboc.1024           TIME_WAIT
tcp       0      0   *.1028               *.*                  LISTEN
tcp       0      0   *.6000               *.*                  LISTEN
```

This extract shows that there are two established TCP connections (to
`merlin.1034` and `treijs.1036`), one of which is sending information and the
other receiving. The connection to `reboc.1024` is waiting to hang up. There
are two ports waiting for a connection.

3. What is the `ping` utility used for?

The `ping` utility is used to query another system. It sends an ICMP message to
the remote and waits for a reply. The `ping` command is very useful for testing
connections.

Day 7

1. Define the roles of gateways, routers, bridges, and brouters.

A *gateway* performs routing functions between networks and can translate
protocols. A *bridge* connects two or more networks using the same protocol. A
router is a network device that forwards datagrams around the network. A
brouter performs the same functions of both the bridge and router.

2. What is a packet-switched network?

A packet-switched network is one wherein all transfers of information are based
on self-contained packets (like TCP/IP's datagrams).

3. What is the difference between interior and exterior neighbor gateways?

Interior gateways connect LANs of one organization, whereas exterior gateways
connect the organization to the outside world.

4. What are the advantages and disadvantages of the three types of routing tables?

The three types of routing tables are fixed, dynamic, and fixed central. The
fixed table must be manually modified every time there is a change. A *dynamic*
table changes its information based on network traffic, reducing the amount of
manual maintenance. A *fixed central* table lets a manager modify only one table,

which is then read by other devices. The fixed central table reduces the need to update each machine's table, as with the fixed table. Usually a dynamic table is the least problem for a network administrator, although the table's contents can change without the administrator being aware of the change.

5. What is the HELLO protocol used for?

The HELLO protocol uses time instead of distance to determine optimal routing. It is an alternative to the Routing Information Protocol.

Day 8

1. What protocol is used by DNS name servers? Why is that a good choice?

DNS uses UDP for communications between servers. It is a better choice than TCP because of the improved speed a connectionless protocol offers. Of course, transmission reliability suffers with UDP.

2. What is a DNS resource record?

A resource record is an entry in a name server's database. There are several types of resource records used, including name-to-address resolution information. Resource records are maintained as ASCII files.

3. Show a sample entry in an IN-ADDR-ARPA file and explain what the fields mean.

An entry in an IN-ADDR-ARPA file would look like this:

```
merlin    IN    A    143.12.2.46
```

The line contains the machine name, the class of machine (IN means Internet), A to show it is an address resource record, and the IP address.

4. BOOTP helps a diskless workstation boot. How does it get a message to the network looking for its IP address and the location of its operating system boot files?

BOOTP sends a UDP message with a subnetwork broadcast address and waits for a reply from a server that gives it the IP address. The same message can contain the name of the machine that has the boot files on it. If the boot image location is not specified, the workstation uses another UDP message to query the server.

5. What is the Network Time Protocol? Why is it used?

The Network Time Protocol is used to ensure that all internal timers are synchronized and have similar settings.

Day 9

1. Show how the NFS layers compare to the OSI Reference Model.

This is shown in Figure 9.1. The NFS layers comprise the top three layers of the architecture, including the application layer protocols (Mount, yp, and so on), XDR (External Data Representation) in place of the presentation layer, and RPC (Remote Procedure Call) in place of the session layer.

2. Explain how a port mapper assigns ports.

The port mapper controls assignment of ports based on requests from applications. The port mapper maintains a table of ports, and the RPC programs that are using them. When the port mapper receives a request for a port, it checks for an available port and then completes a table entry for the port and application, returning the port number with a status message.

3. What is External Data Representation?

"External Data Representation (XDR)" is a method of encoding data within an RPC message, used to ensure that the data is not system-dependent.

4. What does the Mount protocol do?

The Mount protocol returns a file handle and the name of the file system in which a requested file resides. The message is sent to the client from the server after reception of a client's request.

5. What is REX? What advantage does REX offer over similar utilities?

The Remote Execution Service (REX) is designed to enable users to run commands on other machines without logging in and without the overhead of larger utilities like Telnet. Since REX preserves the full shell environment, it is better than other remote procedures.

Day 10

1. What components make up a Medium Attachment Unit (MAU), and what are their roles?

   The MAU is composed of the Physical Medium Attachment (PMA) and the Medium Dependent Interface (MDI). The MAU manages the connection of the machine to the network medium itself.

2. What is FDDI? Why is it popular?

   FDDI, Fiber Distributed Data Interface, is popular because it provides very high transmission speeds over a fiber-optic cable.

3. What is the role of the Discard service?

   The Discard service discards everything it receives, returning nothing back to the sender.

4. The Time protocol is often used by network devices. What is its role?

   The Time protocol is used to synchronize devices on a network so their clocks are consistent. If they were not consistent, some packet information involving actual times would be meaningless.

5. Does the presence of a second network protocol (like IPX) affect the basic TCP/IP protocol suite's operations?

   TCP/IP can function over other network protocols (like IPX) by replacing parts of the TCP/IP layered architecture with the other network protocol's layers. Some duplication and crossover of functionality can be expected, but TCP/IP will function properly with many different networks.

Day 11

1. How many devices are allowed on a Class B network (the most common)?

   Class B networks use 2 bytes for the device portion of the IP address. This allows 65,534 different devices.

2. What is the difference between the BSD UNIX TCP/IP broadcast address setting and the one normally used?

F

The BSD UNIX TCP/IP broadcast address was set to use all 0s, whereas the Internet standard (and most other TCP/IP implementations) use all 1s. The Internet system is the most widely used except in locations that have run BSD UNIX for many years and have not made the switch.

3. What is a pseudo tty?

   A pseudo tty, or false terminal, enables external machines to connect through Telnet or rlogin. Without a pseudo tty, no connection can take place.

4. What does the following .rhosts file do?

   ```
   # .rhosts
   artemis tparker
   artemis goof
   artemis aarmenakis
   mig rmaclean
   ```

   This file enables three users from the system artemis and one user from the system mig to log into the host system without using passwords. The user IDs that can be used are specified after the machine name.

5. What is anonymous FTP, and why would you use it?

   Anonymous FTP enables users to connect to a host without using a valid login and password. Usually, anonymous FTP uses a login called anonymous or guest, with the password usually requesting the user's ID for tracking purposes only. Anonymous FTP is used to allow a large number of users to access files on the host without setting up logins for them. Anonymous FTP systems usually have strict controls over the areas an anonymous user can access.

Day 12

1. Why is it preferable to have Windows for Workgroups packets encapsulated by IP, rather than the reverse?

   By encapsulating Windows for Workgroups packets within IP packets, the packets can be sent over a wider network. Routers, for example, cannot handle Windows for Workgroups (WFW) packets. This enables a WFW system to communicate with another WFW system anywhere along the internetwork.

2. Why is the SHARE command necessary when using TCP/IP on a DOS network?

   SHARE enables more than one request for the same file to be processed by the operating system. If SHARE were not active, a system would hang while the file request is processed. Even if only one user is using a system, it is advisable to load SHARE in the AUTOEXEC.BAT file.

3. Use a diagram to show how Windows for Workgroups and TCP/IP co-reside on a layered architecture for DOS.

   A diagram that shows the layered DOS architecture is shown in Figure 12.2.

Day 13

1. What are the five parts of the OSI Reference Model dealing with network management (called the Specific Management Functional Areas)?

   The OSI-RM defines the five aspects of network management as accounting, configuration, faults, performance, and security.

2. What is a Management Information Base (MIB)?

   A Management Information Base is part of every SNMP-managed device. Each SNMP agent has the MIB database, which contains information about the device's status, its performance, connections, and configuration. The MIB is queried by SNMP.

3. What is ping?

   ping is the Packet Internet Groper. It sends out an ICMP request to a destination and waits for a response. ping is a simple utility used to check connectivity.

4. Assume a LAN has some machines using Ethernet and others using IEEE 802.3. Will they be able to communicate?

   Not unless there is a translation system in place. The datagrams for Ethernet and IEEE 802.3 are slightly different. This is a common problem because most users think that IEEE 802.3 is Ethernet.

5. What is Kerberos?

   Kerberos is a network security system developed at MIT. It provides encryption and validation services that are very difficult to break.

Day 14

1. What are the six basic socket commands?

   The basic socket commands are open, send, receive, status, close, and abort.

2. A Transmission Control Block performs what function?

   A TCM is a complex data structure that contains a considerable amount of information about a connection. There is a TCB for each connection.

3. What is the difference between an unspecified passive open and a fully specified passive open?

   An unspecified passive open has the server waiting for a connection request from a client. A fully specified passive open has the server waiting for a connection from a specific client.

4. What command will display status information about a socket?

   The command getsockopt queries a socket and displays all information returned about the socket.

5. What is a fork?

   A fork is a UNIX process that creates a copy of the existing application and then executes it.

Index

Symbols

A

V-W

X-Y-Z

Add to Your Sams Library Today with the Best Books for Programming, Operating Systems, and New Technologies

The easiest way to order is to pick up the phone and call

1-800-428-5331

between 9:00 a.m. and 5:00 p.m. EST.
For faster service please have your credit card available.

ISBN	Quantity	Description of Item	Unit Cost	Total Cost
0-672-48440-4		UNIX Networking	$29.95	
0-672-22773-8		The Waite Group's UNIX Communications, 2nd Edition	$29.95	
0-672-48494-3		UNIX System Security	$34.95	
0-672-30571-2		UNIX Security for the Organization	$35.00	
0-672-30551-8		Exploring the UNIX System, 4th Edition	$29.99	
0-672-30402-3		UNIX Unleashed	$49.99	
0-672-30460-0		Absolute Beginner's Guide to UNIX	$19.99	
0-672-30594-1		Programming Winsock (Book/Disk)	$35.00	
0-672-30519-4		Teach Yourself the Internet: Around the World in 21 Days (Book/Disk)	$25.00	
0-672-30466-X		Internet Unleashed (Book/Disk)	$39.95	
0-672-30473-2		Client/Server Computing, 2nd Edition	$40.00	
0-672-30485-6		Navigating the Internet, Deluxe Edition (Book/Disk)	$29.95	
❏ 3 ½" Disk		Shipping and Handling: See information below.		
❏ 5 ¼" Disk		TOTAL		

Shipping and Handling: $4.00 for the first book, and $1.75 for each additional book. Floppy disk: add $1.75 for shipping and handling. If you need to have it NOW, we can ship product to you in 24 hours for an additional charge of approximately $18.00, and you will receive your item overnight or in two days. Overseas shipping and handling adds $2.00 per book and $8.00 for up to three disks. Prices subject to change. Call for availability and pricing information on latest editions.

201 W. 103rd Street, Indianapolis, Indiana 46290

1-800-428-5331 — Orders   1-800-835-3202 — FAX   1-800-858-7674 — Customer Service